PROCEEDINGS

ACM SIGMICRO NEWSLETTER
Volume 14, Number 4
December 1983

*THE 16th ANNUAL
MICROPROGRAMMING
WORKSHOP*
DOWNINGTOWN, PA

**IEEE
COMPUTER
SOCIETY
PRESS** Φ®

SPONSORED BY

ASSOCIATION FOR COMPUTING MACHINERY
SIGMICRO

IEEE COMPUTER SOCIETY
TC-MICRO

ACM ORDER NUMBER 520830
IEEE CATALOG NUMBER 83CH1928-1
LIBRARY OF CONGRESS NUMBER 83-81647
IEEE COMPUTER SOCIETY ORDER NUMBER 497
ISBN 0-89791-114-8

THE INSTITUTE OF ELECTRICAL
AND ELECTRONICS ENGINEERS, INC.

Prepaid Price
Members $18.75
Nonmembers $37.50

Library of Congress Number 83-81667
ISBN 0-89791-114-8 (paper)
ISBN 0-8186-4494-X (microfiche)
ISBN 0-8186-8494-1 (casebound)

Additional copies may be ordered from:

ACM Order Department
P.O. Box 64145, Baltimore, MD 21264
ACM Order No. 533831

IEEE Computer Society
P.O. Box 80452
Worldway Postal Center
Los Angeles, CA 90080
Computer Society Order No. 494

IEEE Service Center
445 Hoes Lane, Piscataway, NJ 08865
IEEE Catalog No. 83CH1925-7

acm **Association for Computing Machinery**

Preface

Some years ago, one of my mentors took a hard line on the study of micropro-gramming, which I paraphrase as follows:

> Microprogramming is just an implementation technique, a way to get the end built,
> rather than an end in itself. There is no more reason to have a Workshop on Micropro-
> gramming than to have one on, say, binary decoders.

In an important sense, this is true. There is no good reason I can think of for having a workshop on any well-understood implementation technique, which leaves us with Micro-16, part of the continuing effort to understand microprogramming.

The production of any artifact typically goes through several stages: art, craft, engi-neered routine, and mechanization. This holds equally well for clay pots, binary decoders, and microcode. Any implementation technique that remains an art is not going to suc-ceed without the artist; artists are generally in short supply, and difficult to create. Crafts-men are easier to train: by making microprogramming a craft we increase its applicability. If we can master the routine production of microcode, and automate that process, then we will indeed have a well-understood technique, and no more workshops; the binary decoder analogy will finally apply.

This year's workshop has an emphasis on firmware engineering and methodology, which indicates to me that while we may have mastered the art of microprogramming (well, now and then, one or two of us), and maybe even the craft of microprogramming, we have not yet mastered the routine production of microprograms. But a look at the papers indicates we're making progress.

Putting together a workshop requires a great deal more than booking a site and collecting a bunch of papers and people. As general chairman, I found myself constantly being surprised at how much the organizing committee had to do, and constantly grati-fied that the job was being done. Without the help of these good people, there wouldn't be a workshop. The institutional support we have received has also been indispensable, and is gratefully acknowledged. Special thanks go to Karen Jones and Marie DiLabio for deciphering my scrawl, and to Linda Torchia for creating the logo and producing the artwork well and quickly.

Bill Hopkins
General Chairman

506956

Foreword

As with its predecessors, MICRO-16 continues to explore the art, science, and technology of microprogramming. As the reader of these Proceedings will note, a major emphasis of the present Workshop is the evolving discipline of firmware engineering which may be 'defined' as the application of scientific principles to the design, development, and production of microcode. It is pleasing to note, however, that some of the more 'classical' problems, related to architectural issues and migration, continue to draw attention.

As program chairman it is my pleasure to acknowledge the support of a number of persons who helped in putting together the technical program. I would like to thank in particular, the referees and the members of the Program Committee who, working within a very tight schedule, managed to review and produce meaningful reports on the submitted papers. These referees are listed on a separate page. It was a pleasure to work with the general chairman, Bill Hopkins. Scott Davidson and Rich Belgard provided psychological and logistic support when most needed. Cathy Pomier provided her usual cheerful and competent secretarial help. And, finally, my thanks to the authors who, of course, are the central focus of this Workshop.

Subrata Dasgupta
Program Chairman

MICRO-16 Workshop Committee

Chairman
William C. Hopkins
Burroughs Corporation

Program Chairman
Subrata Dasgupta
University of Southwestern Louisiana

Tutorial Chairman
Will Tracz
IBM/FSD

Publications
C.G. Stockton
IEEE Computer Society

Local Arrangements
Robert C. Smith
Burroughs Corporation

Publicity Chairman
Ann Marie McCabe
Burroughs Corporation

Treasurer
Michael Horton
Burroughs Corporation

Program Committee

Subrata Dasgupta
University of Southwestern Louisiana

Scott Davidson
Western Electric Research

Josh Fisher
Yale University

Gideon Freider
University of Michigan

Glenford Myers
Intel Corporation

Alice Parker
University of Southern California

Bruce D. Shriver
University of Southwestern Louisiana

Will Tracz
IBM

Nick Tredennick
IBM

MICRO-16 Referees

Takanobu Baba
Rich Belgard
Subrata Dasgupta
Scott Davidson
Josh Fisher
Gideon Frieder
Ratan Guha
Stan Habib
Lou Hafer
John Hennessey
Rick Hobson
David Landskov
Joseph Linn

Robert Mueller
Glen Myers
Christos Papachristou
Alice Parker
Bruce Shriver
John Stankovic
Steven Sutphen
John Tarter
Will Tracz
Nick Tredennick
Walter Wallach
Tom Weidner
Robert Winner

Call for Participation

The Seventeenth Annual WORKSHOP ON MICROPROGRAMMING

is tentatively scheduled October 30–November 2, 1984

at the
Hyatt Regency
New Orleans, Louisiana

Anyone interested in lending a hand
is urged to write or call the general chairman or
the program co-chairmen

Bruce D. Shriver
Computer Science Department
Box 44330
University of Southwestern Louisiana
Lafayette, Louisiana 70504
MICRO-17

Joseph L. Linn
Computer Science Department
Box 44330
University of Southwestern Louisiana
Lafayette, Louisiana 70504
MICRO-17

Robert I. Winner
Department of Computer Science
Box 74, Station B
Nashville, Tennessee 37235
MICRO-17

IEEE COMPUTER SOCIETY

THE INSTITUTE OF ELECTRICAL AND ELECTRONICS ENGINEERS, INC.

acm
ASSOCIATION FOR COMPUTING MACHINERY

MICRO 17

Table of Contents

Session I
Keynote Address

Chairman

M.J. Flynn
Stanford University

TOWARDS BETTER INSTRUCTION SETS

Michael J. Flynn[*]

Stanford University, Stanford, CA and Palyn Associates, San Jose, CA

Abstract

An effectively designed instruction set is the result of many considerations. These include not only obvious measures such as code size, performance and implementation cost, but also issues such as compatibility and especially design complexity.

In an effort to reduce the design complexity, flexible or universal base designs have been used to realize various instruction sets or source problem requirements.

Using either a dedicated or universal host, language oriented DEL architectures may offer some significant performance advantages over more traditional architectures.

Towards Better Instruction Sets

Probably few areas of computer system design are as controversial as the architecture or instruction set of a processor. As Professor Wilkes observed in last year's keynote address (1), the instruction set is a primary force and influence upon the microprogrammer. Many things are implied by instruction set, including software functionality, software structure, hardware cost, design effort, etc.

A great deal of recent discussion has centered on the merits of reduced vs complex instruction sets. While this focus may be useful, I believe that there are other issues in architecture at least as important as RISC vs CISC. Some of these include dedicated host designs vs universal host designs; design time vs performance; evaluation of various universal host proposals; language oriented vs host oriented instruction sets. We will look at some of these after considering the factors influencing instruction set design.

[*]   work supported in part by Army Research Office Durham, under contract #DAAG29-82-K-0109

A Model (2)

The instruction set lies at the boundary between compilation and interpretation. One can regard a computer as consisting of three parts: an architecture or instruction set, a storage, and an interpretive mechanism. The interpretive mechanism is programmed to execute the instruction set and cause the specified state transitions in the memory. Since the interpretative mechanism may itself be a machine - with storage and (micro) instruction set we have a notion of two machines, the host or micromachine doing the interpretation of the image machine or the instruction set processor.

The question of whether the image machine is "high level" or "low level" is deceptively simple sounding. Presumably a low level architecture requires few host instructions to execute its state transitions, while a high level machine requires many more. This, of course, ignores the potential sophistication of the host itself, what resources it has and what constraints have been placed upon it. In the absence of being able to standardize on a particular host configuration, I prefer to classify instruction sets as being either language oriented or host oriented with the distinction being that a language oriented architecture describes storage transformations in semantics similar to those used in a high level language source program while a host oriented architecture uses objects present or presumed to be present in the host; memory cells, registers, etc. One might expect that a language oriented instruction set would necessarily be more complex than a host oriented one, i.e. would take more host cycles to interpret a given instruction. This is not necessarily true, as many recent host oriented instruction sets have extensive interpretation requirements (therein lies the basis of much of the RISC vs CISC argument (3)).

What Makes a Good Instruction Set?
Primary Factors

There have been many proposals to evaluate instruction sets (4), usually on a quantitative basis. Unfortunately, these evaluations may be misused since the evaluation process usually restricts the scope of test material to small problem state programs. Whatever the limitations of such measurements they do form at least a partial basis for instruction set evaluation. Some of these measures include:

1. Static measures - In the absence of other considerations, smaller static code size is better. More concise code can be emitted more rapidly by a compiler, should have better locality in the memory hierarchy and require less memory bandwidth for the instruction stream.

2. Compilation time - An item frequently overlooked in many evaluations is the time it takes to compile a source program into an instruction set. A typical processor spends perhaps half its time in compilation and the other half in problem execution. While compile time implications are just as important as run time implications, it is difficult to measure the influence of instruction sets on a compilation process. One compiler may attempt elaborate optimization while another one is "compile and go." Some generalities are possible: architectures that require register usage optimization and large program size, for example, would require more compilation time than those without the same requirements. However, these generalities are of limited use. The evaluation of an instruction set for ease of compilation is confused by the complexity of the compilation process itself. Compilers differ in their debugging functionality, their attempt at source to source optimization (rearranging the original source program in its best possible form), and simply the skill of the compiler writer.

3. Run time - Dynamic measures of an architecture include such artifacts as number of instructions executed, number of data references required for reads and writes, and memory traffic required as measured in bytes transferred. Ultimately, one would like to include a measure of the number of host cycles required to execute an image program. Like compile time this is difficult to do on a comparative basis, since different hosts have different degrees of support for various image machines.

4. Predictability - Related, at least indirectly, to both compilation time and run time is the predictability of finding (decoding) and executing fragments of an instruction. Predictability comes at the expense of code size since information is by definition directly related to uncertainty. However, many architectures are created in such a way as to require needless serial interpretation of fields as part of the execution process. The interpretation of field B may depend upon the result of the interpretation of field A. The use of variable width codes to encode a given field is another difficulty. Huffman codes, for example, require a serial inspection of the

contents of a field on a bit by bit basis to determine even the width of the field. Predictability in an instruction set allows successful overlapping and lookahead on the part of the host in the interpretation of the image instruction stream.

In addition there are other types of dependencies which inhibit execution predictions by the host.

1. Interinstruction dependencies where the execution of the present instruction depends upon the past instruction. While much of this is unavoidable, several of the worst interlock difficulties in high speed machines such as store into the instruction stream can be eliminated by disciplined instruction set design.

2. Process to process dependencies - here again a well defined call and return mechanism minimizes the process entry costs.

5. Transparency - by definition transparency is a property of the architecture that allows it to represent source state transitions on a one for one basis. If program execution is viewed as a sequence of non-interruptible atomic actions, then at end of each non-interruptible event the transparent interpreting machine has the same state as that specified by the program being interpreted. Clearly an optimizing compiler destroys transparency between the source and the image machine. A high speed host that executes instructions out of order destroys transparency between the image instruction and the host. Transparency, as such, has not been much sought after in either architecture or compiler development efforts. Its advantages are subtle. It eases the burden - perhaps makes possible - program verification. It is also a valuable property in verifying the coordination of the execution of concurrent processors. Several paradoxes in concurrent execution arose from a failure in transparency.

While the value of transparent execution may be debatable, it is clear that language oriented architecture can more easily support such execution than host oriented instruction sets (regardless of their level of complexity).

Secondary Factors Influencing the Design of Instruction Sets

In addition to the straight forward tradeoffs between compiler technology and host technology, there are a number of additional, seemingly secondary issues whose importance frequently overwhelms the primary and more academic considerations mentioned in the previous section. These secondary issues include such issues as compatibility, environmental stability, design time and technology.

Compatibility

All platitudes to the contrary, the primary level of transportability and compatibility of programs is the instruction set, not the higher level language. Frequently for older programs the source simply does not exist any longer. Even where the source exists the multitude of dialects of the same source language creates obvious problems.

Since most traditional instruction sets are host oriented, they were created under then current premises of host technology - the cost of a register, the speed of memory, etc. The more successful an architecture is, the more implementations it has, the longer its life, the more certain the need for continued compatibility, and finally the more difficulty in providing competitive measures of static and dynamic performance; an obvious problem in comparing architectures.

The Environment

Processes can be designed for single applications or for a universe of applications. In an age of "cheap" hardware it seems obvious that hardware should be dedicated toward an environment insofar as the application is stable and known. To use a universal processor will naturally give a poorer performance. On the other hand, economy of manufacturing scale allows such processors to be produced at extremely low costs. The cost for the design can be amortized over a much larger quantity of processors. The hardware may be cheap, but the design costs are not, unless the applicability is vast. Of course, this leads to an interest in universal structures which we will discuss in a later section.

Ever recognizing that processor costs include both design and production costs (i.e. total processor costs), one must also consider the total system cost. Memory costs, I/O, power supply, and housing each typically exceed the cost of a microprocessor and thus dominate the total cost picture.

Design Time

Complicated architectures require complicated development programs for both design and development, verification and production. The recent interest in academic institutions in reduced instruction sets stems as much from the possibility of being able to do a design of a simple architecture and being unable with the same meager resources to accomplish the implementation of a more complex instruction set using the

same host technology. Here again universal structures may used to ease the design problem at the expense of the primary performance measures.

Technology

Technology provides both a direct and an indirect influence on the architecture and its resultant performance. Presently chip area constraints require an implementation to fit a fixed area and performance may be severely limited in order to force an a priori defined instruction set to fit on a particular chip. With conventional packaging techniques, pin constraints may severely restrict access to memory, placing a premium on those architectures which make best use of memory bandwidth. Just as System 370 was a child of its times in its register and memory specification, present microprocessor technology constraints are similarly products of today's limitations. Upcoming wafer technologies which package a complete wafer rather than a chip may radically alter much of the current thinking about chip oriented or area constrained processor architecture.

Three Universal Hosts

There are various ways a computer designer can create host structures without committing the design to a particular image architecture and environment. The basic difference among approaches arises from tradeoffs among compiler technology, design time, and compile and run time performance. Three more or less universal (or at least general purpose) host structures are:

1. The universal host machine (UHM) is an interpretive machine designed to emulate various high level architectures. The architecture can be specialized for particular environments, such as a particular high level language. The UHM's limitation is that it takes additional cycles to interpret the unsupported image architecture.

2. The universal executing host (UEM) relies on compiler technology to adapt the universe of environments to the processor, the IBM 801 (5) or the RISC (3) are examples of the UEM approach. From our point of view, the high level language source is compiled into a type of microcode.

3. Gate array. Initially a gate array may seem to be a strange type of host, yet when it is personalized with wiring layers - a relatively simple design process - it emulates a desired image machine. Like all universal approaches the gate array pays a price for its flexibility. A given area of silicon

must be depopulated by at least a factor of two - probably more than 4 - when compared to a custom lay out.

Each of these approaches pays a price for their flexibility, but the price is paid in different ways and at different times. In each of the above cases a single host design is adapted to multiple environments by either compiler, interpreter, or routing technology.

UEMs and UHMS of recent vintage are much more similar than different. They usually share at least the following characteristics:

1. A large read/write microstore, accessible in one internal cycle. This microstore may be used in different ways. In the UHM it would be used for microprogram storage and perhaps cache, whereas in the UEM it is used almost exclusively for cache.

2. Main memory is a block oriented device for bulk storage in a multi-level storage hierarchy. Movement of environments from remote executable levels of storage may require support ranging from simple to elaborate.

Indeed the instruction sets at the host level are quite similar. They are both designed to be executed in one ALU cycle controlling a small number of working registers. A recently designed VLSI UEM at Stanford called MIPS (6) uses an instruction format with some limited horizontal parallel capabilities. Indeed it has an instruction format very similar to the Stanford EMMY (7), a 32 bit UHM designed for experimental purposes and now in use at Stanford for several years. The MIPS processor is particularly interesting as a state of the art UEM. It has an overlapped organization with a four stage pipeline; the interlocks are handled by the compiler. The EMMY design has a three stage pipeline with interlocks handled by the emulator (interpreter).

The most significant difference between the UEM and the UHM environment is the way the microstorage is used: in the UHM there is a separate micro-program storage. UHMs and UEMs are both improved by use of a cache type high speed storage for data and programs. The UHM simply pays the price of larger program static size with a larger cache, whereas the UEM pays the price of the micro program storage.

The limited differences between UEM and UHM might well argue for a Universal machine (UM) with a reconfigurable microstorage to be (partially) used as either micro-program storage or cache.

In a recent experiment at IBM, the System 370 architecture was implemented in a gate array (8) technology. The processor chip consisted of an all bipolar gate array using 4,923 bipolar gates out of a possible (available) 7,640. The

chip was a $49mm^2$ die with 200 I/O pins. A gate array provides an interesting alternative to personalizing an architecture in contrast to the preceding two approaches which customize through more traditional software. Actually the complete System 370 consisted of multiple chips consisting of the gate array processor chip, a control store ROM chip, a register chip, and main memory chips. The processor implementation was area limited and thus the host was realized with only an 8 bit ALU execution (with full 24 bit address arithmetic, however). It is important to note that the purpose of this experiment was to test CAD tools and not to optimize chip design tradeoffs. The experiment was successful in that the design was accomplished in a relatively short period of time with limited manpower. In an experiment organized to develop a true custom architecture, perhaps different chip arrangements would emerge perhaps using custom macro ALUs and on chip micro-storage of some smaller size.

Custom (Language Oriented) Architectures

At Stanford in the past several years, we have developed what we call the DEL - Directly Executed Language - approach to high level architecture. DEL is actually a misnomer since the source HLL program is not directly executed. Perhaps a better acronym would be DCA - Direct Correspondent Architecture. Objects in the source are represented as single objects in the image program. A basic objective of this research was to find better ways to customize architectures to environments. As such, most of our studies have been limited to particular source languages. We have completed studies on Fortran, Pascal, and Cobol. The Fortran and Pascal architectures (called Deltran (9) and Adept (10), respectively) were fully emulated using the Emmy UHM in our emulation laboratory. Deltran was not supported with the complete compilation facility, however, Adept is fully supported. Among the number of techniques used in the creation of DEL architectures two are particularly important:

1. A robust (or complete) set of formats
2. A contour based implementation of object specification

A robust set of formats gives concise code by eliminating both memory overhead instructions (load, store, push, pop, etc.) and redundant identifiers (as in a fixed three address format). All redundancy and overhead instructions can be eliminated with 21 formats, however, for practical purpose much smaller sets (about 8) will accomplish most of the advantages of completeness. The complete format set uses an internal evaluation stack, for example consider the statement:

$$A = B + C * D$$

In a stack machine this would be executed with the following instructions:

```
push      C
push      D
*
push      B
+
pop       A
```

This would be replaced simply by two DEL instructions.

```
F1,C,D  *
F2,A,B, +
```

Where F1 is a format that identifies the two operand sources as being explicit, i.e. contained in the instruction and the result as being stack. When the result is the top of the stack, the stack is automatically pushed. The F2 format identifies the stack as the right hand source, the left hand source and the result are explicit. When the stack is a source, it is automatically popped.

The contour model is based on a description of programming languages originally proposed by Johnson. Each procedure has its own contour and at least for dynamic languages a contour which contains data values used in the called procedure is loaded from main store into high speed contour storage at procedure entry time. For both Deltran and Adept, the specified width for an object varied from contour to contour. Its size was determined simply by using the smallest integer that contains $\log_2$ of the number of unique objects present in that particular environment or scope of definition. A procedure with 7 unique variables would have 3 bit fields to identify a variable. Addressing a particular variable consists of adding the three bit field to an environmental pointer which contains the base for the contour being executed. If the value is known, as in the case of constants and locals, it is simply contained in the contour. The first access to other variables, such as array elements will create an indirect reference, the address is determined by using a descriptor contained in the contour (9, 10).

Some Observations and Data

1. The RISC vs CISC tempest. Many traditional and fairly complex instruction sets (e.g. S/370 or VAX) include "reduced" instruction sets in their repertoire. The complexity comes about from extended functionality - managing large and segmented memory spaces, operating system support, file and character handling primitives, etc., and of course compatibility. These are not measured by small single test programs.

One may observe, however, that small, single user operating systems environments may be an increasingly important processor application (e.g. workstations).

2. Universal hosts provide a general purpose framework for matching environments to hardware. All such hosts pay a price for this flexibility - and this flexibility may exist only at design time (gate arrays - or UHMs with ROMs) or come at the expense of compile time (UEM) or require run-time overhead in loading a R/W UHM microstore.

3. Gate arrays vs UHM: System 370 emulation. A UHM of comparable bipolar technology to the 370 gate array was designed and simulated at Stanford. The UHM was a custom MSI design. Comparing this to the previously described gate array experiment:

	System 370 Chip	Comparable UHM Emulating 370
Number of Gates	4,923	11,000 (est.)
Cycle time	100 ns	125 ns (est.)
Data Paths	8^b (partially mapped)	32^b UHM
Control Store	54^b X 4^k (approx.)	32^b X 4^k
	ROM	RAM
Emulator Size (System 370)	NA	2,200 words
Av. Cycle/image Instr.	50	22

In both cases the number of gates does not include either microprogram storage or the bulk of the image registers. The estimate of 125nsec was based on T^2L Schottky MSI for the UHM. Note that if the designers of the 370 chip had 11,000 at their disposal, they would have certainly been able to realize a well-mapped host - with about 8-10 cycles per image instruction. The 11,000 gates of the UHM would fit on the same $49mm^2$ chip as the 370 in a completely custom design. The significant trade-off is not area but design effort and CAD support.

A custom designed UHM chip is another way of providing a flexible host and may in complex systems, provide superior results to gate arrays.

4. Language oriented vs Host oriented architectures. Extensive tests on EMMY emulating Adept (our Pascal architecture) illustrate the significant advantage that DELs offer over conventional host oriented architectures in both static and dynamic measures. For a suite of programs including FFT, Kalman filter and maze runs, the following data (10) is referenced to Adept (Adept = 1).

Measure	IBM/360	HP1000	P-Code
Code size	2.40	2.22	3.60
Instructions executed	3.42	3.55	3.57
Inst. bytes fetched	3.29	2.57	4.12
Data bytes fetched	5.82	4.80	5.81
Data bytes stored	20.15	12.56	9.19

If experience on EMMY is used as a guide, the DEL architectures are no more complex than familiar host oriented architectures (e.g. S370 emulator size is 2200 words while Adept emulator size is 1500 words - with comparable functionality).

5. While specialized custom designs can yield significant performance/functional advantages over a universal host based design, presently the design cost of such systems is excessive. In many ways the future of architecture is bound to the future of design tools.

6. There is a significant need for continued research in architecture - so as to know how to shape an instruction set to an environment. The "art" should be removed from computer architecture.

Indeed there are many new approaches possible, such possibilities as run-time expansion of a concisely encoded instruction into an expanded form can be done as a cache is loaded. Heuristic architectures could record an execution history of program execution to improve host performance.

Conclusions:

Many factors influence instruction set design over and above the obvious compile-execution tradeoff.

Design time is an especially serious problem as much of the potential of the technology must

be "derated" to accommodate limitations of either the design tools or universal hosts.

Language oriented architectures provide an important basis for the understanding of customizing an architecture to an environment. DEL derived data seems highly promising when compared with familiar host oriented instruction sets.

References

(1) Wilkes, M. V., The Processor Instruction Set, Proc. of the 15th Workshop on Microprogramming, Pub. by - IEEE Computer Society 1982 pp 3-5.

(2) Flynn, M. J., Customized Microprocessors, Microcomputer System Design Lecture notes in Computer Science No. 126, Springer-Verlay 1981, pp 182-220.

(3) Patterson, D. A. and Ditzel, D. R., "The Case for the Reduced Instruction Set Computer," Computer Architecture News, 5, 9,3, (1980) p 25.

(4) Fuller, S. H. and Burr, W. E., Measurement and Evaluation of Alternative Computer Architectures, Computer, Oct. 77, p 24-35.

(5) Radin, G., "The 801 Minicomputer," Computer Architecture News, 10, 2, (1982)

(6) Hennessy, J. L., et al, "MIPS: A VLSI Processor Architecture," Proc. CMU Conference on VLSI Systems, Oct. 81.

(7) Davis, C., et al, Gate Array Embodies System/370 Processor, Electronics, Oct. 9, 1980, pp 140-143.

(8) Flynn, M. J., Neuhauser, C. J., and McClure, R. M., EMMY - an Emulation System for User Microprogramming, AFIPS, Vol. 44 (NCC 1975) pp 85-89.

(9) Flynn, M. J., Hoevel L., W., Execution Architecture - the Deltran Experiment, IEEE Transactions on Computers, Feb. 1983.

(10) Wakefield, S. W., Studies in Execution Architecture, Ph. D. thesis, EE Dept. Stanford University 1983.

Session II
Microcode Compaction and Optimization

SRDAG Compaction - A Generalization of Trace Scheduling to Increase the Use of Global Context Information

Joseph L. Linn (1)

University of Southwestern Louisiana
Computer Science Department
P.O. Box 44330
Lafayette, Louisiana 70504

ABSTRACT - Microcode compaction is the process of converting essentially vertical microcode into horizontal microcode for a given architecture. The conventional plan calls for a microcode compiler to generate vertical code for a given architecture and then use a compaction system to produce horizontal code, thereby greatly reducing the complexity of horizontal code generation.

This paper attempts to extend the existing techniques used to perform the compaction process. Specifically, the procedure presented generalizes the "trace scheduling" method of [Fisher81] by using more global context information in compaction decisions. A number of definitions from classical compaction are generalized to encompass this expanded scope.

Further, the paper presents two example classes of problems for which the new method outperforms the trace scheduling technique in terms of the execution time efficiency of the generated code. A number of unresolved questions are noted involving the class of global compaction procedures.

1.0 Introduction

This paper presents an extension to the trace scheduling microcode compaction method [Fisher81] called "SRDAG compaction". The history of classical microcode compaction has so far been marked by two epochs. In the first epoch, the primary thrust of research was aimed at discovering reasonable solutions to the local compaction problem. The goal of any compaction algorithm is to transform an input vertical microprogram into an equivalent compacted horizontal microprogram. For the local compaction problem, the input program is restricted to be a single (basic) block, that is a program with a single entry, a single exit, and no branches.

---

(1) This work is supported, in part, by a grant from the RCA Corporation.

When it was discovered that this problem is NP-complete (for the most general case where the register assignment is not known a priori) [DeWitt76], attention turned to the discovery of algorithms not guaranteed to produce the optimal compaction but whose execution time is within practical limits. A number of such algorithms have been discovered and tested [Landskov80, Davidson81]. It has been determined that these algorithms achieve solutions within a few percent of the optimal in virtually all cases. However, error bounds on the performance of these algorithms have never (to the author's knowledge) been established. In the case of one algorithm, microinstruction list scheduling [Fisher79], one would assume that the well known list scheduling bounds would carry over in a reasonable way. Thus, the first epoch in classical compaction ended with the discovery of a number of algorithms running in quadradic time achieving very good solutions to the local compaction problem.

The current epoch began with attention turning to the problem of exploiting parallelism beyond block boundaries. It was immediately apparent that the the global compaction problem could not be effectively solved by merely compacting individual basic blocks autonomously; the interplay among the basic blocks of a program exerts great influence on local compaction decisions. The solution offered by [Fisher81] is trace scheduling, a technique by which a path, or trace, of the program is essentially treated as a single block to be compacted. In this way, the scheduler has a more global view of the program and interactions among blocks on the trace are taken into account. Unfortunately, interactions with blocks off the trace are not considered. In addition, compacting the entire trace is not as general as compacting only the first block of the trace. This is because a major emphasis in trace compaction is that the trace under consideration is in some sense the most likely uncompacted path through the graph. However, moving instructions from later blocks of the trace into the first may have the effect of changing which trace through the graph is the most likely. Thus, it seems reasonable that the trace should be reselected after the first block has been compacted.

11

SRDAG compaction works in a manner that is very similar to trace compaction (1) except that the subgraph considered is a singly rooted directed acyclic graph (SRDAG) instead of a path. Moreover, the entire SRDAG is not compacted simultaneously; in fact, only the root block of the SRDAG is compacted in each iteration. The primary advantage of SRDAG compaction over trace compaction is that some important improvements are considered that are not considered when the global view is restricted to a path. For example, a particular microinstruction may be free at the top (i.e. movable to a higher block, see DEFINITION 7 below) of several blocks in the SRDAG. The SRDAG compaction algorithm prefers to move up such duplicated microinstructions whereas the trace compactor is not aware of this possible improvement.

The presentation here will assume that the program graph is a directed acyclic graph (DAG), i.e. that there are no loops. The technique used for introducing loops in [Fisher81] should apply equally well to SRDAG compaction.

2.0 The Model

This paper utilizes nearly the identical model as [Fisher81]. There are a few differences that are pointed out as the appropriate definitions are given. The most fundamental unit of execution for a computing engine is a microoperation. On a horizontal machine, several microoperations may be packed together to form a microinstruction. A basic block, or just block, is a sequence of microinstructions where only the last one is permitted to be any type of branch. Thus, we are led to the following definitions:

DEFINITION 1: For any given microengine, MOP is the set of all legal microoperations for that engine.

DEFINITION 2: For any given microengine, there is a function

is_instruction : powerset(MOP) -> Boolean.

The is_instruction function replaces the resource_compatible function of [Fisher81] in the loop-free case. Further, if I1 and I2 are microinstructions with I3 equal the union of I1 and I2, I1 and I2 can be combined exactly when is_instruction(I3). As explained in [Fisher81], this function is easily calculated using a resource vector.

---

(1) The terminology "trace scheduling" from [Fisher81] stems from the fact that list scheduling is the selected local compaction technique and from the fact that the scheduling paradigm and terminology are utilized in the presentation. This presentation does not utilize the same list scheduling basis; thus, the more generic "trace compaction" is used.

DEFINITION 3: A block is a sequence of microinstructions where only the last microinstruction is permitted to contain a branch microoperation, and no branch is permitted to any microinstruction in the sequence except the first.

DEFINITION 4: Microinstructions are assumed to operate by reading and writing certain registers (memory elements) of the microengine. If REGISTERS is the set of memory elements directly accessible by microoperations we can define:

readreg, writereg:
    powerset(MOP) -> powerset(REGISTERS)

The functions readreg and writereg are properties of the particular microengine being considered. Not all of the registers need actually be memory elements; indeed registers are also introduced to model the effects of microoperations on busses and other data paths of the engine. The purpose of the readreg and writereg functions is to specify in an unambiguous way how microinstructions can be rearranged while preserving the semantic meaning of the program. A relation may be defined in terms of these functions that allows us to say that a particular microinstruction must be executed before another one. This relation is defined as follows.

DEFINITION 5: Given is a DAG D of microinstructions. For any unique microinstructions Ii and Ij so that there is a path in D from Ii to Ij:

 * if the intersection of writereg(Ii) and readreg(Ij) contains some register r and there is no microinstruction Ik on any path from Ii to Ij so that r is in writereg(Ik), then Ii directly data precedes Ij.

 * if the intersection of readreg(Ii) and writereg(Ij) contains some register r and there is no microinstruction Ik on any path from Ii to Ij so that r is in writereg(Ik), then Ii directly data precedes Ij.

If Ii is related to Ij by the "directly data precedes" relation, the notation is Ii << Ij. Further, the name of the transitive closure of this relation is "data precedes", i.e. if Ii <<+ Ij then it is said that Ii data precedes Ij. It is possible for there to be Ii, Ij, and Ik so that Ii << Ij, Ij << Ik, and Ii << Ik. These "transitive edges" may be removed since this does not affect the behavior of the compaction procedures.

DEFINITION 6: Given a set of microinstructions, MI, and a partial order, R, defined on MI, the set of successors of a microinstruction I in MI is given by:

successors(I) = {I' in MI | I R I'}.

Of course, if I' is in successors(I) then I' is termed a successor of I.

DEFINITION 7: Given a partial order over the set of microinstructions, microinstruction I is free at the top of a block B if it contained in B and if it is not the successor of any any microinstruction in B. Microinstruction I is free at the bottom of B if I has no successors in B.

DEFINITION 8: A register r is live locally in block B if some microinstruction in B reads register r before any microinstruction writes register r. A register r is live at the top of block B if it is live locally or if there exists a block B' so that (a) there is a path from B to B' in G, (b) no microinstruction in the path from B to B' writes register r except potentially B', and (c) r is locally live in B'.

DEFINITION 9: A program P is a five-tuple <G,edgep,startp,live_reg,cmpct> 5-tuple where

G = <Blocks,Arcs> is a directed graph with the vertices (Blocks) of the graph being blocks and the edges (Arcs) representing a possibility that control can pass between the tail of an arc and its head.

edgep : Arcs -> [0,1] is a function giving the conditional probability that control will flow to the head of the arc, given that control passes to the tail of the arc.

startp : Blocks -> [0,1] is a function giving the probability that the program will start in a given block.

live_reg : Blocks -> (subsets of registers) is a function denoting which registers are live at the beginning of any block. Live_reg need only be given for leaves initially since the compaction procedure recomputes live_reg anyway.

cmpct : Blocks -> {true,false} is a function denoting whether a given block has already been compacted.

3.0 A Global Compaction Procedure

In this section, the algorithm for global compaction is presented. The various steps of the algorithm are represented by pidgen code for expository purposes; the code given should not be understood to be a tested implementation.

Global compaction may be viewed as a procedure that transforms one program into another one. The goal of global compaction is to perform this mapping in such a way as to preserve semantics of the program and also to reduce the execution time of the program by reducing both the length of individual blocks and the number of blocks through which control passes during execution. The procedure normally begins with a program in which few, if any, blocks have been compacted. There are no reported instances where a high level language microcode compiler actually

operates in this fashion. Nevertheless, if a procedural binding concept [Davidson80] is incorporated in the language, the code emitted might be precompacted. Also, in the S* family of microprogramming languages [Dasgupta78, Klassen81] supports the concept of precompacted "regions". Thus, allowing some precompacted blocks simply anticipates already emerging microcode compiler technology.

In addition, the compaction procedure also requires that the program graph G be acyclic and that the program may not begin execution in any block that has a predecessor in G. The process is an iterative one; on each iteration, at least one uncompacted block is compacted yielding a new program. Unfortunately, the compaction of one block may cause other blocks to be built in order to preserve the semantics of the program. Each iteration of the procedure may be described as follows:

```
procedure SRDAG_compaction(inout P:program);
  begin
  reduce_graph_and_compute_livereg(P);
  while some block of P is not compacted do
    begin
    select_compaction_SRDAG(D,P);
    compact_root_of_D_updating_P(D,P);
    reduce_graph_and_compute_livereg(P);
    end;
  end;
```

Several items are noteworthy. First, the steps of SRDAG compaction are essentially the same as those of the trace compaction procedure of [Fisher81]. This is hardly surprising since SRDAG compaction may be viewed as a generalization of trace compaction. One notable difference is that the bookkeeping procedure of [Fisher81] is explicitly integrated into the root compaction procedure. Second, no proof of termination is presented.

In addition, this presentation makes explicit a graph reduction procedure. In the version used here, the procedure reduce_graph_and_compute_livereg effects several important transformations. First, empty blocks are deleted and strings of blocks coalesced when possible. Second, updated live register information is computed; in the same step, useless microinstructions can be eliminated. Although the procedure as shown recomputes live register information for the entire graph on each iteration, execution time might be saved by recomputing this information only for those blocks changed or created in the current iteration and their predecessors. The implementation of this procedure is a standard topic in code generation [Aho77] and is not discussed here.

This presentation concentrates on the root compaction step. However, a few remarks are in order regarding the selection of the SRDAG to be compacted. First, it is determined using the program probability functions which uncompacted block with no uncompacted predecessors is the most likely to be executed. The block becomes the single root of the SRDAG, i.e. the block to be compacted. Given this, the SRDAG selected is simply the maximal SRDAG with the given root in which all the blocks of the SRDAG are uncompacted. Notice that this causes the blocks to be compacted in rather a top-down fashion beginning at the top(s) of the program. Nevertheless, the maximum information in the graph is available in each step for compaction decisions.

In [Fisher81], there are identified a menu of six rules that govern semantic-preserving motion of microinstructions among blocks. These are reproduced here in Figure 1. Fisher reports that trace compaction utilizes rules R1, R3, R5, and R6 implicitly; SRDAG compaction will do the same. However, the use of rule R6 by trace compaction is very limited and rule R4 is not used at all. The advantage of SRDAG compaction over trace compaction is due to its use of rule R4 and its more general use of rule R6.

RULE	∀ I FROM	MOVES TO	WHENEVER
R1	B2	B1 & B4	The ∀I is free at the top of B2
R2	B1 & B4	B2	The ∀I is free at the bottom of B1 & B4
R3	B2	B3 & B5	The ∀I is free at the bottom of B2
R4	B3 & B5	B2	The ∀I is free at the top of B3 & B5
R5	B2	B3 (B5)	The ∀I is free at the bottom of B2 and the ∀I writes no register live at the top of B5 (B3)
R6	B3 (B5)	B2	The ∀I is free at the top of B3 and writes no register live at the top of B5 (B3)

Figure 1

Legal movements of ∀ instructions in a program

4.0 The Root Compaction Step

Thus, we turn our attention to the root compaction procedure. There are two features of the SRDAG compactor's instruction placement that differ from that of local compaction:

1) the need for bookkeeping operations to

preserve the semantics of the program.

2) the need to deal with the sometimes unusual semantics of branch microinstructions, e.g. delayed branching [Gross82].

There are two operations in compaction that cause bookkeeping operations: (a) moving microinstructions up the SRDAG and (b) moving microinstructions down the SRDAG. The task of moving up is further divided into two cases. The complex case of moving up a conditional jump is considered in a later section. The situation of moving nonjump microinstructions up the SRDAG is depicted in Figure 2a. Here, blocks B1 and B2 are considered to be on the SRDAG in question while the rest of the blocks are not. Clearly, if a microinstruction if moved up from B2 into B1, the microinstruction must also be placed so that it will be executed en route from B3 to B2, from B4 to B2, etc. Figures 2b and 2c depict alternative schemes for changing the graph in order to preserve the semantics. Since SRDAG and trace compaction are still relatively new, no work has yet been published on a procedure to make a reasonable selection from all the alternatives. The alternative selected is as in Figure 2d since it delays the creation of extra microinstructions until it is determined that there is some benefit to the duplication. Also, this version simplifies the case of moving up a conditional jump considered later.

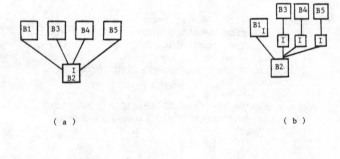

(a)   (b)

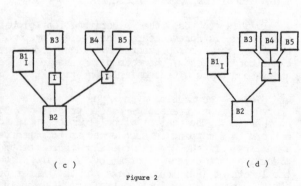

(c)   (d)

Figure 2

Moving up a microinstruction

(a) The original with I in B2. (b) no sharing   (c) partial sharing
(b) Complete Sharing

14

The general case of moving a microinstruction up in the compaction occurs when the microinstruction is free in several blocks, there are several off-SRDAG blocks involved, and the path from the root block to the block containing the microinstructions contains interior nodes. Figure 3a shows a fairly complex case in which the free microinstruction I in blocks B21, B22, and B23 is to be moved up into B1. Note that the path from B1 to B21 is not disjoint from the path from B1 to B22. Figure 3b shows how the situation could be resolved.

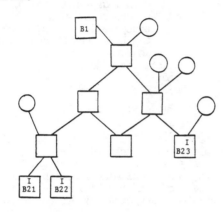

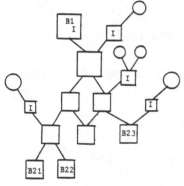

Figure 3

(a) before moving the I in B21, B22, & B23 to B1
(b) after moving the I to B1

Note: The circle block are not on the SRDAG.

The algorithm below effects the desired transformation. It also contains some of the details on how the probability information is updated. Two hints will assist in understanding the algorithm. First, "push_up_blocks" is the set of blocks where a new block will have to be created. Second, all instances of the microinstruction considered are deleted from the original blocks and that the "data_ready_set" is updated.

```
procedure
    consider_move_up(I,BP,D,inout P
                      ,inout data_ready_set);
```

```
-- I   is the microinstruction
--     to be moved up
-- BP  is a set of <block,pointer>
--     pairs locating I in each block
-- P   is the current program
-- D   is the current SRDAG
begin
define P=<G,edgep,startp,live_reg,cmpct>;
push_up_blocks:= {};
for each <B,PI> in BP do
 begin
  for each successor <I',{<B',PI'>}> of I
            at PI in B do
     begin
      if pred(<I',{<B',PI'>}>)-- = 0 then
        then add <I',{<B',PI'>}>
                  to the data_ready_set;
     end;
   delete from B the copy of I located by PI;
   ancestors:=
      {B' | there is a B',B path in D};
   push_up_blocks:=
        push_up_blocks+ancestors-{root(D)};
 end;
for each B in push_up_blocks do
          push_up_a_microI(I,B,D,P);
end;
```

```
procedure push_up_a_microI(I,B,D,inout P);
  begin
  define P=<G,edgep,startp,live_reg,cmpct>;
  create a new block H so that
       the only instruction in H is I;
  add an edge <H,B> to G
       with edgep(<H,B>)=1.0;
  for each edge <B',B> in G
            with B' not in D do
     begin
     add edge <B',H> to G
          with edgep(<B',H>)=edgep(<B',B>);
     delete <B',B> from G
     end;
  end;
```

The second bookkeeping operation involves code moving down the SRDAG. The discussion of this operation is included only for completeness since this operation is not used explicitly in SRDAG compaction. Instead, the procedure for moving up conditional jumps implicitly moves code down whenever it is needed. Specifically, this downward code movement is needed when a sequence of microinstructions that originally appears before a jump has not been scheduled within the time before the jump takes effect. In such a case, the microinstruction must be duplicated in a block that executes before each successor of the block containing the jump. If the original graph contained the graph in Figure 4a, Figure 4b shows one way of performing this duplication. If we assume that the sequence writes only registers that are not live at the top of the starred blocks, the situations in Figure 4c and Figure 4d are alternatives. Again, there has not been any work published on choosing from among these alternatives except in an arbitrary way. The alternative of Figure 4c has been arbitrarily chosen to allow the most opportunity for compaction; ostensibly, the block being pushed down could potentially be subsumed by the lower blocks.

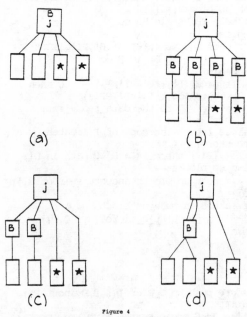

(a) the sequence B is to be moved down; the sequence writes no registers live at the top of the starred blocks.
(b), (c), (d) alternative rearrangements.

Figure 4

In general, not all of the instructions in the sequence manipulate live registers for the succeeding block. It is straightforward to determine the appropriate subsequence to push down into a new block by examining the sequence in reverse and keeping track of the live registers at each point. At each point, a microinstruction is retained if it writes some register in the current live set and discarded otherwise. If the microinstruction contains more than a single microoperation, it is possible that it could be split apart yielding a smaller microinstruction and thereby increasing the opportunity for compaction. This operation is not considered here. The appropriate algorithm for moving down follows; in the algorithm, B is the block with the instruction sequence to be moved down, and P is the current program.

```
procedure move_sequence_down(inout B,inout P);
  begin
  define P=<G,edgep,startp,live_reg,cmpct>;
  define LLReg = local_live_reg;
  S:= reverse(inst_sequence(B));
  for each <B,B'> in G do
    begin
    newS:= empty_sequence;
    LLReg:= live_reg(B');
    for each I in sequence from S do
```

```
    if writereg(I) and LLReg
        are not disjoint then
      begin
      newS:= I,newS;
      LLReg:= LLReg - writereg(I);
      LLReg:= LLReg + readreg(I);
      end;
    if newS not empty do
      begin
      create a new block H
        with inst_sequence(H)=newS;
      add an edge <H,B'>
          with edgep(<H,B'>)=1.0;
      add an edge <B,H> with
          edgep(<B,H>)=edgep(<B,B'>)
          and fixup the branch (if any)
          in B to address H;
      delete the edge <B,B'>;
      end;
    end;
end;
```

The other difference from local compaction, dealing with delayed branches, is discussed briefly in the next section. Having dispensed with many preliminaries, the algorithm for compaction of the root may now be presented. A detailed discussion follows the algorithm.

```
procedure
  compact_root_of_D_updating_P
                    (D, inout P);
  begin
  define P=<G,edgep,startp,live_reg,cmpct>;
  define DRS=data_ready_set;
  define Delay_Length=number_delay_cycles;
  create a new empty block C
    with cmpct(C)=true;
  change all edges in G <B,root(D)>
    into <B,C> with the same probability;
  create an edge e=<C,root(D)>
    with edgep(e) = 1.0;
      -- C is the block into which the
      -- compacted instruction sequence
      -- is placed
  compute << and <<+
    using D as a model for the partial order;
      -- for this computation, the readreg set
      -- for any conditional jump is assumed
      -- to contain all the registers live at
      -- any successor to the jump.
  form_initial_DRS_and_init_preds(DRS,D,<<);
  cycle:= 0; branch_cycle:= 0;
  compacted_sequence:= empty_sequence;

  while DRS not empty and
    cycle-branch_cycle<=Delay_Length do
    begin
    select_next_microI(nextI,DRS,D,G,<<,<<+);
    DRS:= DRS - nextI;
    append {I|<I,BP> in nextI}
        to the inst_sequence of C
    for each <I,BP> in nextI do
      consider_move_up(I,BP,D,P,DRS);
        -- recall that the instances of the
        -- microinstructions are deleted here
```

16

```
        -- and that the DRS is updated
if nextI contains a branch then
  begin
  branch_cycle:= cycle;
  jumpI:= the branch microoperation;
  jumpBP:= {free instances of jumpI};
  end;
cycle:= cycle + 1;
end;

if branch_cycle <> 0 then
  rearrange_for_a_jump(jumpI,jumpBP,D,P);
end;
```

Initially, this procedure may seem very formidable; fortunately, it is divided into three distinct steps. In the first step, we initialize the procedure. First, a new header block is created above the root of the SRDAG and all control into the root is changed to flow through this block. Next, the << and <<+ relations are computed with the partial order based on the SRDAG D. Continuing, the initial data_ready_set is formed; in the same step a "pred" value is set for each microinstruction I to indicate the number of microinstructions that directly data precede I, i.e. that must be placed into the compacted sequence before I. Clearly, the initial data_ready_set consists of those instances of microinstructions whose "pred" value is zero initially. Any particularmicrooperation is represented only once in the data_ready_set; a list of pointers is maintained to locate the instances of the microinstruction.

The second step of the root compaction procedure is the compaction loop. Here, a new compacted instruction is obtained on each iteration with the data_ready_set being updated to reflect any new instructions now data_ready and the program being updated whenever instructions are moved up. This continues until the data_ready_set is exhausted or until the scheduling of a branch microoperation signals the end of the newly compacted basic block.

In the last step, a check is made to determine if a branch microoperation was actually placed. If so, the more complicated sequence of accounting for a jump placement must be invoked. The rearrangement procedure makes use of the "moving down" concept discussed earlier. The details are presented in a later section.

In terms of obtaining a reasonable compaction, the crucial step is the select_next_microI procedure. Thus, this topic is addressed next.

5.0 Selecting the Next Microinstruction

There are many ways in which the next microinstruction might be selected. A very good review of many that have already been discovered and experimented with is given in [Davidson81]. The algorithm most widely recommended is microinstruction list scheduling [Davidson81,

Fisher79, Fisher81, Landskov80]. Perhaps this is because the algorithm is so easily parameterized by a priority assignment function that produces a linear ordering of the microinstructions. Thus, the following is a simple implementation of the selection procedure based on list scheduling.

```
procedure select_next_microI
        (out nextI,DRS,P,<<,<<+);
  begin
  DRS':= DRS;
  nextI:= {}; nextI_justI:= {};
    -- nextI has the instructions and
    -- the pointers, nextI_justI has
    -- just the instructions
  while DRS' not empty do
    begin
    <I,BP>:= the microinstruction in DRS'
              with the highest priority;
    DRS':= DRS' - <I,BP>;
    if is_instruction(nextI_justI+{I}) then
      begin
      nextI:= nextI+{<I,BP>};
      nextI_justI:= nextI_justI+{I}
      end;
    end;
  end;
```

The ability of this procedure to produce effective compactions depends on the selection of a good priority function. Note that in this algorithm, a great deal of data is readily available on which to base a priority. Note the each <I,BP> pair may represent several instances of the same microinstruction. In such cases the actual priority used is the sum of the individual priorities. In [Fisher81], it is reported that giving higher priorities to higher levels in the DAG induced by << gives excellent result for local compaction.

These results do not carry over directly when global compaction is the goal. For example, consideration should be given to always scheduling the microinstruction with the highest probability of being executed regardless of the data precedence relations. Of course, the program is a parameter to the selection process and the priority function could easily use the program's probability functions to order the instructions according to expected execution probability. Also, one might want to determine how much space would be used if a microinstruction is pushed up and to decrease the priority if it is too much space is used. So many possible priority functions exist that further research seems warranted to discover

a) if there is any correlation between "styles" of microengines or microprograms and certain well performing priority functions, and

b) if there are parameterized priority functions that could be used to tune the compaction process to a given environment and, if so, can the tuning be done

17

automatically.

While this type of selection process might perform very well for a number of microengines, it is likely that all of these "greedy algorithms" will perform quite poorly for engines with delayed branches. This is because the algorithms always try for big profits early so that no instructions are available to be scheduled in the cycle(s) following the instantiation of the branch (but before the branch actually occurs). No results addressing this difficult problem have yet been reported.

6.0 Rearranging for jumps

The most complex program transformation required in compaction is that of exchanging the order of the conditional jumps. However, although the details are complex, the basic idea of the transformation may be grasped by a very simple example. Consider the following program fragment:

    if Predicate1 then S1
    elseif Predicate2 then S2
    else S3

The problem is to find an equivalent program so that the two tests can be reversed. Given no additional knowledge about the predicates involved, the best one can do is the following.

    if Predicate2 then
            if Predicate1 then S1 else S2
    else
            if Predicate1 then S1 else S3

Figures 5a and 5b show this same transformation pictorially on program graphs. In order to get an even better understanding of the process, consider this slightly more complicated fragment

    S1;
    if P1 then S2
    else begin
        S3;
        if P2 then S4 else S5
        end

and the "rearranged version" of the program

    S1;
    if P2 then
        if P1 then S2
            else begin S3; S4 end
    else
        if P1 then S2
            else begin S3; S5 end

which are depicted in figures 5c and 5d. A close inspection of the programs and figures reveals that statement S3 has been "moved down". One more example finishes the preparatory discussion. Consider

    if P1 then S1
    else if P2 then S2
            else if P3 then S3
                    else if P4 then S4 else S5

where are are to move the last test (P4) to the top. The appropriate rearrangement is given in the following.

    if P4 then
        if P1 then S1
        else if P2 then S2
                else if P3 then S3
                        else S4
    else
        if P1 then S1
        else if P2 then S2
                else if P3 then S3
                        else S5

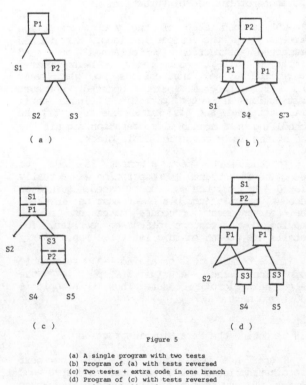

(a)

(b)

(c)

(d)

Figure 5

(a) A single program with two tests
(b) Program of (a) with tests reversed
(c) Two tests + extra code in one branch
(d) Program of (c) with tests reversed and code duplicated

Figure 6 shows the "before and after." When a jump is moved up substantial portions of the graph (or program text) must be copies. How much must be copied? As it happens, the entire graph consisting of all paths from the root of the DAG to the block where the original test resided, the jumpblock, must be copied. In fact, a copy must be made for each outarc of the jumpblock. This leads to the following definition.

DEFINITION 10: Given a SRDAG D and a block B in D, the COPYDAG(D,B) is a SRDAG that contains only the paths from root(D) to B in D.

For each arc that originally connected a block B in the COPYDAG with a block B' off the COPYDAG, an edge is created for each copy CD' of the COPYDAG whose sourse is the image of B in CD', whose destination is B', and whose probability is the same as the ⟨B,B'⟩ edge. Finally, an edge is created from the compaction block C to the appropriate copy of the root(D) for each outarc of the original jumpblock and with the same probability as the original jumpblock arc. The original COPYDAG is now deleted since the copies have been linked into the program.

There are a few extra details that must be considered. First, two jump microoperations are the same only if both the predicate and the destination blocks are identical. Second, the definition of the COPYDAG is only meaningful if there is a single jumpblock. Thus, if multiple instances of a conditional jump are to be placed simultaneously, the jump microinstruction must be pulled down using rule R2 (finally got to use rule R2). If we assume that free microinstructions are pulled down in the graph reduction phase as discussed above, this is no problem; otherwise, select_next_microI procedure will have to be modified to do this.

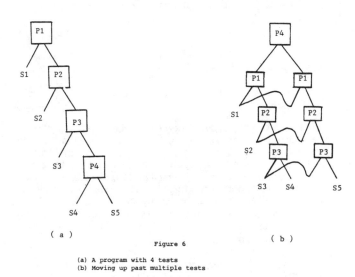

(a)

Figure 6

(b)

(a) A program with 4 tests
(b) Moving up past multiple tests

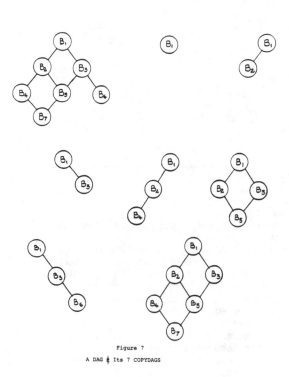

Figure 7

A DAG & Its 7 COPYDAGS

Figure 7 gives an example of an SRDAG and also the COPYDAG for various blocks. Given the concept of a COPYDAG it is reasonably straightforward to define the appropriate transformation. First, a copy of the COPYDAG is made for each outarc of the jumpblock, i.e. the block that originally contained the jump. Recall that the jump has already been removed from the jumpblock by the copying up procedure. Each copy of the COPYDAG is associated with one of the arcs of the original jumpblock. Since there is no longer a jump in the block, there should no longer be multiple outarcs. Rather, the only successor of the copy of the jumpblock is the successor of the original jumpblock along the arc that is associated with this copy of the COPYDAG. The edge probability is always 1.

Third, if there are off SRDAG jumps onto the COPYDAG then the root compaction procedure will have pushed up the microinstruction, but the outarcs will not be correct. Thus, any block B in the COPYDAG may have an off SRDAG predecessor B'; B' is unique because of the implementation of pushing up. In such cases, an arc associated with each outarc of the jumpblock is created. This arc has B' as its source and has as its destination the copy of B in the copy of the COPYDAG associated with this outarc. The probability for the new arc is the same as the probability of the outarc with which it is associated. All of these remarks are folded into the following algorithm; Figure 8 shows a detailed example of the transformation.

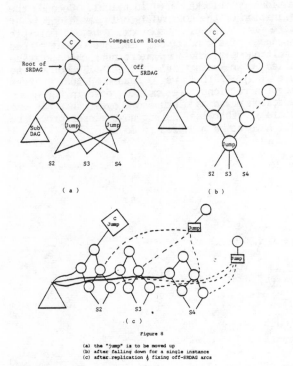

Figure 8

(a) the "jump" is to be moved up
(b) after falling down for a single instance
(c) after replication & fixing off-SRDAG arcs

```
procedure
    rearrange_for_a_jump(jumpI,jumpBP,D,P);
    begin
    define P=<G,edgep,startp,live_reg,cmpct>;
        -- recall that the pushing is already
        -- done and that jumpBP is a singleton
    define jumpBP=<jumpblock,jumpPI>;
    define CD=COPYDAG(D,jumpblock);
    for each edge <jumpblock,B'> do
        begin
        create a copy of CD called CD';
        for each edge <B1,B2> in D
            with B1 in CD and B2 not in CD do
            begin
            define imageB'= image of B' in CD';
            define imageR = image of root(D)
                                 in CD';
            define imageJ = image of the
                                 jumpblock in CD';
            add an edge e1=<imageB',B2>
```

with edgep(e1)=edgep(<B1,B2>);
```
            add an edge e2=<C,imageR> with
                edgep(e2)=edgep(<jumpblock,B'>);
                -- recall that C is the
                -- compaction block as
                -- defined in the
                -- compact_root_... procedure
            add an edge e3=<imageJ,B'>
                with edgep(e3)=1.0;
            end;
        for each block B in CD for which
            there exists an edge <Boff,B>
            with Boff off the SRDAG do
            begin
            delete the edge <Boff,B>;
            define imageB=image of B in CD';
            add an edge e=<Boff,imageB>with
                edgep(e)=edgep(<jumpblock,B'>);
            end;
        end;
    delete the original CD from the graph;
    end;
```

This concludes the presentation of the algorithm for SRDAG compaction.

7.0 Performance

In general, the code produced by SRDAG compaction is no worse than the code produced by trace compaction. This is readily seen in the fact that SRDAG compaction degenerates to trace compaction in the case where the SRDAG chosen is a path and where compacting the blocks in order does not affect the probability of the next block being executed. However, there are cases where SRDAG compaction outperforms trace compaction by a factor of two.

Consider the program graph of Figure 9. In the "root" are two instructions: one to get the opcode of an instruction and another to do a case-type branch. In each of the $n-1$ left subnodes there is a microinstruction to decode two register fields of the instruction and a second one to do some ALU operation (a different one in each branch). In the rightmost subtree, there are also two microinstructions. The first one decodes one register field and an immediate operand. The second performs a transfer microoperation. We assume that the two decodes have a resource conflict, i.e. that they cannot be in the same microinstruction. A program of this sort might arise in emulating an architecture with only register to register arithmetic and an immediate load. The edge probabilities are assumed to be $(1/n+1)$ for the left branches and $(2/n+1)$ for the right branch since we might assume that the immediate instruction is executed more often than any particular register to register instruction.

The trace compactor chooses to move the decode from the right node into the root block since this is the instruction most frequently executed. The average execution time of the trace compacted program is

20

Ave_Time_Trace(n)
```
        = probability(right_block)
            * execution_time(right_block)
        + probability(left_blocks)
            * execution_time(left_blocks)
        = (2/n+1)(2)+((n-1)/(n+1))(3)
        = (3n+1)/(n+1).
```

However, the SRDAG compactor sees the n-1 copies of the other decode microinstruction and therefore chooses to move this into the root instead. Thus, we have that

Ave_Time_SRDAG(n)
```
        = (2/n+1)(3)+((n-1)/(n+1))(2)
        = (2n+4)/n+1.
```

Hence, the performance of the trace compacted program will be 50% worse than the performance of the SRDAG compacted program. Of course, an architect when given this information might try to provide resources for parallel decodes.

As a second example, assume that each of the blocks in Figure 4 contains k/2 microinstructions and that all the left subnodes contain the same code. Assume further that all the instructions from all the blocks can be compacted to run in k/2 cycles; admittedly, this situation is not very likely. But, in this case, the trace compactors average execution time will be (k(n+1)-1)/(n+1) whereas the SRDAG compacted version will always run in (k/2) cycles. Clearly, the ratio of trace compacted vs SRDAG compacted runtime is approximately 2:1; it is conjectured that this is the highest ratio possible.

It is reasonable to note here that moving up microinstructions has a chance of reducing the space requirements as well if not too many off-SRDAG blocks are created. Trace compaction has some of this benefit but the results are magnified for SRDAG compaction especially when duplicated instances of a microinstruction are moved up simultaneously. Note that in the last example the space of the trace compacted version is O(nk) whereas the SRDAG compacted version uses only O(k).

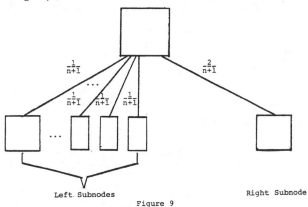

Left Subnodes   Right Subnode

Figure 9

An example graph of a program

8.0 Conclusions

This paper has presented an procedure that compacts code to run as much as 100% faster than trace compacted code. Further, if the trace compacted code occupies O(n) space, the SRDAG compacted code could use as little as O(sqrt(n)) space. In addition, it seems that the SRDAG compaction procedure will never do worse than trace compaction. Thus, we believe that SRDAG compaction is the method of choice for the global compaction of microcode.

A number of unresolved questions in the compaction arena have been noted. SRDAG compaction provides an excellent framework for considering these problems. Of particular interest is the selection of the next microinstruction when delayed branches are considered. We conjecture that, unlike the classical problem, the epsilon approximation problem [Horowitz78] for local compaction with delayed branching is NP-hard.

As was noted earlier, SRDAG compaction makes use of five of the six rules for code motion. However, SRDAG compaction still makes little use of rule R2. Perhaps, it would be reasonable to incorporate a routine to "pull down" all such free microinstructions into the graph reduction procedure. The compaction process would then have the opportunity to pull them back up if desired. Further work into resolving this question seems warranted.

Also, a great deal of emphasis in the past has been placed on local compaction algorithms with local parameterizations. In other words, the parameterizations sought did not consider concepts from global compaction. For example, the compaction procedure should be sufficiently parameterized that microinstructions can be prevented from moving up if the cost of doing so would be too high. This type of parameterization has not yet been studied even for the best known underlying local compaction procedures.

Finally, we believe that the current decomposition of the horizontal code generation is not the only one that should be considered. The ability to move microinstructions around in the graph depends critically on the fact that different blocks in the program use different resources. If code is generated initially without regard for the needs of global compaction, it is unlikely that different resources will be used. What is truly needed is research to address the difficult problem of generating code that has a particular shape so that code generation and compaction may be integrated.

REFERENCES

[Aho77]
A.V. Aho and J.D. Ullman Principles of Compiler Design, Bell Laboratories, Murray Hill, N.J., 1977. Published by Addison-Wesley, Menlo Park, California.

[Dasgupta78]
S. Dasgupta "Towards a Microprogramming Language Schema," Proc. 11th Annual Workshop on Microprogramming, pp. 144-153, November, 1978.

[Davidson80]
S. Davidson "Design and Construction of a Virtual Machine Resource Binding Language," Ph.D. Dissertation, University of Southwestern Louisiana, Lafayette, Louisiana, August, 1980.

[Davidson81]
S. Davidson, D. Landskov, B.D. Shriver, and P.W. Mallett "Some Experiments in Local Microcode Compaction for Horizontal Machines," IEEE TC, vol. c-30, no. 7, pp. 460-477, July, 1981.

[Dewitt76]
D.J. Dewitt "A machine independent approach to the production of optimal horizontal microcode," Ph.D. Dissertation, Univ. of Michigan, Ann Arbor, Tech. Rep. 76 DT4, August, 1976.

[Fisher79]
J.A. Fisher "The optimization of horizontal microcode within and beyond basic blocks: An application of processor scheduling with resources," Courant Math. Comput. Lab., Ph.D. Dissertation, New York Univ., New York, New York, October, 1979.

[Fisher81]
J.A. Fisher "Trace Scheduling: A Technique for Global Microcode Compaction," IEEE TC, vol. c-30, no. 7, pp. 478-490, July, 1981.

[Gross82]
T. Gross and J.L. Hennessy "Optimizing Delayed Branches," Proc. 15th Annual Workshop on Microprogramming, pp. 114-120, October, 1982. IEEE TC, vol. c-30, no. 7, pp. 460-477, July, 1981.

[Klassen81]
A. Klassen and S. Dasgupta "S*(QM-1): An Instantiation of the High Level Microprogramming Schema S* for the Nanodata QM-1," Proc. 14th Annual Workshop on Microprogramming, pp. 124-130, November, 1981.

[Horowitz78]
E. Horowitz and S. Sahni Fundamentals of Computer Algorithms, Computer Science Press, Rockville, Maryland, 1978.

[Landskov80]
D. Landskov, S. Davidson, B.D. Shriver, and P.W. Mallett "Local Microcode Compaction Techniques," ACM Computing Surveys, vol. 12, pp. 261-294, September, 1980.

TREE COMPACTION OF MICROPROGRAMS

Jehkwan Lah and Daniel E. Atkins

University of Michigan
Department of Electrical and Computer Engineering
Ann Arbor, Michigan 48019

Abstract

Although Fisher's *trace scheduling* procedure for global compaction may produce significant reduction in execution time of compacted microcode, the growth of memory size by extensive copying of blocks can be enormous. In the worst case, the memory size can grow exponentially [FIS81a] and the complex bookkeeping stage of the trace scheduling is an obstacle to implementation.

A technique called *tree compaction*, which is based on the trace scheduling, is proposed to mitigate these drawbacks. Basically, it partitions a given set of microprogram blocks into tree-shaped subsets and applies the idea of trace scheduling on each tree-shaped subset separately. It achieves almost all of the compaction of the Fisher's trace scheduling procedure except that which causes copying of blocks. Preliminary tests indicate that tree compaction gives almost as short execution time as trace scheduling but with much less memory. The paper includes such an example.

1. Introduction

For the last ten years or so, the use of and interest in microprogramming have increased rapidly [AGE76] not only as an implementation tool for instruction set interpreters but also as a way to reduce overhead for processors using parallelism at the lowest level. Several high level microprogramming languages (HLML) have been proposed and are reviewed in [SIN80]. One of the critical issues in developing a HLML, particularly to control parallel resources, is how to generate efficient microcode. It is a common belief that microcode generated by a machine (or a compiler) cannot be more efficient than one written by a highly skilled microprogrammer, but as the size of microprograms grows, it becomes beyond human intelligence to handle all opportunities to optimize a microprogram [PAT76].

A major way to generate efficient microcode is through microprogram compaction. Microprogram compaction is the process of exploiting parallelism to combine microoperations (MO's) into microinstructions (MI's) to reduce the time and/or space needed for the execution of a microprogram. In solving microprogram compaction problem, optimality is not

----

This work is supported by the Air Force Office of Scientific Research under contract F49620-82-C-0089.

pursued since the microprogram optimization (optimal compaction) problem has been proved to be NP-complete both in microword dimension [DEW76] and in bit dimension [ROB79].

The microprogram compaction problem has been approached in two ways: local compaction and global compaction. Local compaction deals only with a straight line microcode (SLM) section also known as a basic block. A SLM is a sequence of MO's with no jump into the microcode except at the beginning and no jump out except possibly at the end. Global compaction deals with microprograms which have more than one basic block with conditional jumps, joins and loops.

The local compaction problem is considered to be essentially solved and several methods are reviewed in [LAN80, DAV81]. In [VEG83], there is a reference to a thesis result which reportedly proves that the classical compaction problem, which does not consider reordering of source microcode, can be solved in $O(n^v)$, where v is a bounded number of registers in the machine. However, the author conjectures that the general compaction problem - that is, the problem that considers all semantics-preserving partial orderings - is still NP-complete even with the bounded-register assumption, because the problem of finding a semantics-preserving partial ordering which yields optimum compaction is NP-complete.

Four methods have been proposed to solve the global compaction problem [DAS79, WOO79, TOK78, TOK81, FIS79, FIS81a] as summarized in [FIS81b]. The trace scheduling by Fisher [FIS79, FIS81a] is the most general and appears to give the fastest execution of compacted microcode.

Although Fisher's trace scheduling procedure for global compaction may produce significant reduction in execution time of compacted microcode, the growth of memory size by extensive copying of blocks can be enormous. In the worst case, the memory size can grow exponentially [FIS81a], and the complex bookkeeping stage of the trace scheduling is an obstacle to implementation.

In [FIS81a], Fisher suggests modifications to mitigate the memory growth effect. These modifications are based upon selection of a probability threshold below which (with some exception) MO's are not allowed to move across block boundaries. Both memory size and execution time appear to be very sensitive to changes in the source microcode. See section 3.5 for more discussion on the modifications.

In this paper a technique called tree compaction, based on the trace scheduling, is proposed to mitigate the drawbacks of the trace scheduling. Basically, it partitions a given set of microprogram blocks into tree-shaped subsets and applies the idea of trace scheduling on each tree-shaped subset separately. It achieves almost all the compaction of the Fisher's trace scheduling procedure except that which causes copying of blocks.

In this paper, after a simple microprogram model is presented, the trace scheduling is reviewed briefly. Next the tree compaction algorithm is described followed by a detailed example. The trace scheduling is done on the same sample microprogram and a comparison with tree compaction is presented.

In the descriptions of trace scheduling and the tree compaction algorithm, a loop-free code is assumed. In his recent report concerning trace scheduling [FIS82], Fisher proposed unwinding of loops. In the tree compaction algorithm, similar loop unwinding is possible but is probably too costly in space except for small inner loops.

2. Simple Model of Microprograms

This section defines a simple model of a microprogram which will be used to illustrate the essence of the tree compaction algorithm. For a more thorough model of microprograms, see [LAN80].

Def: A microinstruction (MI) is an ordered set of all control signals in a machine at a given (quantized) time.

Def: A microprogram is a time-ordered sequence of MI.

Def: Each separate machine activity specified in an MI is called a microoperation (MO).

Thus an MI can be characterized as a set of MO's.

Def: An MO is represented by a six-tuple (name, instruction, next-address, destination-registers, source-registers, resource vector). The name is a number to identify each MO, the instruction is a command to the microsequencer (microaddress controller), for example, CONT, CJMP, GOTO, etc. and the next-address is a target address for a branch. The destination-registers and the source-registers are the registers written and read respectively in a given MO. A resource vector is a vector in which each component corresponds to an individual resource available in the hardware. The value of each component is either 1 or 0 depending on whether the corresponding resource is used in a given MO.

Def: A register is live at some point in a program if its contents will be read in the future prior to being overwritten. Otherwise, the register is dead.

Def: In a given sequence of MO's mo_1, mo_2, ..., mo_i, ..., mo_j, ..., mo_t, we say mo_i data-precedes mo_j if either or both of following hold.

(1) mo_i writes a register and mo_j reads that value.

(2) mo_i reads a register and mo_j writes on it.

Note that the case where mo_i and mo_j write the same register is not included. In such a case, mo_i writes a dead register and therefore is redundant and should have been eliminated.

Def: The data precedence relation defines a directed acyclic graph on the set of MO's. We call this the data precedence graph (DPG). Since the data precedence relation is transitive, we represent only direct data precedence in drawing the DPG.

A loop free program can be represented as a connected directed graph with one node of in-degree zero (entrance) and one node of out-degree zero (exit).

Def: A top tree is a connected subgraph of the program graph which is itself a tree and has a unique node r with in-degree zero in the tree. Node r is the root of this top tree.

Def: A bottom tree is a connected subgraph of the program graph which is itself a tree and has a unique node r with out-degree zero in the tree. Node r is the root of this bottom tree.

Note that a path is both a top tree and a bottom tree. So is a single node.

Def: A trace is a set of blocks which forms a path of execution and has higher probability of execution than any other path in a given microprogram or a part of it.

Def: A weighted execution time of a microprogram is the sum of execution time of each block multiplied by the probability of that block executed.

3. Brief Review of the Trace Scheduling

3.1. Overview

Four different approaches have been proposed to solve the global compaction problem as reviewed in [FIS81b]. Dasgupta's approach [DAS79] allows MO's to move across block boundaries as symmetric pairs only. Tokoro [TOK79, TOK81] identified general rules for MO motion across block boundaries. Wood [WOO79] assumed a structured microprogram and allowed MO's to move between the blocks of the same nested level. The trace scheduling by Fisher [FIS79, FIS81a] is the most general and appears to give the fastest execution of compacted microcode.

Informally, trace scheduling proceeds as follows.

Each block in the microprogram is assigned a probability of execution which can be either measured by a benchmark run of uncompacted microprogram or handed down by the programmer. The trace is determined and then compacted as if it is a single block using a local compaction technique called list scheduling. During that compaction, some MO's might have been moved below and/or above conditional jumps and/or joins. With few exceptions, these MO's need to be copied to other blocks off the trace to preserve the semantics of the given microprogram. In some cases, several blocks need to be copied.

Next another trace is selected from the rest of the microprogram not including the trace just compacted, and the same process continues until all blocks in the microprogram are compacted.

Loops are handled simply by unrolling them [FIS82] to yield a stream, which may be compacted as above. All the intermediate loop tests will now be conditional jumps in the stream.

The following is a more precise description of the trace scheduling procedure. For a complete description of the algorithm, see [FIS81a] and [FIS79].

Note that Fisher did not distinguish between MI and MO. Instead he used the term MI through out with a flag called *compacted* defined on each MI.

```
For all MI's to be compacted, compacted := false;
For all entrances and exits, compacted := false;
While at least one MI has compacted=false do;
{
        /* T : a trace of MI's;  S : a trace schedule */
        Call Pick_trace(T);
        Call Schedule(T);
        Call Bookkeep(S);
}
```

3.2. Pick_trace

Picks the uncompacted MI with the highest probability of execution, calling that m. Builds a trace around m by working backward and forward. To work backward, it picks the uncompacted leader of m with the highest probability of execution and repeat the process with that MO. It works forward from m analogously.

3.3. Schedule

Builds a DPG with all MI's on the trace. Once the DAG is built, list scheduling (see section 4.5) is done just as it is in local compaction.

3.4. Bookkeep

Revise the given set of MI's, with operations duplicated where necessary to make the code semantically equivalent to the original set of MI's. Two major sources of the revision are *joins* and *conditional jumps*. Since the whole trace has been compacted as if it is a SLM, there can be many MO's which were moved over the block boundaries (joins and conditional jumps). Many of these have to be copied to off-trace blocks to preserve the original semantics. This bookkeeping stage is the cause of implementation complication and possible memory explosion.

3.5. Modifications

To prevent possibly exponential growth of memory size, Fisher suggested modifications of trace scheduling [FIS81a].

(1) If the block ends in a conditional jump, we draw an (DPG) edge to the jump from each MO which is above the jump on the trace and writes a register live in the branch.

(2) If the start of the block is a point at which a rejoin to the trace is made, we draw (DPG) edges to each MO free at the top of the block from each MO which is in an earlier block on the trace and has no successors from earlier blocks.

Fisher recommended the above to be used if the expected probability of a block's being reached is below some threshold. However, we suspect that there are some difficulties. First, the major source of extensive copying of blocks is from initial long traces which therefore have higher probabilities of being executed. Thus, fixing blocks with lower probability of being executed, after possibly extensive copying has already been done, helps relatively little. If, however, the threshold is raised to include blocks of high probability of execution, then it becomes close to compacting each block separately. Second, in long traces, the memory size growth is so sensitive to minor changes in source code that it is possible one small change in source code would almost double the size of compacted code.

4. Tree Compaction Algorithm

4.1. Overview

A global compaction technique called the *tree compaction* algorithm, which is based on the trace scheduling, has been developed. It does almost all the compaction that the trace scheduling does except those which cause copying of blocks. Therefore it achieves almost the same level of execution time reduction without drastic increase of micromemory size.

Informally, the tree compaction algorithm proceeds as follows.

Blocks are partitioned into *top* tree-shaped subsets of blocks. Trace scheduling is applied to each tree-shape subset of blocks separately. In other words, on each tree-shaped subset of blocks, a trace is repeatedly selected, treated as if it is a single block, and compacted using list scheduling with copying of MO's as necessary. Next the blocks are partitioned into *bottom* tree-shaped subsets of blocks and the compaction proceeds as before.

A more detailed description follows. In Section 5.1, a working example of tree compaction is given.

Input:
    Sequence of MO's (name, instruction, next_address, dest_reg, src_reg, resource_vector).
Output:
    Sequence of MI's where each MI contains one or more MO's.
Procedure:
1) Identify blocks (MO sequence bounded by joins and conditional branches).

2) Perform live register analysis and determine live registers at the beginning and end of each block.

3) Partition the flow graph (where each node is a block identified in step 1) into top trees.

4)

```
For each tree DO
{
        Repeat until all non-single-block traces
        are compacted
        {
                Pick_Trace
                List Scheduling
                Bookkeeping
        }
}
```

5) Partition the flow graph into bottom trees.

6) Perform 4) until all blocks are compacted, as described in the following sections.

4.2. Live register analysis [AHO77]

Def: The depth-first-ordering of the nodes of a graph is the *reverse* of the order in which we *last* visit the nodes in the preorder traversal. Depth-first-numbers DFN(n) assigned to each node indicate the depth-first-ordering of the nodes.

Def: IN[n] is the set of registers live at the point immediately before block n and OUT[n] is the same immediately after the block.

Def: DEF[n] is the set of names assigned values in block n prior to any use of that name in block n, and USE[n] is the set of registers used in block n prior to any definition thereof.

Input:
    Set of blocks where each block contains a sequence of MO's.

Output:
    List of live registers at the beginning and end of each block.

1) Compute a depth-first ordering of the nodes. Let the nodes be n_1, n_2, ..., n_N, such that $DFN[n_i] = i$.

2)

```
begin
        for i := 1 to N do
        begin
                IN[n] := USE[n];
                OUT[n] := empty;
        end
        while changes occur do
                for i := n to 1 by -1 do
                /* in reverse depth-first order */
                begin
```

$$OUT[n_i] := \bigcup_{s\ a\ successor\ of\ n_i} IN[s];$$

$$IN[n_i] := (OUT[n_i] - DEF[n_i]) \cup USE[n_i];$$

```
                end
end
```

4.3. Partition into trees

For the rest of this section, the algorithm description regarding the second phase of the tree compaction (dealing with bottom trees) is shown inside parentheses.

Input:
    List of blocks

Output:
    List of trees where each node is a block

1) Find all the blocks where the exits (entrances) are conditional branches (joins) and call the set Bf.

2) Among Bf, identify blocks that have a join (conditional jump) at their entry (exit) or, whose predecessor (successor) is not in Bf. Call the set of each blocks Br. Blocks in Br are roots of trees.

3) For each block in Br, build a tree by repetitively adding each of the tree's successors (predecessors) that has no join (conditional branch) at its entry (exit). Call this set of trees Bt.

The trees identified by this process do not cover the whole microprogram. When identifying top trees, for example, some blocks with bottom tree shape are left. However, those blocks are covered when identifying bottom trees and then compacted. The whole microprogram is covered by top and bottom tree identification with some middle blocks covered by both.

4.4. Pick_Trace

Input:
    A tree-shaped set of blocks.

Output:
    A trace

1) Start from the root block and take the most likely path at each conditional branch (join) down (up) to a leaf block.

2) For each conditional branch , add the IN registers of off-the-trace blocks as conditional source_registers.

4.5. List Scheduling

Input:
    Sequence of MO's in a basic block or in a trace

Output:
    Sequence of compacted MI's

1) Build DPG on MO's starting from the first MO. Conditional source_registers are used when considering data interaction between a conditional jump and the MO's that follow but not the MO's that precede.

This constraint is to prevent movement of MO's above a conditional jump which may overwrite live registers at off-the-trace blocks but still allow movement of MO's below a conditional jump. In the case of a join, list scheduling is done on trace with no constraint and new joining points are identified at the bookkeeping stage.

2) Assign priority value (# of successors in DPG) to each MO.

3) CYCLE = 0

4) Data Ready Set (DRS) is formed from all MO's with no predecessors on the DPG.

5)

    While DRS is not empty, DO
    {

        CYCLE = CYCLE + 1
        The MO's in DRS are placed in iteration CYCLE
        in order of their priority until DRS is exhausted
        or no more resources are available for CYCLE.
        All MO's so placed are removed from DRS.
        All unscheduled MO's not in DRS whose
        predecessors have all been scheduled are added
        to DRS.

    }

4.6. Bookkeeping

Input:
    List of compacted MI's in a trace.

Output:
    Modified microprogram.

1) Identify blocks for compacted MI's. For traces from top trees, this is trivial since conditional branches form natural block boundaries. For traces from bottom trees, it is not as simple. New block boundaries, or new joins, have to be found where below which points, no MO's, which were originally above old joins, are allowed.

2) Check MO's in trace. Each MO that has been moved below a conditional branch (above a join) is copied to the other block(s) off the trace from that conditional branch (join). If a MO has been moved below more than one conditional branch (above more than one join) it has to be copied for each such branch (join).

3) If any MO's have been copied in step 2), do live register analysis again to update IN registers and OUT registers of each block.

5. An Example and Discussion

5.1. An Example

    Here is an example of how the tree compaction algorithm works. Fig. 5.1 is a microprogram with 21 MO's in 7 blocks. The letters A through G are assigned to each of the 7 blocks and the numbers 1 to 21 indicate MO's. Fig. 5.1(b) is a list of MO's represented by the six-tuple. MO 3 and MO 12 are conditional jumps. Throughout all figures in the example, conditional jump MO's are underlined. It is assumed that the probability of block B executing is 0.7 and that of block E is 0.6. Accordingly, the probability of block C executing is 0.3 and that of block F is 0.4. The probability of blocks A, D and G executing is all 1's, naturally. Therefore, the trace in this example microprogram is blocks A, B, D, E and G.

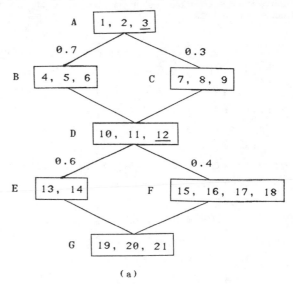

(a)

block	name	inst	next_addr	dest_reg	src_reg	resource_vec
A	1	CONT		1	2, 3	0 1 1 0
	2	CONT		10	1, 5	0 0 1 0
	3	CJMP	7	2	3, 4	1 0 1 0
B	4	CONT		8	9, 5	0 1 0 0
	5	CONT		2	2, 5	0 0 0 1
	6	GOTO	10	15	4, 8	0 1 0 0
C	7	CONT		9	8, 8	0 1 0 1
	8	CONT		1	1, 5	0 1 0 0
	9	CONT		8	11, 12	0 0 0 1
D	10	CONT		14	2, 13	0 1 0 1
	11	CONT		7	3, 5	0 1 0 0
	12	CJMP	15	6	4, 10	1 0 0 0
E	13	CONT		9	3, 4	1 0 1 0
	14	GOTO	19	6	3, 6	0 1 0 0
F	15	CONT		2	6, 8	0 0 0 1
	16	CONT		7	2, 14	0 1 0 1
	17	CONT		4	2, 5	0 1 0 0
	18	CONT		14	11, 12	0 0 1 0
G	19	CONT		9	6, 10	0 0 0 1
	20	CONT		13	7, 3	0 0 0 1
	21	STOP		3	4, 11	0 1 1 0

(b)

Fig. 5.1 An example microprogram

The first step of the tree compaction algorithm is to perform live register analysis and the result is shown in Fig. 5.2. Next, blocks are partitioned into top tree-shaped subsets as shown in Fig. 5.3(a). In tree-shaped subset T1, blocks A, B are the trace, so they are compacted together as if a single block. The compaction is done first by building DPG with MO's in blocks considered. When building DPG, IN[C] is assumed to be read at MO 3 which is a conditional jump. However, those registers are used only when considering data interaction between MO 3 and the MO's in block B, but not between MO 3 and other MO's of block A.

The DPG is shown in Fig. 5.4(a). Note that no edge is drawn between MO 2 and MO 3 to allow possible movement of MO 2 below MO 3, and an edge between MO 3 and MO 4 prevents the movement of MO 4 above MO 3. Next list scheduling is done and the result is shown in Fig. 5.5(a). Since MO 2 is scheduled below conditional jump MO 3, MO 2 is copied to block C.

```
  inreg[A]  = 2 3 4 5 8 9 11 12 13
 outreg[A]  = 1 2 3 4 5 8 9 10 11 12 13
  inreg[B]  = 2 3 4 5 9 10 11 12 13
 outreg[B]  = 2 3 4 5 8 10 11 12 13
  inreg[C]  = 1 2 3 4 5 8 10 11 12 13
 outreg[C]  = 2 3 4 5 8 10 11 12 13
  inreg[D]  = 2 3 4 5 8 10 11 12 13
 outreg[D]  = 3 4 5 6 7 8 10 11 12 14
  inreg[E]  = 3 4 6 7 10 11
 outreg[E]  = 3 4 6 7 10 11
  inreg[F]  = 3 5 6 8 10 11 12 14
 outreg[F]  = 3 4 6 7 10 11
  inreg[G]  = 3 4 6 7 10 11
 outreg[G]  =
```

Fig. 5.2 Live registers

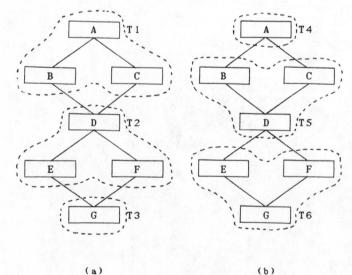

(a)   (b)

Fig. 5.3 Partition into trees

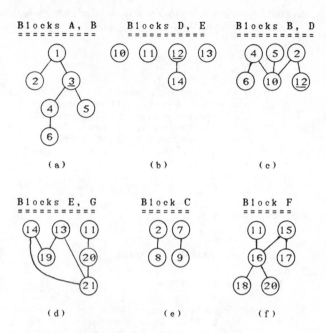

(a)   (b)   (c)

Blocks A, B   Blocks D, E   Blocks B, D

Blocks E, G   Block C   Block F

(d)   (e)   (f)

Fig. 5.4 Data precedence graphs

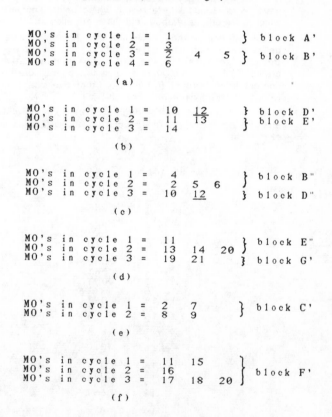

```
MO's in cycle 1 = 1          } block A'
MO's in cycle 2 = 3
MO's in cycle 3 = 2    4   5 } block B'
MO's in cycle 4 = 6
```
(a)

```
MO's in cycle 1 =   10  12   } block D'
MO's in cycle 2 =   11  13   } block E'
MO's in cycle 3 =   14
```
(b)

```
MO's in cycle 1 =   4        } block B"
MO's in cycle 2 =   2   5  6
MO's in cycle 3 =   10  12   } block D"
```
(c)

```
MO's in cycle 1 =   11         } block E"
MO's in cycle 2 =   13  14  20
MO's in cycle 3 =   19  21     } block G'
```
(d)

```
MO's in cycle 1 =   2   7    } block C'
MO's in cycle 2 =   8   9
```
(e)

```
MO's in cycle 1 =   11  15     }
MO's in cycle 2 =   16         } block F'
MO's in cycle 3 =   17  18  20 }
```
(f)

Fig. 5.5 Intermediate results

Similar compaction is done for blocks D and E in tree T2. The DPG is shown in Fig. 5.4(b) and the result is shown in Fig. 5.5(b). Notice that MO 11 is copied to block F. Left-over single blocks C, F and G are not compacted in the first phase since they will be compacted in the second phase.

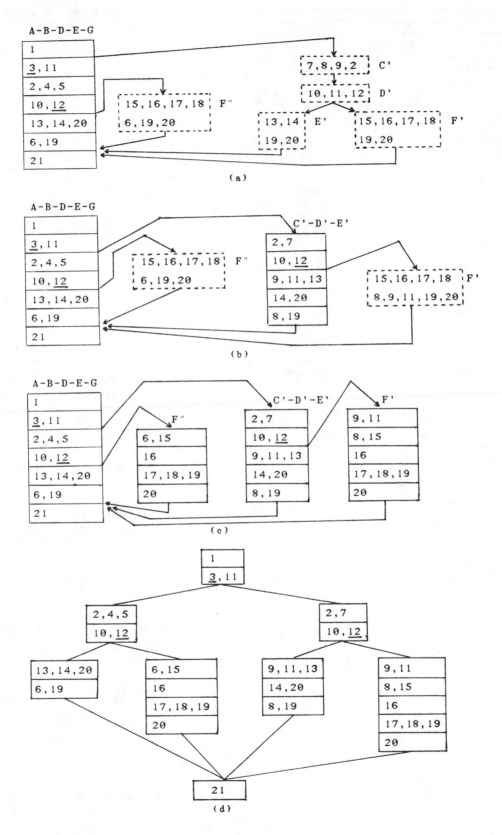

Fig. 5.7   Trace scheduling

The second phase of the tree compaction algorithm is similar to the first phase except the blocks are partitioned into bottom-tree shaped subsets. The traces are blocks B, D and blocks E, G. The compaction already done in the first phase on the blocks covered by both top and bottom trees is redone in the context of bottom tree trace. Note that the top tree compaction added MO 2 to block B and MO 11 to block E. The left-over single blocks C and F are also compacted this time. The DPG's are shown in Fig. 5.4(c),(d),(e),(f) and the results are shown in Fig. 5.5(c),(d),(e),(f). In Fig. 5.5(c), new join is between cycle 2 and cycle 3, since cycle 3 does not contain any of the MO's from block B while cycle 2 contains some. Similarly, in Fig. 5.5(d), new join is between cycle 2 and cycle 3.

The final result of the tree compaction done on a given example microprogram is shown in Fig. 5.6. Execution time of the trace blocks A, B, D, E, G is 8, and weighted execution time is 8.4. 13 MI's are used to hold the compacted micro-code.

The trace scheduling done on the same example is briefly described in Fig. 5.7. Fig. 5.7(a) shows the state after the list scheduling and bookkeeping on the first trace (blocks A, B, D, E, G) is done. Since MO 6 has been scheduled below MO 12, the join from block C to block D had to be moved down with blocks D, E and F copied as shown. The second trace of blocks C', D' and E' is compacted and some more copying is done as shown in Fig. 5.7(b). Next the remaining single blocks F' and F" are compacted. The final result is shown in Fig. 5.7(c) and it is redrawn in Fig. 5.7(d) in a more conventional form.

Here the execution time of the trace blocks A, B, D, E, G is 7 and weighted execution time is 7.52. A little more than 10% improvement over the tree compaction algorithm. However, space used to make that 10% improvement in execution time is 21 MI's, a 60% increase. The space time product of

trace scheduling result is about 45% bigger than that of the tree compaction result. These are summarized in Fig. 5.8.

This specific example shows the advantages of tree compaction algorithm, i.e., it saves memory space with minimal penalty in execution time. More analysis and experimentation are underway in an effort to generalize this result.

	time in trace	weighted time	space needed	space time product
tree compaction	8	8.4	13	109.2
trace scheduling	7	7.52	21	157.92

Fig. 5.8 Comparison summary

5.2. A Discussion

While Fisher's trace scheduling can give short execution time for a particular trace, the growth of memory size by extensive copying of blocks in some cases can be enormous. In the worst case, the memory size can grow exponentially with respect to the number of branches as Fisher mentioned in [FIS81a]. In contrast, increase in memory size of the tree compaction algorithm, in the worst case, is of $O(n^2)$ where n is the number of conditional branches. Still the tree compaction algorithm does almost all the compaction that the trace scheduling does except those which yield copying blocks. See sections 5.2.1 for a case of exponential memory growth in trace scheduling and 5.2.2 for the worst case space complexity analysis of tree compaction.

The tree compaction algorithm does not change the topological structure of blocks. In trace scheduling, a compacted program may have a totally different structure from the original program because of creating many new blocks when repairing joins in the bookkeeping stage. If the compacted microprogram has totally different structure on top of many rearranged MO's, the already difficult debugging process may become close to impossible.

In the tree compaction algorithm, by partitioning a given microprogram into top and bottom trees before compaction, the bookkeeping stage of the algorithm is very much simplified. By compacting each tree separately, one type of possible compaction is prohibited but that is the very kind of compaction which requires copying of possibly many blocks. In the previous example, movement of MO 6 below the conditional jump MO 12 is such a case.

As an extension of the tree compaction algorithm, if a given microprogram is structured, it is allowed to compact MO's between the blocks at the same structure level as long as it does not violate data dependency rule including the blocks between them which are lower in level. This is an adoption of Wood's idea [WOO79].

5.2.1. A case exhibiting exponential memory growth in trace scheduling

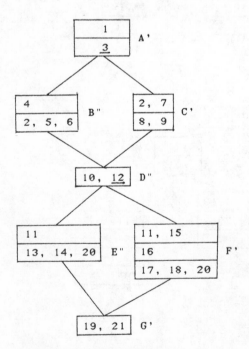

Fig. 5.6 Final result

One microprogram shown in Fig.5.9 is analyzed to demonstrate that the memory requirement of trace scheduling can grow exponentially.

For the purpose of the analysis, it is assumed that each block contains large unspecified but equal number of MO's and the blocks $A_1, B_1, A_2, B_2, \cdots A_n, B_n, A_0$ form a trace. Furthermore, it is assumed that, after the trace blocks are compacted, one MO from each blocks $B_1, B_2, \cdots, B_n$ has been combined with MO's in block A_0 so that it is necessary to make copies of blocks as shown in Fig. 5.9(b). Since it is assumed that the number of MO's in each block is equal and larger than one, and the only over-the-block-boundary movements of MO's are the ones from blocks $B_1, B_2, \cdots, B_n$ to A_0, it is reasonable to assume that the size of each block does not change. Let the size of each block be unity for convenience.

Now the rest of the microprogram except the first trace has to be compacted and it is assumed again that the similar situations arise as the first trace and copies are made.

Let $f(n)$ be the size of the microprogram shown in Fig. 5.9(a) after compaction in terms of number of blocks. n is the number of conditional branches.

$$f(n) = 2n + 1 + f(n-1) + 1 + f(n-2) + 1 + \cdots + f(0) + 1$$

$$= 3n + 1 + f(n-1) + f(n-2) + \cdots + f(0)$$

It is obvious that $f(0) = 1$.

$$f(n) = 3n + 1 + f(n-1) + f(n-2) + \cdots + f(0)$$

$$-)\ f(n-1) = 3(n-1) + 1 + \quad + f(n-2) + \cdots + f(0)$$

$$f(n) - f(n-1) = f(n-1) + 3$$

Therefore,

$$f(n) = 2f(n-1) + 3$$

This and $f(0) = 1$ give

$$f(n) = 2^{n+2} - 3$$

i.e. $f(n)$ is exponential function of n, or the number of conditional branches in the microprogram shown in Fig. 5.9(a).

This is of course a pathological case which is not likely to happen in real microcode. However, the implication that movements of MO's below joins cause extensive copying of blocks, is serious. In real microcode, it is possible that movements of MO's below joins happen frequently enough to increase the memory size forbiddingly large. Just note that a single movement of an MO from block B_1 to A_0 would approximately double the memory size.

5.2.2. Worst case space complexity analysis of tree compaction

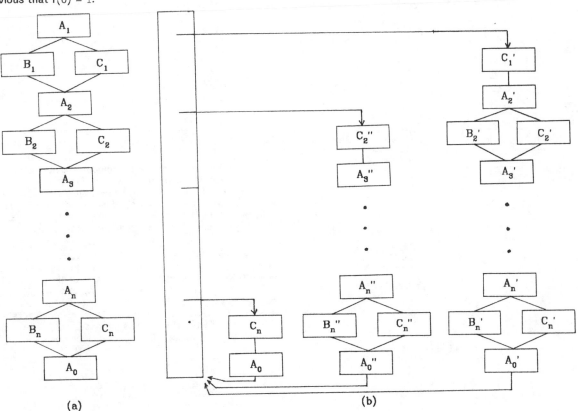

(a)   (b)

Fig. 5.9 Exponential memory growth in trace scheduling

In tree compaction, the worst case in memory space growth happens when a given microprogram has the structure shown in Fig. 5.10. An informal proof by induction that this tree shape microprogram gives the worst space complexity follows.

Adding one conditional branch to a SLM yields 4 blocks A_0, A_1, B_1 and A'_0 -- the only case, thus the worst case. Since we are concerned only about the topology of the microprogram, the size of each block is assumed to be unity and blocks newly created by adding a conditional branch are still assumed to be of size unity. Let's assume that the set of blocks shown in Fig. 5.10 except the 3 blocks A_n, B_n, A'_{n-1}, and block A_{n-1} connected to block A'_{n-2}, gives the worst space complexity with respect to n-1 conditional branches. Adding one more conditional branch to either block A_{n-1} or B_{n-1} increases the space complexity the most. If the conditional branch is added to one of the blocks A_0, A_1, ..., A_{n-2} or A'_{n-2}, A'_{n-3}, ..., A'_0, then a join is introduced inside the top tree or the bottom tree, and so either tree is forced to be partitioned into smaller trees, therefore space complexity is reduced. If the conditional branch is added to one of the blocks B_1, B_2, ...,

B_k, ..., B_{n-2}, then the increased size of the microprogram is $2(k+2)-(k+1)+1$ blocks instead of the $2(n+1)-n+1$ blocks required when adding the conditional branches to either A_{n-1} or B_{n-1}. By adding a conditional branch to one of the blocks B_k, $1 \leq k \leq n-2$, 3 new blocks will be created. After the compaction, the original block, the size of which used to be (k+1), becomes empty except for a conditional branch MO, and the sizes of 3 added blocks are (k+2), (k+2) and 1 respectively. The same reasoning applies to blocks A_{n-1} or B_{n-1}. Therefore, a microprogram with the topology shown in Fig. 5.10 requires the largest possible memory space after the tree compaction is performed.

Now, in calculating the worst case memory growth, let's assume that in any conditional branch, the "left" branch has higher probability of execution than "right" branch for convenience. Without this assumption, the result would still be the same, except that the tree would contain more than one trace. Here, only the top tree (upper half of the program) will be analyzed. Similar analysis for the bottom tree (lower half of the program) will yield the same space complexity.

Since it was assumed that A_0, A_1, ..., A_n form a trace, after compaction of the trace, the worst possible scenario is that blocks A_0, A_1, ..., A_{n-1} are copied to block B_n, blocks A_0, A_1, ..., A_{n-2} are copied to block B_{n-1}, and so forth through block A_0 being copied to block B_1. As a result of this compaction, blocks A_0, A_1, ..., A_{n-1} become empty except for one conditional branch MO, the size of A_n and B_n is (n+1), and the size of B_k, $1 \leq k \leq n-1$, is (k+1). Therefore, the size of the whole microcode after compaction is

$$S = 2(n+1) + \sum_{k=1}^{n-1} (k+1)$$

$$= \frac{n^2}{2} + \frac{5n}{2} + 1$$

$$= O(n^2)$$

6. Conclusion

A technique to solve the global compaction problem of microprogram based on trace scheduling has been presented. By partitioning blocks into tree-shaped subsets first and applying the idea of trace scheduling on each tree separately, it seems possible to achieve a speedup similar to that of trace scheduling but with much less memory space used.

A preliminary version of the tree compaction algorithm has been implemented using PASCAL on a VAX-11/780 running UNIX. The example given was actually produced by the implementation and used about 1 second of CPU time. The current version at the time of this writing assumes the abstract model of microprogram. More extensive testing and evaluation of the algorithm is planned using a microprogram model and a simulation of a realistic machine.

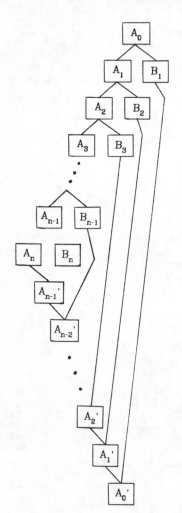

Fig. 5.10 Worst case in tree scheduling

References

[AGE76]
T. Agerwala, "Microprogram Optimization: A Survey", *IEEE Transaction on Computers* Vol. C-25(10) pp. 962-973 (October, 1976).

[AHO74]
A. V. Aho, J. D. Ullman, *Principles of Compiler Design*, Addison-Wesley (1974)

[DAS79]
S. Dasgupta, "The Organization of Microprogram Stores", *ACM Computing Surveys* Vol. 11(1) pp. 39-65 (March, 1979).

[DAV81]
S. Davidson, D. Landskov, B. D. Shriver, P. W. Mallett, "Some Experiments in Local Microcode Compaction for Horizontal Machines", *IEEE Transaction on Computers* Vol. C-30(7) pp. 460-477 (July, 1981).

[DEW76]
D. J. DeWitt, "A Machine Independent Approach to the Production of Optimal Horizontal Microcode," *Ph. D. Dissertation*, University of Michigan, (August, 1976).

[FIS79]
J. A. Fisher, "The Optimization of Horizontal Microcode within and beyond Basic Blocks: An Application of Processor Scheduling with Resources," *Ph. D. Dissertation*, New York University, (October, 1979).

[FIS81a]
J. A. Fisher, "Trace Scheduling: A Technique for Global Microcode Compaction," *IEEE Transaction on Computers* Vol. C-30(7) pp. 478-490 (July, 1981).

[FIS81b]
J. A. Fisher, D. A. Landskov, B. D. Shriver, "Microcode Compaction: Looking Backward and Looking Forward", *National Computer Conference*, pp. 95-102 (1981)

[FIS82]
J. A. Fisher, "Very Long Instruction Word Architectures", and the ELI-512", *Research Report #253*, Yale University, Department of Computer Science (December, 1982)

[LAN80]
D. Landskov, S. Davidson, B. Shriver, and P. W. Mallett, "Local Microcode Compaction Techniques," *ACM Computing Surveys* Vol. 12(3) pp. 261-294 (September, 1980).

[PAT76]
D. A. Patterson, "STRUM: Structured Programming System for Correct Firmware", *IEEE Transaction on Computers* Vol. C-25(10) pp. 974-985 (October, 1976).

[ROB79]
E. L. Robertson, "Microcode Bit Optimization is NP-complete", *IEEE Transaction on Computers* Vol. C-28(4) pp. 316-319 (April, 1979).

[SIN80]
H. J. Sint, "A Survey of High Level Microprogramming Languages", *Proceedings of the 13th Annual Workshop on Microprogramming* pp. 141-153 (1980)

[TOK78]
M. Tokoro, T. Takizuka, E. Tamura, I. Yamaura, "A Technique of Global Optimization of Microprograms", *Proceedings of the 11th Annual Workshop on Microprogramming* pp. 41-50 (1978)

[TOK81]
M. Tokoro, E. Tamura, and T. Takizuka, "Optimization of Microprograms," *IEEE Transaction on Computers* Vol. C-30(7) pp. 491-504 (July, 1981).

[VEG83]
S. R. Vegdahl, "A New Perspective on the Classical Microcode Compaction Problem", *SIGMICRO Newsletter*, Vol. 14(1) pp.11-14 (March, 1983)

[WOO79]
W. G. Wood, "The Computer Aided Design of Microprograms", *Ph. D. Dissertation*, University of Edinburgh, Scotland (1979)

LOCAL AND GLOBAL MICROCODE COMPACTION
USING REDUCTION OPERATORS*

Steven G. Henry
Hewlett-Packard, GLD
Greeley, CO 80634

Robert A. Mueller   Michael Andrews
Department of Computer Science - Colorado State University
Fort Collins, CO 80523

ABSTRACT

The problem of compacting microcode has received considerable attention, but there remains much room for improvement. The major obstacle is the NP-completeness of the associated optimization problem and the coupling between code generation and compaction. Reduction operators are one form of heuristic technique that have been used effectively in scene analysis. By abstracting the microcode compaction problem as a constraint satisfaction problem, we can utilize some developed heuristic techniques. This approach is demonstrated along with experimental results obtained from a computer implementation. A comparison is made with several existing methods.

1.0 INTRODUCTION

The problem of compacting microcode has received considerable attention[3], but there are many areas still needing consideration[23]. One obstacle is the NP-completeness of the associated optimization problem[6], which requires the use of heuristic techniques that trade "compactness" for practical algorithm speed and space. An additional obstacle is the coupling that exists between code generation and compaction[24]. Code compaction could be improved if code was generated so that it could be efficiently compacted.

*This work was supported in part by NSF Grant #MCS-8107481. Adapted from a thesis submitted to Colorado State University in partial fulfillment of requirements for a Master of Science degree.

Reduction operators are one form of heuristic technique that have been used effectively in scene analysis, a major area of artificial intelligence. They provide an effective technique in dealing with the NP-complete compaction problem. In addition, the framework within which the reduction operators are applied may prove useful in attacking the coupling problem.

Haralick et. al.[9] have addressed scene analysis as a "constraint satisfaction problem", the goal of which is to find a subset of objectives satisfying certain criteria. The set of potential candidates is a search space implied by an instance of the problem, and the subset satisfying the constraints represents a "feasible solution". The problem becomes an optimization problem when we attempt to minimize (maximize) some "objective function" on the set of feasible solutions.

Constraint satisfaction has been reformulated to solve scene analysis problems as the "Consistent Labeling Problem"[9][10][11]. The consistent labeling problem can be informally stated as follows: "Given a set of objects (U), a set of labels (L), and a compatability relation on U x L (R), find an assignment of labels to units which satisfy R."

This paper will show how the microcode compaction problem can be solved as a consistent labeling problem, and demonstrate the application of reduction operators to solving instances of microcode compaction represented as instances of consistent labeling. The general ideas behind the method, examples of its application to microcode compaction, and a comparison of the complexity and performance of this method to several previously reported methods are the major topics discussed. Detailed time and space complexity analyses, experiments, and interpretations of the experimental results can be found in the M.S. thesis of Henry[13].

The reduction operator technique will be useful in several situations. It is useful where code optimality is critical. This is because the algorithm is probabilistically optimum. In other words, optimal results are always obtained (with respect to the initial ordering) in usually polynomial time. The technique is also useful in situations involving wide horizontal microcode formats (>60 microoperations per word) and multiple constraints. This is because the representation scheme is fairly flexible. Finally, the representation scheme may prove useful in reducing the coupling between code generation and compaction. (This is suggested as an area for future research).

The major disadvantage of the method lies in its time complexity, which is typically a factor of N or N^2 greater than existing methods when applied in the classical fixed data dependency ordering context. Its viability in the more general context of microcode optimization[23] remains open.

For brevity, it is assumed that the reader is familiar with fundamental terminology and concepts of microprogramming, the microcode compaction problem, and important previous work in microcode compaction. (For more information on these topics, the reader may refer to [25] and [3] for discussions of microprogramming and microcode compaction, and [23] for a recent critical overview of the state of the art in microcode compaction).

2.0 THE CONSISTENT LABELING PROBLEM

Many problems are encountered in scene analysis and related areas where a match must be made between an unknown object and the correct name or description of the object subject to certain constraints. For example, given a scene to be analyzed by a computer, the task faced is to correctly identify and match the observed objects with their correct names. The names are matched to the objects with respect to a world model. This world model specifies allowable relations between named objects. For example, an object with the label "vase" must be above an object with the label "table".

Haralick and others have presented several papers about the problem of matching labels to objects. They formulate these and other constraint satisfaction problems in terms of the "consistent labeling problem" [9][10][11][12]. This problem is to discover all possible mappings of units into labels such that the assignments satisfy all of the constraints. For example, in the scene analysis problem, the units become the objects to identify and the labels become the names to attach to the objects.

The consistent labeling problem consists of units, labels, and a unit-label constraint relation.

The units and labels form two sets; U and L respectively.

$$U = \{u_1, u_2, \ldots, u_m\}$$

$$L = \{l_1, l_2, \ldots, l_j\}$$

In order to explain how U and L are formed, the n-queens problem is used as an example. The n-queens problem is well known from the study of algorithms. The problem is to place n queens on an nxn chessboard such that no two queens can capture one another. This problem can be expressed in terms of the consistent labeling problem by letting the columns of the chessboard be the units and the rows of the chessboard be the labels. A labeling of a unit (row) with a label (column) indicates that a queen occupies that square. The constraints of the problem are that a unit cannot be assigned a label (potential queen placement) if an existing unit-label assignment (occupied square) would allow a capture to take place.

Figure 2.1 shows some examples of of consistent and inconsistent labelings for the 6-queens problem. Also are shown the sets U and L for this example.

The major difficulty in solving the consistent labeling problem is that there are an exponential number of possible assignments that could be checked. To reduce the magnitude of this problem, Haralick provides a heuristic algorithm that uses known constraint information in order to reduce the overall search effort. This technique requires developing a compatibility model.

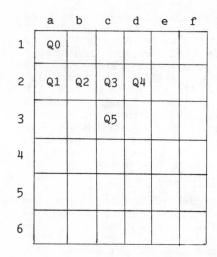

	a	b	c	d	e	f
1	Q0					
2	Q1	Q2	Q3	Q4		
3			Q5			
4						
5						
6						

```
1,a,2,a   is not a consistent labeling
1,a,2,b   is not a consistent labeling
1,a,2,c   is a consistent labeling
1,a,2,d   is a consistent labeling
2,c,3,c   is not a consistent labeling

U = {1,2,3,4,5,6}
L = {a,b,c,d,e,f}
```

Figure 2.1. Partial 6-queens problem
formulation using U and L.

A world model is the compatability model used in scene analysis algorithms. It is developed to express allowable relations between named objects. This world model serves as a reference of all allowable relations of named objects during the course of the scene analysis algorithm. In the consistent labeling problem, such allowable relations are expressed using the unit-label constraint relation R. R specifies compatible combinations of units and labels taken N at a time, where N is the order of the constraint relation.

The value of N is an important consideration. Most constraint problems are based on N = 2 and as such are binary constraint problems. For example, in the n-queens problem, the constraints are binary since pairwise combinations of queens must be checked for compatability to determine if the overall solution to the problem is correct. As will be seen later, the microprogram compaction problem can be expressed such that only binary constraints are involved.

As mentioned, R specifies the compatible combinations of units and labels taken N at a time. It therefore consists of N-tuples of unit-label pairs. It contains all N-tuples of unit-label pairs that are compatible given the constraints of the problem. R is a subset of $(U \times L)^N$ since not all unit-label pairs may be compatible.

Entries in the R relation are determined from the nature of the problem. Figure 2.2 shows some of the entries in and not in the R relation for the 6-queens problem.

```
(1,a,2,c) in R.
(1,a,2,d) in R.
(1,a,2,e) in R.
(1,a,2,f) in R.
(2,b,3,d) in R.
(2,e,4,a) in R.
(5,a,6,b) not in R.
(4,a,6,c) not in R.
```

Figure 2.2. Partial R relation
for the 6-queens problem.

The sets U, L, and R form a compatability model (U,L,R) for the problem to be solved. This compatability model is used to find a solution to the problem.

The problem solution to the consistent labeling problem is known as a globally consistent labeling. A globally consistent labeling is a labeling of all of the units with their associated labels that satisfy the constraints of the problem. Once a globally consistent labeling is found, the solution to the problem is known since each unit will have a unique label that is compatible with the labels held by each of the other units. (Note that there can be more than one globally consistent labeling for a given problem.)

To find a solution to the consistent labeling problem, a tree search will be modified to make use of the R relation. Figure 2.3 shows a partial tree-search for the 6-queens problem without the modifications.

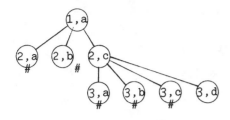

Figure 2.3. Tree-search for solution
for 6-queens without using reduction
operators.

The modifications to the tree search
require referring to the R relation to
make choices of potential labels for units
and to adjust the R relation based on both
the selection made and on the use of
reduction operators.

Only labels appearing with units
somewhere in the R relation are chosen as
a potential assignment. For example, let
us assume that the R relation as shown in
figure 2.2 represents the R relation
during a search. If the algorithm were
searching for a label for unit 4, then the
only possible choice would be label a
since 4,a appears in the R relation.

Reduction operators are applied to
the R relation to "winnow out" false
combinations of N-tuples of unit-label
pairs that are not part of any globally
consistent labeling. These operators
check combinations of entries from the R
relation and based on the results, discard
members of R that are not possibly part of
an eventual solution. By making R as
small as possible, the search for a
solution becomes much quicker than an
exhaustive search of all possibilities
since the potential labeling choices
become more limited.

Reduction operators are applied at
each level of a tree search to the current
R relation which gets smaller as the tree
search progresses. It gets smaller for
two reasons. First, a label is chosen for
a selected unit when moving to the next
level of the tree search. The R relation
is updated to involve only the selected
label for the chosen unit. Entries in R
having the unit in question paired with a
different label are deleted. At any time,
the R relation thus represents the choices
made during the tree search since all
choices of a label for a unit must be made
with respect to the R relation. Secondly,

the R relation is reduced through the
application of the reduction operators. As
mentioned, the reduction operators remove
from R any combinations of N unit-label
pairs that are not part of any globally
consistent labeling with respect to that R
relation.

Therefore, by reducing the size of R,
the potential choices are limited. If R
can be reduced in an intelligent fashion,
then only the correct choices will be
made. (However, reducing R to a minimal
relation with only the correct choices is
an NP-complete problem [10].)

There are two reduction operators
presented by Haralick that reduce the
number of entries in the R relation.
These are the ϕ_{kp} and the Ψ_{kp} operators.
The two reduction operators can be shown
to work in an equivalent fashion for
identical k and p values. The only
differences arise when actually
implementing the reduction operators. For
brevity, only the ϕ operator will be
discussed. The interested reader is
referred to [13] for further discussion of
the Ψ operator.

The k and p parameters supplied with
the reduction operators govern the ability
of the reduction operators to remove
inconsistent entries from the R relation.
The k parameter specifies the number of
units that are fixed to labels during the
test. The p parameter specifies the total
number of units that must be checked in
the test.

There are several conditions that
must be satisfied in the test. First,
every combination of the unit-label pairs
in the R relation taken k at a time must
pass a test. The test requires p-k free
units to have at least one label listed in
R such that the combination of k fixed
unit-labels and the p-k free unit-label
pairs is itself a consistent labeling
(verified by checking the current R
relation). Figure 2.4 shows an example
and description of the application of the
reduction operator ϕ_{23} to a small R
relation.

One additional condition of the test
is that if the reduction operator removes
any entries from R, it must be re-applied
to all the remaining entries in R until no
more entries can be removed.

The reduction operators are applied
at each level of the tree search to arrive
at a globally consistent labeling. Pseudo
code and an example of a tree search in a
microcode compaction will be shown in a
following section.

```
U= {1,2,3,4}   R = { (1,a,2,b)
                     (1,a,3,a)
L= {a,b,c}           (1,a,3,c)
                     (2,a,3,a)
K = 2                (3,a,4,b)
                     (1,a,2,a)
P = 3                (1,a,4,b)
                     (2,a,4,b)
                     (2,b,3,c)}
```

1. Pick an entry from R to
   see if it is part of a
   potential globally consistent
   labeling.

   Choose entry (1,a,2,b).

2. Since k = 2, both units in the
   entry are fixed to their labels.

3. Since p-k = 1, 1 unit is a free
   unit. All such single free units
   that are not already chosen as a
   fixed unit must be checked for
   compatability with the selected entry
   from the R relation.

   Start with unit 3.

4. See if there exists label(s) for unit
   3 appearing in the R relation.

   There exists two, a and c.

5. See if there exists at least one label
   such that when paired with the free
   unit is compatable with the labels
   held by the fixed units.

   (1,a,3,a) in R? - no.

6. Try another label for unit 3 since
   (1,a,3,a) is not compatible.

   Test 3 with label c.

7. (1,a,3,c) in R? - yes.
   (2,b,3,c) in R? - yes.

8. Now test unit 4 (all possible free
   units must be checked).

   available labels for 4: b

   (1,a,4,b) in R? - yes.
   (2,b,4,b) in R? - no.

   Since there are no other labels for
   unit 4, and no label when paired with
   unit 4 is compatible, then entry
   (1,a,2,a) must not be part of any
   globally consistent labeling. (Such
   a labeling would certainly have a
   label for unit 4 which would be
   compatible with (1,a,2,b) when unit
   1 is assigned label a and unit 2
   is assigned label b).

9. Discard (1,a,2,b) from R.

10. Select another entry.

    Choose (1,a,2,a).

11. Apply the test.

    available labels, unit 3: a,c

    (1,a,3,a) in R? -yes
    (2,a,3,a) in R? -yes

    *Note since there exists at least one
    label when paired with unit 3 is
    compatible with the selected R entry;
    label c does not need to be tested.

    now try unit 4: potential labels: b

    (1,a,4,b) in R? - yes
    (2,a,4,b) in R? - yes

12. (1,a,2,a) can be part of a globally
    consistent labeling.

13. Test all other entries in a similar
    fashion. Then, if any entries have
    been deleted from R (as one was in
    step 9, repeat the application of the
    reduction operator until either R is
    empty, or no more entries are
    removed.

Figure 2.4. Application of
ϕ_{23} to a small R relation.

3.0 MICROPROGRAM COMPACTION
AS A CONSTRAINT RELATION

     This section will show how the
microprogram compaction problem can be
solved using the consistent labeling
formalism and algorithm. To do so, the
constraints of a microprogram must be
identified.

     A mop can be scheduled at a time
level if (1) it is compatible with other
mops scheduled at that level, and (2) if
the mops upon which this current mop is
dependent have already been scheduled at
earlier time levels.

The components of the compaction problem can be mapped into unit and label sets in many ways (alternatives are discussed in [13]). In this approach, microoperations and resources are combined as units and the time levels are taken to be labels. The labeling problem becomes the assignment of time levels to microoperations and their associated resources subject to data dependencies and resource constraints.

The U and L sets in the (U,L,R) model are easily constructed by including in them all of the mops and time levels. An entry is placed in R if the unit and labels of the entry satisfy the constraint relation. That is, if $(\langle mop_1, t_1 \rangle, \langle mop_2, t_2 \rangle)$ is an element of R, then mop_1 and mop_2 are compatible when scheduled at time levels t_1 and t_2 respectively. All such combinations need to be in the R relation to express the complete relation as defined by the microprogram.

The algorithm to build R requires several steps. Several intermediate stages help to define the constraints. First, a precedence relation is constructed that describes the data precedence ordering of the microoperations. Then, a connectivity matrix takes the data dependency information from the data precedence ordering and constructs two time partitions. These two partitions will describe the minimum and maximum time levels at which a given microoperation can be scheduled (E and L partitions). Finally, the resource usage and compatibility will be calculated which includes the other constraints that need to be considered. An algorithm for computing R is given in [13]. An example is shown in figure 3.1.

Note that the R relation is initialized based on the traditional data dependency graph. However, at a space penalty the R relation can be initialized considering all possible pairwise combinations of microoperations. Therefore, any problems in compaction due to anti-dependencies can be avoided. (See [23] for a full discussion of source order precedence problems in compacting microcode.)

Micro Operation	Write Regs	Read Regs	Resources Used
1	R2	R1,R4	ALU 1
2	R4	R2,R3	ALU 2
3	R5	R2	ALU 2
4	R1	R4	ALU 2

$U = \{1,2,3,4\}$
$L = \{t1,t2,t3\}$
$R =$
$\{(1,t1,2,t2)$
$(1,t1,3,t2)$
$(1,t1,3,t3)$
$(1,t1,4,t3)$
$(2,t2,3,t3)$
$(2,t2,4,t3)$
$(3,t2,4,t3)\}$

*Note that R is both a reflexive and a symmetric relation. Therefore, $(2,t2,1,t1)$ need not be shown even though a member of R. Also $(1,t1,1,t1)$ also need not be shown.

Figure 3.1. Example R initialization.

4.0 COMPACTION ALGORITHM

A high-level pseudo-code description of the compaction algorithm is shown in figure 4.1. The procedure for building R is discussed briefly in the previous section. Mobility adjustment connotes the addition of time levels, which adds flexibility to the R relation. The heart of the algorithm is the consistent labeling procedure, which is given in figure 4.2. Figure 4.3 shows an example of the algorithm in solving a small microcode compaction problem as initialized in figure 3.1.

```
Compacted := False;
WHILE NOT Compacted DO
 BEGIN
  Build_R_relation;
  Consistent := False;
  Find_consistent_labeling(Consistent);
  IF NOT Consistent THEN
   Adjust Mobility by adding a
   time level.
  ELSE
   Compacted := True;
 END;
END;
```

Figure 4.1. High-level
pseudo-code description.

1. Choose a unit not already assigned.
2. Choose a label to assign to the unit
   that is a valid choice for the unit
   based on the R relation.

   IF none exist, then set Result to Null
   and RETURN.
3. Eliminate from R any entries consisting
   of the selected unit and labels not
   chosen for the unit.
4. Check to see if labels still exist
   for all units.
5. If no labels exist, THEN
   a. Set Result to No consistent labeling.
   b. Restore the R relation and the labels
      to their original state when this
      procedure was entered.
   c. RETURN to calling procedure.
6. Apply the Reduction operator to the
   R relation restricted to the label
   assigned in step 3.
7. Check to see if labels still exist for
   all units.
8. If no labels exist, THEN
   a. Set Result to No consistent labeling.
   b. Restore any deleted labels and the
      R relation to its original state
      when this procedure was entered.
   c. RETURN to calling procedure.
9. If every unit at this point has
   exactly one label THEN Set Result to
   Consistent Labeling and RETURN.
10.If any units have more than one label
   remaining and every unit has at least
   one label THEN
   a. Recursively CALL Algorithm Find
      Consistent Labeling, passing to it
      the restricted R relation, U and L.
   b. IF the returned Result is Consistent,
      then RETURN.
   c. IF the returned Result is Null, then
      delete the label from
      consideration and go to step 2.

Figure 4.2. Find Consistent Labeling
Algorithm.

choose unit 1, label t1

restrict R relation so that
unit 1 has only label t1.

(R is the same- no entries
 deleted).

Apply reduction operator.

R={(1,t1,2,t2)
   (1,t1,3,t2) - delete (unit 2 fail)
   (1,t1,3,t3) - delete (unit 4 fail)
   (1,t1,4,t3)
   (2,t2,3,t3) - delete (unit 4 fail)
   (2,t2,4,t3) - delete (unit 3 fail)
   (3,t2,4,t3)
   (3,t2,4,t3)}- delete

Reapply to smaller R.

R={(1,t1,2,t2) - delete (unit 3 fail)
   (1,t1,4,t3) - delete (unit 3 fail)

R is now empty. Backtrack; but no more
labels left for unit 1. Thus, must
increase the mobility by adding a
time level. R is rebuilt and the
process repeated.

R = {(1,t1,2,t2)
     (1,t1,2,t3)
     (1,t1,3,t2)
     (1,t1,3,t3)
     (1,t1,3,t4)
     (1,t1,4,t3)
     (1,t1,4,t4)
     (1,t2,2,t3)
     (1,t2,3,t3)
     (1,t2,3,t4)
     (1,t2,4,t3)
     (1,t2,4,t4)
     (2,t2,3,t3)
     (2,t2,3,t4)
     (2,t2,4,t4)
     (2,t3,3,t4)
     (2,t3,4,t4)
     (3,t2,4,t3)
     (3,t2,4,t4)}

etc. as shown above.

Figure 4.3. Partial compaction example
using reduction operators.

40

5.0 MICROPROGRAM COMPACTION
EXPERIMENTS

A 55K byte PASCAL program for the HP9816 computer was developed to test and analyze the algorithm. It collected compaction statistics on 2 reduction operators with varying k and p parameters.

The experiments run using the program used the microprogram model presented by Fisher[8], with the following variables: (1) number of mops to compact, (2) number of available resources, (3) number of resources used per microoperation, (4) number of available registers, (5) number of read registers available, and (6) number of write registers available.

Several hundred experiment sets were executed, each designed to evaluate a different characteristic of the problem. This allowed a comparison of the essential properties of the reduction operators when applied to microcode with varying critical path lengths and probabilities of resource conflict. The results were encouraging. Either every problem compacted at Fisher's theoretical lower bound[8] or the lower bound was verified to be incorrect and the solution generated optimal. This was to be expected since the reduction operators are probabilistically optimum.

It was interesting that the lower bound was incorrect in some cases. Fisher mentions that this occurs when there are several critical paths that are constrained by different resources. This was precisely the case in each example found. Another interesting observation was that the problems that experienced backtracking did so because of local bottlenecks.

An analysis of the algorithm performance results in an interesting conclusion. As the probability of two microoperations having a resource conflict increased and the probability that two microoperations were data dependent decreased; the consistent labeling algorithm began to backtrack significantly. (For a detailed presentation, see [13].) It is believed that microprograms having these characteristics are rare in actual practice.

For a problem consisting of 20 mops, the best heuristics that Fisher evaluated were about 3.8% above the theoretical lower bound. The worst heuristics were at about 8% above the theoretical lower bound. Figure 5,1 shows a comparision between the average lower bound for Fisher's best heuristic and the reduction operator heuristic.

	Fisher	Reduction Operator
Avg soln	12.390	14.46
Avg bound	11.935	14.27
% delta	3.8%	1.33%

Average number of microoperations in the final solution to a 20 mop compaction.

Table 5.1. Comparison between techniques.

As can be seen from the data, the reduction operators produce compactions that are much closer to Fisher's theoretical lower bound.

There is some disparity in the comparison. The average solution for these experiments was several mops higher than the average solution for Fisher's problems. The average solution should have been the same since the same models and experiment ranges were used. All aspects of the test were double checked and no difference could be found in the test case generation procedures. However, assuming that the percentage difference in results can be compared, it would seem that about 1.3% of the percent difference was due to lower bound error. Therefore the best previous heuristics are about 2.5% above an actual bound whereas the reduction operators are exactly at the true lower bound.

6.0 SUMMARY OF RESULTS

The results of the research are fairly encouraging. First of all, it was possible to express the microprogram compaction problem in terms of the constraint satisfaction problem using the Haralick (U,L,R) framework. This framework resulted in a worst-case space complexity of N^4 where N is the number of microoperations input. The worst-case space constraint occurred when the number of time levels required to compact the microprogram was equivalent to the number of microoperations. For typical compaction problems the actual space complexity was between N^2 and N^3. The average time complexity to compact microprograms was N^3 for typical samples of microcode.

Another encouraging result was that the compaction algorithm using reduction operators was shown to be feasible and implementable. A 55K byte PASCAL program was developed to run the experiments and was a good tool in evaluating the reduction operator performance.

The resulting algorithm was probabilistically optimum rather than approximately optimum as are most other known heuristics. The probabilistic nature was seen to occur when the nature of the problem caused significant backtracking.

The cases where the heuristic began to backtrack occurred in samples of microcode that had a high probability of resource conflict and very little data dependency. These cases of microcode are not found much in practice. Thus, in practical cases the solution was obtained in polynomial time.

One discouraging discovery was that there existed no convenient tradeoff between the optimality of the results and the amount of time it took to arrive at the results. Future modifications to the algorithm could provide this flexibility.

There are two other areas that could be investigated. There is some potential in using reduction operators to address the issues of code generation and compaction. The R relation and reduction operators provide a convenient representation scheme that could allow code generation and compaction to occur simultaneously. Another improvement would be to search the R relation in parallel, which could make up for this algorithm's performance penalty. We are currently considering enhancements to the algorithm and its role in a phase-coupled retargetable microcode synthesis system.

In conclusion, the scene-analysis reduction operator heuristics hold good promise in compacting microprograms that do not have a high probability of resource conflict and short critical paths.

7.0 BIBLIOGRAPHY

[1] AGERWALA,T., "Microprogram optimization: A survey," _IEEE Trans. Comp._ C-25,10 (Oct. 76), 962-973.

[2] ASTOPAS, F., AND PLUKAS, K. "Method of minimizing computer microprograms," _Automatic Control_ 5,4 (1971), 10-16.

[3] DAVIDSON, S., LANDSKOV, D., SHRIVER, B., AND MALLET, P., "Some experiments in Local Microcode Compaction for Horizontal Machines", _IEEE Trans. Comp._ C-30,7 (July 81), p 460-477.

[4] DASGUPTA, S., AND TARTAR, J. "The Identification of Maximal Parallelism in Straight-Line Microprograms," _IEEE Trans. Comp._ C-25,10 (Oct. 76), 986-991.

[5] DASGUPTA, S. "Comment on the identification of maximal parallelism in straight-line microprograms," _IEEE Trans. Comp._, C-27, 3 (March 78), 285-286.

[6] DeWITT, D. "A Machine Independent Approach to the Production of optimal Horizontal Microcode," Ph.D. Dissertation, Univ. of Michigan, Ann Arbor, Tech. Rep 76 DT4, Aug. 1976.

[7] FERNANDEZ, E.B; AND BUSSEL, B. "Bounds on the number of processors and time for multiprocessor optimal schedule," _IEEE Trans. Comp._ C-22,8 (Aug. 73) 745-751.

[8] FISHER, J.A., The Optimization of Horizontal Microcode Within and Beyond Basic Blocks: An Application of Processor Scheduling with Resources, Ph.D. Thesis, Department of Mathematics and Computing, New York University, October 1979.

[9] HARALICK, R., DAVIS, L., ROSENFELD, A., AND MILGRAM, D., "Reduction Operations for Constraint Satisfaction", _Information Sciences_ 14, (1978) 199-219.

[10] HARALICK, R., AND SHAPIRO, L., "The Consistent Labeling Problem: Part I", IEEE Trans. on Pattern Analysis and Machine Intelligence, PAMI-1, No. 2, (April 79), 173-184.

[11] HARALICK, R., AND SHAPIRO, L., "The Consistent Labeling Problem: Part II", IEEE Trans. on Pattern Analysis and Machine Intelligence, PAMI-2, No. 3, (May 80), 193-203.

[12] HARALICK, R., AND ELLIOT, G., "Increasing Tree Search Efficiency for Constraint Satisfaction Problems", Artificial Intelligence 14 (1980), 263-313.

[13] HENRY, STEVEN G., Microprogram Compaction Using Reduction Operators, Masters Thesis, Department of Electrical Engineering, Colorado State University, July, 1983.

[14] KLEIR, R. L., AND RAMAMOORTHY, C.V., "Optimization Strategies for Microprograms," IEEE Trans. Comp. C-20,7 (July 71), 783-794.

[15] LEWIS, T., AND SHRIVER B., "Introduction to Special Issue on Microprogramming Tools and Techniques", IEEE Trans. Comp., C-30,7 (July 81), 457-459.

[16] PATTERSON, D., "V-Compiler: A next-generation tool for microprogramming", National Computer Conference, (1981), 103-109).

[17] POE, M., "Heuristics for the Global Optimization of Microprograms", (SIGMICRO) 13th Annual Workshop on Microprogramming, (1980) 13-22.

[18] RAMAMOORTHY, C.V.; AND TSUCHIYA, M., "A High-Level Language for Microprogramming," IEEE Trans. Comp. C-23,8 (Aug. 74), 791-801.

[19] TOKORO, M., TAMURA, E, TAKASE, K, AND TAMARU, K., "An approach to microprogram optimization considering resource occupancy and instruction formats," in (SIGMICRO) 10th Annual Workshop on Microprogramming, (1977), 92-108.

[20] TOKORU, M., TAMURA, E., AND TAKIZUKA, T.; "Optimization of Microprograms", IEEE Trans. Comp. C-30,7 (July 81), 491-504.

[21] TSUCHIYA, M., AND GONZALEZ, M.J., "An approach to optimization of horizontal microprograms," (SIGMICRO) 7th Annual workshop on microprogramming preprints (Sept. 30-Oct. 2, 1974) 85-90.

[22] TSUCHIYA, M., AND GONZALEZ, M., "Toward Optimization of Microprograms", IEEE Trans. Comp. C-25,10 (Oct. 76) 992-999.

[23] VEGDAHL, S., Phase Coupling and Constant Generation in an Optimizing Microcode Compiler, Ph.D. Dissertation, Dept. of C.S., Carnagie-Mellon University, Dec. 1982.

[24] YAU, S.S., SCHOWE, A.C, AND TSUCHIYA, M. "On Storage Optimization of Horizontal Microprograms," (SIGMICRO) 7th Annual workshop on microprogramming preprints (Sept. 30-Oct. 2, 1974) 98-106.

[25] ANDREWS, M,. Principles of Firmware Engineering In Microprogram Control, Computer Science Press, Potomac, Maryland, 1980.

[26] GAREY, M., AND JOHNSON, D., Computers and Intractibility: A Guide to the Theory of NP-Completeness, W.H. Freeman and Co., San Francisco, 1979.

Session III
Architectural Issues

EXPERIMENTATION WITH A TWO-LEVEL MICROPROGRAMMED MULTIPROCESSOR COMPUTER

Takanobu Baba*, Katsuhiro Yamazaki, Nobuyuki Hashimoto,
Hiroyuki Kanai, Kenzo Okuda, and Kazuhiko Hashimoto**

Department of Information Science
Utsunomiya University
Utsunomiya 321, Japan

ABSTRACT

MUNAP (MUlti-NAnoProgram machine) is a two-level microprogrammed multiprocessor computer designed and developed at a university as a research vehicle. This paper describes the experiences with the implementation of MUNAP. We start with a brief overview of the machine. We then describe the system organization both on hardware and support software. The architectural hierarchies defined on the basic hardware and software systems are described in detail. We conclude the paper with a list of the lessons we have learned from the experience.

1. Introduction

After the introduction of user microprogrammable machines, many open research questions were suggested. These include alternatives for supporting higher level languages, emulation of "environments" as well as extant computers, the representation and preparation of microprograms [12]. The idea also has impact on computer architects as a systematic approach to design and develop a user microprogrammable machine with innovative architecture [6, 7, 13].

MUNAP is a two-level microprogrammed, multiprocessor computer, intended primarily to be used as a user microprogrammable machine and further applied to various areas for study about the open problems. In the MUNAP system, a microinstruction simultaneously drives several nanoprogram streams in the four 16-bit processor

*Visiting at the College of Business and Management, University of Maryland, College Park, MD 20742
**HITACHI Software Engineering, Japan

units. Under these two levels of control, it provides highly parallel and distributed functions for nonnumeric processing, such as variable length word addressing, data permutation at the microprogram level, and bit operation and field handling at the multinanoprogram level. A detailed description of the hardware organization of MUNAP is presented in [1, 4]. The purpose of this paper is to describe the implementation of MUNAP and our experiences during the implementation. The description of the implementation decisions that we have made and a summary of our experiences will most certainly aid future microprogrammable machine implementors in their work.

In the following sections, we begin with a brief overview of the machine; then, we describe the historical perspective of the MUNAP project. In particular, the effort for developing a hierarchical microarchitecture on the bare hardware machine is described in some detail, referring to several experimental results. We conclude the paper with a list of the lessons we have learned from this experience.

2. An Overview of the MUNAP Machine

MUNAP employs a new two-level microprogrammed multiprocessor architecture, as shown in Fig. 1. One microprogram memory specifies the nanoprogram addresses of several processing units. The microprogram also coordinates the execution of multi-nanoprograms. This scheme is expected to have the following effects.

1) flexibility for meeting a wide range of system requirements through writeable microprogram and nanoprogram memories.

2) utilization of maximum parallelism between multiprocessor units under single microprogram control; and

3) savings in total control storage requirements by having nanoinstructions which are common to more than one microinstruction.

The first two factors allow a single microinstruction to be applied to any combination of the processing elements for each unique applications of the operation.

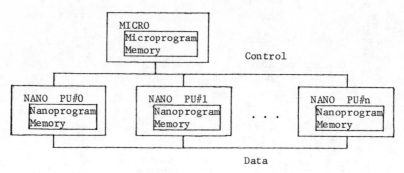

Fig. 1 Two-level microprogrammed multiprocessor architecture.

I-bus

O-bus
(64-bit)

Fig. 2 outlines the data flow of MUNAP. There are one microprogram memory (MPM) and four nanoprogram memories (NPM) within four identically constructed processor units (PU). A 28-bit microinstruction simultaneously drives several nanoprogram streams in the four 16-bit processor units. A 40-bit nanoinstruction has a 1-bit field to specify the end of a nanoprogram at each execution step. When all the nanoprograms end, the next microinstruction is activated. Since the nanoprogram memory is also reloadable as the microprogram memory, this allows the user to specify any combination of nanoinstructions in multiprocessor units.

Several hardware units are distributed among the microprogram level and nanoprogram level. The microprogram-controlled units are the four levels of 16-number, 4-bit segment shuffle exchange network (SEN) with exchange and broadcast cells for interconnection between processors and main memories and for data permutation, and the 8 banks of main memory modules (MM) with address modifier (AM) for variable length word access and two dimensional table access. The nanoprogram controlled units are the arithmetic and logic unit (ALU), the bit operation unit (BOU) for bit count, bit test and priority encode, and the field division and concatenation unit (DCU). The other units include the micro stacks (MSTK) and general registers (REG) at the micro level, and the register file (RF), scratchpad memory (SPM), counter (C), flag register (FLR), and port registers (IPR and OPR) at the multi-nano level.

The ECLIPSE S/130 minicomputer is attached to MUNAP as a console processor. MUNAP has been designed and constructed with about 2500 IC's at our laboratory. For the detail of MUNAP organization, see [4].

3. The MUNAP System Architecture

The MUNAP project organization is depicted in Fig. 3. It may be divided into the following three stages:

1) Architecture design and hardware development;

2) Support software systems development; and

3) Application to research problems.

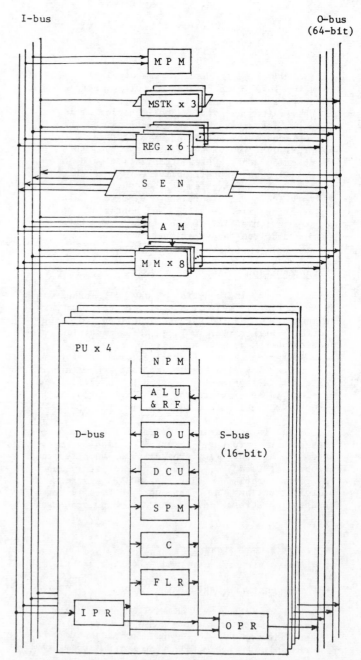

Fig. 2 MUNAP hardware organization.

Actually, these stages did not progress serially. The development of micro-assembly language for two-level microprograms started just after fixing the architecture, in parallel with the development of hardware. The application part of the last item is now under development, in parallel with the development of system description language. In this section, we will briefly outline the first two items.

A. Architecture Design

The MUNAP project began in 1978. The design objectives of the machine were defined as follows: 1) the system should support basic functions for a wide range of nonnumeric processing through firmware and hardware; and 2) as a research vehicle, the system should provide a powerful, yet flexible, architecture. The first objective is based on the fact that existing computer architecture and hardware do not provide efficient nonnumeric computation. In order to attain these objectives, we decided to utilize microprogramming technologies as effectively as possible. In particular, our attention was attracted by a new, two-level microprogramming scheme combined with a multiprocessor architecture which offers flexibility and parallelism in constructing a research-oriented multiprocessor computing system.

The design of the architecture was done by a professor and an undergraduate student in half a year. This small number enabled us to design a machine with well-defined principles. The detailed design of hardware and the development of a prototype of a processor unit (one of the multiple processor units) was done the next year, mainly by a group of five persons. After checking the logic of the PU, with that of two-level control scheme, we extended the number of processors to four, using the same wiring list as in the first prototype processor. This part is one of the most successful aspects of the hardware development of multiprocessor computer. MUNAP has been constructed of 2500 IC´s and the development required 9 man-years of effort.

B. Support Software Systems

Our initial experiences with the MUNAP led us to feel that some good support software are necessary for utilizing MUNAP.

The first attempt was a microprogram debugger, developed on the console processor, ECLIPSE S/130 minicomputer. It allows users to do console operations, such as general reset, load/store microprograms, start/stop the execution, read/write the facility values, and step run the microprograms for debugging [3]. As the size of microprograms grew, a relocatable loader for two-level microprograms became necessary and was developed. The loader receives object microprograms of a micro-assembler and relocates them both at micro- and nano-program levels without changing the sequences of microprograms and nanoprograms or the logical relation between a microinstruction and its nanoprogram. An evaluator has also been developed to get data while running the machine.

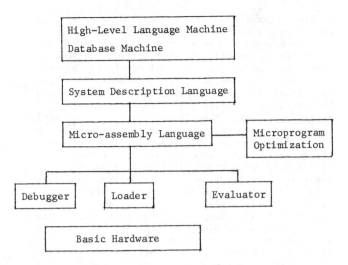

Fig. 3   MUNAP project organization.

The evaluator monitors the step-wise execution and produces the data for evaluating dynamic properties of the machine, such as micro- and nano-instruction usages.

Based on these support software systems, attempts to define relatively higher architectures have been made for future applications. These include the design and implementation of languages at micro-assembly and system description language levels, as described in the next section. The issue of optimization of two-level microprograms is discussed in [3].

4. Hierarchical Micro-Architectures

4.1 Basic concepts

At the initial stage of hardware development for MUNAP, we were required to do hand-coding for checking the hardware by running test microprograms. The experience taught us that it is very difficult to describe a microprogram with multiple nanoprograms. The nanoprogram level MIMD feature makes the process more complicated. At times, we had to write 28-bit microinstruction with 4 40-bit (i.e. 160-bit) nanoinstructions to specify the control for one machine cycle. Based on the experience, we decided to develop an architecture that is not only easy-to-use but efficient. To satisfy these contradictory requirements, the hierarchical micro-architecture concept was developed.

Fig. 4 shows the basic idea of hierarchical micro-architectures. At the lowest level, the multiple nanoinstruction sets are defined for multiple processors. The meaning of a microinstruction is partially determined by the nanoprograms. The microinstruction set is defined on the nano-level architecture. This micro-level instruction set, combined with the nanoinstruction sets, represents the visible micro-architecture of the machine (Level 0). On the Level 0 architecture, we define a higher level, enhanced view of the machine to make it easier to develop microprograms by utilizing symbolic expressions for arithmetic operations and sequencing, and providing the user a facility for describing the combined micro-nano operations in one statement (Level 1). The key for defining the Level 1 architecture is that it should not lose the flexibility for specifying micro-nano combinations and the parallelism among multiple processors. When we met a decision point for designing the language, that is, usability or efficiency, we chose efficiency or prepared two types of expressions, one for efficiency and the other for ease of use for the same operation. At the next level, a higher view is defined by a system description language level (Level 2). This level provides problem solving capabilities by including several data types, operators, and functions, as in usual system description languages [9]. Further, a tagged architecture is defined to aid the user's debugging process and realize dynamic data type transformation. An additional layer to be considered is derived from the varieties of user specialties that may surround the system (Level 3). By using the Level 2 facilities, we can describe a high level language processor, such as the PASCAL compiler for Level 3.

In the following sections, we will concentrate our discussion on the language features and experimental results of Levels 1 and 2. The detailed discussions will be deferred to [5].

4.2 Language features and experimental results

(1) Micro-assembly language level

A register-transfer-level language has been designed and implemented [2, 3] to obtain an efficient microprogram, allowing the user to utilize the hardware features. Table 1 shows the statements of the language. Fig. 5 shows a sample description of a bit count microprogram. The language features are summarized in the following two types:

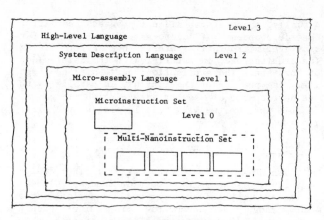

Fig. 4 Basic concepts of hierarchical micro-architectures.

(a) Description of two-level microprograms: Basically, the user can describe any combination of a microinstruction and multinanoprogram, activated by the microinstruction, in order to efficiently make use of the flexibility of two-level microprograms. The microprogram and nanoprograms are described in sequence and distinguished by indentation. At this level, the hardware functions are uniform and frequently used micro-nano combined functions may be described in one statement, called micro-nano statement. ST-NO. 8 is an example of one statement description. The statement is translated into one microinstruction that reads data from MM and controls the SEN to send the data to four PU's, and four nanoinstructions, that write the data on the port registers to SPM (10)'s in four PU's. The user does not need to be aware of the operations of elementary micro- and nano-instructions. The definition of the virtual flag is an example of the uniformity. It enables the test of positive data at Level 1, although there is no positive flag at Level 0.

```
ST-NO.          STATEMENT

  1  MICRO MAIN BITCOUNT (100);          /* BIT COUNT MICROPROGRAM */
  2     EXT NEXT (2);                    /* DECLARE EXTERNAL SYMBOL NEXT */
  3     *;                               /* ACTIVATE NANOPROGRAMS */
  4        RF(2) := 0;                   /* CLEAR BIT COUNTER */
  5        CXO := 0;                     /* CLEAR COUNTER CXO */
  6  L1:   AM MODE M8 (X,H) PU(3-0);     /* SET MM ADDRESS WITH SUM OF
  7        OPRO := RFO(1) <+> CXO;          RFO(1) AND CXO */
  8     SPM(10) := MM;                   /* READ DATA INTO SCRATCHPAD */
  9        RF(3) := <BCT,1> SPM(10);     /* COUNT ONES IN SPM(10)'S */
 10        RF(2) := RF(2) <+> RF(3)  CXO+1;  /* COMPUTE PARTIAL SUM */
 11     *IF CXO MOD4 <> 0 THEN GOTO L1;  /* TEST COUNTER */
 12     IPR := <SRL16> OPR;              /* ADD RFO(2)-RF3(2) AND SET
 13        OPRO := RFO(2);                  RF3(4) BY SERIAL PU
 14        OPR1 := RF1(2) <+> IPR1;         OPERATION */ †
 15        OPR2 := RF2(2) <+> IPR2;
 16        RF3(4) := RF3(2) <+> IPR3;
 17     GOTO NEXT;                                       + see [4]
 18  END;
```

Fig. 5 Bit count microprogram in micro-assembly language (Level 1).

(b) Description of parallel processing: The parallel processing of MUNAP is divided into three categories: (i) microinstruction and multiple nanoinstructions are tightly coupled to perform a single task; (ii) SIMD operation, in which multiple PU´s do the same operation; and (iii) MIMD operation. ST-NO.8 is an example of (i). Although the MIMD operation should be described in several statements, the SIMD operation may be described in one statement. ST-NO´s from 13 to 16 and ST-NO´s 4 and 9 show examples of MIMD and SIMD operations, respectively.

The micro-assembler receives the source statements and performs the following:

1)   divide a micro-nano combined statement into a microinstruction and nanoinstructions and assign the nanoinstructions to appropriate PU´s.

2)   extend a statement for multiple PU´s to several statements and assign them to appropriate PU´s.

3)   optimize the two-level microprograms.

For example, ST-NO. 8 in Fig. 5 is decomposed into one microinstruction (m) and four nanoinstructions (n0-n3) during the first and second steps as follows.

$$m: MM \rightarrow \langle SEN \rangle \rightarrow IPR$$

n0: IPR0 -> SPM0(10)   n2: IPR2 -> SPM2(10)
n1: IPR1 -> SPM1(10)   n3: IPR3 -> SPM3(10)

The third optimization step tries to make microinstructions utilize as much of the same nanoprogram as possible. An example is illustrated in Fig. 6. If the nanoprogram (d, g, and h) activated by microinstruction B is included in the nanoprogram for microinstruction A, B can utilize a part of A´s nanoprogram by activating the necessary part of A´s nanoprogram (indicated by dotted lines). The detailed optimization conditions are found in [3].

To evaluate the effectiveness of the architecture, we performed an experiment. Ten problems were given to the members of our laboratory who were knowledgable about the language. The results are summarized as follows.

-   The micro-nano statements account for 33.1 % of the total microinstructions. This significant usage demonstrates the effectiveness of the micro-nano combined statements for describing tightly coupled micro-nano operations.

-   The description of parallel processing is 27.0 % of total descriptions. According to the classifications of (b) above, we can classify them into three categories: (i) micro-nano statements (33.3 %), (ii) the same nano statements (41.9 %), and (iii) different nano statements (24.8 %).

Table 1 Micro-assembly language statements

	Statement Name (Meaning)
Declaration	EXT (External Address)
	ADDR (Internal Address)
	EQU (Name for a SPM or RF word)
Execution	
Micro (activate nano)	*GOTO, *IF (2-way/5-way branch), MPM Write, AM (MM Address Modification)
Micro (not activate nano)	Assignment (including Read/Write MM), GOTO, IF CASE (Functional Branch), CALL, RETURN, Literal Flag SET, RESET, HALT, NOP (No operation)
Nano	ALU, DCU, BOU, Nano-literal, IF, Flag Set, NOP, MICRO (Data transfer to Port Register)
Micro-Nano Combined	Assignment (Data Transfer between Micro and Nano) *IF (Micro-level Branch Based on Nano-level Test Results)

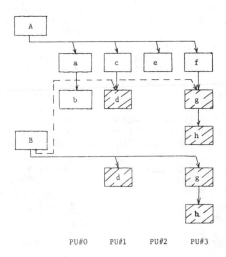

PU#0   PU#1   PU#2   PU#3

Fig. 6 An example of nanoprogram utilization.

A, B: microinstruction
a, b, ..,h: nanoinstruction

(2) System description language level

The micro-assembly language has provided a relatively high-level micro-architecture to the user. However, it is still difficult to describe large, utility programs or application programs in such a language.

The following objectives are defined for designing the MUNAP System Description Language (MSDL):

(a) Definition of high-level architecture: On the Level 1 architecture, we defined a rich set of data types, operators, and functions. These are summarized in Tables 2, 3, and 4. Included are, in particular, the data types of array and structure, the control statements IF, WHILE, FOR, and SWITCH, operators for data exchange and concatenate, and functions for bit and character string operations.

(b) Utilization of hardware features: To utilize the hardware features of MUNAP, we represent some of them in the language. Examples are string functions for nonnumeric function units such as BOU and DCU (Table 4), and shift and exchange operators for the SEN (Table 3). This is a compromise between the high-level, problem-oriented architecture and low level hardware organizations.

(c) Tagged architecture: The goals of an effective computer architecture are not only the efficient processing of large amounts of data but also the enhancement of the debugging process and the enhancement of reliability of the computing system [11]. Higher processing capability, obtained by parallel processing, should be applied not only for processing large amounts of data at high speed but also for improving the user interface by semantic checking during program execution. To implement these concepts at the system description level, we designed a tagged architecture. This architecture is expected to provide the facilities for (i) detecting several kinds of errors at run time such as refering to an unassigned data value, and (ii) automatically transforming the data types of operands. These two items aid the development process of programs.

The source program written in MSDL is translated into an intermediate form by the host processor, and then interpretively executed by MUNAP. In order to make use of the MUNAP micro-architecture features, the intermediate language has one-to-one correspondence with the MSDL source program. The interpreter consists of 3.2 K microinstructions and 7.6 K (1.9 K for each PU) nanoinstructions.

The experimental results are summarized as follows:

(a) The static data from the interpreter shows the ratio 1:0.9:1.9 for the average numbers of micro-statements (M), nano-statements (n), and micro-nano statements (MN) for realizing a module of the interpreter. (It mainly corresponds to one of the operators, control statements, or functions.)

(b) The average number of active PU´s for all the microroutines in the interpreter is 2.2.

(c) The overhead caused by type check and type transformation occupies the major part of overhead for tag processing. They are 75 % of total overhead for tag processing.

Further, to get dynamic data, we made a MSDL program of integral computation for the equation:

$$S = \int_0^2 (x^3 + 2x - 1)\,dx.$$

Table 2 Data types

Integer	SHORT (16), INTEGER (32), LONG (64)
Real	FLOAT (32), DOUBLE (64)
Bit	SBOOL (16), BOOL (32), LBOOL (64)
	LBOOL N (64+16N)
Character	CHAR N (8N)
Flag	FLAG (1)
Operator	OPERATOR (8)*

*number in parenthesis represents bit length.

Table 3 Operators

Arithmetic	$*$, $/$, $\%$, $+$, $-$
Logical	! (not), & (and), | (or), ^ (xor), !&, !|, !^
Shift	SLL, SRL, SLA, SRA, SLC, SRC
Exchange	M8, M16, M32, M64 (Mirror transformation), XX, ** (Data exchange)
Relation	$>$, $<$, $>=$, $<=$, $==$, $!=$
Concatenation	&&, ||

Table 4 String functions

Bit String

BSUBSTR(BIT,POS,N)	N-bit extraction from POS-bit
PEC(BIT,{L/M},{0/1})	Bit position detection of {0/1} from {LSB/MSB}
BCT(BIT,{0/1})	{0/1} count
BCON(B1,B2,..,BN)	Concatenation of B1, B2, ..,BN

Character String

CSUBSTR(CHAR,POS,N)	N-character extraction
INDEX(CHAR,{L/M},C)	Character position detection
CCT(CHAR,C)	Count character C
CCON(C1,C2,..,CN)	Concatenate C1, C2,.., CN

The source program is shown in Fig. 7. The experimental results are summarized as follows:

(a) The total number of machine cycles is 744738; the corresponding execution time is 0.45 second.

(b) the average number of dynamically active PU´s is 2.14.

(c) the ratio of M, N and MN is 1:1.2:31

The detailed data and discussions will be found in [8, 14].

4.3 Effects of Architecture Hierarchies

Summarizing the characteristics of three micro-architecture levels, the following items are observed.

(1) The higher the level of language, the richer is the facility. This can be generalized to all the aspects of language, such as data structure, arithmetic and logical operators, and control functions.

(2) At the lowest level of Level 0, the user must take care of the parallelism and two-level control scheme of the bare machine. At Level 1, the frequently used micro-nano combina-

tions, and the instructions with the SIMD feature, may be described in one statement. But these features do not completely hide the hardware features, such as parallelism among multiple processors and two-levels of control, from the user. At Level 2, such hardware features are almost hidden from the user, and problem-oriented functions are provided.

(3) The utilization of multiple processor parallelism does not change between Levels 0 and 1, because they have the same description capability. However, it slightly decreases from Level 1 to Level 2, in exchange for independence of parallelism recognition by the user.

(4) The error check function is only provided at Level 2 to aid the programming process and enhance system reliability.

(5) The extensibility of the language differs from Levels 1 and 2. The extensibility at Level 1 corresponds to the extensibility of hardware such as the addition of a new microinstruction field or micro-order. The Level 2 extension is in the addition of new functional modules.

The above comparison shows that we have defined a reasonable interface as a compromise between the user's requirements and multiprocessor system throughput.

5. Lessons Learnt from the MUNAP Machine

This section briefly presents what we feel to be the important lessons from our work on MUNAP in the past several years.

(1) Parallelism

Using the architecture of a two-level microprogrammed multiprocessor, we can select an arbitrary number of processors, especially as multiples of 2. Needless to say, the greater the number of multiprocessor units, the larger the possibility of parallelism. Then, the question is: Is the number of the MUNAP processor units, i.e. 4, appropriate? We would say yes. The reasons are:

1) It is difficult to find out inherent parallelism of 8 or above from "ordinary" problems like language processing [10].

2) It is not practical to describe microprograms of a computer with eight or more "independent" PUs for each machine cycle.

3) The experimental results described in 4.2 show that the average PU utilization is around 2, and multiple processors from 2 to 4 are activated in most of the machine cycles. This means that parallelism obtained with two processors is not enough even for ordinary problems.

```
PROCEDURE SIMPSON;
LOCAL INTEGER  SPM  I,M=20;
     FLOAT  SPM  (S,X)=0.0,F,H,A[3]=-1.0,2.0,0.0,1.0;

  PROCEDURE FX(X,F);
    FLOAT X;
    VAR FLOAT F;
    LOCAL DOUBLE  SPM  Y;
         INTEGER  SPM  I;
  {   Y=0.0;
      FOR ( I=3; I>=1; I=I-1)
        {    Y=(Y+A[I])*X;
        }
      F=Y+A[0];
  }

{   H=2.0/M;
    FOR (I=2; I<M; I=I+2)
      {   FX(X,F); S=S+F; X=X+H;
          FX(X,F); S=S+4.0*F; X=X+H;
          FX(X,F); S=S+F;
      }
    S=H*S/3.0;
}
```

Fig. 7 Integral computation program in MSDL.

Notice that the above claims are on ordinary problems. The situation may be different if we apply it to parallel problems, like matrix computation. However, this would decrease the need for the MIMD feature of a two-level microprogrammed multiprocessor architectures.

Thus, we prefer to extend the word length and capacity of facilities of each processor unit rather to increase the number of processors, if more computation power is required.

(2) Nonnumeric processing functions

Our primary intention in providing nonnumeric units such as bit operation and field handling units, and variable length word access from MM is to use them for special purpose processing such as database applications. However, our experience has taught us that the functions are also useful for ordinary processing. For example, these units are used for tagged data processing (i.e., extraction and test) and for intermediate language decoding in the MSDL interpreter.

Thus, we think these functions should be provided in general purpose computers as usual operations. Such hardware units with basic nonnumeric operations combined with flexible microprogrammed architecture will result in a comprehensive machine.

(3) Two-level microprogramming

The two-level microprogramming scheme, combined with the parallelism among multiple processors, are the most successful part of our

53

research. The advantages of two-level controls over one-level controls on the control storage requirements, etc, are discussed in [4]. They also result in a flexible architecture by reloadable microprogram and multiple nanoprogram memories. The shuffle exchange network and 8 banks of main memory modules also result in a flexible architecture by providing a parallel and reconfigurable hardware organization under the control of microprograms.

Our experience has taught us about some relationships between micro and nano levels for decentralized control ("partial join mode" [4]), which are a little complicated, and are seldom used by ordinary users. Therefore, after evaluating the usage of such functions, we might be able to reduce the complexity of hardware units and the constraints on timings.

6. Concluding Remarks

We have reported on the first several years of a research program on a two-level microprogrammed, multiprocessor computer. We have discussed the present hardware organization, the design of hierarchical architectures, and the lessons we have learned by working on the project. The results show the effectiveness of the current MUNAP organization. However, this should not be considered a post mortem. Work continues on development of application programs on the machine with innovative architecture as the advanced phases of the research program. They include database machine and high level language machine projects. The results of this research will yield a comprehensive framework for future design and development of innovative computer architectures.

REFERENCES

[1] Baba, T, Ishikawa, K., Okuda, K., and Kobayashi, H.: "MUNAP - A Two-Level Microprogrammed Multiprocessor Architecture for Nonnumeric Processing," Proc. IFIP Congress 80, (Oct. 1980), pp. 169-174.

[2] Baba, T., and Hagiwara, H.: "The MPG System: A Machine-Independent Efficient Microprogram Generator," IEEE Trans. Comput., (June 1981), pp.373-395.

[3] Baba, T., Hashimoto, N., Yamazaki, K, and Okuda, K.: "Microprogramming Support System for a Two-Level Microprogrammed Computer MUNAP," Trans. IECE Japan, (Oct. 1982), pp. 1265-1272.

[4] Baba, T., Ishikawa, K., and Okuda, K.: "A Two-Level Microprogrammed Multiprocessor Computer with Nonnumeric Functions," IEEE Trans. Comput., (Dec. 1982), pp. 1142-1156.

[5] Baba, T.,Hashimoto, N., Kanai, H., Okuda, K., and Hashimoto, K.: "Hierarchical Micro-Architectures of a Two-Level Microprogrammed Multiprocessor Computer," to be published in the proceedings of International Conference on Parallel Processing, Aug. 1983.

[6] Barr, R.G., Becker, J.A., Liinsky, W.P., and Tantillo, V.V.: "A Research-Oriented Dynamic Microprocessor," IEEE Trans. Comput., (Nov. 1973), pp. 976-985.

[7] Fisher, J.A.: Very Long Instruction Word Architectures and the ELI-512, Proc. of the 10th Annual Int. Symposium on Computer Architecture, (June 1983), pp. 140-150.

[8] Hashimoto, N.: "Micro-Architecture Description Languages for a Two-Level Microprogrammed Computer MUNAP," Master thesis of Dept. Inf. Sci., Utsunomiya University, Japan, (March 1983).

[9] Kernigham, B.W. and Ritchie, D.M.: The C Programming Language, Prentice Hall, Inc., (1978).

[10] Moto-oka, T.: "Future Aspects of Computer System," IECE Japan, (1979), pp. 1204-1207.

[11] Myers, G. J.: Advances in Computer Architecture, New York: Wiley, (1978).

[12] Rosin, R.F., Frieder, G., and Eckhouse, R.H.: "An Environment for Research in Microprogramming and Emulation," Commun. Ass. Comput. Mach., (Aug. 1972), pp. 748-760.

[13] Tomita, S., Shibayama, K., Kitamura, T., Tanaka, T., and Hagiwara, H.: "A User-Microprogrammable Local Host Computer with Low-Level Parallelism," Proc. of the 10the Annual Int. Symposium on Computer Architecture, (June 1983), pp.151-159.

[14] Yamazaki, K., Hashimoto, N., Kanai, H., Baba, T., Okuda, K., and Hashimoto, K.: A System Description Language for a Two-Level Microprogrmmed Computer MUNAP: MSDL, Tech. Rep. of IECE Japan, EC82-60, (Dec. 1982).

A DESIGN APPROACH FOR A MICROPROGRAMMED CONTROL UNIT WITH BUILT IN SELF TEST

Jordi Duran
Universitat Politecnica
de Barcelona
Barcelona, Spain

Tulin E. Mangir*
UCLA Computer Science Dept.
Rm3532F Boelter Hall
Los Angeles, CA 90024
(213) 206-6542
825-1322 (msgs)

ABSTRACT

We present an architecture for concurrent testing of a microprogrammed control unit. This approach is compared with other control unit testing strategies. The advantages of this approach are: a) it allows testing of the control unit independent of the operational section, b) minimizes the hardcore, c) it is easily incorporated in microprogrammed control units, d) since it is concurrent, probability of detecting intermittent errors is high, e) it is incorporated into the specification and therefore amenable for VLSI implementations.

I. INTRODUCTION

Testing of the control unit has been dependent on the correct working of the operational, or data, section of a processor. Based on the behavior of the operational section, 'good' or 'badness' of the control section is deduced. Some of the methods can be used concurrently with normal operation and others used off-line [MANG 80, MANG 82, MANG 83a, MANG 83b].

Self-testing microprogrammed control units can be classified in the following way:

1- The control unit is monitored through the outputs of its operational section [ROBA 78]. To determine the correct (or incorrect) operation of the control unit, special test patterns have to be applied in an off-line fashion and monitor the outputs of the operational section (ALU, shift register, stack, etc.)

This method, (applying commands and data that determine the states of the control unit), seems attractive, but has the following drawbacks:
- The test is not concurrent with execution of the application (unless we consider concurrent execution using idle periods of the CPU).

- Since both the control section (microinstruction, microsequencer, MAR and MIR) and the operational section are tested through the outputs

of the operational section, the hardcore (i.e., the part of the hardware which must be working correctly) of the system is constituted by the overall control unit and the diagnosis of the faulty module becomes more difficult.

On the other hand, this method has the following advantages:

- No internal modification of the control unit is needed. Hardware to generate and store test patterns and to observe the outputs is needed.

-Both *hardwired* and *microprogrammed* control units can use this method.

The solution presented by El-Lithy and Husson [E1LI 80] also follows this method, but only for bit-sliced control units.

2- All control unit internal signals are encoded so so that an error generates an incorrect word that can be detected by a decoder [COOK 73]. Outputs of the operational section need not be monitored since control signals are monitored directly. The control unit is tested at the data transfer level and not at the functional level. This approach has the following disadvantages:

- Since all the signals issued by the control section have to be encoded, the microstore has to be modified (in both its control and address part). This results in a larger microstore and wider signal paths.

- The encoders and/or decoders placed on the signal paths delay the signals.

- The hardware is significantly increased due to the added encoders, decoders, microstore, and signal path width.

This method has the following advantages:

- The signals issued by the control section are directly monitored and no external inputs have to be applied to determine the correct operation. Outputs are not monitored because internal hardware (self-checking checkers) issues a good/bad signal.

- Control unit testing is concurrent with the application program.

---

*The person to whom all correspondence should be addressed.

3- Sridhar and Hayes [SRID 81] propose the design of a CI-testable control unit. CI-testable arrays facilitate testing of control units, but have these drawbacks:

- The control unit usually must be redesigned to get a CI-testable structure.

- It applies only to bit-sliced control units.

- Operation of the control unit is monitored through the operational section output signals. Test patterns must exercise the hardware correctly.

- The test method is off-line with the application program.

A self-testing approach based on BILBO techniques has been proposed by Daniels and Fasang, for the *external test* of microprocessors [DANI 83], [FASA 82], [FASA 83]. The external test of a microprocessor, or in a more general case of a CPU, presents the following problems:

- Signals can be inaccessible therefore cannot be monitored.

- Hardcore of the system is constituted by the overall CPU plus the additional logic needed to implement the self-testing mechanism.

- Operation code and some status signals (i.e., fetch cycle signal) must be observable.

- Most important of all, control unit signals, used to verify or test the control unit, must be generated by fault secure units.

Our method avoids or diminishes, the drawbacks of the above methods while conserving their virtues. Basically, it is built-in self-test [MANG 83a, MANG 83b]. This method is based on the application of parallel signature analysis to the internal signals.

Signature analysis cannot detect all possible errors, but an n bit signature finds more than $100 \left(1 - 2^{-n}\right)$ % of all possible errors (that is, deviations from the correct data sequence).

Our method has the following characteristics:

- It only monitors the control section (and not the operational section) of the CPU, i.e., a self-testing control part of the CPU is designed.
As a result, the hardcore of the system is minimized. Having asserted the proper operation of the control part, the operational part can be tested and verified by the former using microprogrammed test and diagnostic procedures.

- The control section is directly observed. No special encoding of control and address signals is needed.

-The self-testing procedures run concurrently with the application program.

- Since it can be run concurrently, it has a high coverage of the intermittent errors.

II. DESIGN OF A MICROPROGRAMMED CONTROL UNIT WITH BUILT IN SELF TEST

We consider the control unit, (CPU) divided into two functional sections: control section and operational section (Figure 1).

The control section is the microstore, the microinstruction register, and the sequencer. It translates a macroinstruction into a sequence of microinstructions and control signals for the operational section.

Our goal is a self-testing control section. We want a control section that either behaves correctly and issues a "good" signal or, in case of improper behavior, issues an "error" signal.

The control section operates correctly if, and only if:

1) each macroinstruction activates the correct sequence of microinstructions; and
2) for each microinstruction, the control signals are proper for that instruction.

Alternatively, the control part operates correctly if, and only if:

1) each macroinstruction causes a branch to the correct microstore location;
2) each subsequent microinstruction generates the correct address, (that is, the address that guarantees the correct sequencing of the microprogram corresponding to the macroinstruction);
3) each microinstruction issues the proper control signals to the operational section in order to realize the operation corresponding to the microinstruction.

The control section signals and the sequencer addresses have to be monitored. This method differs from methods in which either the control section is controlled indirectly through the outputs of the operational section or the data/control signal transfer is monitored using error detecting codes. The proposed control unit is shown in Figure 2.

At the beginning of execution of a macroinstruction, the (decoded) operation code of the macroinstruction is loaded into the macroinstruction latch and both the Address Signature Register (ASR) and Control Signature Register (CSR) are cleared.

For each microinstruction the sequencer address and the control signals (only those issued to the operational part) are loaded into the ASR and CSR respectively. This is a compact signature of both the address sequence and the control signal sequence generated by the microprogram.

The macroinstruction latch addresses the test memory for the reference address and control signatures.

At the end of each microprogram, the actual values of the address and control signatures are checked against the reference values in two fault secure checkers. If the values match, we can assert the correct behavior of the control section during the execution of the macroinstruction.

The Address Signature Register (ASR) is placed just at the output of the sequencer for the following reasons:

- the address field of the microinstruction (when it is clearly differentiated from the rest of the macroinstruction) usually does not contain the address of the next microinstruction (as in the original proposal by Wilkes), but it contains a set of control signals that lead the sequencer to generate the next address. Therefore, the address appears, in a more manageable form, only at the output of the sequencer.

- by placing the ASR at the output of the sequencer, the "address control" bits of the microstore and the MIR, and the sequencer are tested. Some registers of the operational section maybe tested as well, (in an indirect manner), since these registers may contain data used to calculate by the sequencer to generate the address of the next microinstruction.

The Control Signature Register (CSR) is placed just between the MIR and the operational section. In this way it tests the corresponding bits of the microstore and the MIR. For horizontal or diagonal microinstructions with clearly differentiated fields, several CSRs can be used, one for each field or for a group of fields. This improves diagnosis capabilities of the self-test mechanism are greatly improved.

Detection of the Conditional Branches

Since the self-testing mechanisms are implemented in the control unit, we can assume, without loss of generality, that all status flags are accessible. Status flags determine the sequencer address for conditional branches.

For conditional macroinstructions we assume two possible sequences of microinstructions. We must determine which sequence has been executed (because they have different reference signatures).

Our solution is shown in Figure 2. The opcode of the conditional macroinstruction is one input to the flag multiplexer. The selected flag is the most significant bit of the test memory address, so the signature selected depends on the branch taken. For unconditional macroinstructions, flag values do not affect the multiplexer address.

Other designs detect the branch taken by counting the number of (micro) cycles for execution of the (micro) instruction [DANI 83]. These solutions can reduce the hardware. We have chosen "direct status control" because it has more direct and local control over the source of the decision.

III. IMPLEMENTATION DEPENDENT ASPECTS

A) Influence of the microstore organization

The actual architecture of the control unit influences heavily the hardware needed and the diagnostic capabilities of the self-testiong mechanisms.

Horizontal organizations need more testing hardware to track a sequence of wider bit patterns but diagnosis is better. The microinstruction can be divided into several fields. By independently controlling these different fields using several signature analysis registers, the origin of the fault can be determined with higher precision.

Vertical organizations need less hardware, but, since the microinstruction is highly encoded, diagnostic capabilities are reduced. If the signature analysis registers are placed after the decoder, the characteristics of the self-test are similar to the horizontal organization.

B) A practical case

In this section, we will discuss how to add self-test to an existing control unit. For this example, we have used the control unit of the PERQ minicomputer.

PERQ uses a 48 bit microinstruction organized in 12 fields. The structure of the microinstruction and the self-testing logic is shown in Figure 3.

The X, Y, A, B, and ALU fields control the source of the operands and the function realized by the ALU. The Z field can be either a constant (for ALU operations) or a jump address. The CND and JMP fields control the operation of the sequencer. The W, H, and F fields contain control bits that enable writing and interruptions, and control the interpretation of the SF and Z field contents. The SF can be either the most significant part of an address or the code of a special function.

The implementation shown in Figure 3 permits a fairly accurate determination of the origin of the fault. The CND and JMP fields are not checked at the output of the MIR because they are always tested implicitly in the address signature register. Note that the F,SF, Z, and H fields do not always determine the operation of the sequencer. If the diagnostic capabilities are to be increased, an additional direct testing of these bits can be done just after the MIR. Since the sequencer is not self-contained (it takes jump offsets from registers in the operational section) it cannot be determined if an address fault has been produced in the sequencer or in the operational section. Additional hardware would be needed to do so. In the PERQ code, instructions can be 1 or 2 bytes long. We suppose that the detection of 2 byte instructions is done in the starting address decoder.

Test Store. The test store has to contain a 40+12 bit signature for each possible microprogram (assuming 4K 48-bit words of microstore). Since PERQ has 284 instructions (9 of which are conditional branches) we need a test store of 293x52 bits, approximately 2K bytes. (Case jump can be included in this category since it can be executed by one of two microprograms).

Considering a 4Kx48 bits microstore (PERQ can have up to 16K of microstore to implement user written microprograms), the overall memory requirements of the control unit are increased approximately 8%

If self-testing is implemented outside the control section CPU test memory of approximately $\frac{1}{2}$K byte would be needed. The diagnostic capabilities would be reduced and the hardcore of the system increased.

CONCLUSION

We described a microprogrammed control unit architecture with built-in self-test. We showed how to modify a PERQ for self-test. This method enables concurrent verification and testing of the control section independently of the operational section. It also minimizes the hardcore required to verify correct behavior of the control section. Actual implementation depends on instruction format and control section microarchitecture.

ACKNOWLEDGEMENT:

The authors would like to thank Ms. Vicki Graham for the preparation of the manuscript.

REFERENCES

[COOK 73] R.W. Cook, W.H. Sisson, T.F. Storey, W.N. Toy, "Design of a Self-Checking Microprogram Control", IEEE Trans. Computers, Vol.C-22, No.3, March 1973, pp. 255-262.

[DANI 83] S.F. Daniels, "A Concurrent Test Technique for Standard Microprocessors", COMCON 83, February 1983, pp. 389-394.

[DASG 79] S. Dasgputa, "The Organization of Microprogram Stores", Computing Surveys, Vol.11, No.1, March 1979, pp. 39-65.

[ElLI 80] M. El-Lithy, R. Husson, "Bit-Sliced Microprocessor Testing - A Case Study", FTCS-10, October 1980, pp. 126-128.

[FASA 82] P.P. Fasang, "A Fault Detection and Isolation Technique for Microcomputers", 1982 IEEE Test Conference, pp. 214-219.

[FASA 83] P.P. Fasang, "Microbit Brings Self-Testing on Board Complex Microcomputers", Electronics, March 10, 1983, pp. 116-119.

[KONE 79] B. Konemann, J. Mucha, G. Zurehoff, "Built-in Logic Block Observation Techniques", IEEE 1979 Test Conference, pp. 37-41.

[MANG 80] T.E. Mangir, "Failure Modes for VLSI and Their Effect on Chip Design", Proc, ICCC80.

[MANG 81] T.E. Mangir, "Use of on Chip redundancy for Fault-Tolerant VLSI Design", Ph.D. Dissertation, UCLA, June 1981.

[MANG 83] T.E. Mangir, "Wafer to System Requirements for BIST", BIST Workshop, March 15-17, 1983. South Carolina.

[MANG 83] T.E. Mangir, "An Integrated Approach to VLSI Testing", to be published, Proc. ICCAD 1983, Santa Clara, CA.

[ROBA 78] C. Robach, G. Saucier, "Dynamic Testing of Control Units", IEEE Trans. Computers, Vol.C-27, No.7, July 1978, pp. 617-623.

[SRID 81] T. Sridhar, J.P. Hayes, "Design of Easily Testable Bit-Sliced Systems", IEEE Trans. Computers, Vol.C-30, No.11, November 1981, pp. 842-854.

[WILL 82] T.W. Williams, K.P. Parker, "Design for Testability - A Survey", IEEE Trans. Computers, Vol.C-31, No.1, January 1982, pp. 2-15.

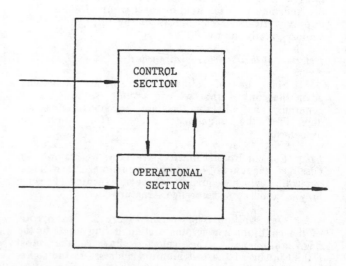

Figure 1. Functional sections of CPU

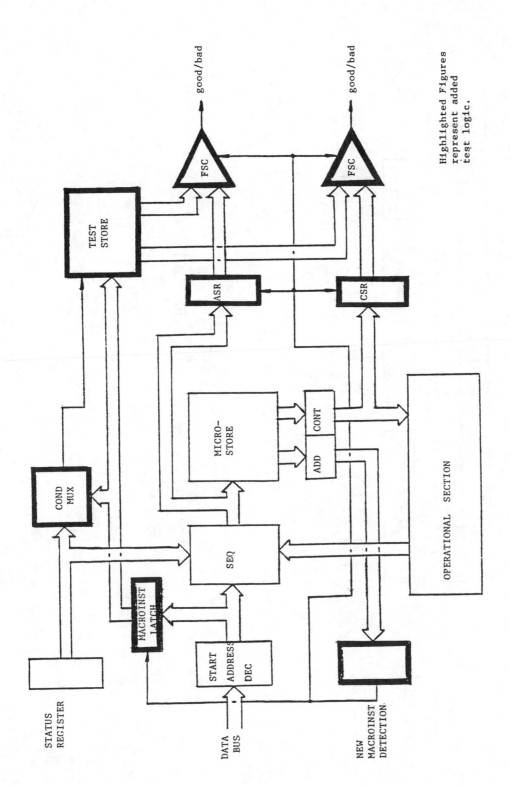

good/bad

good/bad

Highlighted Figures
represent added
test logic.

Figure 2. Proposed design of a microprogrammed control section with built-in self-test

59

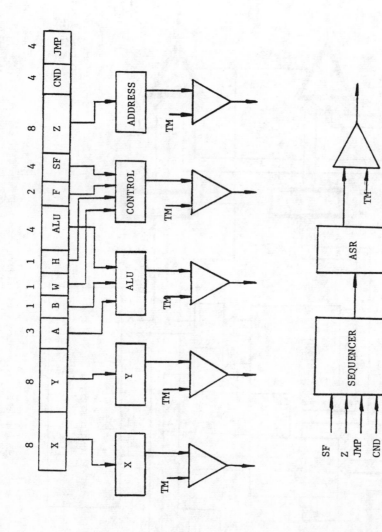

TM: Test Memory

Figure 3. Possible implementation of built-in self-test for microprogrammed control section of PERQ minicomputer.

MODIFICATIONS TO THE VAX-11/780 MICROARCHITECTURE TO SUPPORT IEEE FLOATING POINT ARITHMETIC

DAVID B. ASPINWALL and YALE N. PATT

University of California, Berkeley and San Francisco State University

ABSTRACT

The VAX-11/780 was designed specifically to implement the VAX architecture. As such, it does not support the IEEE standard for floating point arithmetic. A project was undertaken to provide this support by modifying the 11/780 microarchitecture. Our objective was to produce a microengine that would efficiently execute a modified VAX instruction set, in particular, one that executes VAX floating point instructions consistent with the IEEE standard. We made minimal changes to the 11/780 hardware, relying primarily on changes to the microcode. This paper describes the work of this project.

1. Introduction

A microarchitecture is usually designed to implement a specific target machine. The VAX-11/780, which implements the VAX-11, is such a microarchitecture. Changes in the microarchitecture to accommodate unintended uses are usually cumbersome, expensive, and incur a great loss in performance.

Recently, a standard for binary floating point arithmetic has been adopted by the IEEE. We wished to implement this standard within the context of the VAX architecture, so that experimentation of the VAX with IEEE floating point arithmetic could take place. Consequently, a project was undertaken to modify the 11/780 microarchitecture so that it would support the IEEE standard.

This paper is divided into five sections. Section 2 delineates the IEEE standard. Section 3 describes portions of the VAX-11/780 microarchitecture that are pertinent to the execution of floating point instructions. Section 4 lists modifications to the microarchitecture required to support the IEEE standard. Finally, Section 5 presents some preliminary conclusions.

This work was supported, in part, by the U.S. Department of Energy under Contract DE-AM03-76SF00034, Project DE-AT03-76E10358, through the University of California, Berkeley.

UNIX is a trademark of Bell Laboratories. VAX is a trademark of Digital Equipment Corporation.

David Aspinwall is currently with Cyclotomics, 2120 Haste St., Berkeley, CA.

2. The IEEE Standard for Binary Floating Point Arithmetic

In 1981 the IEEE (Institute for Electrical and Electronics Engineers) first published its proposed standard for binary floating point arithmetic[4]. The IEEE standard defined floating point data types, listed instructions which must be included in a conforming implementation, specified various modes which must be implemented, and defined what types of faults could occur and how these faults should be handled. This section gives a brief introduction to the standard.

2.1. Data Types and Formats

The standard lists several data types, some of which must and some of which should be implemented. The data types implemented by this project are: **floating**, **double**, and **(double-)extended**. Floating and double, 32 and 64 bits wide, correspond closely to floating and double data types in the VAX architecture except for the differences described below. Extended is 80 bits wide, with a 15 bit exponent and a 64 bit fraction, which includes an explicit leading bit. The extended data type is intended for guarding against loss of precision during a series of floating point calculations.

The formats of the data types in our implementation are different from those specified by the standard in the positions of the exponent and fraction field, due to a decision made during the design of the floating point accelerator hardware.

There are several ways in which floating point data types in the standard differ from the floating point data types in the VAX-11. There are representations for **positive and negative infinity**. Infinities behave as would be expected, for instance $\infty \times \infty = \infty$. Both **positive and negative zero** are possible. There is a set of numbers called **NaNs** (Not a Number) used either for debugging or to represent the result of certain operations that result in faults. It is possible to have **denormalized numbers**, i.e. numbers where the leading bit of the fraction is not a one. This is used to implement "gradual underflow", which makes it possible to ignore underflow conditions more often than if using other underflow mechanisms[2].

2.2. Rounding Modes

The standard defines four **rounding modes** which specify the direction of rounding (to nearest, up, down, or truncate). In round to nearest, which is the default mode, ties are broken in favor of a zero in the least significant bit. The user must be able to specify which rounding mode to use.

2.3. Faulting

The exceptions that occur as a result of IEEE floating point instructions are specified by the standard. Five basic exception types are defined: invalid operation, inexact result, divide by zero, underflow, and overflow. The user must be able to enable or disable each of the above exceptions. Users should be able to write their own exception handlers if their programming language allows it.

2.4. Predicates and Branching

Numbers in IEEE format do not obey the law of trichotomy. A number is either less than, equal to, greater than, or unordered with respect to another number. The unordered relation occurs when at least one of the numbers being compared is a NaN (even if the other is also a NaN). The standard requires that the user should be able to branch based on the truth value of several predicates which are logical combinations of these four relations. For some predicates a fault should be taken if the two numbers being compared are unordered with respect to one another.

3. The VAX-11/780 Microarchitecture

The VAX-11/780 is a processor designed specifically to emulate the VAX-11 architecture[3]. The VAX-11/780 microarchitecture[5] is horizontal, having 96-bit microinstructions. Control store addresses are 13 bits, allowing up to 8K words of microcode, with the lower 4K in PCS (PROM control store) and the upper 1-4K in WCS (writable control store). The first 1K of WCS is known as WDCS (writable diagnostic control store), since it contains diagnostic routines, along with some microcode to fix mistakes in the original microprogram, and code to interface with the floating point accelerator. This section discusses details of the VAX-11/780 microarchitecture that are used in implementing the IEEE standard or that influenced the design portion of the project.

3.1. The Data Path

The data path of the VAX-11/780 is divided into four parts: the arithmetic, data, address, and exponent sections. The arithmetic section includes a 32 bit ALU and three scratch pad register sets, two of which are used to emulate the VAX-11 general purpose registers. The data section includes two often used temporary registers (D and Q), the ID (Internal Data) bus, which provides the main interface between the CPU and the floating point accelerator, a barrel shifter which can be used to normalize fractions, and logic to determine how far a fraction stored in the D register must be shifted to normalize it. The exponent section contains three 10 bit registers which are used for (among other things) storing exponents, two flip flops for storing signs, and a 10 bit ALU used to manipulate exponents in parallel with operations on the fractions. Note that the 10 bit data path within the exponent section is not large enough to operate on exponents of double (11 bit exponent) or extended (15 bits) data types.

In addition to the ID bus, the DFMX (data format multiplexer) bus may be used to send data between the CPU and the accelerator. There are also four registers accessible via the ID bus which are physically located in the accelerator, and which can be used to store control, status, and maintenance information.

3.2. The Microsequencer

At certain times in the flow of microcode emulating a VAX instruction, the low eight bits of the next microaddress are determined as a function of the current opcode and operand specifiers. This is called a decision point fork. The value of these eight bits comes from ROMs and combinational logic. A three bit counter called the execution point counter keeps track of how many decision point forks have occurred so far in the emulation of the current VAX-11 instruction. Decision point forks guide the microcode flow to the proper place for specifier decoding and instruction execution. This means that information about the number and types of operands associated with each opcode is hardwired into the machine. This had a significant impact on the opcodes and operand specifier types which were used to implement the IEEE floating point instructions.

The FPA can set the high bit of the next microaddress, sending the microcode flow into WCS, by raising a signal called ACC OVERRIDE. This signal is used to force the CPU to the appropriate microcode when the floating point accelerator is present. This can only happen at a decision point fork.

The FPA also transmits to the CPU three status bits (ACC UB0, ACC UB1, and ACC UB2). These signals are used to indicate that a result from the accelerator is ready, or that an exception has occurred. The use of these bits is explained further in section 3.4.

3.3. The Instruction Buffer

The Instruction buffer (IBUF) is an eight byte instruction prefetch buffer. It does several things which help in executing floating point instructions. It transmits to the floating point accelerator the opcode, operand specifier types, source register numbers, and literal operand data. The IBUF also transforms floating point short literals into VAX-11 floating point format.

3.4. The Floating Point Accelerator

A floating point accelerator (FPA) is an attached processor designed to perform floating point arithmetic quickly. It operates as an attached processor with the CPU, receiving operand values and returning results and status information. The CPU can disable the FPA if it wishes to.

An FPA[6] is being built at Berkeley which does IEEE standard addition, subtraction, multiplication, division, floating remainder, and square root in floating, double, and extended data types. It also does 32 bit signed magnitude integer multiplication. As mentioned above, it raises the ACC OVERRIDE signal to force the microcode to a different flow during floating point instructions. The FPA maintains some status information. Also, it returns the results of floating point operations to the CPU over the DFMX bus, and signals whether or not the results being transmitted are correct, by raising or not raising the ACC UB1 flag.

There are several things within the emulation of floating point instructions which the FPA does not handle. Since the FPA is only an attached processor with no connection to main memory, it cannot do operand specifier decoding, fetching of data, or storing of results. The CPU sends any operands stored in memory to the FPA, waits for the FPA to send its results back, and then stores the results in memory or in registers. The FPA does not initiate faults, although it does signal the CPU when a fault has occurred. It also does not handle non-arithmetic instructions such as moves, compares, and converts. These are executed by the CPU in microcode.

Data items are sent from the IBUF to the FPA, from the CPU to the FPA, and from the FPA to the CPU. The IBUF sends immediate and short literal data to the FPA over the ID (internal data) bus. The FPA maintains its own copy of the general purpose register set. Therefore, register operands for floating point instructions need not be sent to the FPA. However, every time the CPU changes a general purpose register, it sends a copy of the new register contents to the FPA via the DFMX bus. The CPU sends operand data that is not register mode, immediate, or short literal to the FPA via the ID bus. The FPA returns results to the CPU over the DFMX bus.

Since the CPU and FPA work asynchronously, some **handshaking mechanism** is required for the exchange of data. When the accelerator is waiting for operand data from the CPU, it loops waiting for the **CP_SYNC** signal. The CPU raises this signal as it sends the data over the ID bus. Similarly, when the CPU is expecting a result from the FPA, it raises the CP_SYNC signal, and loops waiting for one of two signals (**ACC UB0** or **ACC UB1**) from the FPA. When the FPA has a result to send to the CPU, it sends its data over the DFMX bus, raises ACC UB0, and waits for the CP_SYNC signal. It continues sending the data and raising ACC UB0 until it receives CP_SYNC. If an exception occurs and the FPA does not have a result to send to the CPU, it raises the ACC UB1 signal instead.

There are two ways in which the CPU controls the FPA. There is a bit in the accelerator control and status register called **ACC ENABLE** which, when cleared, prevents the ACC OVERRIDE signal from having any effect. This effectively turns off the accelerator. There are also two fields in the VAX-11/780 microinstruction (ACF and ACM) which allow the CPU to trap the FPA to a given microaddress.

3.5. User Microprogramming Capabilities

Although we chose not to, we should point out in this introduction to the 11/780 microarchitecture that it is possible for a user to microprogram the VAX-11/780 without changing any hardware at all by using the XFC (extended function call) instruction. There are, however, two problems with doing so. First, it is slow; it takes 16 microcycles (3.2 microseconds) from the time it starts processing the XFC instruction to the time it begins executing the user-written microcode. It is also very difficult to use the common operand specifier microcode using the XFC instruction.

4. Modifications to the Microarchitecture

This section discusses what had to be done to implement the IEEE standard within the context of the VAX-11/780. It includes a description of the opcodes used, operand specification, storage of status information, how faults are handled, what the floating point accelerator does, and how the microcode flow is controlled. More details of the implementation and a discussion of some of the issues involved and possible alternative solutions are given in [1].

4.1. Instruction Set

One of the first things that had to be done was the modification of the VAX instruction set to handle the IEEE standard. This was constrained by the number of opcodes available for use, by the types of operands required by various instructions, and by the self-imposed requirement that IEEE floating point instructions should have the same basic format as other VAX instructions. It was also influenced by what operations the FPA is able to perform.

There are 65 IEEE floating point instructions. The four basic **arithmetic operations** are available in two and three operand versions for floating and double data types, and in three operand instructions with the extended data type. There are instructions to perform **floating remainder, square root, clear, compare, test** (compare with 0.0), **move,** and **move negated** with floating, double, and extended data types. A wide variety of **convert instructions,** including five that convert to and from extended, are included. There is a new **branch instruction,** and two instructions dealing with **floating point status information.** A list of all instructions added or modified is given in the appendix.

4.2. Opcodes

For those IEEE floating point instructions directly corresponding to a VAX-11 instruction, for example ADDF2 (add floating 2 operand), the corresponding VAX-11 opcode is used. However, there are several instructions without any VAX-11 equivalents for which opcodes had to be provided. These include instructions with extended operands, remainder and square root instructions, a new branch instruction, and instructions having to do with the floating point status register. This section describes how opcodes for these instructions were provided.

Six VAX-11 floating point instructions were dropped from the IEEE-VAX implementation, leaving their opcodes available for re-use. These instructions were POLYF and POLYD (polynomial evaluation), EMODF and EMODD (extended multiply and integerize), and ACBF and ACBD (add, compare, and branch floating and double). The VAX-11 ACBF and ACBD opcodes were used for the floating remainder instructions. The EMODF and EMODD opcodes were used for the square root instructions.

Opcodes in the VAX-11 architecture are generally one byte in length, but there is a set of **escape opcodes** included to allow extension of the instruction set. One of these opcodes, **ESCE,** was used to implement the following IEEE floating point instructions: extended format clears, compares, and moves; convert instructions where one operand is in extended format; the floating point status register instructions; and the branch on floating conditions instruction. In each case the opcode consists of an escape byte (hexadecimal FE) followed by another opcode byte. Use of the escape opcode requires extra microcode to clear this byte out of the instruction buffer, so that a decision point fork can be taken with the low 8 bits of the destination microaddress dependent on the second opcode byte.

A third mechanism was used for arithmetic instructions (i.e. those handled by the FPA) with extended format operands. In this approach, the opcode for another instruction is used, with the first operand having an illegal addressing mode. For example, the opcode for ADDE (add extended) is the same as that for ADDF3 (add floating 3 operand), with the first operand having short literal addressing mode. Since short literals are illegal for IEEE floating point instructions, the opcode is taken to mean "add extended" rather than "add floating". When the FPA sees the ADDF3 opcode followed by a short literal mode specifier, it immediately raises the ACC OVERRIDE signal.

4.3. Operands

Operands and operand specifiers were kept as much as possible like those in normal VAX-11 instructions. In some cases, however, differences were necessary or desirable. As mentioned above, short literal addressing mode is not allowed. This is because short literals are converted into VAX-11 floating point format by the 780 hardware. Since the formats of VAX-11 data types and those in the IEEE standard are different, the values which would be produced after the hardware conversion of the short literals are not very useful. Other than this, operand specifiers are the same as before for those IEEE floating point instructions with direct counterparts in the VAX-11. However, for IEEE floating point instructions with no VAX-11 counterparts, there are several differences.

Extended format operands must always be in register mode. Since extended operands are used mainly for intermediate results, which would usually be in registers anyway, this is not a major problem. For CLRE, CMPE, TSTE, MOVE, and MNEGE, this is the only difference from the operand specifiers in the VAX-11. For convert instructions with one extended operand, both operands must be in registers. For two of these instructions, the second operand specifier is indicated as being register deferred mode, although the operand is actually contained in the registers. This was done to make the microcode flow to the correct location.

A more complicated method of operand specification was used for arithmetic instructions with extended operands. For ADDE, SUBE, MULE, and DIVE, two operand specifiers follow the opcode: the first in short literal mode and the second in register mode. The short literal mode specifier serves two purposes: short literal addressing mode is illegal for IEEE floating point instructions, so the short literal indicates that the operation is on extended format operands; and the short literal value indicates the register number of the first of three registers in which to store the extended result. The register number of the second operand indicates the source register numbers. There are four "extended format registers" used for extended format instructions. These are R0, R1, and R2; R3, R4, and R5; R6, R7, and R8; and R9, R10, and R11. The four bit register number in the second operand specifier is divided into two two-bit fields, each of which indicates one of the sources. For REME and SQRTE, the same method is used to specify the destination registers, but the source registers are specified in the usual way.

The BFLT (branch on floating conditions) instruction has a mask operand which must be in short literal mode, and a branch displacement. The two floating point status register instructions have only implicit operands.

4.4. Condition Codes

The VAX-11 processor status longword (PSL) contains four **condition code bits** which are set or cleared as a side effect of most instructions. The bits are N (negative), Z (zero), V (overflow), and C (carry). For VAX-11 floating point instructions, the N, Z, and V bits are usually set to indicate whether the result was negative or zero, and whether an overflow occurred. The C bit is cleared by most VAX-11 floating point instructions. A different mapping of condition code bits to relations was necessary for IEEE floating point instructions because of the unordered condition. In IEEE floating point instructions, less than is represented by PSL<N>, equal or zero by PSL<Z>, unordered or NaN by PSL<V>, and greater than by PSL<C>.

4.5. Microcode Control Flow - Extra Override Signals

The ACC OVERRIDE signal and an additional signal (ACC UB2) provided by the FPA were used to ensure that the flow of microcode always wound up at the right location.

In the VAX-11/780 implementation of the VAX-11, the ACC OVERRIDE signal was raised at a certain decision point fork during the emulation of arithmetic floating point instructions handled by the FPA. For those arithmetic floating point instructions carried over into the VAX-IEEE instruction set, such as ADDF2, the signal is raised at the same fork as before. For new arithmetic floating point instructions, such as extended format instructions, square root, and remainder, the ACC OVERRIDE signal is raised when the illegal operand specifier is seen by the FPA.

The ACC OVERRIDE signal must also be raised at some point during the execution of instructions not handled by the accelerator. This is done because the microcode to emulate those instructions is mostly stored in a ROM, so it could not easily be changed. In the absence of the ACC OVERRIDE signal, the microcode would emulate the VAX-11 instruction associated with the opcode, not the IEEE standard instruction, giving meaningless results.

When the FPA raises ACC OVERRIDE at a point where the original VAX emulation microcode had not intended, the CPU often winds up at a location already occupied by an instruction which is part of another flow. For this reason, the accelerator raises another signal, ACC UB2, at the same time it raises ACC OVERRIDE. The CPU branches on the value of this bit to see whether it got to the location via the old flow or via the ACC OVERRIDE signal.

4.6. Control and Status Register

The ACCS (accelerator control and status) register is used to store various bits of status information, as it is in the implementation of the VAX-11. There is more status information to keep track of in the IEEE floating point architecture than in the VAX-11, so many more of the bits in the register are used. Programs may use the ACCS register to specify which of four rounding modes to use and to enable or disable the five different types of faults. Consequently, the status information must be maintained as part of the process context, which is not the case in the VAX-11. The ACCS also contains five fault indicator bits, which specify which fault condition has just occurred, and five error flag bits, which accumulate information about what exceptions have occurred.

The ACCS register is physically located in the floating point accelerator, and is addressed by processor address 28 using the MTPR (move to privileged register) or MFPR (move from privileged register) instructions.

Since the MTPR and MFPR instructions are privileged, new instructions were provided to allow the user to read from and write to the ACCS register. The new instructions are: **MTFPS** (move to floating point status register), and **MFFPS** (move from floating point status register). The MTFPS instruction stores the contents of VAX-11 register 0 into ACCS. The MFFPS instruction stores the contents of ACCS into register 0.

Since the ACCS register is not part of the process context as defined by the VAX-11 architecture, status information would be lost on a process context switch. In order to keep this from happening, the **LDPCTX** (load process context) and **SVPCTX** (save process context) instructions were changed to make use of the fact that the VAX-11 executive stack pointer (ESP) is part of the context of a process, but is not used by UNIX. Thus, the SVPCTX instruction is modified to store the contents of the ACCS register in the executive stack pointer before saving the process context. The LDPCTX instruction restores the contents of the ACCS register from the executive stack pointer saved in the process control block by SVPCTX. This solution was suggested by Keith Sklower.

4.7. Faulting Mechanisms

How the presence of a fault condition is recognized by the CPU and what happens after recognition depends on whether or not the instruction is being executed by the FPA. If it is, the FPA raises the **ACC UB1** flag when the CPU is expecting the result data. The FPA also sets error flags and fault indicator bits in the floating point control and status register (ACCS) to indicate the kind of error that occurred. If the instruction is being emulated in microcode, the microroutine recognizes the fault condition and sets the flags itself.

In either case, the microcode then checks the fault enable bits in the status register to see if the exceptions that occurred are enabled. If the exceptions are disabled, a result is stored. If an enabled exception occurred, the microcode sets an internal register to the vector for IEEE floating point faults. The microcode then jumps to common code to handle the exception.

5. Conclusions and Project Status

This section gives some preliminary conclusions and discusses the current status of the project. Detailed measurements and analysis are contained in [1].

Currently, the hardware is still under development. For this reason, we have not yet been able to make detailed measurements. Also, some work still has to be done on various code generators so that they will emit code for the IEEE-VAX architecture. Once these two projects are completed, we can begin to fully test the system. One purpose of this experimentation will be to determine how the presence of the new features in the IEEE standard will affect users. By running identical source programs on a normal VAX and on a VAX augmented with IEEE arithmetic, it will be possible to see whether the features of the IEEE standard make programming and debugging easier or more difficult for users.

Some preliminary timings have been done. It appears that the IEEE-VAX will execute some test routines about 5-8% slower than a normal VAX. Most of the additional overhead is due to checking of special cases which exist in the standard. For some instructions, special case handling required by the standard slows execution considerably. Also, the execution of some instructions takes an extra microcycle because the microcode has to branch on ACC UB2 to see if it got to a certain location via the ACC OVERRIDE signal (see Section 4.5). For most arithmetic instructions, however, the speed is roughly the same.

We have demonstrated that it is feasible to modify an existing microarchitecture to emulate a large set of new instructions efficiently. It is clear, however, that the use of an existing microarchitecture results in significant costs in terms of the number of microcycles required to perform a specific operation and the amount of actual physical microcode required, as compared to what might be achieved by designing a new microengine to accommodate the modified architecture.

ACKNOWLEDGEMENT

This project was part of a larger undertaking to run software on a VAX augmented by an IEEE floating point accelerator. The interaction with others working on the "larger project" was indispensable. In particular, we wish to acknowledge our interaction with Prof. Richard Fateman, Prof. W. Kahan, Keith Sklower, and George Taylor. We would also like to acknowledge, posthumously, the contribution of David Cary, who, as a graduate student, did some of the early work and provided a great deal of the early enthusiasm.

REFERENCES

[1] David B. Aspinwall, "An Implementation of the IEEE Floating Point Standard on the VAX-11/780", Master's Thesis, San Francisco State University, 1983.

[2] Jerome T. Coonen, "Underflow and the Denormalized Numbers", *Computer* 14, No.3, pp. 75–87, March 1981.

[3] Digital Equipment Corp., "VAX Architecture Handbook", 1981.

[4] IEEE Computer Society Microprocessor Standards Committee Task P754, "A Proposed Standard for Binary Floating Point Arithmetic", *Computer* 14, No.3, pp. 51–62, March 1981.

[5] Yale N. Patt, "Introduction to the VAX-11/780 Microarchitecture", Digital Equipment Corporation, internal technical report, in preparation.

[6] George S. Taylor and David A. Patterson, "VAX Hardware for the Proposed IEEE Floating-Point Standard", *Proceedings 5th Symposium on Computer Arithmetic*, IEEE, pp. 190–196, 1981.

List of Instructions

Opcode	Instruction	Description
40	ADDF2	Add Floating 2-operand †
41	ADDF3	Add Floating 3-operand †
60	ADDD2	Add Double 2-operand †
61	ADDD3	Add Double 3-operand †
41	ADDE (ADDF3)	Add Extended * †
42	SUBF2	Subtract Floating 2-operand †
43	SUBF3	Subtract Floating 3-operand †
62	SUBD2	Subtract Double 2-operand †
63	SUBD3	Subtract Double 3-operand †
43	SUBE (SUBF3)	Subtract Extended * †
44	MULF2	Multiply Floating 2-operand †
45	MULF3	Multiply Floating 3-operand †
64	MULD2	Multiply Double 2-operand †
65	MULD3	Multiply Double 3-operand †
45	MULE (MULF3)	Multiply Extended * †
46	DIVF2	Divide Floating 2-operand †
47	DIVF3	Divide Floating 3-operand †
66	DIVD2	Divide Double 2-operand †
67	DIVD3	Divide Double 3-operand †
47	DIVE (DIVF3)	Divide Extended * †
4F	REMF (ACBF)	Remainder Floating * †
6F	REMD (ACBD)	Remainder Double * †
6F	REME (ACBD)	Remainder Extended * †
54	SQRTF (EMODF)	Square Root Floating * †
74	SQRTD (EMODD)	Square Root Double * †
61	SQRTE (ADDD3)	Square Root Extended * †
D4	CLRF	Clear Floating
7C	CLRD	Clear Double
FED4	CLRE (ESCE+CLRF)	Clear Extended *
51	CMPF	Compare Floating
71	CMPD	Compare Double
FE51	CMPE (ESCE+CMPF)	Compare Extended *

Opcode	Instruction	Description
53	TSTF	Test Floating
73	TSTD	Test Double
FE53	TSTE (ESCE+TSTF)	Test Extended *
50	MOVF	Move Floating
70	MOVD	Move Double
FE50	MOVE (ESCE+MOVF)	Move Extended *
52	MNEGF	Move Negated Floating
72	MNEGD	Move Negated Double
FE52	MNEGE (ESCE+MNEGF)	Move Negated Extended *
4C	CVTBF	Convert Byte to Floating
6C	CVTBD	Convert Byte to Double
4D	CVTWF	Convert Word to Floating
6D	CVTWD	Convert Word to Double
4E	CVTLF	Convert Long to Floating
6E	CVTLD	Convert Long to Double
48	CVTFB	Convert Floating to Byte
49	CVTFW	Convert Floating to Word
4A	CVTFL	Convert Floating to Long
56	CVTFD	Convert Floating to Double
68	CVTDB	Convert Double to Byte
69	CVTDW	Convert Double to Word
6A	CVTDL	Convert Double to Long
76	CVTDF	Convert Double to Floating
4B	CVTRFL	Convert Rounded Floating to Long
6B	CVTRDL	Convert Rounded Double to Long
FE76	CVTDE (ESCE+CVTDF)	Convert Double to Extended *
FE6D	CVTED (ESCE+CVTWD)	Convert Extended to Double *
FE4D	CVTEF (ESCE+CVTWF)	Convert Extended to Floating *
FE32	CVTREL(ESCE+CVTWL)	Convert Rounded Extended to Longword *
FE6C	CVTREQ(ESCE+CVTBD)	Convert Rounded Extended to Quadword *
FE01	MTFPS (ESCE+NOP)	Move To Floating Point Status Register *
FE02	MFFPS (ESCE+REI)	Move From Floating Point Status Register *
FEE8	BFLT (ESCE+BLBS)	Branch Floating *

An asterisk means that the instruction has no equivalent in the VAX-11 architecture. A dagger (†) means that the operation is performed by the FPA.

"<opc1> (<opc2>)" indicates that VAX opcode <opc2> is being used in our microengine to do operation <opc1>.

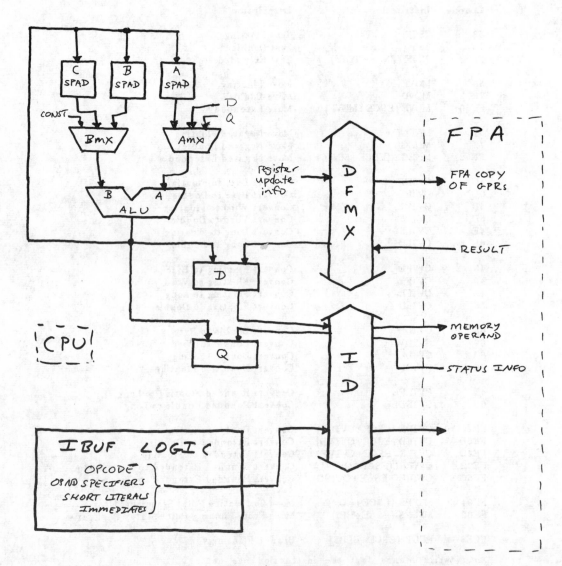

FIGURE 1 — VAX-11/780 DATA PATH

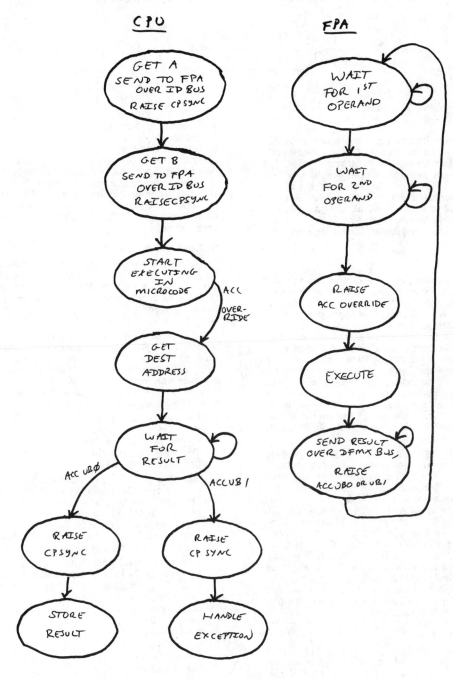

FIGURE 2: EXAMPLE —
ADDF3 A, B, C

HLLDA defies RISC: Thoughts on RISCs, CISCs, and HLLDAs

William C. Hopkins
SDC - A Burroughs Company
P. O. Box 517,
Paoli, Pennsylvania 19301

Abstract

High Level Language Directed Architectures (HLLDAs) are usually intended as ideal hosts for programs written in the supported languages. Patterson et al. [1] have claimed that, in general, a Complex Instruction Set Computer (CISC) is less efficient than a simpler computer with a sophisticated compiler. We claim in this note that HLLDAs should not all be lumped into this generalization, outline some HLLDA design criteria to avoid previously observed inefficiencies, and propose a unification strategy.

I. Introduction

In a series of papers [1-3], Patterson and his colleagues at Berkeley have demonstrated a Reduced Instruction Set Computer (RISC) to be a faster execution engine for a set of benchmark programs than many of the available processors that have more complex instruction sets. The central reason for this improvement is the removal of run-time overhead, either by moving it to compilation time, or by tailoring the architecture to avoid inefficiencies. By providing a simple, uniform instruction set, the RISC allows the compiler to specify precisely the instruction sequence needed to perform a computation, rather than using more general (i.e., time-consuming) instructions that check for conditions that are known to the compiler not to be possible.

The inefficiency of existing computers is surely lamentable, and the RISC approach to architectural design is a welcome tonic. We must be careful, however, to consider which classes of architectures are being denigrated, and not to include architectures for which the arguments in favor of RISCs do not apply. To this end, Section II discusses three overlapping classifications of architecture (CISCs, RISCs, and HLLDAs) and section III compares them with respect to the sources of run-time inefficiency. Section IV argues that HLLDAs are not inherently as inefficient as many examples have been found (or claimed) to be, and proposes criteria for designing HLLDAs that are efficient. Finally, Section V outlines a strategy for unifying the HLLDA and RISC concepts.

II. Classes of Architectures.

The distinction between Complex and Reduced instruction sets is useful, and we will accept it without quibbling. The RISCs group's characterization of CISCs, however, does not necessarily apply to all computers with "non-simple" instruction sets; the class of complex instruction set computers is quite large and varied,

and needs further subdivision. We shall not attempt a full taxonomy; rather, we shall characterize a useful subset. In this discussion we will use the term CISC to refer to the class of machines to which RISC I has been compared; the broader class will be referred to with the spelled-out phrase. Section II is the author's interpretation and elaboration on the work of others; it is intended to provide an intuitive feel for the classifications . Perhaps a more formal treatment can come later.

CISCs: What are they?

Since Patterson's group has popularized the term, we will take their guidance in characterizing CISCs. In general, CISCs can be thought of (not entirely facetiously) as small machine instruction sets that have been spoiled by success, or as instruction sets designed by committee.

CISCs are mainly evolutionary products. Simple instruction sets have been expanded, for a variety of reasons. Evolutionary trends must, however, allow for compatibility with existing object programs. The result is a machine with a "rich" instruction set, but one often lacking in symmetry. Some of the identifiable problems with complex instruction sets are:

- Generality. In many cases, the available data manipulation instructions cover a breadth of cases in a single instruction that is usually not necessary. The overhead of checking for infrequent cases is incurred by all instances of the instruction.

- Specificity. In other cases, the instructions are tied to specific registers or register relationships. This requires that any program that wishes to use the instructions' capabilities must conform to the arbitrary requirements, usually at some cost in execution time, and always at the cost of compiler constraints and complexity.

- Register limitations. With typically no more than 16 registers, often fewer, CISCs are often register-limited, resulting in "register spilling" and excessive register/memory traffic. This problem is often exacerbated by restrictions on register usage, effectively decreasing the available register pool for any particular use.

- Instruction format. Older designs were heavily influenced by the then-high cost of memories, with the emphasis on encoding the operators in a minimum of bits. The effects of this are often costly in other areas, as short displacements require multiple base registers and an extra literal load for addresses, short register fields preclude expansion of the register set, a two-address format requires extra data movement operations, etc.

- Assembly language orientation. The existing CISCs are all designed to be programmable at the assembly level, with the result that the instruction sets are not well-suited for compilation; the needs of a human programmer are vastly different from those of a compiler.

Lack of high-level abstractions. Since the evolution of the instruction sets is from an assembly language orientation, there is no solid basis for support of high level language abstraction to grow on. Introduction of such support must therefore be revolutionary, and is unlikely to fit well with the existing instruction set. Perhaps as a result, there has been little innovation of this type. Instead, a sort of local optimization is performed, what might be called vertical migration of existing (i.e., assembly language coded) constructs, in which a sequence of existing instructions is replaced by a new, usually faster instruction. While this is useful, it ignores the more important issues of global optimization, and complicates the instruction set.

Some of the computers classified as CISCs are the IBM 360/370, DEC VAX-11, and the initial crop of 16-bit microprocessors (Intel 8086, Motorola MC68000, Zilog Z8000, etc.). Some of the above comments apply to each of these.

RISCs: Better than CISCs?

The RISC approach is two-pronged: improvements to the architecture (the instruction set and the visible state) and VLSI implementation on a single chip. The architectural improvements include:

- a multiplicity of registers.
- a simple and elegant procedure call mechanism requiring little data movement (the register window).
- a reduced and regularized instruction set, including;
  - a register-oriented 3-address instruction format.
  - isolation of the memory interface to a single instruction each for load and store.
  - a longer (32-bit) instruction, allowing more instruction parameters to be specified without a memory access.

The effects of the architectural changes are significant:

- The compiler is freed from the constraints of the CISC architecture, allowing a more efficient compilation process.
- Since instructions do not have parameters of unknown characteristics, there is less decoding overhead in executing them.
- Since instructions are generally not tied to specific registers, code generation involving these operations need not become embroiled in ensuring that the necessary initial state is set.
- Since attempts to support the HLL abstraction directly in hardware are limited, there are fewer possibilities for design "mistakes" for the code generator to overcome.
- Code size is increased marginally over existing CISCs [3].
- The speed penalty for HLL use is decreased markedly (10% vs. 100% to 200%) [2].

The RISC I implementation [3] exploits these architectural changes and VLSI technology, resulting in a single chip processor with 138 registers and single-cycle (400 nsec) execution for all but a few instructions. In a comparison of execution times for a family of benchmark programs, RICS I's speed was reportedly twice that of a VAX/11-780 and four times that of a Z8000.

HLLDAs: Another solution?

The guiding principle behind the design of HLLDAs is the preservation of the HLL abstractions, at what might be called the "compiler primitive" level. This reduces the semantic gap between the source and object forms of the language, simplifying the compiler and making debugging and run-time checking easier. In addition the object code size is sharply reduced. [See reference 4, which uses the term "language oriented image."]

Some of the characteristics of an ideal HLLDA are:

- Each primitive object of the source language is represented by an identifiable run-time object.
- Each primitive operation on objects is represented by a single machine language operator.
- The domain of an operator is restricted to those objects on which the operation is defined in the source language.

One result of this object-orientation is that operators are defined to have the maximum effect, that is, to invoke as much of the processing as feasible by a single op-code. Where the source language involves low level operations, there will perforce be low level machine operators. (This puts a limit on the level of HLLDAs for languages like C that allow low-level operations on high-level abstractions, i.e., that specify the mapping of the abstractions onto the hardware and do not protect them.) The relationship of the language, the design of the corresponding HLLDA, and its performance is, of course, very complex, but it is reasonable to expect that careful design of the source language can significantly improve the performance of the HLLDA that supports it.

A Model for HLLDAs.

In an idealized HLLDA, the HLL program to be executed is compiled to the HLLDA's object form and saved. The compiler may perform whatever optimization is feasible and desired, or it may preserve the sequentiality specified by the source program.

Execution of the program involves loading the program code (perhaps on a demand basis) into the HLLDA code space and interpreting the instructions. (We make no assumption about the form of instructions; they may be linearly encoded conventional operation codes or they may be more closely related to the programming language constructs [see, for instance, reference 5].) Program data is maintained in the HLLDA's data space. We assume that the state of the HLLDA is consistent whenever we examine it (such as between instructions), and contains all information necessary to specify the state of the computation.

Models for HLLDA implementation.

Two implementation models are used below: a general implementation model (the default), and a high-performance implementation model.

The general implementation model involves a general microprogrammable host which is microprogrammed to interpret HLLDA programs. The microprograms are reloadable, and the host is not overly biased towards any particular HLL, but provides general hardware and software support for all. Examples of such hosts are the Nanodata QM-1 [6], the Burroughs B1700 [7], and the Stamford EMMY [8]. The interpreter performs the HLLDA instructions sequentially, leaving a consistent HLLDA state between instructions.

High performance implementations are assumed to provide extra hardware support for particular HLLs, perhaps to the extent of eliminating the need for microcode altogether. There is, of course, a wide variety of possibilities, and the design may be aimed at a single HLL (as in the classic Burroughs B5500 [9] and the more recent Intel iAPX-432 [10]) or at a set of languages (as in the unique Standard Computer MLP-900 [11]).

Telling the Fish from the Fowl.

These classifications, of course, are not precise; they are suggestive of archetypes that seem useful. Any complete architectural design will not fall unambiguously and uniquely into any one of the classes, but will probably contain features that fit several, or all. It thus remains a subjective process to classify architectures, and the ensuing arguments should help develop clearer criteria for this judgment. (As a starter, consider in what respects RISC I differs from a HLLDA for C.)

Architectural taxonomy remains a form of butterfly collecting. Every innovation in computer architecture requires that current taxonomies be redrawn to include the features that make the innovation unique. Perhaps the best we can hope to do is come up with classifications that make useful distinctions. To this end, the next section compares the archetypes of RISCs and HLLDAs.

III. Comparison of HLLDAs to RISCs.

Both HLLDAs and RISCs have advantages; the choice of an HLL implementation strategy depends on the desired characteristics of the resulting system. We can contrast the approaches in a number of different areas:

Portability.

Given the cost of software development, it is a fact of economic life that program portability is required, across a product line and over time. Portability can be achieved in several ways:

- Source compatibility. If programmed only in a high level language, most programs can be made portable to a new machine (either a different slot in the product line or a successor product) by implementing the HLL on it. This requires that source programs be maintained by all users; it is an unfortunate characteristic of some DP markets that the source is often unavailable.

- Object code portability. With an existing well-documented object language (including the operating system interface) supported on a new machine, both source and object portability are easily achieved. New or high-performance computers, however, are constrained by the existing instruction set.

- Emulation. This is really a special case of object code portability, in which the new machine does not naturally provide the portability. Instead, an "emulation package" is added to support the old machine language and interpret the old operating system interface, usually at a marked performance cost over equivalent "native" machine code.

HLLDAs provide a particularly attractive form of object code portability. Since the machine language deals with the HLL abstractions, it is free of any bottom-up design features that might limit the implementation strategy. A wide variety of implementations is easily possible: different strategies can be used depending on the cost/performance requirements, the processing

requirements of the target market, the available technology, and so on.

CISCs partake of these advantages to a certain extent, but are lower in level, reducing the breadth of possible implementations. One cannot efficiently implement an 8086, for instance, with a B1700 interpreter, its level is too low to map onto such a host.

Preservation of abstractions.

Abstractions are the essence of programming; much of the programmer's debugging time is spent trying to find the images of his abstract entities after they are mapped into the programming language and then onto the hardware, and then verifying that the operations performed on them are what was intended. By preserving the language abstractions as identifiable objects, HLLDAs greatly reduce the complexity of this task. In addition, soft implementations can, as a run-time option, perform comprehensive validity checking, trace the operations on selected objects, and generally reduce the effort (and hence cost) of developing and maintaining software. The trend in programming language technology has been to foster the use of abstractions in programs. It seems reasonable to preserve the abstractions where they can be useful.

A RISC needs a separate interactive debugger to perform these functions, where they are even possible. It requires recompilation or extra hardware for tracing and trapping, and where registers are used to optimize variable access, it may not be possible to detect all changes to a given variable.

Complexity Management.

One of the motivations for introducing HLLDAs is to divide the program processing problem into two independent parts, compilation and interpretation, with a well-defined interface between them, the HLLDA instruction set; the complexity of the overall task is similarly divided. The total complexity of translating an HLL to a low level machine depends in part on the richness of the HLL. For languages that are designed for simplicity of compilation (e.g., C and Pascal), the overall task is manageable, as the RISC results demonstrate. For HLLs with a richer set of underlying concepts (e.g., Ada, Cobol, full PL/I), or with deferred binding of objects (APL, Lisp, Snobol), there is complexity inherent in the run-time mechanism. Code generation for these languages is complicated by the inability of the compiler, in the general case, to identify the full implication of an operation. As a result, the compiler must generate code that handles all cases whenever the binding cannot be forced. At this point, the RISC approach is rendered inapplicable, as the run-time processing cannot be moved to compilation time. Practically, RISCs would have run-time libraries of these operations, which approximate the high-level instructions of the HLLDA.

When complexity of this magnitude is forced upon the run-time environment, HLLDAs are immediately appealing. The complexity is absorbed into the HLLDA interpreter, and the compilation process is simplified. In addition, the process of validating compilers for new implementations is greatly simplified, and replaced by the simpler task of validating new HLLDA interpreters.

Execution speed.

HLLDAs have often suffered, particularly in soft implementations, from excessive interpretive overhead. We claim below that this is avoidable, for at least some languages, with proper design. High performance implementations, in any case, can use extra hardware to minimize the overhead. The remaining speed issues are:

- Global optimization. This can be done as well for a HLLDA as for a RISC; the only requirement for the HLLDA is that the required operations (in the optimized code) be available as operators.

- Local optimization. The HLLDA approach imposes somewhat arbitrary divisions, the operator boundaries, across which local optimization is difficult. Here a RISC has an initial advantage which, if exploited, may prove to be lasting. There are, however, several countervailing trends to be considered:

  - These boundaries are relatively infrequent if the operators are at a high enough level.

  - Optimization across boundaries is possible (even if complex) for very high performance implementations.

  - Parallelism within individual operators can be exploited by parallel hardware, and may more than offset the RISC's initial speed advantage. Identification of the parallelism is done once, and built into the implementation, rather than being identified separately for each program during compilation, as a RISC approach would require. (At some point, compilation time does become important.)

Compilation Time.

HLLDA compilers have a much easier task than RISC compilers; the target language is optimized for the source language and every object in the language is represented by a single object or operator in the HLLDA. The RISC compiler, on the other hand, must map the objects onto the architecture and transform the operations into the proper sequences of RISC instructions. The HLLDA compiler also avoids many of the time-consuming processes of the RISC compiler, including local optimization, register allocation processing, parallelism detection, etc.

The balance between compilation speed and execution speed, and trade-offs between them, must always be made with knowledge of their relative importance. This may vary greatly among languages and even among applications, so no static solution is likely to succeed.

IV. Inefficiencies in HLLDAs.

Many HLLDAs have been proposed, and a number of them implemented. Some general criticisms, which surely do not apply to all, can be made:

- Overambitious domain. A HLLDA should be directed to the specific HLL it is to support. An attempt to support several HLLs, even if similar, is bound to lower the level of the operations to a common support level. Attempting to combine support for several dissimilar languages in one architecture leads at best to a set of independent overlapping structures; usually the interaction of the structures is a problem.

- Too low a level. The fetch and decode phases of instruction execution can create a great deal of overhead, particularly in microprogrammed implementations of machines. By increasing the level of the operators, that is, maximizing the processing that an operator invokes, the interpretive overhead can be kept small.

- Generality in the design. This shows up in such

characteristics as descriptor-driven operators, separate operand-form specifiers, and automatic allocation of local variables for a called procedure (even if none is needed). This often appears to be the result of ignoring the restrictions on the HLL being supported and the optimizations that can be made in many cases.

Design Criteria for HLLDAs.

In order to avoid most of the inefficiencies traditionally associated with HLLDAs, we need only examine the source of the inefficiencies and avoid those characteristics in the HLLDA design. To recapitulate the resulting criteria:

- Each language should (initially, anyway) have its own HLLDA. No attempt should be made to collapse even similar languages onto the same interpreter until the efficiency of the individual architectures can be determined and the effect of combining them analyzed.

- The abstractions of the language should be preserved in the HLLDA. Nearly identical concepts (e.g., increment operator for integers and successor operator for enumerated types) should be maintained, rather than collapsed (and necessarily decomposed into separate increment and range-check operators).

- Run time binding should be avoided whenever the compiler can specify the binding. In particular, separate operand specifiers should not be used for high-frequency operations, but a family of equivalent instructions with bound operand forms can be provided. The compilation process can be eased by allowing both the general and specific forms of the same instruction. (This particular prescription can be ignored if parallel evaluation of the operands is supported, as apparently is (or should be) the case with the BELLMAC-32 [12].) For some HLLDAs, this may require two-level decoding for some operators; it clearly should be arranged so that the more frequently executed operators decode the fastest .

- Finally, and most important, the problem must be well understood. Dynamic measurements of the relative frequency of operations (including operand types) are the only valid basis for many of the design decisions that must be made. (These can often be predicted from knowledge of the language construct frequencies and the code generation strategies.) Care must also be taken to ensure that the dynamic data are not based on biased samples; applications and environments that cover the target range of the processor must be measured.

V. Synthesis?

Classifying architectures or architectural features in these categories serves to assist the architect or analyst in evaluating the design. It is not the intent of these distinctions to promote "ideological purity" in architectural design, to divide the world into sheep and goats to segregate them. It therefore seems useful to attempt to unify at least some of the classifications we have been discussing.

One hint of the direction of this was the earlier commment about RISC I being a C-directed architecture. Since C allows low-level access to data structures, a RISC-level instruction set is necessary. By restricting the comparison of RISC I with other processors to a set of small benchmark programs written in C, the poor match of the other architectures to C has been demonstrated. In the case in the Intel 432 this is particularly evident [13]. If we accept the RISC I instruction set as being a superior primitive set for C, we should then expect the limits of its performance advantage to show up in processing higher-level abstractions.

For a more object-oriented environment than C or Unix provides, such as the Ada language and its view of the universe, the primitive set is more complex. The 432 has apparently been designed to cope with the higher-level abstractions that this environment supplies, and appears to do a good job of manipulating multiple processes and inter-process operations, while failing to be competitive in simple computations. It is merely conjecture, but it seems likely that the mechanisms for dealing with the complex abstractions have been generalized to the extent that they get in the way of simpler modes of processing.

The crux of the problem is that most programming languages are not uniform in their treatment of abstractions, and that some abstractions are farther removed from hardware primitives than others. A short integer is inherently simpler and easier to manipulate than a file, at least as they are implemented in our current technology. Without recognizing and allowing for this range of abstraction, no architecture is going to be ideal for the full range of programs in any language.

The synthesis of the RISC and HLLDA approaches appears to lie in the installation of a RISC-like mode of processing within a HLLDA, allowing local computations to proceed without invoking the time-consuming mechanisms of, for instance, the environment-handler. Whether this is possible for existing languages is not clear, but is certainly a good area for research. If nothing else, we could perhaps discern some criteria for language and system design to allow this architectural approach.

There have been several interesting efforts that appear to be approaching this synthesis from opposite directions. The BELLMAC-32 [12] appears to be a RISC integrated with some higher-level concepts derived from operating systems considerations. The Mesa processor [13] is a more object-oriented design, but adds an emphasis on local processing that has been missing in other HLLDAs. Both architectures are claimed not be restricted to one language, but to a class of similar languages, indicating that are not pure HLLDAs. The similarities among the languages cited, however, are notable, and the result of Mesa's collapsing of frequent sequences into single operations should approximate the result of the top-down derivation of operations that would define a HLLDA.

VI. Summary.

The choice of an implementation strategy for an HLL system requires that the designer specify the goals of the implementation and evaluate the available strategies in light of these goals. We have provided some discussion of some of the possible goals in light of two different strategies, argued that HLLDAs provide distinct advantages over RISCs in many of them, and indicated a route to a synthesis of the two approaches.

VII. References.

There has been much work in the areas of RISC and HLLDA design. This listing includes several that are not cited in the text (denoted by [NC] in the entry) that the author considers important to an understanding of the area.

1. David A. Patterson and David R. Ditzel, "The Case for the Reduced Instruction Set Computer," *ACM SIGARCH Newsletter*, Vol. 8, No. 6 (October 1981).

2. David A. Patterson and Richard S. Piepho, "RISC Assessment: A High-Level Language Experiment," *Proc. 9th Annual Symp. on Computer Architecture* (April 1982) [*ACM SIGARCH Newsletter*, Vol. 10, No. 3].

3. David A. Patterson and Carlo Sequin, "A VLSI RISC," *IEEE Computer*, Vol. 18, No. 9 (September 1982).

4. Michael Flynn, "Directions and Issues in Architecture and Language," *IEEE Computer*, Vol. 13, No. 10 (October 1980).

5. William C. Hopkins and Gary Davidian, "A Microprogrammed Implementation of an Architecture Simulation Language," *Proc. 10th Annual Workshop on Microprogramming* (October 1977) [*ACM SIGMICRO Newsletter*, Vol. 8, No. 3 (September 1977).

6. Nanodata Corporation, *QM-1 Hardware Manual* (1975).

7. W. T. Wilner, "Design of the Burroughs B1700," *Proc. FJCC-72, AFIPS Conf. Proc.*, Vol. 41 (1972).

8. M. J. Flynn, C. J. Heuhauser, and R. M. McClure, "EMMY -- an emulation system for user microprogramming," *Proc. NCC-75, AFIPS Conf. Proc.*, Vol. 44 (1975).

9. Elliot I. Organic, *Computer Systems Organization: The B5700/B6700 Series*, Academic Press, New York (1973).

10. Intel Corp, *Introduction to the iAPX-432 Architecture*.

11. H. W. Lawson and B. K. Smith, "Functional Characteristics of the Multilingual Processor," *IEEE Trans. Computers*, Vol. 20, No. 7 (July 1971).

12. Alan D. Berenbaum, Michael W. Condry, and Priscilla M. Lu, "The Operating System and Language Support Features of the BELLMAC-32 Microprocessor," *Symp. on Architectural Support for Programming Languages and Operating Systems* [*ASPLOS*] (March 1982) [*ACM SIGARCH Newsletter*, Vol. 10, No. 2].

13. Richard K. Johnsson and John D. Wick, "An Overview of the Mesa Processor Architecture," *ibid*.

14. [NC] George Radin, "The 801 Minicomputer," *ibid*.

15. [NC] Douglas W. Clark and William D. Strecker, "Comments on 'The Case for the Reduced Instruction Set Computer,' by Patterson and Ditzel," *ACM SIGARCH Newsletter*, Vol. 8, No. 6 (October 1980).

Session IV
Microcode Development and Support Systems

A CONCURRENT MICROPROGRAMMING FACILITY

John F. Fedak

IBM Corporation, Tucson, Arizona 85716

ABSTRACT

Control-unit microcode is characterized by the control of multiple asynchronous devices. This paper describes the Concurrent Microprogramming Facility (CMF), a general-purpose microcode operating system that applies recent advances in programming technology to define a uniform method of expressing this inherent asynchrony. This method is shown to be the basis for the partition of the microcode function and to provide a framework for communication between programmers as well as programs. CMF provides an environment where microcode is viewed as disjoint asynchronous processes that communicate with each other and hardware adapters using a small set of primitives based on the concept of message passing. A uniform process interface both streamlines documentation and accommodates multiprocessor designs. A macro-based system definition facility drives the system and allows the structure of a large microprogram to be specified on a single page.

INTRODUCTION

An examination of the microcode structure inside a computer-peripheral control unit suggests that it may benefit from recent advances in programming technology. A control unit's microcode typically controls a number of asynchronous devices; such asynchrony is difficult to express in most programming languages, with the result being the ad-hoc development of control algorithms for each new product. This, in turn, is reflected in microcode documentation, with each microprogram taking a unique approach to describing program component interaction.

Consider what comprises the microcode structure. It is generally accepted that the specification of interfaces between components is of primary importance. There is, however, no uniform mechanism in which to specify such components or their interfaces. This paper proposes such a mechanism in the form of a facility that acts as the interface between the components of a microprogram. Such a facility can provide the

basis for the partition of functions in the microcode and be the basis for the description of its design.

Consider the microcode structure of a hypothetical, computer-peripheral control unit, as illustrated in Figure 1. The function is partitioned in what could be considered a typical fashion: components for host-system interaction, allocation of a storage buffer, control of the device mechanics, and control of data transfer. Such a model, although somewhat simplistic, could easily represent a printer, tape, disk, or similar control units, in which data is moved between a host system and a storage device.

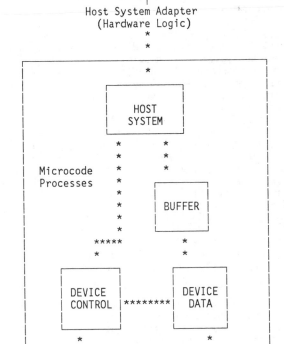

(* = message path)

Figure 1. Hypothetical Peripheral Control Unit

Each of the four boxes pictured can be thought of as independent asynchronous processes, perhaps even running on different processors. It would appear desirable for both the microcode and its description to directly reflect this asynchrony. A procedure-based protocol is not suited for this; procedure calls assume a hierarchical control flow with a single thread of execution. What is needed is an asynchronous process protocol where multiple processes exist in various states of execution, each performing a single synchronous task. The idea of program partition based on asynchrony has been used in large operating systems for many years; more recent research[1,2,3,4] has focused on the use of high-level structures for interprocess communication, such as message passing. An additional benefit of this approach is the potential for unifying design and documentation; a simple concise way of expressing the interface between two asynchronous processes would be a valuable part of a system-level design description.

What should be the characteristics of a facility that provides such a protocol? As suggested, it should allow the ready expression of the concurrent execution of asynchronous programs. Stated differently, it should permit a large program to be partitioned into disjoint asynchronous processes that communicate in a simple, yet disciplined manner. The microprocessor-based computer peripheral environment, characterized by hardware interaction and the need for efficiency, must also be considered. A view of hardware devices as asynchronous processes would allow the use of a single set of communication primitives. An efficient implementation reduces the temptation to revert to faster, less-disciplined process communication (that is, code that is more difficult to maintain). Expandability is also important to permit the use and easy reconfiguration of multiple processors in a control unit.

The remainder of this paper describes a microcode run-time support facility that embodies these characteristics. Subsequent sections examine the technique of message passing, consider hardware-related issues, and present a description of an implementation.

CONCEPTS OF MESSAGE PASSING

Within the last several years, a variety of proposals for concurrency in programming have been submitted. Early techniques, ranging from semaphores[5] to the programming languages Modula[4] and Concurrent Pascal[1], strove for efficiency of implementation. In general, such techniques are based on global access to shared resources, such as the control variable of semaphores or the monitor procedures in Concurrent Pascal. These schemes are efficient but geared to single-processor systems or multiprocessor systems that have shared storage.

This limitation has been removed in more recent proposals, starting with Hoare's Communicating

Sequential Processes language[3]. His was the first description of a technique that has generally become known as message passing. This technique introduces into a programming language new operators or primitives that are used specifically for interprocess communication. These operators are ideally built into a language but may be adapted to existing languages by defining them as user-called system procedures. In addition, there is the need for methods of defining processes and using them to structure a system.

Although there are variations in terminology and implementation, all message passing systems implement what are called the SEND and RECEIVE primitives. SEND allows a process to send data to another process; RECEIVE allows a process to receive data from another process. A number of possible interpretations of these primitives exist; for example, when a process sends data to another process, it may be blocked (not allowed to continue execution) until the receiver has issued a corresponding RECEIVE. Another approach defines queues at each process so that a sender may continue execution after sending a SEND whether or not the receiver has accepted the message. Another approach introduces the notion of mailboxes into which messages are sent and received, thus allowing processes to own a variety of mailboxes each to be used for a specific purpose.

A significant advantage of message passing from a programmer's viewpoint is that its use is independent of the system's configuration. Ideally, each process may be programmed without knowledge of the number or configuration of processors in the system. This abstraction, however, does entail some cost: the implementation must support the automatic transfer of a message to any processor in the system. In addition, a scheduler is required if multiple processes are to be executed on a single processor.

From a system's viewpoint, the use of message passing enables the development of simple, concise, process-interface definitions: a process is defined by the messages it accepts and generates. This is analogous to techniques in data abstractions that define a program component in terms of the procedures it provides. The difference with a process protocol is the notion of asynchrony supported by queueing. For example, if two processes simultaneously send a message to another (to obtain a resource, for example), one process is placed in a queue to wait until the other has been processed. Hence, critical sections may be avoided without the use of timing and implementation-dependent techniques, such as interrupt masking.

Inside a process, the familiar subroutine is used for program partitioning. The result is a system with two distinct types of module interfaces (and hence descriptions): asynchronous process interfaces and synchronous procedure interfaces. A framework is thus provided for microcode documentation consisting of three layers:

1. A system description of the interaction of processes
2. Process descriptions of the interaction of procedures
3. Procedure implementation descriptions.

While layers 2 and 3 are common in microcode documentation, a uniform method of defining the highest level can be most useful in the early phases of system design and review.

HARDWARE ISSUES

Control-unit microcode is characterized by its close interaction with hardware. Hardware can range from relatively simple devices, such as buttons or LED displays, to more complex hardware, such as a CRT or character generator. To encourage a system view of design, it is useful to apply microcode-communication techniques to hardware as well. We can start by viewing each hardware device in the system as an asynchronous process. Since the cost in adapting hardware devices to support message passing is prohibitive, a message passing implementation must accommodate hardware limitations.

Consider first the potential benefits. A single set of message passing primitives appears sufficient for all interprocess communication, whether hardware or software. If so, hardware design and documentation could be tied in with microcode development. While many issues of hardware development cannot and should not be considered in this context, the important hardware-microcode interface can be. Hence, this interface, frequently the source of problems in any large system design, is subject to the same review process in the same language as all microcode reviews. Also, the advantages of a clear definition of relevant interfaces are extended to the benefit of hardware designers in their desire for more cost-effective hardware.

Consider now the integration of hardware communications into a message passing system. A hardware device receives data from microcode in one of two ways: coded I/O instructions (either specific or storage-defined) or hardware-initiated I/O (such as cycle steal and direct storage access). Write I/O instructions are handled by having a run-time kernel convert a SEND primitive into one or more write I/O instructions, as defined by a hardware-description table set up at IPL time. Hardware-initiated I/O (usually used for larger data blocks) is best handled by a requirement that such transfers be preceded by a coded I/O instruction, that is, the hardware does not access storage unless instructed to do so by the microcode. Similar rules apply for data transferred from hardware to microcode. Cycle steal to write data into storage is handled by having I/O instructions initiate data transfers; read I/O instructions from RECEIVE primitives work well for short messages. Interrupts become messages (albeit short ones) received by a process like any other. Thus, if truly hardware-initiated I/O is desired, it follows the sequence of interrupt, coded I/O instruction, and data

transfer. While such a scheme may influence the design of the hardware, we argue that such a protocol yields a simpler, more understandable result.

The next issue in this area is the structuring of a processor network to minimize the effect of a processor reconfiguration on the microcode. A system structure to accomplish this that is independent of the interconnection hardware is shown in Figure 2. Each processor must have access to the network and provide a scheduler, if required, to time share its resident processes. The essential idea is to define a communications process. When the message passing support kernel receives a message destined for a process on another processor, it passes the message to the communications process, which forwards it to a similar communications process on the destination processor. When the communications process receives a message bound for a process on its processor, it sends it to its destination via the system kernel. The communications process itself is largely programmed like any other process; there is some special handling required, however, to indicate the source and destination of messages that pass through it.

Hence, if processor reconfiguration is necessary, theoretically only the communications process is affected. Of course, this assumes that there are enough processes to occupy each processor--more processors are only useful if there are enough asynchronous processes to use them all. The end result is that, from the microcode's viewpoint, the entire system can be seen as a set of disjoint asynchronous processes; a process that communicates using a simple set of primitives (SEND, RECEIVE) with all other processes in the system, whether they are hardware or software, and whether they reside on the same processor or on another one.

CMF: AN IMPLEMENTATION

The Concurrent Microprogramming Facility (CMF) is a general-purpose microcode operating system developed to meet the requirements stated in the previous sections. It consists of a set of programs that serve as a run-time support facility; these programs perform interrupt handling and provide procedures through which processes communicate. In addition, a set of system-definition macros are provided to allow a system designer to define the processes and hardware in a system. The macros are used in a system-definition module that defines the system to CMF.

Each process in the system is defined as a main program, which may contain as many subroutines as desired. The processes communicate with each other using the message passing primitives. The entire system is created at link time when the main programs, the CMF support routines, and the system-definition tables are linked together. At initial microprogram load time, each process is started at its main entry point to allow some initialization. Processes frequently become blocked (via RECEIVE) but never terminate; such termination is considered a programming error.

Program efficiency plays a significant role in the semantics of SEND and RECEIVE primitives. The design exploits the nature of microprogramming, especially its use in dedicated systems, to simplify the implementation and make it more efficient.

Communication Primitives

From the programmer's standpoint, CMF is best viewed as an extension to an existing, sequential programming language that allows process communication. It is visible as a set of procedures used by a process to communicate with another process. For simplicity, a significant assumption is made: a microcode is a closed, dedicated system. As such, it is expected that its processes are determined at development time with no requirement for their dynamic creation and destruction and the resulting storage management. We argue that this is a reasonable assumption for computer-peripheral control units; the microcode exists to perform a specific unchanging function and interacts with a host system only through a well-defined command interface. The result is a system of processes defined statically at IPL time, thereby simplifying the management of tables that govern their execution.

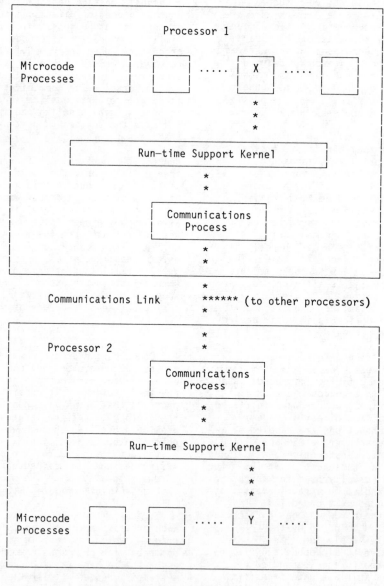

* shows the path taken by a message
  from process X on processor 1
  to process Y on processor 2

Figure 2. Interprocessor Communications Control

It is within this static framework that the communication primitives are implemented. Each process is defined as having a single mailbox, or port, from which it receives messages. Hence, a sending process specifies a process ID as the destination for a message. This technique avoids the introduction of separate mailboxes, which require additional names and allocation strategies, keeping things simple and somewhat more intuitive (we think of sending a letter to people, not to their mailbox).

When a process has to send a message to another process, it issues the following command:

    CALL SEND(destination,command,message,length);

where destination is the process ID of the destination process, command and message comprise the message to be sent, and length is the length of the message in bytes. The SEND primitive is defined as nonblocking. This means that the sender continues execution after issuing the SEND, because the receiver will ultimately receive the message. This scheme implies the existence of a message queue for each process in which messages sent to it are stored while it was busy; furthermore, it implies that the queue is big enough to hold as many messages as could ever be queued--a number that can be determined in a static system and designated at system-definition time. A queue overflow is thus treated as an unrecoverable programming error.

When a process has to receive a message from another process, it issues the command:

    CALL RECEIVE(source,command,message);

where source, command, and message are variables to receive the message. A process issuing a RECEIVE is blocked (suspended from further execution) until a message is received from another process (blocking never actually occurs, however, if a message is immediately available in its message queue). Note that RECEIVE does not specify the process in which messages are received but rather receives them in the order in which they arrive in the queue (that is, FIFO); this significantly simplifies the management of the message queues. The function of receiving messages from a specific process is still quite useful, however. Consider a process that runs out of storage while performing a job. It issues a SEND to a storage manager to obtain more storage and awaits a reply before it can continue. Intervening messages from other processes (perhaps requesting the next job) should not yet be received. Such messages can be delayed with the introduction of a CALL primitive that acts like a SEND followed by a RECEIVE that must come from the same process. The use of this primitive to obtain storage results in other messages waiting until the storage manager has responded. Such a scheme allows the queue to remain FIFO, yet provides the necessary function and introduces efficiency into the system: often, especially in resource allocation (for example, files and storage), a process issues a SEND and awaits a reply with RECEIVE; using CALL performs both

functions with only one system call. It is worth mentioning that an additional primitive, CONDREC (for Conditional Receive), is provided to enable a process to query its message queue without blocking.

In addition to handling process communication primitives, CMF performs process scheduling. A variety of scheduling schemes are possible; the processor architecture influences the specific one chosen. Note, however, that each process is programmed without knowledge of the specific scheduling discipline (other than general knowledge of relative priorities). As currently implemented, CMF exploits the multilevel interrupt structure of a particular microprocessor family. This structure is characterized by eight independent, prioritized levels with support for state switching between them (that is, registers and status are saved or restored on level changes). The support package in this environment runs on all levels in a reentrant manner, scheduling each level independently with no priority among the processes on a given level. To further simplify things, CMF never explicitly interrupts a process; a process executing on a level controls that level until it calls a communication primitive. This scheme could readily be modified for processors that have fewer interrupt levels to allow programs a larger priority space.

An Example

At this point, it is worthwhile to give an example that illustrates the use of these primitives. Consider Figure 1 as the control unit for a page printer. The device control could be named print control and device data could be named print data. Initially, at IPL time, each of the four processes is given control to perform some initialization; each, when complete, issues a RECEIVE to await something to do.

The first message received is the result of an interrupt. For this example, the operator presses a START key. A message is sent to the print control process by the CMF interrupt handler; print control determines that a START key was, in fact, pressed and sends a message to the host process. It then issues a RECEIVE to await more work. The host process receives the message and informs a host system (via some hardware adapter) that the printer is ready to accept commands and data. It, too, issues a RECEIVE to await more work. Later, the host system sends print commands and data to the printer for output. These commands arrive as interrupts converted to messages to the host process. The host process executes each command when received, informs the system of its results, and suspends its operation by issuing a RECEIVE to await more work.

The processing of commands containing print data requires the host process to send messages to the buffer process to allocate storage in which to place the print data. When enough data has accumulated to print a page, the host process sends a message to print control to effect the printing of the data before it suspends operations to await more data. At the completion of each page, print data sends a message to the buffer process to free storage used by that page and print control sends a completion message to the host process to ask for more pages. In addition, messages are passed between print data and print control to synchronize their operation.

In this scheme the receipt of data from the host is asynchronous to its printing. Each process executes independently of the others, except when they synchronize. For example, when the host process is awaiting data from the host system, the print data and print control process may be executed to control the mechanical operation of the device. Similarly, when the printer requires no direct control, the host process may be executed to process commands received from the host. A priority scheme is used to decide which process gets the processor when more than one wants to be executed.

It is significant that no special handling is required as a function of the input data rate. This derives from the fact that RECEIVE is time-independent; a process is suspended until a message is available regardless of how long that may take. (Note that a hardware timer would be useful here, as in any such microcode, to ensure that the processor is still functional.) The system fully benefits from the use of buffering and consists of simple processes, each responsible for one part of the machine. The function has been partitioned in a typical manner; the benefits are derived from the fact that each process is essentially disjoint: no variables are shared between them, except the print data itself. All interprocessor communication is explicitly specified (with no shared flags or critical sections) and there are no special cases.

Note that this example does not mention the number or configuration of processors in the system or where the processes reside. Certainly, one approach is the use of a single processor; performance, however, may dictate the use of multiple processors. There is some limitation to this in that host and print data must have access to the buffer; a shared storage scheme would likely be an expensive solution but is quite possible. In fact, print control could be moved completely to another separate processor with just a simple interface (serial, bus, etc.). In any such scheme, there would be the expense of interprocessor connection, but the four processes presented would require no microcode change.

System Specification

Consider now the specification of a peripheral control-unit system. How is the information such as process IDs, processor assignments, and message queue lengths known by the run-time support? Each processor in the system is required to have a system-definition module that completely specifies the microcode processes that execute on it and the hardware adapters that are attached to it. Furthermore, the communications process must be able to handle messages for processes on other processors.

The handling of nonresident processes by the communications process is dependent on the system; this process is not defined as part of CMF. CMF supports it only by reserving a specific process ID for it to which it routes messages destined for processes not on the same processor. System-definition macros are used to define the microcode processes and hardware adapters owned by a processor. These macros are declarative in nature and are used only in the system-definition module for each processor. Specific macros provide for the declaration of a microcode process or a hardware adapter. Parameters for process declarations specify the process ID, processor priority, and message queue size. Parameters for adapter declarations specify the process ID, interrupt level, and a table that drives I/O operations (for example, mapping commands to adapter addresses). The macros produce data structures that drive the CMF kernel for both interrupt handling and message control. The specific macros used and their parameters are, like the scheduling algorithm, dependent on the microprocessor architecture. This is true of the interrupt handler as well; machines with storage-mapped I/O require different hardware-interaction code from those with a specific I/O command set, although the message format remains the same.

Another feature of the system-definition module is the macro input itself. Typically, the macro input specifying the processes for a processor fits on a single page and thus provides a concise system overview. This overview provides the starting point for system-level documentation. Another part of this same layer is a description of the process interfaces. This starts with a complete list of all messages each process accepts and generates.

The use of a document formatter such as DCF[6] simplifies this job by allowing the use of a common file (embeds in DCF) for each message in the system. Taken even further, the data-structure declarations for messages could be incorporated directly into the documentation, thus ensuring that it is updated along with program interfaces.

CONCLUSIONS

This paper has presented CMF, a run-time support environment for peripheral control-unit microcode. CMF applies the programming technique of message passing to the microprocessor-based, peripheral control-unit environment characterized by hardware interaction and multiple processors. It permits the ready expression of concurrent algorithms inherent to peripheral control units and provides a language for program description.

The general concepts embodied by CMF encourage the development of structured microcode consisting of disjoint components. A uniform process-communication method streamlines communication between programmers while maintaining simplicity and program efficiency. The technique has application across a wide spectrum of microcoded applications, thus encouraging uniformity in the development process. Consideration of hardware issues works toward a systems view of design to bring together those responsible for both hardware and microcode. The overall results is microcode that is easier to develop, maintain, and describe.

ACKNOWLEDGMENTS

The author acknowledges the assistance of many members of the IBM GPD Tucson community, including Dick Ide, Roger Foreman, and the past and present members of the Future Printer Microcode department for their criticisms and suggestions during CMF development.

REFERENCES

1. P. Brinch Hansen, "The Programming Language Concurrent Pascal," **IEEE Transactions on Software Engineering**, Vol. SE-1, No. 2, pp. 199-207, June 1975.
2. P. Brinch Hansen, "Concurrent Programming Concepts," **Computing Surveys**, Vol. 6, No. 4, December 1973.
3. C. A. R. Hoare, "Communicating Sequential Processes," **CACM**, Vol. 21, No. 8, pp. 666-677, August 1978.
4. N. Wirth, "Modula: A Language for Modular Multiprogramming," **Software Practice and Experience**, Vol. 7, pp. 3-35, 1977.
5. E. W. Dijkstra, "The Structure of the Multiprogramming System," **CACM**, Vol. 11, No. 5, pp. 341-346, May 1968.
6. IBM SH20-9161-1, **Document Composition Facility User's Guide**.

The Logic Engine Development System
Support for Microprogrammed Bit-Slice Development

Franklin Prosser and David Winkel

Logic Design, Inc., 1200 Longwood Drive, Bloomington, IN 47401
and
Computer Science Department, Indiana University, Bloomington, IN 47405

ABSTRACT

The Logic Engine Development System is an integrated hardware and software system that aids the designer in many phases of microprogrammed bit-slice hardware design. It is the first commercially-available system to provide direct support for the microprogram sequencer, or to supply a built-in host computer for the designer's use. The Logic Engine includes a new microassembler that encourages structured coding while remaining simple to use.

Microprogramming permits the designer to tackle complex control tasks, but this ability to deal conceptually with complex designs brings with it numerous implementation problems. On what type of breadboard should we build the architecture? How will we debug the architecture? How will we produce the microcode? How will we load the microcode into a control store? How will we design and build the microinstruction sequencer? How will we debug the microcode? How will we modify the microcode?

These questions imply that the designer will need a powerful support system to allow him to manage microprogrammed control. The control unit itself is only one part of a good development system. Such a system must provide support for the development and debugging of both the architecture and the control algorithm. The system should suppress the usual design headaches and subtleties of hardware construction. A development system should provide the convenience of wire-wrap for initial testing. It should provide lights and switches to assist the designer in displaying and controlling individual signals during the testing stages of design. Of course, it should give powerful support to the development, debugging, and modification of the control program.

The Logic Engine Development System, manufactured by Logic Design, Inc., offers a high standard of performance for development systems for microprogrammed bit-slice design.

THE LOGIC ENGINE

Figure 1 shows the components of the Logic Engine Development System. The base unit houses the microprogrammable controller, a

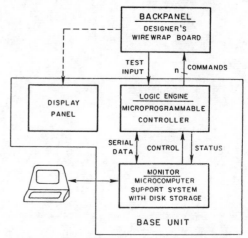

Figure 1. Logic Engine Development System

microcomputer-based debugging support system, and a debugging display panel. Attached to the base unit is a large, detachable backpanel for wirewrap assembly of the hardware architecture.

Base Unit

The Logic Engine microprogrammable controller contains a microprogram sequencer based on the 2910, writable control store (WCS) of 1K or 4K words, a microinstruction register ("pipeline") to deliver command signals to the designer's architecture, and a buffer register to support communication between the controller and the microcomputer-based monitor. Figure 2 shows the internal structure of the Logic Engine. The task of the controller is to present a properly-sequenced set of control signal voltages to the designer's architecture. Therefore, a Logic Engine microinstruction has two primary fields: a fixed-format sequencing field of 20 bits to direct the 2910 in the production of the address of the next microinstruction, and an open-ended field (up to 104 bits) for specifying command signals to the designer's circuit. In automatic mode, the controller loads microinstructions from WCS into the microinstruction register under the control of the

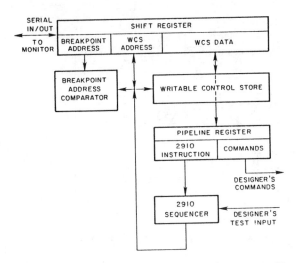

SHIFT REGISTER

SERIAL IN/OUT
TO MONITOR

BREAKPOINT ADDRESS | WCS ADDRESS | WCS DATA

BREAKPOINT ADDRESS COMPARATOR

WRITABLE CONTROL STORE

PIPELINE REGISTER

2910 INSTRUCTION | COMMANDS

DESIGNER'S COMMANDS

2910 SEQUENCER

DESIGNER'S TEST INPUT

Figure 2. Architecture of Logic Engine controller

2910 sequencer. In debugging mode, the designer has several ways to influence the delivery of command signals to his architecture, using features of the debugging monitor.

The support system consists of software running on a 6809 microcomputer contained within the base unit. The 6809 system has 64K memory, with dual 5 1/4-inch floppy disk drives, two serial input-output ports, and one parallel port. The parallel port provides the interface between the support system and the Logic Engine controller. One serial port is dedicated to the designer's display terminal; the other port is available for connecting a serial printer, remote computer, or other device. Logic Engine support software is organized around a debugging monitor running under the FLEX[1] operating system. Software includes an editor, Logic Engine microprogram assembler, and various utility programs.

The Logic Engine display panel provides 96 LEDs for data display, 29 pushbuttons and toggle switches for data entry, and a variable-speed clock which includes a manual mode. The designer has access to these facilities whenever the backpanel is attached to the base unit. The base unit provides power at +5V, -5V, +12V, and -12V for the Logic Engine and for the designer's circuit.

Backpanel

The Logic Engine backpanel is large: 16 inches wide and 20 inches high. It has a large, general purpose work area to handle DIP chips of 8 to 64 pins, on .3-, .6-, and .9-inch centers. There is a prebussed work area for 100 14- or 16-pin DIP chips, and a prebussed area for up to 2 megabytes of dynamic RAM. The designer can access both sides of the board without extenders. Ground and +5V appear as power grids on opposite sides of the board, with extensive provisions for attaching power bypass capacitors. Connections with the display panel are through two 100-pin connectors. Along one side of the backpanel is an area committed to the microinstruction register and writable control store for the designer's command

signals. This permits easy wrapping of the command signals onto the architecture, and allows the designer to implement as many command signals (up to 104) as the design requires.

Support Software

The Logic Engine development and debugging monitor supports detailed control of the WCS contents and of the operations of the microprogram sequencer and microinstruction register. Single-letter monitor commands provide quick and easy access to the monitor features. The designer may load and read the WCS, either as single words, groups of words, or through bulk transfer from disk. Any portion of a WCS word may be modified without disturbing the remainder. Since the 2910 microprogram sequencer is an integral part of the Logic Engine, the monitor knows its detailed structure and operating characteristics, and can provide full and convenient means of displaying and modifying all of the sequencer's internal registers. Also, the designer may view the microinstruction register and may modify any portion of the register. Further, the Logic Engine monitor permits the designer to specify whether, with each manual change of the register, a designer's clock signal is to be issued. This gives the designer a significant debugging tool: the manual entry of microinstructions into the pipeline register without modifying the writable control store. Since the microinstruction register's command field is wired to the designer's architecture, the designer may perform detailed manual control of his circuit. This ability to exercise the architecture without modifying the basic microcode in WCS is a major advantage of Logic Engine-based circuit development.

Table 1 summarizes Logic Engine monitor functions available to the designer. The communication between the monitor and the Logic Engine controller uses full-handshake synchronization sequences to assure trouble-free interactions at any Logic Engine clock speed. In executing microcode from WCS, the most powerful debugging features are single-step and breakpoint. Single-step permits the designer to execute one instruction at a time (of his choosing) from WCS, with a complete Logic Engine register dump accompanying each instruction. Breakpoint is used when the designer is running microcode at high speed. The designer announces a particular WCS address that, if it becomes the candidate for next microinstruction, will cause the controller to idle. This permits the designer to stop instruction execution at any address, and then observe the current status of his system.

The Logic Engine microprogram assembler provides powerful microprogram development features, while remaining simple and straightforward. The assembler supports symbolic naming of single bits and fields of bits. There is a convenient syntax for invoking desired values of command bits. The assembler provides full mixed-logic capabilities, giving the designer the freedom to specify signal values as voltages or as logic levels, and to

Table 1. Logic Engine Monitor Functions

H Help! Display summary of functions
A Assemble a microprogram source file
L Load WCS from object file
D Dump WCS to object file
X Execute a FLEX operating system command

M Display and modify WCS
E Examine a block of WCS
R Display and modify Logic Engine registers

P Load microinstruction register and issue
   designer's clock (manual execution)

C Clear 2910: next instruction from location 000
B Set or clear breakpoint
G Go: run microcode from WCS
I Idle Logic Engine
S Single step: one instruction from WCS

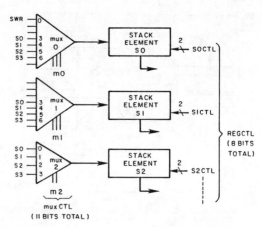

Figure 3. Design example: Architecture

describe the voltage convention for truth of each
signal². The designer may specify the default
values for all command signals, so that in writing
microcode the designer need only describe command
signals that must deviate from the normal default
values. For the sequencing portion of the
microinstruction, the full instruction set of the
2910 is supported, with convenient mnemonics and
with a straightforward symbolic way to designate
any incoming status signal to be tested by a
microinstruction.

DESIGNING AND DEBUGGING WITH THE LOGIC ENGINE

To illustrate the use of the Logic Engine in
digital design, let's do an example. We will
follow the design of a small portion of a machine
that can directly execute the FORTH language³ in
hardware. (Although the actual FORTH Machine uses
bit-slice technology, to suppress irrelevant
detail we are using discrete technology in this
example. It's not necessary to know anything
about FORTH to follow the example.)

Initial Design

In the first step, we work out the architecture --
the registers, busses, and data paths. FORTH is a
stack-oriented language, and several of its
important operations involve manipulations of the
elements on the stack. In this example, we will
focus on the stack operations. In our design, we
wish to have the top several elements of the stack
available for direct use, with the deeper elements
of the stack kept in a RAM. Figure 3 shows a
portion of the top three elements of the stack
architecture. Each stack element (which may
contain as many bits as necessary) receives its
input from a multiplexer (actually, a set of
multiplexers, one for each bit, controlled
identically). Each desired source for a given
stack element becomes an input to that element's
multiplexer. For testing purposes, in addition to
the stack elements, inputs include the switch
register on the display panel. We shall call the
select signals for the multiplexers M0, M1, and
M2, and we shall refer to the entire collection of

multiplexer select signals as MUXCTL. In the full
design, each stack element requires two control
inputs; we call them S0CTL, S1CTL, and S2CTL, and
we call the collection of stack element controls
REGCTL.

The next step in the design is to work out in
rough form the algorithms to control the
architecture. The thought put into this
preliminary control algorithm step will often
suggest modifications to the architecture. The
design process involves iterating between
increasingly refined paper versions of the
architecture and control until we feel reasonably
confident that we understand our problem
thoroughly. Then there is hope that when we build
our machine, it might actually work!

At this stage in the algorithm design, we can
determine what signals from the architecture we
will need to test in our microcode, in order to
direct the flow of control of the instructions.
The 2910 sequencer accepts a single signal as a
test input. 2910 instructions may interrogate
this signal and branch based on its value. There
are often many signals that, at some point in the
microcode, must be tested. The designer of a
microprogrammed system faces the problem of
directing the desired signal from the architecture
into the sequencer at the proper time. Of the
several mechanisms for selecting one signal from
many, perhaps the easiest and simplest is to
construct a multiplexer in the architecture.
Since for each microinstruction we will know
which, if any, signal is required for testing, we
may use some of the microinstruction command bits
to serve as the select code for the multiplexer.
In our full design, we require about a dozen test
inputs, so a 16-input multiplexer with a four-bit
select code is appropriate. Figure 4 shows the
structure of the test input selection apparatus.
You will notice that we have decided to allocate
the first four microinstruction command bits (bits
0-3) to the control of the test multiplexer. This
is an arbitrary choice.

Initial Testing of the Architecture

Now it is time to construct and test the

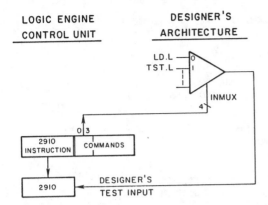

LOGIC ENGINE
CONTROL UNIT

DESIGNER'S
ARCHITECTURE

Figure 4. Design example: Test input selection

architecture. On the Logic Engine backpanel, we lay out the chips required to implement the architecture, assemble the appropriate sockets and chips, and wirewrap the design. The backpanel is large, permitting us to develop and debug the architecture without requiring a partitioning of the components among small printed circuit board modules.

At this point, we usually will wish to make some preliminary tests of the registers and data paths. The Logic Engine display panel has numerous lights and switches to assist in this and later debugging steps. We will wirewrap or jumper important outputs to any of the display panel's LEDs, and connect switches to key inputs as desired. A disposable cardboard overlay for the display panel allows us to label the lights and switches. We may use the display panel's variable-speed clock to provide clocking signals to our design. The manual clocking mode permits us to debug statically -- we deliver clock transitions only when we wish. This is a powerful debugging technique.

Now we exercise the architecture with the display panel's switches, and observe the results on the lights. In effect, we are manually delivering rudimentary control to the architecture prior to developing the actual control program, thus allowing early detection of gross errors in wiring or design.

Developing the Control Program

Once we are satisfied that the architecture is working at our present level of testing, we turn to the detailed development of the control algorithm. We will rely on the Logic Engine to help us with the control development in two ways: by providing a standard environment for developing and executing microprograms, and by giving human-oriented aids for the programming and testing of the code. Although the Logic Engine gives a standard environment, our microprogram code will of course be specific to our particular design.

The Logic Engine microprogram assembler has two parts. In the declaration phase, we specify

symbolic names for all variables and quantities of interest, and we describe the structure of the microinstruction. The program phase contains the microcode itself, in symbolic form. The use of symbolic notations whenever possible is of great value, not only because of their descriptive power, but also because later changes in the design may usually be made with a minimum of disturbance of the program. During the earlier phases of the design, we will have developed symbolic names for the important signals that control the architecture. It is natural to use these names in developing the microcode.

We organize the collection of command signals into a useful order, and then commit them to specific bits in the command portion of the microinstruction. As a part of the declaration phase of the microprogram, we will describe to the assembler (and for ourselves!) the structure of the microword. At this point or later, we may wire each dedicated command bit into the corresponding point in our architecture.

Figure 5 shows a small portion of FORTH Machine microcode created to load data from the display panel switch register and test the FORTH Rotate instruction. This code includes all the necessary declarations and microinstructions to support our example, and uses a variety of notations to illustrate features of the microprogram assembler. Command bits are defined with the COM directive. In Figure 5, the definition of MUXCTL provides the following information: MUXCTL is a field of 11 bits, which we choose to refer to in our program with indices running from 10 (for the leftmost bit) to 0. In the command area of the microinstruction, MUXCTL occupies bits 4 through 14. Thus MUXCTL(10) occupies bit 4 of the microinstruction. We have chosen to describe the control in terms of logic (true or false), rather than in terms of voltages. In the definition of MUXCTL, we specify that, for each bit, truth is to be implemented as a high voltage (T=$7FF, hexadecimal 7FF). Further, we declare that, whenever any bit or bits of MUXCTL are not specifically mentioned in a microinstruction, the default values for the bits are true logic levels (D=%TTTTTTTTTTT).

In many instances, we wish to deal with the set of command signals that controls a particular multiplexer in Figure 3. For our convenience, with the next three lines of the program we define three variables M0, M1, and M2. M0 is declared to be a field of three bits, numbered 2 to 0, which is equivalent to bits 9 to 7 of MUXCTL. M1 and M2 are declared similarly to be equivalent to bits 6 to 4 and bits 3 to 2 of MUXCTL. With these definitions, we may refer to the field MUXCTL as a whole, or to subfields M0, M1, and M2, or to any bit in any of the fields. In similar fashion, we declare the attributes of the collection of stack control signals REGCTL.

In examining Figure 3, you will see that, in order to select stack element S0 as the output of multiplexer 1, we must supply the code 3 (binary %011) into the Mux 1 select inputs. For

```
                                ID     FORTH_TEST
                  * FORTH ENGINE
                  * SAMPLE DECLARATIONS AND SAMPLE MICROCODE
                                SIZE 23; NUMBER OF COMMAND BITS
                                MODE LOGIC
                  * TEST MUX CONFIGURATION
                  INMUX(3:0)    COM    (0:3),T=%HHHH,D=0
                  LD.L          INV    INMUX=0,T=%L
                  TST.L         INV    INMUX=1,T=%L
                  * COMMAND FIELD DECLARATIONS
                  MUXCTL(10:0)  COM    (4:14),T=$7FF,D=%TTTTTTTTTTT
                  M0(2:0)       EQU    MUXCTL(9:7); MUX 0 SELECT SIGNALS
                  M1(2:0)       EQU    MUXCTL(6:4); MUX 1 SELECT SIGNALS
                  M2(1:0)       EQU    MUXCTL(3:2); MUX 2 SELECT SIGNALS
                  M0S2          INV    M0=5; SELECT REG S2 THRU MUX 0
                  M0SWR         INV    M0=0; SELECT SWITCH REG THRU MUX 0
                  M1S0          INV    M1=3; SELECT REG S0 THRU MUX 1
                  M2S1          INV    M2=1; SELECT REG S1 THRU MUX 2
                  REGCTL        COM    (15:22), T=%HHHHHHHH,D=%FFFFFFFF
                  LOAD3         EQU    %11111100; LOAD S0,S1,S2
                  ROTATE        INV    M0S2,M1S0,M2S1,REGCTL=LOAD3; ROTATE STACK
                                PROG
LOC XDDDI CCCC CC
          000                   ORG    0
          000     BEGIN         EQU    *
000 10033 0FFE 00 LOAD          JUMP   TEST IF LD.L=%F
001 50013 0FFE 00               JUMP   *    IF LD.L=%T
                                JUMP   BEGIN;M0SWR,M1S0,M2S1,
002 30003 086F F8                      REGCTL=LOAD3; **PUSH SWITCHES ONTO STACK
003 10003 1FFE 00 TEST          JUMP   LOAD IF TST.L=%F
004 50043 1FFE 00               JUMP   *    IF TST.L=%T
005 30003 0D6F F8 ROT           JUMP   BEGIN;ROTATE; **ROTATE TOP 3 STACK ELEMENTS
                                END
0 ERROR(S) DETECTED
```

Figure 5. Design example: Microprogram assembler output

convenience, we define a symbol M1S0 that will invoke (INV) the value 3 on the field M1. If in a microinstruction we wish to pass element S0 through multiplexer 1, we simply write M1S0, thus assigning the value 3 (%011) to the field M1 in the microinstruction. In the microcode in Figure 5, the instruction at location 002 illustrates this usage. The symbol ROTATE shows how we may easily develop complex invocations. The use of ROTATE in the instruction at location 005 invokes the previously-defined invocations M0S2, M1S0, and M2S1, and invokes the value LOAD3 in the command bits defined for REGCTL.

The illustrative microprogram performs two operations: loading the contents of the display panel switch register into stack element S0 (and pushing the stack), and performing a rotation of the top three elements of the stack. Two pushbuttons on the display panel, LD and TST, control the actions. When LD is pressed and released, the load and push operation will occur; pressing and releasing TST will enable the rotate operation. For each button, it is necessary to assure that the microcode performing the loads and rotates will be executed only once per button push. The code at locations 000 and 001 performs a "single pulser" function[4] for the LD button; the

code at locations 003 and 004 performs a similar function for the TST button. In the development phase, we have specified that a use of TST.L, such as at locations 003 and 004, should invoke the value 1 for command field INMUX; the assembler will take care of generating the proper values for the test multiplexer select lines. Based on the declarations and on the test condition ("IF TST.L=%F", for instance), the microprogram assembler will determine the logic level (false) entering the 2910 sequencer that should cause a jump, and will translate this logic level into the proper voltage.

With this informal description of the language, you should be able to follow the test program. In the Logic Engine's microassembly language, we have tried to encourage use of high-level structured coding, while retaining a simple syntax.

Testing the system

Having written the test program, we assemble it and load it into the Logic Engine WCS, using the appropriate monitor commands. We clear the Logic Engine, to cause the next microinstruction to be taken from location 000. Feeling bold, we enter the automatic run mode, causing the Logic Engine to execute the instructions at locations 000 and 003, waiting for us to press LD or TST on the display panel. We set a desired data value into the display panel's switch register, and press and release the LD button. Assuming that we have wired the outputs of the stack elements to LEDs on the display panel, we may observe the results. If, as is likely, there is some problem with the behavior of the load-and-push operation, we must debug the architecture and the code. The single-step mode is useful at this point; it allows us to execute our microcode, but freeze the system after each instruction, so that we may observe at our leisure the status of any signals in the architecture.

If we isolate a problem, and wish to supply a particular set of command signals to the architecture, we may use the monitor's manual execution mode, in which we present manually-generated command bit patterns for loading into the microinstruction register. During manual execution, we may (in fact, must) specify whether we wish the Logic Engine to issue a clocking signal to our architecture. We have detailed control of the entire debugging process.

If we determine that a particular microinstruction is incorrect, and the error does not warrant a re-assembly at this time, we may manually change the microcode in the WCS.

Usually, the designer will write several small test microprograms such as in Figure 5, to verify that the architecture is reacting properly to sequences of test commands. From there, tests of more complex portions of the microcode are in order. Here, we will find occasion to use the breakpoint feature, in combination with single-stepping and manual execution. At every stage, the Logic Engine provides valuable assistance in developing and debugging the design.

Going into Production

To retain the debugging capabilities of the Logic Engine environment, the designer may include a Logic Engine controller board in production models. This board is identical with that in the Logic Engine base unit, and contains both the controller and the 6809 microcomputer. Even with ROM-based production systems, retaining the Logic Engine environment offers many advantages. Field and factory maintenance personnel would have access to all the debugging features except those that require modification of the control store. Single-stepping, breakpointing, manual execution of instructions from the microinstruction register, and displays of the microinstruction and sequencer registers -- all would be available. One could develop a powerful set of microdiagnostics for use during maintenance.

INSIDE THE LOGIC ENGINE

Architecture

Let's take a closer look at the Logic Engine's internal architecture, which is shown in Figure 2.

Table 2. Monitor Directives to the Logic Engine

0   Exercise 2910 sequencer from pipeline register
1   Shift left: dump 1 bit from shifter to monitor
2   Shift right: load 1 bit from monitor to shifter
3   Load shifter from WCS
4   Write WCS from shifter
5   Load pipeline register from shifter
6   Execute single instruction from pipeline register; load pipeline register from WCS
7   Run: continual execution from pipeline register, with pipeline loaded from WCS

Transfer of data between the Logic Engine and the monitor is through the shift register, using a one-bit serial path SIN/SOUT. The shifter has three major fields: a breakpoint address, a WCS memory address, and a data field for a microinstruction. The breakpoint address and WCS address fields are each 12 bits in size; the length of the data field is determined by the designer, since it is a function of the number of command bits required by the design. Two busses provide the principal data paths within the Logic Engine. An address bus permits either the shifter's WCS address field or the 2910 address output to be the source; destinations may be the WCS address inputs, the shifter's WCS address field, and the breakpoint comparator. A data bus connects the shifter, WCS, and microinstruction register. The shifter's data field and the output of the WCS may be sources on this bus; destinations may be the WCS data inputs, the shifter's data field, and the microinstruction register. You will notice that the shifter's WCS address and data fields and the WCS itself are bidirectional, serving as either sources or destinations as appropriate.

Monitor Control of the Logic Engine

Control of Logic Engine activities is through directives from the monitor. Table 2 shows the eight directives that the monitor may issue to the Logic Engine controller. The two shift directives (1 and 2) allow movement of one bit of data from or to the Logic Engine shifter. The pipeline load directive (5) allows loading of the microinstruction register from the shifter's data field, independent of the WCS. The two WCS directives (3 and 4) require that the shifter's WCS address field contain an appropriate WCS address; these directives permit movement of data between the shifter and the WCS. Directives 6 and 7 assume that the current instruction in the microinstruction register is causing the 2910 to produce the WCS address of the next instruction. These directives cause the microinstruction register contents to be replaced with a new instruction from the WCS, with the concurrent issuing of a designer's clock signal. Upon loading of the microinstruction register, the old command bits that have been presented to the designer's architecture are replaced with new bits, and the 2910 receives a new instruction. The single instruction directive (6) loads only one new instruction into the microinstruction register. Directive 7 is the automatic run command: new instructions are loaded into the microinstruction register at the full speed of the Logic engine system clock, until the monitor cancels the run directive. The final directive, 0, is used internally within the Logic Engine to help in extracting the contents of the 2910's registers; it is also used in allowing the designer to issue designer's clock signals directly from the control terminal.

The implementation of these monitor directives requires that the monitor deliver control signals to the Logic Engine controller and receive status information in return. In addition to the monitor directive, which requires 3 bits, the monitor sends several other signals to the Logic Engine. These include a breakpoint enabling signal, a signal to control the issuing of designer's clocks, and, of special interest, a synchronization signal IDLE. The Logic Engine responds with signals such as breakpoint-found and its own synchronization signal EXECUTING.

The principal task of the Logic Engine's control unit is to present proper control signals to the shifter, WCS, microinstruction register, and 2910 sequencer, and to deliver the designer's clock signal. The basis for the internal control of Logic Engine activities is a two-state ASM chart[5], implemented with PALs (Programmable Array Logic elements). Figure 6 shows the structure of the Logic Engine control unit.

From Table 2's primitive directives, the powerful operations in Table 1 may be constructed. The monitor software must contend with a number of difficult and subtle issues, such as the problem of extracting the contents of the 2910 sequencer's internal registers for display, and the restoring of these registers to their original values.

Also, the monitor must take great care that the command bits being presented from the microinstruction register to the designer's architecture do not undergo spurious changes during the performance of the designer's debugging operations. Furthermore, the correct issuing of designer's clock signals requires considerable analysis. The Logic Engine allows the designer to have the benefit of a "friendly" environment without having to construct it himself.

Monitor - Logic Engine Synchronization

Among the knotty problems that must be solved to implement a microprogram control unit for debugging is the synchronization of monitor and controller activities. In the Logic Engine system, the monitor's IDLE signal and the Logic Engine's EXECUTING signal form the basis for full-handshake synchronization. A full-handshake sequence helps assure that, no matter what the relative speeds of the two cooperating processes, all operations will proceed correctly.

Figure 7 shows the handshaking sequences for the monitor (running in the 6809 microcomputer) and for the Logic Engine (implemented in hardware). During periods of inaction, the monitor's IDLE signal is true, and the Logic Engine is looping in its idling configuration in state 0. To execute a monitor directive, the monitor will ascertain that the Logic Engine is idling, will present the new directive, and will then bring IDLE to false. To complete the execution of the directive, the monitor will, after verifying that the Logic Engine has received and is executing the directive, bring IDLE to true. Finally, upon checking that the Logic Engine is idling, the monitor has completed the performance of its directive.

The Logic Engine is performing its own version of the handshake sequence. When the idling Logic Engine senses that IDLE is false, it will begin the execution of the directive present on the input lines, and will assert EXECUTING. Upon subsequently sensing that IDLE has become true, the Logic Engine will complete the execution of the directive, cease to assert EXECUTING, and return to its idling configuration.

THE LOGIC ENGINE PHILOSOPHY

Most microprogramming development systems view the design task from the perspective of the WCS. The focus is on providing efficient access to the control store, while leaving to the designer the problems of developing and implementing the controller. The Logic Engine philosophy is to provide a useful control environment for the designer -- the focus is on the controller, rather than on the control store.

The design and construction of a microprogram sequencer involves much more than simply selecting a sequencer chip and inserting it into a circuit. The problems of constructing a useful controller and observing and directing its activities during development and maintenance are not trivial. The

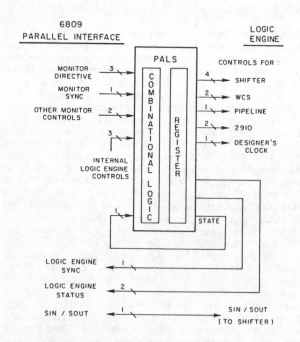

Figure 6. Logic Engine control unit

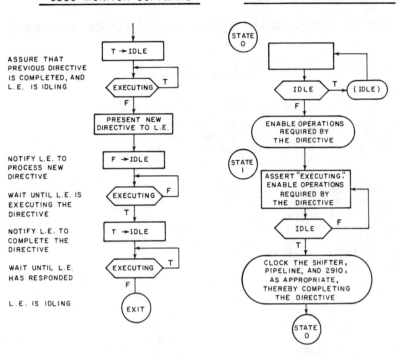

Figure 7. Logic Engine monitor-controller synchronization

considerable hardware and software engineering requirements argue strongly in favor of packaging as much of the process as possible into a standard system. Not only must the microprogram control store be available for designer's use -- a feature of all microprogramming development systems -- but also the sequencer itself should be treated with similar care and attention. The Logic Engine is the only commercially available development system to offer explicit support of the sequencer. Considering the complexity of making efficient use of the control sequencer, the commitment to a particular sequencer, the 2910, is a great advantage for many designers, in that the development system manufacturer has done the difficult work.

Digital circuit packaging usually takes one of two forms: everything on a large board, or a system partitioned into a number of small boards connected by a backplane. Each form has its merits and drawbacks. For the initial design of most systems, and for the final version of many systems, we prefer the single-board approach. The single board is more reliable, because it has fewer connectors; it is smaller, because it has fewer bus transceivers. The single board is easier to design, because the designer need not physically partition the system at too early a stage in the design process. A single board is easier to debug, and it is cheaper. Most uses of the Logic Engine are for developing bit-slice systems, although some microprocessor system designers find the large board size and prewired memory convenient.

The Logic Engine philosophy is to provide as complete a design system as possible for microprogrammed bit-slice development: breadboard, prepackaged controller, human-engineered debugging apparatus, self-contained host microcomputer system. The Logic Engine provides support of hardware design during development in the lab, during production checkout, and in field and factory service.

REFERENCES

[1] --, 6809 FLEX Operating System, Technical Systems Consultants, Inc., West Lafayette, IN, 1979. FLEX is a trademark of Technical Systems Consultants, Inc.

[2] D. W. Winkel and F. Prosser, The Art of Digital Design, Prentice-Hall, Inc., Englewood Cliffs, NJ, 1980, Chapter 2.

[3] L. Brodie, Starting FORTH, Prentice-Hall, Inc., Englewood Cliffs, NJ, 1981.

[4] D. W. Winkel and F. Prosser, The Art of Digital Design, Prentice-Hall, Inc., Englewood Cliffs, NJ, 1980, Chapter 6.

[5] D. W. Winkel and F. Prosser, The Art of Digital Design, Prentice-Hall, Inc., Englewood Cliffs, NJ, 1980, Chapter 5.

M29 - An Advanced Retargetable Microcode Assembler

Michael J. Eager

Advanced Micro Devices, Inc.
Microcomputer Systems (M/S 6)
P.O. Box 3453
Sunnyvale, CA 94088

Abstract

The M29 Assembler is a retargetable microcode assembler which produces relocatable microcode. It provides a straightforward means of describing the microinstruction format, a very general method of specifying field contents, a comprehensive macro facility, and a multifunction relocating linker which permits overlays and libraries of microcode. Several features support improved productivity and reduction of coding errors.

1.0 Introduction

Why Another Microcode Assembler

There are several microcode assemblers available commercially [10] and several more which have been described in the literature [7]. It appears that a new one is announced each year. One might easily ask what purpose there might be in developing another one.

Myers [4, p. 304] gives a list of desirable attributes for microprogram assemblers. In summary he lists the following features:

1. Flexible description language.
2. Able to describe many architectures.
3. Default values.
4. Flexible, simple, readable syntax.
5. Comment support.
6. Alignment of microinstructions.
7. Listing format control.
8. Common syntactic errors detection.
9. Device independence.

Existing commercial microprogram assemblers do not meet Myers' requirements: Cromis is device dependent; Rapid has a very awkward syntax; AMDASM allows many common errors to slip through undetected; the HP 64000 assembler [12] requires the user to design and write the assembler including all error checking; Micro-8 [1] does not complain if the user assigns values to incompatible fields in a microinstruction. Additionally, none of the existing retargetable microcode assemblers supports relocatable microcode and independent assembly of routines.

Another question that might be asked is why not develop a microprogram compiler? There have been many articles about high-level, intermediate-level and low-level retargetable microprogram compilers [2, 5, 6, 9, 11]. I believe Rauscher's evaluation in 1974 continues to be accurate today:

"Although high level microprogramming languages have been proposed and discussed in the literature, these remain for the most part research projects." [8]

There are a number of areas to be addressed in developing a retargetable microprogram compiler: hardware description, resource allocation, optimization, code compaction, and validation. Each of these topics has been addressed to some degree, but each appears to be a significant problem.

In keeping with our design goals, discussed below, we set aside the development of a microcode compiler as a long term research project.

Design Goals

Although Myers' goals were not our design goals, the M29 Microprogramming System does have these attributes. Our goals for M29 are:

1. Support a wide range of microinstruction formats and architectures, including current and future AMD products.

2. Increase programmer productivity.

3. Reduce clerical or coding errors.

4. Allow diverse programming styles.

5. Support relocatable and linkable microcode.

6. Create a microassembler and linker which is practical, reliable, marketable and may be developed in a reasonable amount of time.

It is this last point which dictates that an assembler be constructed rather than a microcode complier. We feel that within existing constraints of our schedule and budget, a working and usable microprogram compiler cannot be created.

M29 Overview

M29 consists of four programs:

M29DEF -- Microinstruction Definition
M29ASM -- Microprogram Assembler
M29LINK -- Relocating Linker for
           Microcode
M29LIB -- Microcode Library Manager

M29DEF is used to create a definition file which describes the microinstruction field by field. It is this definition file which allows the assembler to be retargeted to support many different instruction formats. The definition file, along with optional macro libraries, is used by M29ASM to assemble the users microprogram. M29ASM produces relocatable microcode which may be saved in a library by M29LIB or passed directly to M29LINK. M29LINK assigns addresses to each assembly segment and resolves linkages between segments. It can search libraries created by M29LIB to resolve external references.

The flexibility of M29DEF in describing a wide range of microinstructions allows the assembler to be retargeted to produce code for a many different machines. Additionally, M29 is written in C in a portable fashion to allow it to be executed on different host systems. To avoid problems of limited memory on some systems, the symbol tables are organized to overflow to disk when memory is exhausted.

The next sections will describe M29DEF (Microinstruction Definition) and M29ASM (Microprogram Assembler) in detail. M29LINK will be discussed only briefly, inasmuch as relocating linkers are quite common, and M29LIB will not be described. Complete descriptions of these are contained in [13].

2.0 M29DEF — Microinstruction Definition Program

The microinstruction definition defines a name for the instruction, the length of the instruction, the fields of the instruction and variations in format, allowable values for each field and default values for each field. The name and length of the microinstruction is specified in a single statement as follows:

Hex29: INSTRUCTION LENGTH(64);

Following the initial specification of the instruction name and length, the fields of the microinstruction are described. This consists of field descriptions and case statements. The case provides a method of describing alternate formats for a microinstruction, such as when bit steering is used.

Field Description

A field in a microinstruction is a group of bits which are logically related (perhaps only in the mind of the hardware designer) and which are manipulated as a unit. They need not be contiguous, but they are treated as if they were. Figure 1 gives the description of the operation code field of the Am2901.

```
Op: LENGTH(3),
       VALUES(  B'000' : ADD,
                B'001' : SUBR,
                B'010' : SUBS,
                B'011' : OR,
                B'100' : AND,
                B'101' : NOTRS,
                B'110' : EXOR,
                B'111' : EXNOR),
       DEFAULT (OR);
```

Figure 1. Am2901 Op code definition.

The name of the field (as well as that of values or macros, described below) may be any sequence of characters, including non-alphabetic characters, which can be distinguished from literal values or predefined operators. Constants may be specified in hexidecimal, decimal, octal, binary or as ASCII characters. Figure 2 shows examples of valid names and constants.

Addr	A<-B
Call	Long.Identifier
Continue	<-Mem.Data
BR_C=0	12BReg

Binary:	B'11,111,100'	B'1000,0011'
Octal:	Q'374'	O'203'
Decimal:	1234567	D'1,234,567'
Hexidecimal:	X'FC83'	H'304A'
ASCII:	'Cats Meow'	'Dogs Bark'

Maximum length of constants is 256 bits.

Figure 2. M29 identifiers & constants.

The descriptive entries specify the size and location of the field and specify valid values for the field. It is also possible to specify a default value and to indicate whether the value is to be modified before being saved in the field.

Valid descriptors are as follows:

BITS	--	Bits which make up the field
LENGTH	--	Length of field
DEFAULT	--	Default value for field
VALUES	--	Definitions of names for field values
INVERT	--	Invert (one's complement) field value
COMPLEMENT	--	Two's complement field value
MASK	--	Use low bits of value, ignoring high order bits
REVERSE	--	Reverse order of bits in field
VALID	--	A list of valid values for the field
DISPLAY	--	Display mode for debugging

Symbolic Values

Each of the values in the **VALUES** definition consists of a constant followed by a colon and a symbol which will represent the constant's value when assigned to the field.

The value specifications provides one of the strongest and at the same time simple means of detecting and avoiding errors. The value is associated only with the field for which it is defined. It is not an equate or macro substitution, which might be assigned to another field erroneously, and it may not participate in arithmetic expressions.

The same identifier may appear as a symbolic value for another field, with a totally different value associated with it. For instance, an ALU might have an increment operation code with the value 6, defined as the symbolic value **INC**. The program counter might also be able to increment its value when a control bit is set to 1. **INC** might be defined for this value, also. **ALU = INC** would be equivalent to **ALU = 6** and **PC = INC** to **PC = 1**. If **ADD** were defined for the ALU but not for the PC, **ALU = ADD** would be valid, but **PC = ADD** would be flagged as an error.

Note that using symbolic values in expressions makes little sense. The meaning of **ALU = INC + 1**, if it were possible, would assign 7 to the ALU control field, which might be another completely unrelated operation, or illegal. Clarity and the ability to detect very common errors would be lost. If there is a need to use identifiers in an expression, they may be defined in the assembly program as equates.

Case Definitions

The case statement is used to describe multiple formats for the microinstruction word. The statement is structured similar to case statements in Pascal, but it is a descriptive structure, not a control structure. The case describes alternate, mutually exclusive formats of an instruction, along with an optional selector field. The specification is such that if the selector field has a specific value, only one of the alternate field definitions is valid and all others are undefined.

The case statement is introduced by the reserved word **CASE** and followed by an optional selector field name. Following this are one or more case entries. A case entry consists of a value or list of values of the selector field (or an arbitrary unique value if the selector is omitted) and a BEGIN-END block containing the descriptions of the fields which are defined (selected) for this value.

Figure 3 shows the part of the structure of a hypothetical microinstruction. It has two formats, one which specifies a sixteen bit data value and one which specifies a eight bit sequencer control field and an eight bit address field. One bit (**Sel**) specifies which format is being used.

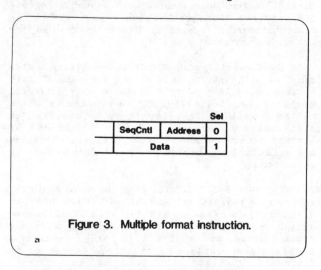

		Sel
SeqCntl	Address	0
Data		1

Figure 3. Multiple format instruction.

Figure 4 gives the description of this portion of the microinstruction. The **Sel** field is defined first and then each of the formats is defined, indicating which value of **Sel** selects the format.

```
Sel : LENGTH(1);
CASE Sel OF
    0 : BEGIN
            Address : BITS(0:7);
            SeqCntl : LENGTH(8), ... ;
        END
    1 : BEGIN
            Data : LENGTH(16);
        END
ENDCASE
```

Figure 4. M29 description of fig. 3.

Case statements may be nested so that a microinstruction with several sub-formats may be described. A case statement may appear wherever a field may be defined. A field may be used as a selector only once.

When an assignment is made to a field defined within a case statement, the value of the selector field is set to reflect the correct selection value. Any subsequent assignment to a field defined in an alternate entry will be flagged as an incorrect entry. Thus

SeqCntl = CALL,

will also assign the value 0 to **Sel**. If an assignment to **Data** is made in the same microinstruction, an error message will be generated. Similarly, if an explicit assignment of 0 is made to **Sel**, an assignment to **Data** will be flagged as an error.

The position of the next bit to be assigned in a microinstruction word is maintained automatically. This value is the same at the beginning of each BEGIN-END block in a case statement. The position at the end of the case is one higher than the highest position specified in the case statement.

It is also possible to specify a case statement which does not have a format selector field. This is needed to describe certain instruction structures such as AMD's Am29116 ALU. This component has a 16 bit control word which is divided into five fields. The operation to be performed may be specified in one of three different fields, depending on the operation type, or may be implied by the other operands as happens in shift instructions. The component actually determines the operation based on decoding all 16 bits.

While it might be possible to explicitly enumerate all operations, the result would be very large and difficult to understand. A case statement without a selector allows the different formats to be grouped together and appropriate fields defined for each format. When assignments are made to field values they are checked to insure that they are consistent with each other.

Definition Validation

Several checks are made on the definition program to insure that it is consistant and complete. These include verifying that each bit in the instruction has a field defined for it and that the total length of fields is the same as the instruction length. Field names must be unique unless the names are reused within mutually exclusive case entries. Symbolic value names are unique within the fields for which they are defined, although the same value may have multiple names.

Case entries are checked to insure that there will not be any ambiguities in the assembly. This could happen if one case entry defined a set of fields with the same names as another case entry and there were no possible way to distinuish one from the other.

3.0 M29ASM -- Microcode Assembler

The M29 Microcode Assembler is designed to be flexible in use. It allows the user to create microcode in several different styles, depending on the amount of effort he wishes to put into designing macros or his preferences in the structure of microprograms. The assembler provides several advanced features including extensive error checking, relocatable output, multiple program sections, conditional assembly, and an extensive macro facility.

Instructions

An instruction consists of one or more phrases separated by commas and terminated by a semicolon. A phrase may assign a value to a field of the instruction or invoke a macro. In the first case a phrase consists of the name of a field in the microinstruction, an equal sign, and a value to be assigned to the field. For example, to assign a value to the Am2901 operation code field defined in Figure 1 the following phrase could be used:

Op = 4,

Alternately, the value specified in the definition of the field could be used to better document the meaning:

Op = AND,

The value may be an expression (either absolute or relocatable) and may consist of constants (numbers in decimal, hexadecimal, octal or binary, or ASCII text constants), symbols defined in the assembly (labels or equates), or it may be a symbolic value. The operations which may be performed on these values include addition, subtraction, division, multiplication, remainder (modulo), negation, shift, and, or, and xor. All operators must be preceded and followed by blanks to allow them to be distinguished from symbols which contain a character like plus or minus. Similarly, the equal sign must be separated from the field name and the value by at least one blank.

If a symbolic value is specified, it must be one of the values defined in the field specification. If **VALID** is not specified, only the values in the **VALUES** list are considered valid for the field.

Examples of valid phrases using expressions are as follows:

```
Addr = Lab1 + 2,
A-REG = R5 - 1,
Addr = LabelA - LabelB,
B-REG = R5 * 2 + 1,
```

The second assignment takes the value of a symbol defined in an equate (R5) and subtracts one from it. If the value were written R5-1 an error would be issued since there was no symbol defined which consisted of those four characters.

When a value is assigned to a field, it is validated based on information given in the definition file. Values will be padded on the left with zeros to fill out the field if needed and any indicated operation (reversal, complement, etc.) performed on the value before being assigned to the field. If the field is too small for the value, a warning message is issued.

Macros

A phrase may also invoke a macro. When invoked, actual arguments may be specified which are substitiuted for formal arguments in the macro body. Macro names must be distinct from field names. Arguments are separated by blanks. An argument may optionally precede the macro name. Macros may generate one or more phrases or complete instructions. Figure 5 shows the definition of an Am2901 macro.

```
MACRO
    AM2901 &AReg &BReg &Op &Dest &Src;
    BEGIN
      OUTPUT('A-Reg = &AReg,  B-Reg = &BReg,');
      OUTPUT('ALU = &Op,  SRC = &Src,  DEST = &Dest');
    END
```

Figure 5. Am2901 macro definition.

The phrase

    AM2901 R0 R1 ADD QREG AB,

invokes the **AM2901** macro, which expands into the following fields:

    A-REG = R0, B-REG = R1, ALU = ADD,
    Src = AB, Dest = QREG,

Macros may be used to group values together as in the AM2901 macro or to insure that when one field is set to a value, another field is set to a corresponding value.

A macro need not have any arguments. This may be used to make the microcode more symbolic and readable. Figure 6 shows a macro **Write** which sets the value **Write** in the **Rd/Wr** field. Using this macro, the microcode can be made more readable and eliminate the ambiguity of what zero or one in the **Rd/Wr** field means, or what values are valid.

```
MACRO
    Write;
    BEGIN
      OUTPUT('Rd/Wr* = Write');
    END
```

Figure 6. Operation definition using macro.

The body of the macro may contain macro time variables and operations comparable to those used for expressions on these variables. These variables are identified by their first character being an ampersand (&). The macro variables may be either local to the macro or defined to be global and therefore accessable by any other macro which defines the same global variable name. Conditional statements and block structuring permit extensive macros.

The **OUTPUT** function specifies the text which is to be placed in the input where the macro is invoked. The argument of **OUTPUT** will be evaluated by replacing macro variables with their values. **OUTPUT** may be called any number of times to construct the output text. If a semicolon is output, the current microinstruction will be terminated and a new one begun.

The functions **WARN** and **ERROR** may be invoked with a text string to report a warning or an error to the user of a macro. Errors indicate that the assembly output is not usable; warnings are informational messages only and do not prevent the assembly output from being linked.

The macro facility allows the user to create microprograms in the style he desires. It is possible, using the M29ASM macro facility, to develop a set of macros which resemble a register-transfer language or one which resemble vertical microcode rather than horizontal. Examples of macro use will be given below in section 4.

Conditional Assembly

Conditional assembly commands are used to select portions of the input to assemble based on the values of assembly time variables. All assembly time variables are identified by beginning with an ampersand (&).

Assembly time variables are defined by being named in a **GLOBAL** statement and are given values in assignment statements. For example:

GLOBAL &DEBUG;
&DEBUG = 1;

This creates a symbol &DEBUG which is then set to have the value 1. This symbol can be tested later in the assembly or within macros and used to include or exclude statements or otherwise control the generation of microinstructions.

IF and GOTO allow assembly variables to be tested and the order of the instructions assembled altered. For instance, to generate debugging instructions if DEBUG is set to one, the following statements could be used:

```
IF    (&DEBUG == 0) GOTO &NoDebug;
    .
    .               (Debugging instructions)
    .
&NoDebug:           (Regular instructions)
```

Note that the destination of the GOTO is also an assembly variable and must be preceded by an ampersand. It does not need to be declared in a GLOBAL statement.

Relocation Control

Several features of the microassembler support producing microcode which may be relocated. These are program segments, relocatable label values, entry points and external references. Program segments allow the programmer to identify a section of microcode as being independent from other microcode. Each segment has its own location counter and may be independently relocated by the linker. It is possible to switch between segments and intermix the microcode for different segments in the assembly. The code for each segment will be collected together and will be contiguous when output is produced.

A program segment is entered (or re-entered) when a control statement of the form

SEGMENT seg-name;

is encountered. In this example, seg-name is the name of the segment being entered. If this is the first reference to this segment, the location counter will be initialized to zero. If it is a re-entry into this segment, the last location

If in developing a program, it is decided that a subroutine is to be written but located in a different program segment, the instructions in Figure 7 can be used to define or reenter the program segment for the subroutine and then resume the original segment. A global symbol &SEGMENT contains the name of the current segment for use within macros. Note that while the calling routine and the subroutine are in different segments, the name of the subroutine need not be defined as an entry point (described below). This gives a measure of information hiding and improved reliability.

SEGMENT Main;
    ⋮
Seq = Call, Addr = Subr, ...;
SEGMENT Utility;
Subr: ...;
    ⋮
SEGMENT Main;
    — continue program —

Figure 7. Using two program segments.

All labels are relocatable without any action required on the part of the programmer. When a label is used in an expression, the expression's value then becomes a relocatable value. When this value is assigned to a field, the location and size of the field is noted and identified as being relocatable. When actual memory locations are assigned by the linker, this field will be updated to reflect the correct value.

Entry points are labels which may be referenced outside of the current assembly. If a label is not defined as an entry point, it may not be referenced in another assembly and may not appear in an external specification.

An entry point is defined by the label appearing in an entry statement, as is shown by this example:

ENTRY IFetch, PgmCheck;

This example defines two entry points. The actual labels and microinstructions for these labels must appear in the assembly.

External references are handled in a fashion similar to entry points. They are defined in an external statement, as follows:

EXTERNAL SupvCall, DivZero, MchError;

In this example, three external names are defined. These must appear as entry points in another assembly or be defined to the linker. These labels may not appear in the current assembly. When these names are used in an expression, the expression becomes a relocatable value and will be adjusted by the linker when actual locations are assigned.

4.0 Assembler Use

The M29 assembler is very flexible and may be used to develop microprograms in several different styles. The simplest use would be to explicitly assign the value of each field in the microinstruc-

```
       CONTNUE & AM2901 R0 , R0 , QREG , ADD , AQ
   /          & NOINE   & NOSDMA & NOVMA   & READ
   /          & BA      & NOLAD  & NORMM   & LMM     & NOCLB
   /          & NOSWP   & NODIN  & NOSDA   & NORCC   & LCCLCV
   /          & NOLDI   & NOSTR  & MWAWMB  & NOFTCH  & NOCIB
   /          & NOCIA   & RCLMUL & NOLIN

       CONTNUE & AM2901 R0 , R0 , NOOP , AND , DZ
   /          & NOINE   & NOSDMA & NOVMA   & WRITE
   /          & NOBA    & NOLAD  & NORMM   & NOLMM   & NOCLB
   /          & NOSWP   & NODIN  & NOSDA   & NORCC   & LCCLCV
   /          & NOLDI   & NOSTR  & MWAWMB  & NOFTCH  & NOCIB
   /          & NOCIA   & RCLMUL & NOLIN

           & AM2901 R0 , R0 , NOOP , OR , DZ
   /          & INE     & SDMA   & NOVMA   & WRITE
   /          & NOBA    & NOLAD  & NORMM   & LMM     & NOCLB
   /          & NOSWP   & NODIN  & SDA     & NORCC   & LCCLCV
   /          & NOLDI   & NOSTR  & MWAWMB  & NOFTCH  & NOCIB
   /          & NOCIA   & RCLMUL & LIN     & DATA H≠000D
```

Figure 8. Hex29 microcode in AMDASM.
(3 of 250 Instructions.)

```
    AM2901 R0 R0 ADD QREG AQ,
       Bus = Free,  Map = Load;

    AM2901 R0 R0 AND NOP DZ,
       Rd/Wr* = Write;

    AM2901 R0 R0 OR NOP DZ,
       INE = 1, SDMA = 1, Rd/Wr* = Write,
       Map = Load, Lin = 1, Data = H'000D';
```

Figure 9. M29 equivalent of fig. 8.

tion and not use default values. A more sophisticated use of the defaults focuses attention on the interesting and important features of each instruction.

Figure 8 lists a small portion of the HEX-29 microprogram as it appears written using AMDASM [3, p. 309]. The same segment of the microprogram is shown in Figure 9 written using M29 using default values for many fields.

Creating a small set of macros, listed in Figure 10, allows improvement in the programs readability, as shown in Figure 11.

Comparing these examples with the AMDASM microcode for the HEX-29, we can see that the M29 code is much more compact and more readable. Much of the compaction comes from being able to define default values in the definition file. This eliminates many of the field assignments that appear in the AMDASM code. This contributes to the readability of the microcode by eliminating uninteresting and unnecessary text.

The use of macros such as **Bus-Avail** and **Synch-DMA** make the microcode much more readable and understandable. But, in this example, the instruction format of the Am2901 ALU is almost identical to the AMDASM version and provides little insight into the actual function of the ALU.

Further development of macros allows more clarity and ease of program development and debugging. Creating functionally oriented macros for the Am2901 allows us to write code which is both easier to create, since there is reduced need to consult the Am2901 specifications and easier to debug, since it better describes the intended operations.

Figure 12 contains a set of macros which describe a few of the Am2901 functions. If these were used instead of the AM2901 definition, it would be possible to write the microcode which appears in Figure 13. Using these macros, we can write **Y<-D** to indicate that the input on the 2901 D bus is to be copied over to the Y bus without modifying any internal registers, and that **Y<-0** is to zero the Y bus. The corresponding instructions in Figure 11,

```
   MACRO  Synch-DMA;
       BEGIN  OUTPUT('SDMA = 1');   END

   MACRO  Bus-Avail;
       BEGIN  OUTPUT('Bus = Free');   END

   MACRO  Load-Map;
       BEGIN  OUTPUT('Map = Load');   END

   MACRO  Enable-Int;
       BEGIN  OUTPUT('INE = 1');   END
```

Figure 10. Macros for Hex-29.

```
    AM2901 R0 R0 ADD QREG AQ,
       Bus-Avail, Load-Map;

    AM2901 R0 R0 AND NOP DZ,
       Write;                    { Zero Y-Bus }

    AM2901 R0 R0 OR NOP DZ,
       Enable-Int, Synch-Dma, Write,
       Load-Map, Lin = 1, Data = H'000D';
                                 { Copy D-Bus to Y-Bus }
```

Figure 11. M29 code using figure 10.

```
MACRO   AddQ  &Reg;
   BEGIN
      OUTPUT('A-Reg = &Reg, B-Reg = 0,');
      OUTPUT('Dest = QREG, ALU = ADD, Src = AQ');
   END

MACRO   Y<-0;
   BEGIN
      OUTPUT('A-Reg = 0,  B-Reg  = 0,');
      OUTPUT('Dest = NOP, Src = DZ, ALU = AND');
   END

MACRO   Y<-D;
   BEGIN
      OUTPUT('A-Reg = 0, B-Reg = 0,');
      OUTPUT('Dest = NOP, Src = DZ, ALU = OR');
   END
```

Figure 12. Am2901 functional macros.

```
AddQ  R0,
      Bus-Avail, Load-Map;


Y<-0,  Write;


Y<-D, Enable-Int, Synch-DMA,
      Write,  Load-Map, Lin = 1,
      Data = H'000D';
```

Figure 13. M29 code using macros in fig. 12.

AM2901 R0 R0 OR NOP DZ,   (Y<-D)

and AM2901 R0 R0 AND NOP DZ,   (Y<-0)

differ only in the operation of the ALU and reference registers which are not involved in the operation. The M29 instructions show a significant improvement in clarity.

The final example shows what may be developed with extensive macro use. It is possible to design macros with an argument to the left of the macro name so as to make the assembly look like a register transfer language. Figure 14 shows the definition and use of a += macro which adds the value of one register to another. By using conditional statements within the macro, very general operators can be created.

As can be seen from these examples, it is quite possible to design very sophisticated macros which allow the operations of the machine to be described functionally rather than as the contents of bit fields.

5.0 M29LINK - Microcode Linker

M29LINK, the linker for the M29 assembler, is used to relocate assembly modules, link them together, and output the complete block in a format which can be loaded into writable control store or burned into PROMs. The linker accepts various control statements which direct it to link the modules in the form the user specifies.

Each instruction in the assembly output indicates which fields if any are relocatable, the entry point or program segment they are relative to, and an offset to be added to the value of the entry point or program segment. This simple and general method of relocation will satisfy the majority of linker requirements.

Input to the linker may come directly from the assembler or from a library built by M29LIB. One or more libraries can be searched automatically to resolve external references. Control commands may be entered by the user or may be read from an input file. Libraries created by M29LIB may be searched to resolve external references.

The linker allows program segments to overlay other program segments to support paged and reloadable microcode memory. It is also possible to indicate that a given program segment is to be fixed at a specific location in the microcode memory.

To allow ease of customization of a microprogram, the linker will allow the user to specify the values of external symbols. If the user specifies the symbol's value in this way, it may not be defined in any of the program segments to be linked.

The following is a brief description of the commands accepted by M29LINK:

```
MACRO  &Dest += &Src;

   BEGIN   {Add two registers}

      OUTPUT('B-Reg = &Dest, A-Reg = &Src,');

      OUTPUT('ALU = ADD, Dest = RAMA, Src = AB');

   END


Use:   R0 += R1, ...;

Generates:

      B-Reg = R0, A-Reg = R1,

      ALU = ADD, Dest = RAMA, Src = AB, ...;
```

Figure 14. Device independent macros.

ASSIGN   -- assign fixed address to a program
             segment.
INCLUDE   -- include a program segment from a
             library.
LIBRARY   -- specify the name of a library.

LINK   -- specify the name of a file to be linked.
LIST   -- specify options for listings.
OVERLAY -- name an overlay area.
SET   -- define an external symbol and its value.
TRANSFER -- accept control input from another file.

6.0 Summary

The M29 assembler consists of four programs: an instruction definiton program, a macro assembler, a linker and a library manager. Together they provide a comprehensive set of microprogram development tools which support increased productivity in writing microcode and make debugging easier.

The M29 instruction definition program provides the user with a clear and concsise means of describing microinstructions which supports error checking and improved clarity in programming. The assembler is flexible and allows the user to develop macros to extend or tailor the style of the assembly. The linker and library programs support relocatable microcode and modular programming.

M29 is a substantial advance over other commercially available retargetable assemblers and provides many functions which have been lacking in microprogramming tools. It satisfies both the requirements outlined by Myers and the design goals for the project.

References

[1] Greenberg, Kenneth F. "The Micro8 Microcode Assembler," Proc. 14th Annual Workshop on Microprogramming, Chataham, Mass., Oct. 12-15, 1981, pp. 78-82.

[2] Marti, Jed B. and Robert R. Kessler. "A Medium Level Compiler Generating Microcode," Proc. 12th Annual Workshop on Microprogramming, Hershey, PA, Nov. 18-21, 1980, pp. 36-41.

[3] Mick, John and Jim Brick, Bit-Slice Microprocessor Design, NY: McGraw-Hill, 1980.

[4] Myers, Glenford J. Digital System Design with LSI Bit-Slice Logic, NY: John Wiley and Sons, 1980.

[5] Patterson, David A. "The Design of a System for the Synthesis of Correct Microprograms," Proc. 8th Annual Workshop on Microprogramming, Chicago, IL, Sep. 21-23, 1975, pp. 13-17.

[6] Patterson, David A., Karl Lew, and Richard Tuck. "Towards an Efficient, Machine-Independent Language for Microprogramming," Proc. 12th Annual Workshop on Microprogramming, Hershey, PA, Nov. 18-21, 1980, pp. 22-35.

[7] Powers, V. Michael and Jose H. Hernandez. "Microprogram Assemblers for Bit-Slice Microprocessors," IEEE Computer, Vol. 11, No. 7 (July, 1978), pp. 108-120.

[8] Rauscher, Tomlinson G. "Towards a Specification of Syntax and Semantics for Languages for Horizontally Microprogrammed Machines," Proc. ACM SIGPLAN-SIGMICRO Interface Meeting, Harriman, NY, May 30 - June 1, 1973 (published as SIGPLAN Notices Vol. 9, No. 8, August, 1974), pp. 98-111.

[9] Sint, Marleen. "A Survey of High Level Microprogramming Languages," Proc. 13th Annual Workshop on Microprogramming, Colorado Springs, Co., Nov. 30-Dec. 3, 1980, pp. 141-153.

[10] Skordalakis, E. "Meta-assemblers," IEEE Micro, Vol. 3, No. 2 (April, 1983), pp. 6-16.

[11] Tamura, Eiji and Mario Tokoro. "Hierarchical Microprogram Generating System," Proc. 12th Annual Workshop on Microprogramming, Hershey, PA, Nov. 18-21, 1980, pp. 7-21.

[12] Yackle, B. E. "An Assembler for All Microprocessors," Hewlett-Packard Journal, Oct., 1980, pp. 28-30.

[13] M29 Microprogramming System User's Guide, Santa Clara, CA: Advanced Micro Devices, 1983 [in preparation].

AN E-MACHINE WORKBENCH

Gylver Wagnon and Dennis J. W. Maine

Burroughs Corporation
25725 Jeronimo Road
Mission Viejo, California 92691

Abstract

The development environment for microprogramming an implementation (E-Machine) of the Burroughs stack architecture (E-Mode) is discussed with an overview of a supporting hardware organization (the Alpha machine). The set of information-sharing tools in the E-Machine workbench, especially the structured language Ohne, is described and a sample E-Mode operator is used to illustrate several of these tools.

1. Introduction

The Burroughs stack architecture, now known as E-Mode [Allweiss 81], has been around since the 1960s. As each technological advance has allowed faster, denser, cheaper, and more reliable hardware, Burroughs has created new processors supporting the latest version of E-Mode. One of the techniques used since the B5900 [Allweiss 81] is microprogramming.

The workbench described here was created to build a microprogrammed E-Machine. This workbench consists of an information-sharing set of tools used in the creation, editing, and testing phases of microcode development. The workbench made the rapid and straightforward development of this E-Machine possible. Fifty-four thousand lines of microcode were written and simulator tested in less than one year.

Credit for this high productivity goes to the workbench and the relatively frozen specifications of both the E-Mode architecture and the underlying hardware

organization (referred to as the Alpha Machine). The E-Mode specification was the responsibility of an independent, corporate-wide committee. Although still undergoing refinement, the maturity of the architecture and the detail of its documentation were important to the short development time of this E-Machine realization. The Alpha machine organization, although less fixed, was changed only if required for E-Machine implementation.

The Ohne microprogramming language is described in section four. It is shown to include aspects of both high-level and machine dependent languages. A simple example is introduced in the discussion on Ohne. This example is also used throughout the paper to illustrate some of the other tools in the workbench and helps indicate the significant level of tool integration. The workbench itself and its associated files are supported on a large general purpose computer system (in our case, a Burroughs B6900).

2. E-Mode Stack Architecture

E-Mode is often viewed as virtually unchanged since the B5500/B6500 days. In reality, hundreds of changes have been made to refine it. Architectural optimizations such as top-of-stack registers were removed to simplify the specification. Each E-Machine can optimize access to top-of-stack values in any way as long as the E-Mode specification is satisfied. The number of tag bits associated with each memory word has been increased. Fields in control words have been added, enlarged, or rearranged. Operators have been added and/or deleted. These changes reflect the twenty years' experience of building E-Mode processors. It is an evolving architecture.

The E-Mode functional specification is one of the primary tools in the

microprogramming process. This emphasis
is quite deliberate as the quality of the
specification makes the programming
process easier [Wang 82].

The reader is referred to the available
literature [Hauck 68, Brooker 70,
Organick 73, Allweiss 81, Mayer 82] for
more information about the E-Mode
architecture.

3. Alpha Machine Organization

A generalized diagram of the Alpha
organization appears in Figure 3-1 to
assist in the discussion of the Ohne
language and its mapping onto the
hardware. The Alpha machine is
unremarkable, except perhaps for the
complexity of the Condition Multiplexor.
The major hardware modules are described
below.

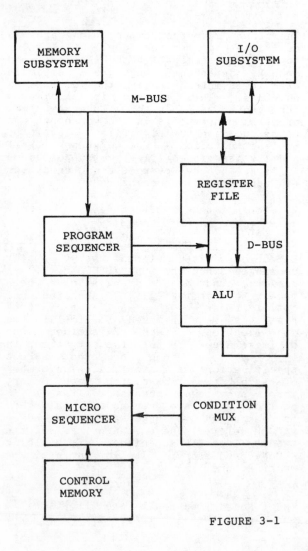

FIGURE 3-1

The M-Bus is a bidirectional path linking
the data, memory, and I/O portions of the
Alpha machine. The data portion of the
machine consists of a dual-ported
register file and an arithmetic logic
unit (ALU). The ALU output on the D-Bus
can be directed back into the register
file or to either the Memory or I/O
subsystems via the M-Bus.

The Program Sequencer recognizes E-Mode
operators and code parameters and directs
the Micro Sequencer to initiate each
operator. Literals or parameters from
the code stream can be transferred to the
ALU data path.

The Micro Sequencer is the central module
of the Alpha machine. It controls the
microinstruction flow by combining
signals from the Program Sequencer, the
Condition Multiplexor, and the Control
Memory to select the next
microinstruction. A return stack
provides nested subroutine calls.
Because operators are initiated without
using this stack, a return with an empty
stack causes the Micro Sequencer to
select the beginning microinstruction of
the next E-Mode operator.

The Condition Multiplexor monitors
conditions throughout the machine and can
test a number of these conditions
simultaneously, signaling the Micro
Sequencer when a test in the
microinstruction is not met and a change
in the microinstruction flow is needed.
The conditions were designed explicitly
for E-Mode and include tests for various
combinations of tag and field values.
There are, in addition to scores of
Boolean (2-way) tests, sets of 4-way,
8-way, and 16-way case conditions.

A fundamental aspect of microprogramming
with the Ohne language is the concept of
a preferred sequence or path of
microinstructions. The Alpha machine
supports this concept with the Condition
Multiplexor. Conditions are tested in
the same clock as the first
microinstruction in the preferred path.
The microinstruction completes execution
normally if the condition is true. If the
condition is false, the microinstruction
aborts. The next microinstruction is
fetched from the alternate path, which is
then executed on the third clock.

4. Ohne Microprogramming Language

The microprogramming language is called Ohne (German for "without") because it is "without" many features of high level languages. Its control structures are few in number and the data types map directly onto the hardware facilities. The language has no branch or "GOTO" instruction. Each underlying hardware implementation has its own variant of Ohne providing additional syntax related to unique hardware features present on that machine. This is similiar to the idea of a microprogramming language schema [Dasgupta 78, Dasgupta 80] rather than having extension statements and operators [Dewitt 76]. There are also some evolutionary changes made in each new version of Ohne that are not incorporated into versions of the language for existing machines simply due to time and manpower constraints. Of course, code generation is unique for each machine, but most of the differences between machines are handled by appropriate values in the source program's declarations. The syntax common to all variants of Ohne provides for these declarations.

Each variant of the language is sufficiently high level to be retargetable [Li 82]. Early Ohne compilers generated simulation code as well as microinstruction files [Allweiss 81]. The Alpha version of the Ohne compiler generates only the microinstruction files and a separate simulator is provided in the workbench. There are advantages and disadvantages to both schemes. Although it is an interesting side issue, it is not discussed here.

The basic units of the language are groups of microinstructions called "operations" and "subroutines." Subroutines are defined in the usual way except that they are parameterless. Operations are special subroutines that implement individual E-Machine operators and whose entry points lie on a vector known to the Micro Sequencer. This relationship permits operations to be invoked directly by the hardware to initiate a new E-Mode operator or by an ordinary subroutine call from other operations or subroutines.

The Ohne language provides for a simple module interconnection mechanism. The modules must be compiled together, and only subroutines can be exported from one module to another.

The unique flavor of Ohne comes from its control structures and from a key syntactical component called a "definition." Definitions are, in a word, macros, but they are much more than that [Sengler 76]. They support the process of top-down programming and step-wise refinement [Wirth 71]. A definition is a method of abstraction with no commitment being made to its implementation. Unlike subroutines, which are normally declared in the program before their calling sequence (or declared forward), definitions naturally follow their invocation in the program. Each definition heading contains a definition number denoting its level of subdefinition and a definition name contained between double left and right bent brackets ("<<" and ">>"). The definition name is composed of any character, with multiple blanks ignored. For example, the definition in the middle of following sequence:

```
reg1 := 0;
<< figure out index >>;
reg3 := index + 4'8000';
```

"<< figure out index >>" should be defined later in the program with

```
#3.2 << figure out index >>:
     index := cp;
     index := index + 6;
```

The control structures in Ohne use a form of the guarded command [Dijkstra 76]. There are three kinds of structures: the alternative statement, the repetitive statement, and the case statement. These structures control access to statement lists through the use of Boolean guards. The alternative statement is a sequence of guarded statement lists surrounded by /IF and \IF. For example:

```
/IF GUARD_1 AND GUARD_2 =>
    << statement list 1 >>
!   GUARD_1 AND NOT (GUARD_2) =>
    << statement list 2 >>
!   NOT (GUARD_1) =>
    << statement list 3 >>
\IF;
```

The statement list associated with the true guard is executed. The "=>" symbol following "GUARD_1 AND GUARD_2" designates it as the primary path as defined in the section on the Alpha machine. The compiler would have chosen a primary path if it had not been noted explicitly. The repetitive statement is quite similiar except that it is repeated until all the guards are false. For example:

```
/DO GUARD_1 =>
    <<statement list 1>>
!   GUARD_2 ->
    << statement list 2>>
\DO;
```

The case statement is slightly different, as the one guard used has more than two values. Each case label corresponds to one of the guard (condition) values. For example:

```
/CASE guard OF
   value1: value2:
       << statement list 1,2 >>
!  value3:
       << statement list 3 >>
!  value4:
       << statement list 4 >>
!  ELSE:
       << error in this case>>
\CASE;
```

Guards are selected from the hardware conditions available, i.e. those provided in the Condition Multiplexor. The correspondence is made known to the compiler through the CONDITION and CONDITION_INDEX declarations as in the following sequence:

```
CONDITION
    GUARD_1;
CONDITION_INDEX
    GUARD_1 [field:value];
```

Hardware dependent functions are made known to the compiler through the use of the COMMAND declaration as in the following example:

```
COMMAND
    function1 fc (f1=x,...,fn=y);
```

The declaration provides microinstruction field encodings (i.e. "f1" to "fn") necessary for the command id or function shown (e.g. "function1"). The data path "fc" is through which the hardware expects to find the input value to the function. Commands with no data path specified' are simply functions with no input parameters. The functions are invoked with various command clauses, such as "COMMAND_PROCESSOR" or "COMMAND_MEMORY." For example, the "function1" command is invoked in the middle of the following sequence.

```
reg := ZERO_EXCEPT (fc: 10);
COMMAND_PROCESSOR (function1, reg);
temp := 0;
```

The Ohne language is a compromise between compiler complexity and ease of programming. Each statement can contain expressions, but the structure is limited to functions that can be performed in one hardware (Alpha) clock. The compiler will check this for the programmer. This restriction eliminates the need for the compiler to generate temporary data storage locations. There is no allocation and deallocation of registers as in the S* family of languages [Dasgupta 80]. The language simply provides a way to symbolically reference hardware facilities such as registers. The compiler still can enforce scoping rules and perform type checking even though the allocation of resources is done by the programmer rather than the compiler. The programmer's knowledge of the Alpha machine is essential to optimize the microprogram, particularly for determining the number of possible concurrent machine operations. The compiler is responsible for assigning most control store addresses and hides the arrangement of fields in the microinstruction.

The largest opportunity for optimization of the microcode is in merging logically adjacent statements into one microinstruction. The most frequent instance of this merging is in the combining of the condition tests (e.g. guards of a IF statement) with the processing of the first statement in the "primary path." If the hardware will not allow this concurrency, then sequential processing of the conditions followed by that statement is done. Attempts are also made to merge subroutine calls with the statement before the call or with the first statement of the subroutine. The compiler also recognizes two or more invocations of the same definition that occur in the same context and merges them by branching to one instance of the code.

Several rules of source code formatting (pretty-printing) are enforced by the Ohne compiler. For example, keyword pairs that bracket a statement sequence (e.g. /IF...\IF) must be positioned in the same column of their respective lines. These rules still provide some diversity of coding style by Ohne users, but eliminate excessive deviations.

Figure 4-1 through figure 4-4 introduce a short example of some Ohne programming. Comments are lines with a non-blank character (e.g. '%') in the first column. All Ohne programs are bracketed by the keyword pair /OHNE ... \OHNE as shown in figure 4-1. Declarations for registers, conditions, commands, etc. immediately follow. The field definition part of these declarations has been omitted for clarity. Modules follow the global declarations.

In figure 4-2, the sample module "branches" is shown. It contains operations and subroutines associated with branch operators. The "static_branch" subroutine is exported to other modules and the "invalid_index_in_temp_interrupt" subroutine is imported from another module for use by this module.

```
/OHNE
  REGISTER temp,..., PBR, PWA, PLI;

  CONDITION less, psi_value_ok;

  COMMAND read_code, step_code_ptr_2_bytes;
     .
     .
     .
%---------insert more declarations and modules here----------%
     .
     .
     .
  \OHNE
```

Figure 4-1: Sample Global Block.

```
/MODULE branches

  EXPORTS static_branch;

  IMPORTS invalid_index_in_temp_interrupt;
     .
     .
     .
%----------insert branch operations and subroutines here---------%
     .
     .
     .
  \MODULE branches
```

Figure 4-2: Sample Module.

In figure 4-3, a branch operation associated with the opcode A2 (in hexadecimal) is shown. It obtains the branch destination from the code stream and calls the "static_branch" subroutine to perform the function.

In figure 4-4, one of the common branch subroutines in the module "branches" is defined for use by several branch operators. This subroutine checks that the branch destination address (i.e. the program syllable (or byte) index (psi) and program word index (pwi) parameters) is valid. If this is true, then the current code pointer is set to this (pwi, psi) couple. Note that the memory read for the word containing the branch destination is done in parallel with the psi check. This is an example of the compiler merging condition tests with the first statement of the primary path.

```
/OPERATION BRUN [PRIMARY 4'A2']


#1 << branch to pwi:psi >>:
    temp := ZERO_EXCEPT (bits_15_to_0: NEXT_2_PARAMETERS),
        COMMAND_PROCESSOR (step_code_ptr_2_bytes);
    static_branch


\OPERATION BRUN;
```

Figure 4-3: Sample Operation.

```
/SUBROUTINE static_branch


#1 << static branch definition >>:
    /IF psi_value_ok (temp) =>
        << read new code word to be executed >>
    ! NOT(psi_value_ok) =>
        temp := isolate_psi_field (temp);
        invalid_index_in_temp_interrupt
    \IF


#1.1 << read new code word to be executed >>:
    COMMAND_MEMORY (read_code, PBR + isolate_pwi_field (temp));
    TEST isolate_pwi_field (temp) - PLI;
    /IF less =>
        << finish processing correct branch >>
    ! geq =>
        temp := isolate_pwi_field (temp);
        invalid_index_in_temp_interrupt
    \IF


#1.2 << finish processing correct branch >>:
    PWA := PBR;
%..................note use of two concurrent operations below.
    COMMAND_PROCESSOR (load_code_ptr, isolate_psi_field (temp)),
        PWA := PWA + isolate_pwi_field (temp)


\SUBROUTINE static_branch;
```

Figure 4-4: Sample Subroutine.

5. Simulator

The simulator is an interactive program that replicates the state and function described by the Alpha machine functional specification. The machine state can displayed in various ways on a terminal screen. Any state item can be altered by moving the cursor to the appropriate field and entering the desired values. Figures 5-1 and 5-2 are sample display pages from the simulator. Myers and Hocker [Myers 81] have written an excellent article on just such a simulator for microcode. Although conceived independently, the two simulators are quite close in concept, features, and use.

The simulator is a cornerstone of the E-Machine microprogramming development workbench; its contribution to the developer's productivity has been identified in eight areas.

1. Early start on microprogramming: Because the simulator was available nearly one year before the hardware prototypes, virtually all of the coding and initial testing of the microcode was completed before the software and hardware integration was attempted.

2. Performance measurement: The running of performance benchmarks permitted alternative design evaluations before the hardware design was committed.

3. Ease of use, ease of change: The simulator presents all of the pertinent machine states, allows the user to alter any state, and traces all changes in state during execution.

4. Simultaneous use: An arbitrary number of copies of the simulator can be in use at any moment. Each programmer and hardware engineer has his own dedicated "machine" any time he wishes it -- no scheduling problems occur.

5. Hardware correctness: The early availability of the simulator permitted the running of special diagnostic and exercise programs, which verified the correctness of complex hardware modules before the

hardware design was committed.

6. Microcode conflict detection: The Alpha machine organization does not prevent the gating of multiple sources or non-valid data onto system buses. Such gating can cause undefined, and possibly damaging, conditions in the hardware. The simulator checks for these occurrences and halts when it detects them.

7. Hardware debug: Firmware/hardware integration is accelerated because doubts about the correctness of the microcode are removed. If correct execution on the simulator is obtained, the problem must lie in the dissimilarity of the simulator and prototype. Reference to the Alpha machine functional specification determines which is correct.

8. Automated testing: The simulator supports an automatic test mode in which it runs a series of checks of microcode correctness, reporting any discrepancies. Each test consists of disk files containing an initial and final machine state. These "state files" can be produced by either the simulator or the script generator (described below). Each test is very specific; thousands of tests for a single operator exist. In automatic test mode, the simulator reads a list (referred to as a "script") that names the tests and performs them serially without further intervention of the user.

Two other features have contributed greatly to the simulator's value. The object file produced by the Ohne compiler contains a procedure name and line number from the source for each microinstruction. The simulator displays these items at all times, permitting easy comparison with the source code. Also, the simulator can interchange machine state, script, microcode, and E-Mode object code files with the processor via the System Control Processor (SCP). The ability to share this information allows all microcode fault isolation to be transferred to the simulator, freeing the prototypes for hardware debug.

```
STATUS:IDLE     SUBROUTINE = static_branch, LINE = 60130000
COMMAND >    "Screen 1"


    ADDRESS    >3DC3<                  REGISTERS
    MICROINSTRUCTION   0 >000000010011<  10 >0<>00000001003D<      AROF  >0<
    CODEADJ    >3<     1 >000000010059<  11 >B<>000000000001<      BROF  >0<
    NEXTADD    >3DF1<  2 >000000010035<  12 >B<>000000000002< CARRYOUT  >0<
    SEQMODE    >0<     3 >00000001003C<  13 >B<>000000000003< EQUALZERO>0<
    OPND1ADD   >12<    4 >000000000000<  14 >B<>000000000004<     ABORT  >0<
    OPND2ADD   >0E<    5 >000000000000<  15 >B<>000000000005<     CNTR0  >0<
    OPND2WR    >1<     6 >000000000000<  16 >B<>000000000006<     CNTR1  >0<
    STRETCH    >0<     7 >000000000000<  17 >B<>000000000007<     GPFF0  >0<
    MODE       >0<     8 >020003010068<  18 >B<>000000000008<     GPFF1  >1<
    ROTALU     >33<    9 >000000000007<  19 >B<>000000000009<    OPCODE >A2<
    CARRYIN    >1<     A >003000010030<  1A >3<>00000000E003<    DYNROT  >0<
    COND1SEL   >00<    B >F00000010044<  1B >3<>00000001003C< DYNSTART  >0<
    COND0SEL   >3C<    C >00000001003C<  1C >0<>000000000000<  DYNSTOP  >0<
    TAGSEL     >0<     D >000000000000<  1D >0<>000000000000<
    LITSEL     >1<     E >000000010068<  1E >0<>000000000000< MEMORY AT
    LITCTRL   >81D4<   F >000000000000<  1F >0<>000000000000<    >10033<
    MEMENABL   >1<    PARENABL >0<   PMEMFUNC >0<       MEMORY>3<>123456789ABC<
    CIDISABL   >0<    STARTBIT>07<   MAMCNTRL >1<          CODE BUFFER
    HDPENABL   >0<    SMEMFUNC >3<   CICNTRL >D4< >A20002FFFFFF95BFFFFFFFFF<
                                     CODEPTR >1<>3<  P1P2OP
```

Figure 5-1: Simulator Screen 1

```
COMMAND >          "Screen 2"
REGISTERS               FLIP-FLOPS        INTERRUPTS      RTRN-STK ADDR LINE
=========               =========         =========       ======== ==== ======
CLOCK >000000000008<  AROF      >0< MEMERROR   >0< F >0000< 3DC2 006001
OPTIMER     >1E83<    BROF      >0< TIMEOUT    >0< E >0000< 3DC6 002572
INTTIMER    >07FF<    CARRYOUT  >0< BADCODE    >0< D >0000< 3DC1 369200
HDPTIMER    >0000<    EQUALZERO >0< STKOVFL    >0< C >0000< 3DC4 369100
CONDCODE    >0<       GPFF1     >1< GLOBALALARM >0< A >0000< 2880 369000
CNTR0       >3<       HDPFF     >0< RUNLITEOUT >0< 9 >0000< 00D1 441000
CNTR1       >9<       CNTRLSTATE >0< HIORQST    >0< 8 >0000<
STKPTR      >0<       EXTADR    >0< SINGLERROR >0< 7 >0000<
PSI         >0<       CODEERROR >0< SFTINT0    >0< 6 >0000<
OPCODE      >00<      CONDHALT  >0< SFTINT1    >0< 5 >0000<
ADDRESS    >3DC3<     HALTCONT  >0< GLOBALATTN >0< 4 >0000<
ELOG    >0000000<     STRCAUGHT >0< INTERVALTMR >0< 3 >0000<
MEMORY IDLE           VERTPARITY >0< CODEFETCH  >0< 2 >0000<
                    CODE BUFFER                     1 >0000<
            >A20002FFFFFF95BFFFFFFFFF<              EMPTY<-
CODEPTR>1<>3<  P1P2OP
```

Figure 5-2: Simulator Screen 2
```
108
```

6. Program Editing

The Editor [Editor 82] is a simple first step toward true tool integration. The editing commands are rather conventional. Two features make the Editor special:

1. The use of the cross-reference and error files created by the Ohne compiler. This information provides the user with a context and search mechanism.

2. The automatic creation of "patch" files used in modifying large Ohne symbolics, which are on the order of 50,000 lines. The Editor displays the workfile (patch) in its merged context while writing only changed records into the workfile.

The cross-reference files provide compiler-generated information on program identifiers. The editing position can be moved directly to the declaration or reference position of the target identifier. This mechanism is inherently faster than the traditional "find" command, which proceeds on a textual basis. One kind of display shows only those lines containing the identifier along with its environment. When the editing window is moved, the "procedural environment" can be automatically displayed.

The error files are used to locate the editing position easily. As each error location is reached, the error message associated with that statement is displayed along with the program text. This facility eliminates much of the need for hardcopy outputs of the compiler run.

The patch files consist of program changes along with editing control records. The changes are made directly with the screen-based editing command. The Editor automatically calculates line number changes, editing control records, and patch numbers as necessary with each edited line. The patch numbers are an integral part of the Releaser mechanism to be described below. All lines associated with a particular patch to the symbolic contain the same patch number. The Editor validates that the patch file corresponds correctly to the program source.

7. Releaser

The purpose of Releaser is to coordinate the development effort of several programmers contributing to a single program. It establishes a patch file database and facilitates version control of the developing software. Individual programmers first develop and test patches to the software. Patches may consist of new code or be modifications to existing code. We have instituted a code review process as a form of quality control. A patch form is completed describing the patch with both a functional and technical analysis. When the patch form is signed off, signifying a successful review, the submitting programmer runs Releaser and, through a simple, on-line interactive process, "releases" the patch to the program database. The patch can now be used by others working on the program.

Releaser automatically assigns a unique number to the patch file, updates the patch database, and generates the files associated with the new program version. Each line in the program added or changed by the patch has the patch number stored with it. These patch numbers are, in essence, a set of pointers to the patch forms describing the patch.

A version card is also automatically generated at the beginning of the program. This information is shared by the Editor, the Ohne compiler, and the simulator. This version control prevents the situation wherein the programmer is unsure of which changes have been made to a particular file. Reports, generated by Releaser, detail all the patches that have gone into making a particular version.

The Releaser user is therefore relieved of all routine coordination problems with other programmers. Releaser handles the issues of program backups, maintenance of multiple versions, and report generation.

8. Scripts

The script generator is a test case compiler. Its development made it possible to produce literally thousands of specific microcode correctness tests. The simulator (described above) and the

System Control Processor (SCP) both
support the automated test facility that
performs these checks. Although the
state files can be produced by the
simulator, the great number of files and
exactness required by these tests make
such a method unattractive.
Additionally, there exists an historical
collection of similiar tests from older
machines. These tests are described in
terms of E-Machine ates rather than
Alpha machine states. The script
generator was developed both to use these
historical tests and to permit the easy
construction of new tests directly from
the E-Mode specification.

The automated test facility requires two
items:

1. A series of disk files that contain
    the initial and terminal machine
    states.

2. The script file that indicates which
    of the state files to use to perform
    the check.

The script generator produces both of
these from the user's input file. The
state files interchange with those
produced by the simulator and SCP. The
script file is in text file format so
that the user can read and edit it if he
wishes; script files can be concatenated
to form a master script file.

The script generator input is an
easy-to-read text description of E-Mode
state, code, etc. Very few Alpha
machine-specific references were included
in the input syntax. Both initial state
and assertions about the final state are
described in the input file. The script
generator maps both of these descriptions
onto the Alpha machine state. The
initial state is set to be that of the
Alpha machine poised to execute an
E-Machine operator; the final state is
set to be the correct state of the
machine after executing the test operator
or sequence of operators.

The script generator makes it possible to
create and use thousands of individual
tests developed specifically for each
E-Machine. The historical tests have
also been run as a confidence measure;
there are more than ten thousand of
these. Figure 8-1 is a sample of the
script generator input.

```
%  +------------------------------------------------+
%  !              Static Branch Tests               !
%  +------------------------------------------------+
TEST BRUN/1
do initialize/test
PSI := 0
code @ PWI:PSI (brun 2:0)
code @ 2:0 (stop)
% end of defining initial state
go
assert pwi = 2
assert psi = 2
% end of defining changes from initial state
%ENDTEST
              .
              .
              .
TEST BRUN/38
%    invalid code parameter (psi) test
do initialize/test
memory[#1006F] := 3 #FFFFFFFFFFFF
% code (brun 7 :6)
memory[#10068] := 3 #A2C007FFFFFF
go
do transcript/do/test/afterint
ASSERT tos[0] is 0      #C007
ASSERT tos[1] is 0      #11020007
ASSERT tos[2] is 3      #000103073
%ENDTEST
```

Figure 8-1: Sample Test Script.

9. System Control Processor (SCP)

The E-Mode architecture describes a
logical entity called the System Control
Processor or SCP. The Alpha machine
realizes the SCP as a physically distinct
microprocessor-based subsystem. This
subsystem has access to and control of
the entire state in the main processor as
well as peripherals. The SCP
communicates with an operator via a
terminal.

The interface that the SCP presents to
the operator is a nearly complete
superset of that presented by the
simulator. The SCP expands the Alpha
machine interface provided by the
simulator to include hardware shift
chains and other items used by hardware
engineers that are not visible to the
microprogram or of interest to
programmers. Display and manipulation of
these items is consistent with the more
common Alpha machine items. The SCP also
provides an E-Machine level display of
state; this interface, although similar
in nature to the Alpha machine interface,
has been made identical for all
E-machines, regardless of their
implementations.

The compatibility of the the SCP and simulator interfaces has increased the productivity of the firmware/hardware integration significantly. All of the tools and methods transfer directly from the programmer's group to the prototype. The simulator's terminal is placed beside the SCP's terminal, and both the hardware and simulator can share or exchange microcode, Alpha machine states and E-Machine code files. Both can be stepped sequentially. If operation is not identical, the state, trace, and last address information of the simulator and the SCP can be compared to discover the cause.

The SCP implementation does not permit some of the features of the simulator; for example, the breakpoint and tracing facilities of the SCP are completely different and not as friendly. The SCP hardware maintains a circular file of clock-edge occurring events. This file can trace only a single sixteen-bit item, which can be switched in software between the micro store address and a second item that is jumper selected. The breakpoint mechanism supports only a single data item.

10. Summary
--- -------

We have described an E-Machine workbench that has facilitated production of reliable and error-free microcode. The existence of relatively unchanging architectural and functional hardware specifications made implementation rather straightforward. The addition of a tool-laden workbench, normally found in other kinds of software development environments, was a prime factor in improving microprogramming productivity. In particular, the tools in the workbench supported a high degree of continuity between the various development phases.

The development of a microprogrammed E-Machine was aided by the use of the Ohne language. The high-level control and data structures in Ohne made it easier to read, write, and assure the correctness of the microprogram. Although detailed knowledge of the Alpha machine was still required, the use of the Ohne language freed the programmer from the myriad of hardware details and allowed concentration on the E-Mode operator algorithms.

Major credit for the rapid development and correctness of the microcode must be given to the decision not to perform any development or debug on the hardware prototypes. All the microcode was fully written and exercised on the simulator before hardware/firmware integration was attempted. This meant that the integration phase was characterized as discovering the differences between the hardware and the simulator. In most cases, these differences were caused by hardware implementation errors.

References.

[Allweiss 81] Allweiss, J. A. & McClintock, J. H., "High Level Language Design," Datamation, April 1981.

[Brooker 70] Brooker, R. A., "Influence of High-level Languages on Computer Design," Proceeding IEE, Vol 117, July 1970.

[B5900 81] B5900 System Reference Manual, Burroughs Corporation, Form 5011034, September 1981.

[Dasgupta 78] Dasgupta, S., "Towards a Microprogramming Language Schema(*)," Proc. 11th Annual Microprogramming Workshop, November 1978.

[Dasgupta 80] Dasgupta, S., "Some Aspects of High Level Microprogramming," ACM Computer Surveys, September 1980.

[Dewitt 76] DeWitt, D. J., "Extensibility - A New Approach for Designing Machine-Independent Microprogramming Languages," Proc. 9th Annual Workshop on Microprogramming, September 1976.

[Dijkstra 76] Dijkstra, E.W., "A Discipline of Programming," Prentice Hall, New Jersey 1976.

[Editor 82] Editor Reference Manual, Burroughs Corporation, Form 5013873, July 1982.

[Li 82] Li, T., "A VLSI View of Microprogrammed System Design," Proc. 15th Annual Workshop on Microprogramming, December, 1982.

[Mayer 82] Mayer, A.J W., "The Architecture of the Burroughs B5000 - 20 Years Later and Still Ahead of the Times?", ACM/SIGARCH: Computer Architecture News, June 1982.

[Myers 81] Myers, G.J. & Hocker, D.G., "The Use of Software Simulators in the Testing and Debugging of Microprogram Logic," IEEE Trans. on Computers, July 1981.

[Organick 73] Organick, E.I., "Computer System Organization: The B5700/B6700 Series," Academic Press, New York, 1973.

[Sengler 76] Sengler, H.E. & Hoare, C.A.R., "On Programs Designed to be Read as Literature," Unpublished Draft, May 1976.

[Wang 82] Wang, D.T., "Defensive Microprogramming," Proc. 15th Annual Workshop on Microprogramming, December 1982.

[Wirth 71] Wirth, N., "Program Development by Stepwise Refinement," CACM, April 1971.

Session V
Vertical Migration

MICROPROGRAMMED ASSOCIATIVE INSTRUCTIONS: RESULTS AND ANALYSIS OF A CASE STUDY IN VERTICAL MIGRATION *)

B. Albert and A. Bode

Institut für Mathematische Maschinen und Datenverarbeitung III,
Universität Erlangen-Nürnberg, Martensstr. 3,
D-8520 Erlangen, West-Germany

ABSTRACT

The microprogrammed implementation of associative instructions on conventional microprogrammable computers with address-based memory-access is introduced as "vertical processing". The implementation on the processors of the EGPA-multiprocessor project is reported as well as runtime comparisons of the microprograms with equivalent HLL-programs. The contribution of the factors vertical migration and associativity to the observed overall speedup is described. Finally, a detailed analysis of the underlying microarchitecture and the handcoded microprograms is given in view of local and global compaction techniques.

1. VERTICAL PROCESSING: ASSOCIATIVE INSTRUCTIONS AND THEIR MICROPROGRAMMED IMPLEMENTATION

The implementation of associative behavior is generally realized as special purpose hardware in systems such as STARAN E (Batcher [5]), DAP (Bird [6]) or lately the SYNFOBASE (AEG-TELEFUNKEN [1]), based on the REM-principle (REcognition Memory, Lamb [19]). This leads to rather efficient associative instructions but enormous cost for the special purpose hardware (content addressable memory and processing element-field) and software (operating system, language compilers ...).

The basic idea of "vertical processing" (Händler [15]) is to implement the associative behavior by microprogramming conventional microprogrammable processors based on an unconventional interpretation of the contents of the conventional address-based RAM (Händler, Klar [17]).

The simplified structure of the special purpose hardware for a bitserial associative processor is shown in Figure 1, along with an example for a

$$RES_{0,i} = ACT_i$$
$$\underline{\text{sequential loop}} \ j = 0,1,2,\dots,n$$
$$\underline{\text{if}} \ REL_j = 1 \ \underline{\text{do}} \ \text{parallel loop} \ i = 0,1,2,\dots,m$$
$$RES_{j,i} = RES_{j-1,i} \ \underline{\text{and not}} \ (AS_{j,i} \ \underline{\text{exor}} \ CRI_j)$$
$$\underline{\text{parallel end}}$$
$$\underline{\text{eif}}$$
$$\underline{\text{if}} \ RES_{j,i} = 0 \ \underline{\text{goto}} \ FIN \ \underline{\text{eif}}$$
$$\underline{\text{sequential end}}$$
$$FIN:\dots.$$

Figure 1: Simplified structure of a bitserial associative processor and sample-algorithm for the execution of the inner loop of an exact match operation in terms of simple logical operations.

*) This project has been supported by the German Federal Ministry for Research and Development (BMFT), contract number DV 4.906 - 081 2070 A, 1978 - 83

personal data base where each associative record comprises a number, name and earnings. Figure 1 also shows that the execution of associative instructions by the PE's and the special purpose registers working on the associative memory may be explained in terms of simple logical operations also available in the microoperation set of every microprogrammable general purpose processor (example: exact match instruction). Figure 2 shows a microprogrammable general purpose processor w bits wide with vertical processing (in our case w = 32).

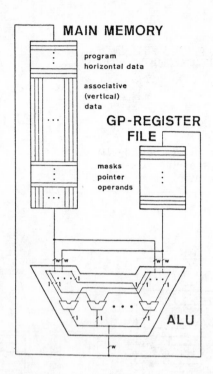

Figure 2: Simplified structure of a general purpose microprogrammable processor and its memory with microprogrammed associative instructions.

The algorithm to execute the associative instructions is implemented by microprogramming the ALU using logical microoperations. Thereby we make the w bit ALU behave as w 1-bit processing elements (PE's) working in conjunction with the special purpose associative registers. These registers are implemented in some registers of the general purpose register set and/or main memory. The contents of the associative memory (Figure 1) is stored "vertically" in the conventional address-based main memory of the system, allowing for associative record-lengths different from w bits. Accessing to one memory address thus supplies a bitslice of w associative records. The only special purpose hardware needed is a small orthogonal memory called "turntable" (Hessenauer [18]) which is used to obtain the vertical data representation in portions of w x w bit during the first data-write phase to the main memory. This may also be implemented by microprogramming but results in very bad runtime characteristics. Of course, larger associative files must be divided into blocks of w records each.

The advantage of the microprogrammed implementation of associativity against the hardware implementation are quite obvious: only a minimum of special purpose hardware and software is needed leading to low cost, better RAS (repairability, availability, serviceability). In the context of our multiprocessor environment this allows for the potential implementation of fail soft behavior. On the other hand, the number of PE's working in parallel on a single processor is restricted to w with w = 32 or 64 according to the wordlength of the processor against

Microprogrammed associative instruction set

1. Associative compares and searches

SAV	associative search, exact match	int, char, fp
MAXMINT	extremum searches (18 dif. types)	int, char, fp
VGLKV	parallel comparison of vector comp.	int

2. Parallel arithmetic

ADDSUBVV	vector-vector arithmetic	int
ADDSUBVS	vector-scalar arithmetic	int
COMPV	complement of a vector	int
SUMV	sum over the components of a vector	int

3. System type operations

INSERT	bitwise write of a record into a vertical vector
EXTRACT	bitwise read of a record from a vertical vector
VMERGE	merging of two vectors
EXIND	pop count of a mask and output of num. indices
Calls to the turntable	

Figure 3: Implemented instruction set of vertical processing.

max. 8 x 256 PE's for STARAN E, i.e. the overall speed will be higher for the special purpose hardware device.

Figure 3 shows the instruction set implemented on the five processors of the EGPA-multiprocessor (Erlangen-General-Purpose Array). The structure and research topics of the EGPA system were published elsewhere (e.g. Händler et al. [16] and Fromm et al. [13]), the processors used are 32-bit highly encoded microprogrammable process computers AEG 80-60, whose microarchitecture is described in more detail in Section 3 of this paper.

Some of the implementation problems of these non-RISC-type instructions have been published in earlier papers (e.g. Bode [7] or Bode, Händler [8]). Currently a new implementation on a bitslice-microprocessor (Am 2900-family) based system with minimally encoded microinstruction format is being undertaken in order to allow a more detailed comparison with the properties of the highly encoded implementation which is reported on here.

The associative instructions were primarily used by the code generator of the language EGFORT, an extension of FORTRAN to a set concept (Schneider [21], Grosch [14]).

2. RUNTIME ANALYSIS OF THE MICROPROGRAMMED ASSOCIATIVE INSTRUCTIONS

The runtimes of the microprograms for vertical processing were compared to equivalent optimized HLL-programs working on the same data but in conventional "horizontal" representation (several versions of random data and real application oriented data have been used). The following results have been obtained (Albert et al. [3]) by software monitoring and using random, application oriented or especially prepared data according to the different investigations.

1. Full associative instructions, delivering a mask as a "pointer" to matching associative records show

Recordlength (bit)	Runtime microprogram (average ms)	Runtime HLL (average ms)	Speedup
8	0.08	6.44	80.50
16	0.09	6.47	71.89
24	0.09	6.43	71.44
32	0.09	6.38	70.89
40	0.09	6.53	72.56
48	0.09	6.48	72.00
56	0.09	6.57	73.00
64	0.09	6.51	72.33
72	0.09	6.64	73.78
80	0.09	6.60	73.33
88	0.09	6.57	73.00
96	0.09	6.66	74.00
104	0.09	6.66	74.00
112	0.09	6.73	74.78
120	0.08	6.68	83.62
128	0.09	6.73	74.78

Figure 4: Runtimes and speedup (averages) for a full associative instruction (arithmetical extremum search with boundary value) against non optimized HLL program for record length between 8 and 128 bit (32 records).

Recordlength (bit)	Runtime microprogram (average ms)	Runtime HLL (average ms)	Speedup
8	0.39	6.29	16.13
16	0.44	6.29	14.29
24	0.45	6.29	13.98
32	0.50	6.28	12.56
40	0.53	6.41	12.09
48	0.66	6.43	9.74
56	0.65	6.42	9.88
64	0.73	6.43	8.81
72	0.80	6.56	8.20
80	0.86	6.57	7.64
88	0.92	6.58	7.15
96	0.91	6.56	7.21
104	0.99	6.70	6.77
112	1.12	6.72	6.00
120	1.03	6.69	6.49
128	1.14	6.71	5.89

Figure 5: Runtimes and speedup (averages) for an associative instruction with bitserial extraction (arithmetical extremum search and extract) against non optimized HLL program for record length between 8 and 128 bit (32 records).

important speedup against the HLL versions. Figure 4 shows the example of one version of an extremum search instruction measured for recordlength varying between 8 and 128 bits. Figure 4 and 5 show runtimes for non-optimized HLL versions (for reference), which are about a factor of 2 slower than optimized code.

2. Associative instructions with microprogrammed bitserial extraction output the matching records instead of pointers to it. In our implementation, this is performed by bitwise access to the main memory of the "extract"-microprogram, which reduces the speedup for larger wordlength (compare Figure 5). This penalty for simulating a CAM on a RAM could be reduced by a faster turntable implementation (orthogonal memory).

3. Parallel arithmetic instructions show only little speedup against HLL versions - especially for standard wordlength - as the operation is hardwired

Record-length (bit)	Runtime microprogram (average ms)	Runtime HLL (average ms)	Speedup
5	0.0868	1.0855	12.51
16	0.1951	1.1500	5.89
32	0.3468	1.1025	3.18
64	0.6481	1.9923	3.07

Figure 6: Runtimes and speedup (averages) for a parallel arithmetic operation (add/sub for two vectors with 32 components) against optimized HLL program for recordlength between 5 and 64 bit.

for conventional "horizontal" data, against its microprogrammed simulation by a sequence of logical operations in vertical processing (compare Figure 6).

4. In the case of the full associative instructions, which were especially usefull for the implementation of the set concept into FORTRAN, we aimed to find out different structural factors contributing to the overall speedup which was calculated to range about 35 for the case of optimized HLL versions (compare Figure 7). By using nearly identical data (except the LSB) the factor associativity, i.e. the possibility to stop the operation before processing the last bitposition, was excluded. In this case, only the factor vertical migration, i.e. reduced macroinstruction fetches, decodes, address calculations etc. ..., was measured ranging around 9. This allows to postulate that the factor associativity contributes to the overall speedup in the case of random data by somewhat around 4.

These measurements allow the following conclusion: the effect of vertical migration is more important for the overall speedup and may also be obtained by conventional "horizontal" microprogrammed block operations. On the other hand, the contribution of associativity is not negligible and makes vertical processing a favourable tool for the extension of the standard instruction set of microprogrammable general purpose computers.

record length (bits)	Vertical Migration			Random Data			Assoc.
	runtime micro-program (ms)	runtime HLL (ms)	speedup vertical migration	runtime micro-program (ms)	runtime HLL (ms)	speedup random	speedup assoc.
32	0.33	3.22	9.76	0.08	2.84	35.50	3.63
64	0.62	5.76	9.29	0.08	2.90	36.62	3.94
96	0.92	8.30	9.02	0.09	3.05	33.89	3.76
128	1.21	10.85	8.97	0.09	2.99	33.22	3.70

Figure 7: Overall speedup (averages) for a full associative instruction (random data) and contributions by factors vertical migration and associativity.

3. MICROARCHITECTURE AND MICRO-PROGRAM ANALYSIS IN VIEW OF THE COMPACTION PROBLEM

The authors' experience in handcoding on the micro-assembler level (for the above mentioned project as well as for bitslice-multiprocessors) confirmed their strong belief that higher level microprogramming languages (HLML's) are a must for applications in which larger pieces of microcode have to be developed. In view of the compaction problem, the microarchitecture and microprograms for vertical processing were investigated, showing that some extensions of the current techniques are needed.

3.1 General description of the microarchitecture of the AEG 80-60

The AEG 80-60 is a 32-bit process computer. It has been designed as a microprogrammed computer. To support our project "vertical processing" the AEG 80-60 was made microprogrammable by extending the control store (2KROM) by 2K reloadable control memory.

The control word is 32 bit wide. This short word indicates encoded microinstructions (almost vertical) with two-level decoding. There are four distinct microinstruction formats. In the first level of decoding it has to be decided what format the current microinstruction has. To make this decision two bits have to be combined, one of them comes from the microinstruction itself, the other is the state of a flipflop whose change of the state is controlled by a microoperation (one microinstruction before!). This is at some extend a kind of residual control. In the second level of decoding the microinstruction is to decode into control signals according to the format specification.

Figure 8 shows the scheme of the microinstruction formats. The 4 formats include all the types of fields but with different lengths. The microprogrammer is able to control the ALU-function with its 2 source operands and its destination as well as the test of a condition and a lot of so called special functions. This field is highly encoded and reaches from NOP to combinations of up to 4 MOs (for example: initiate memory access & load mask register & increment register pointer & decrement shift counter). In spite of the relatively short microword there is the possibility to combine up to 6 MOs into 1 MI. This is the reason why it is meaningful to consider compaction for this almost vertical microarchitecture.

The polyphase microcycle of the AEG 80-60 is variable because there is the possibility of micro-programmed additional clock pulses. In the case of shift operations or for some of the condition tests it is necessary to stretch the microcycle by n phases (controlled by the special function field).

The organization of the microword does not allow the exact separation between controlpart and addresspart. In the "special function" field control- and addressinformation may be mixed (e.g. subroutine call comes from this field).

The microarchitecture consists of:
1. a two port register file with 16 general purpose registers. 12 of these registers can be used by the application microprogrammer after saving the machine programmer's register contents. The 4 other registers are used as base registers and must not be changed by the programmer. Access to a register of this file is done using a register pointer. This pointer is controlled by two microoperations: clear the pointer, increment the pointer. The programmer has access only to the register pointed at and its immediately following register.
2. an auxiliary register file with 4 direct addressable registers. These registers have a connection only to one ALU port, however.
3. an operand register that stores every result of an ALU operation and serves as an inputregister for the specified destination register (from the microinstruction).

The sequencing part of the AEG 80-60 is a little bit unusual. It consists of a control store with its microinstruction register, some decoders and the logic necessary to determine the address of the next microinstruction. Only the unusual address generation will be further described.

One of the four formats has a 10 bit address field. With this format every word inside 1K can be addressed, but to control the rest of the computer there are only 21 bit (10 bit address plus 1 bit format). Therefore a lot of microoperations cannot be encoded in this format.

The other formats permit only a 3 bit address. To address the whole control memory with these 3 bits AEG designed a special addressing method (a kind of two dimensional addressing). A page of 1K words is divided into 128 groups of 8 words (see Figure 9). Every memorycell is defined by a pair (GN, WN) where GN is the group number and WN the word number. The 3 address bits in the microinstruction

| FT | 1.SO | 2.SO | FCT | DEST | COND | SFCT | ADDR |

FT : format type   COND: test condition
SO : source operand   SFCT: special function
FCT : function   ADDR: next address
DEST: destination

Figure 8: Qualitative scheme of the microinstruction's fields.

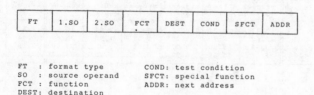

$$GN_{i+1}, WN_{i+1} = \begin{cases} GN_i, WN_{i+1} & \quad WN_i \in \{0, \dots 5\} \wedge \\ & \quad WN_{i+1} \in \{0, \dots, 5\} \\ GN_i+1, WN_{i+1} & \text{if} \quad WN_i \in \{6,7\} \\ GN_i-1, WN_{i-1} & \quad WN_i \in \{0, \dots, 5\} \wedge \\ & \quad WN_{i+1} \in \{6,7\} \end{cases}$$

Figure 9: Microprogram sequencing of AEG 80-60.

specify the WN of the next microinstruction. The GN for the next microinstruction is a function of the current (GN, WN) and the WN specified in the current microinstruction. The GN is either fixed, incremented or decremented by one.

3.2 A review of known optimization strategies from the view-point of vertical processing on the AEG 80-60

Some of the known microcode compaction techniques handle distinct formats (in the case of machine independence), where one specific architecture works with a single format only (Davidson, Shriver [10], Landskov et al. [20], Sheraga, Gieser [22]). Tokoro et al. [24] give an algorithm permitting several distinct formats for one architecture. In this concept it is possible to choose the best format relating to compaction for every microinstruction.

This concept is not applicable to our architecture, however. Since only one bit of the microinstruction is available to specify the format only two formats are selectable without changing the state of the so called format flipflop. If microinstruction (MI n) needs one of the two other formats however, it is necessary to initiate the change of the flipflop in the microinstruction immediately preceeding n (MI n-1). This requests a recompaction of this preceeding microinstruction possibly producing field conflicts that will cause a recompaction of MI n-2 and so on. Such a "feedback" of microinstruction or residual control is not covered by Tokoro et al. [24].

In the literature there are mainly two concepts for the machine independent sequencing of microprograms. Sint [23] proposes a microinstruction description language (MIDL) which provides four operations fetching the next instruction from the control store: JUMP, CALL, RETURN, MULTIJUMP. There is also a default value equivalent to continue. These operations are not powerful enough to model the address generation with 3 bits from the microinstruction and the modified group number.

Baba, Hagiwara [4] designed a microprogram generator (MPG) together with a high-level microprogramming language (MPGL). In this language it is possible to specify an address generation scheme for the next microinstruction. Such a scheme is a pair (B, C_G) where B is a set of (bit position, address generation method) pairs, and C_G is a set of microorders which control B. The following address generation methods are possible (assume the current address is A): retain a part of A, increment a part of A, set a fixed value, set a register value, set 1 or 0 according to the result of the test specified in the microinstruction. Even with this concept it is impossible to model the sequencing of the AEG 80-60 since there is no possibility to build the new address depending on a test of the current content of the microaddress-register, what would be necessary to build the new GN.

The register access mechanism via the pointer is a direct consequence of the effort to shorten the microword. This concept is sufficient for the emulation of the majority of machine instructions.

Most of them work with the register specified in the machine instruction (loaded into the register pointer) and eventually with its succeeding register. However, the application microprogramming needs much more registers.

This register addressing aggravates the anyhow difficult register allocation: The choosen sequence of variables in the register file has an enormous influence to the code generation. E.g. a repeated incrementing of the register pointer will become necessary to access the operands, furthermore it is important that at any label the value of the register pointer is identical for every trace passing this label. We do not know any model to describe this register access method. To some extend this mechanism looks like the known memory access methods, where the memory address register is build as an incrementer which is only resetable. All approaches treat the memory like a single register and therefore all microoperations which access the memory are considered to be datadependent (in the sense of compaction). This means with our architecture a compaction by means of a data dependency graph (Landskov et al. [20]) is useless. We suppose to use the data dependency graph (DDG) to allocate the registers, since the DDG gives a clue to the order in which the variables are used. The phase coupling of register allocation, code generation and compaction (Vegdahl [25]) is much stronger in this architecture than usual. First it seems to be meaningful to take the register allocation before the code generation, since this depends directly on the register allocation (e.g. the number of necessary increments to have access to a register). In this phase it would be desirable to minimize the number of increments necessary between two register accesses. In the compaction phase, however, it could appear that a further increment could be placed in an existing microinstruction what would result in a microoperation at no cost. A register allocation knowing this could lead to a "more optimal" allocation at another place. Fisher et al. [12] require the register allocation to take place during compaction. This requirement can not be maintained with the architecture of the AEG 80-60, since the code to be compacted is strongly dependent of the register allocation.

Summarizing it is possible to say, that the microarchitecture of the AEG 80-60 was choosen to satisfy mainly two requirements:

- reduction of the bitdimension (Agerwala [2]),

- performance.

Obviously there are no automatic methods for code generation and compaction for this machine. To give a statement according the compaction, nevertheless, the handcoded vertical processing microcode has been analysed (compare Figure 10).

All local compaction techniques work only with the so called SLMs (straight-line microprograms), i.e. a sequence of microoperations $S = (m_1 m_2 ... m_t)$ with a single entry point (m_1) and a single exit point (m_t) (Dasgupta, Tartar [9]). The emulation of associativity (vertical processing) shows different average SLM lengths for the distinct instruction types. The miscellaneous instructions possess the

micro-program	P	IT	number of SLMs	number of MIs	number of MOs	average SLM length MI/SLM	MO/SLM	SLM length MO/SLM max	min
AVB	D	p	23	88	141	3.8	6.1	35	0
AVS	D	p	33	108	163	3.3	4.9	29	0
COMPV	B	p	11	60	87	5.5	7.9	26	0
EXIND	E	h	17	33	50	2.0	2.9	12	0
EXTRACT	C	h	29	86	126	3.0	4.3	22	0
INSERT	C	h	18	52	59	2.9	3.3	13	0
MAXMINT	A	h	53	158	229	3.0	4.3	35	0
SAV	C	a	26	68	81	2.6	3.1	12	0
SUMV	B	p	31	90	141	2.9	4.5	23	0
VGLKV	D	a	20	60	100	3.0	5.0	17	1
VMERGE	E	h	36	55	78	1.5	2.2	8	0

```
P:            programmer
IT:           instruction type
A,B,C,D,E:    names of the programmers
a:            associative instruction
p:            parallel arithmetic instruction
h:            miscellaneous instruction
SLM:          straight-line microcode
MI:           microinstruction
MO:           microoperation
```

Figure 10: Some characteristics of the handcoded vertical processing microprograms: only functional microoperations were taken into consideration but no sequencing MO. Therefore some SLMs contain zero MO.

shortest SLMs. These instructions (programs) take a special hardware feature of the AEG 80-60 into consideration, causing many tests. The associative search instructions require also more tests than the arithmetic ones (masks!). These tests are dependent on the algorithms rather than on the hardware.

The maximum length of a SLM is relatively large compared with the average value. That means, that there is a big majority of the short SLMs (70 % of the SLMs have no more than 4 microoperations). This indicates that a local compaction will not lead to a great success.

Looking at the global structure of our application microprograms, statements according prologue/epilogue and main part can be given. Prologue/epilogue will be executed only once (by their nature), while in the main part there are loops often to execute. To "optimize" a program it is therefore necessary to go to much trouble to compact the main part, while the compaction of the prologue/epilogue is not very effective (price/performance). A restriction of the compaction to the main part would lead to a considerable diminishing of the complexity of the optimization, since the main parts of our programs include only 1/3 - 1/4 of all SLMs. This statement corresponds to the intention of the trace scheduling method in the global compaction (Fisher [11]).

The path with the highest "frequency" is chosen first to be compacted, then some house keeping operations are necessary. Then the next path is to be chosen and so on. The programmer is able to give a breakpoint for the compaction.

The evaluation of the two loops with the highest frequency shows the following: the first loop consists of 4 SLMs with a total of 5 microoperations, the second consists of 3 SLMs with a total of 7 microoperations. Both of the loops would be compacted into 4 microinstructions, what is the optimum

for the first loop regarding the local compaction. But we believe that this is far from the optimum concerning the global runtime of the program. To optimize the microprograms, it seems to be advisable to prefer the global compaction techniques together with some other optimization methods like semantic optimization and loop unrolling.

4. CONCLUSION

All these given statements concern the handcoded (!) microcode generated on the AEG 80-60 computer (HLML code should produce larger SLMs). It is rather hard to decide which of the shortcomings of the compaction methods depend on the machine features only and which are real shortcomings. To clear this question a second implementation of the vertical processing is currently undertaken. The host machine of this implementation is a bitslice-based system (AMD 2903/2910) with a nearly horizontal microword and 48 addressable registers.

5. REFERENCES

[1] AEG-TELEFUNKEN, "SYNFOBASE, die Mini-Datenbankmaschine", AEG-TELEFUNKEN, 1983
[2] T. Agerwala, "Microprogram Optimization: A Survey", IEEE Transactions on Computers, Vol. C-25, 10, 962-973, 1976
[3] B. Albert, A. Bode, W. Händler, "A case study in vertical migration: the implementation of a dedicated associative instruction set", Microprocessing and Microprogramming 8, 257-262, 1981
[4] T. Baba, H. Hagiwara, "The MPG-System: A Machine-Independent efficient Microprogram-Generator", IEEE Transactions on Computers, Vol. C-30, 6, 373-395, 1981
[5] K.E. Batcher, "STARAN - Series E", Proc. of the 1977 International Conference on Parallel Processing, J.L. Baer (ed.), 140-143, 1977
[6] A. Bird, "Technical description of the distributed array processor", National Research Region, ICL, Doc. No. AP2, 1975
[7] A. Bode, "Vertical processing: the emulation of associative and parallel behavior on conventional hardware", Proc. EUROMICRO'80, 215-220, North Holland, 1980
[8] A. Bode, W. Händler, "Some results on associative processing by extending a microprogrammed general purpose processor", Proc. 6th workshop on Computer Architecture for Non Numeric Processing, INRIA, 1981
[9] S. Dasgupta, J. Tartar, "The Identification of Maximal Parallelism in Straight-Line Microprograms", IEEE Trans. on Comp., Vol. C-25, 10, 986-992, 1976
[10] S. Davidson, B.D. Shriver, "Specifying target resources in a machine independent higher level language", Proc. NCC, 81-85, 1981
[11] J.A. Fisher, "Trace Scheduling: A Technique for Global Microcode Compaction", IEEE, Transactions on Computers, Vol. C-30, 7, 478-490, 1981
[12] J.A. Fisher, D. Landskov, B.D. Shriver, "Microcode compaction: The State of the Art",

Technical Report TR 82-3-3 University of Southwestern Louisiana, 1982

[13] H.J. Fromm, U. Hercksen, U. Herzog, K.-H. John, R. Klar, W. Kleinöder, "Experiences with performance measurement and modelling of a processor array", IEEE Transactions on Computers, Vol. C-32, 1, 15-31, 1983

[14] J. Grosch, "A language for set-theoretic concepts implemented by microprogrammed associative memory instructions",Wössner (ed.), IFB. Vol. 53, 221-236, Springer, 1982

[15] W. Händler, "Prozessor mit Mikroprogrammsteuerung einer digitalen Rechenanlage", Patent Nr. 2419241, 4/22/1974

[16] W. Händler, F. Hofmann, H.J. Schneider, "A general purpose array with a broad spectrum of applications", W. Händler (ed.), Computer Architecture, IFB, Vol. 4, 311-335, 1974

[17] W. Händler, R. Klar, "Fitting processors to the needs of a general purpose array (EGPA)", Proc. MICRO-8, 87-97, 1975

[18] H. Hessenauer, "Support of vertical dataprocessing by additional hardware", Feilmeier (ed.): Parallel Computers-Parallel Mathematics, Proc. of the IMACS (AICA)-Symposium, 83-86, North Holland, 1977

[19] S. Lamb, "An add-in recognition memory for S-100 bus microcomputers, part 1-3", Computer Design, 8/78: 140-142, 9/78: 162-168, 10/78: 182-186, 1978

[20] D. Landskov, S. Davidson, B.D. Shriver, P.W. Mallet, "Local microcode compaction techniques", Computing Surveys, Vol. 12, 3, 261-294, 1980

[21] H.J. Schneider, "Set theoretic concepts in programming languages and their implementation", Noltemeier (ed.): Graphtheoretic concepts in computer Science, LNCS, Vol. 100, 42-54, Springer, 1981

[22] R.J. Sheraga, J.L. Gieser, "Automatic Microcode Generation for Horizontally Microprogrammed Processors", Proc. Micro 14, SIGMICRO newsletter, Vol. 12, 4, 154-168, 1981

[23] M. Sint, "MIDL - A Microinstruction Description Language", Proc. Micro 14, SIGMICRO newsletter, Vol. 12, 4, 95-106, 1981

[24] M. Tokoro, E. Tamura, K. Takase, K. Tamaru, "An Approach to Microprogram Optimization considering Resource Occupancy and Instruction Formats", Proc. Micro 10, Vol. 8, 3, 92-108, 1977

[25] S.R. Vegdahl, "Phase Coupling and Constant Generation in an Optimizing Microcode Compiler", Proc. Micro 15, Vol. 13, 4, 125-133, 1982

IDENTIFICATION OF MICROPROGRAMMABLE LOOPS
FOR PROBLEM ORIENTED ARCHITECTURE SYNTHESIS

H. Shin and M. Malek

Department of Electrical Engineering
University of Texas at Austin
Austin, Texas 78712

Abstract

The performance of a microprogrammable computer with the writable control memory can be improved by embedding a loop as a single microprogrammed instruction. This paper presents an algorithm for the identification of microprogrammable loops based on the construction of an interval. Also, implementation strategies are discussed with respect to such implementation phases as synthesis of a new instruction and its loading into the control memory. Finally, from the performance point of view, the problem oriented architecture synthesis is compared with the CPU operation overlap.

1. Introduction

In the past two decades, machine instructions have usually been implemented as a sequence of microinstructions in the microprogrammed computer. One way of improving the performance of a microprogrammed computer is to tune or redefine its instruction set so that its architecture supports more efficient execution of a given program. In particular, significant performance enhancement can be accrued by embedding a portion of a problem oriented program as an instruction which is more frequently executed than others. This approach called problem oriented architecture synthesis has been extensively investigated [1-5].

The program loop seems to be, at least intuitively, the most appropriate candidate for such architecture synthesis because of its intrinsic property of repetitiveness in execution. This intuition has been supported by several experiments [1-3], where significant improvements have been obtained by embedding a loop as a single microprogrammed instruction. A program segment or a sequence of instructions which frequently appears in a program is also a candidate suitable for architecture synthesis. It may be difficult, however, to determine the dynamic usage of a segment without collecting run-time statistics

because its static usage is not necessarily the same as its dynamic usage [6]. Nevertheless, without a priori knowledge of dynamic usage of instructions, the use of loops as a synthesis candidate is supported by another experiment [7], where a majority of execution time is spent on a small part of a program.

The performance improvement stems from several factors. Execution of machine instruction requires instruction/operand fetch, instruction/address decoding and execution. By combining the multiple instruction comprising a loop into one instruction, the instruction fetch is obviated, resulting in less frequent main memory access. Operand decoding and fetch phases may be eliminated by allocating local registers to the operands whose addresses remain the same during the period of loop execution. Lastly, the instruction execution phase can be made more effective by optimizing microinstruction streams. In addition, if the called procedure is expanded and microprogrammed in line, operations required for the procedure linkage can be eliminated.

In this paper, a microprogrammable loop is defined as a loop in a problem oriented program whose constituent instructions can be replaced by a single microcoded instruction. Synthesis of the problem oriented architecture on a microprogrammable computer using the program loop requires a knowledge of its bounds and microprogrammability. Despite successful experiments on the architecture synthesis involving program loops, few systematic methods have been developed to locate the microprogrammable loop. In Abd-Alla and Karlgaard [1], the loops were identified from the post execution analysis of the trace file. In a graph theoretic approach, Luque and his coworkers [5] perform abstract algebraic manipulation on the control flow graph to identify the loop. This method is valid only in the structural aspect, lacking functional integrity.

As the second step of architecture synthesis, the candidate loop to be embedded as an instruction is selected, and a new machine instruction is synthesized. Selection criteria are usually the frequency of execution, the size of the loop and writable control memory space available. Finally, the program is modified, incorporating the instructions replacing the loops, and their supporting microprograms are loaded into the control memory. Also, the instruction fetch and decode microprogram is modified to accommodate the new synthesized instruction.

A method for the identification of microprogrammable loops using the interval construct developed by Allen [8] is presented in this paper. Also, various implementation schemes for the architecture synthesis are discussed. Finally, performance of the problem oriented architecture synthesis is compared with the CPU pipelining.

2. The Microprogrammable Loop

A program loop may be loosely defined as a program segment with possibility of repetitive execution. The loop is often implemented in a high level language program using structured constructs such as WHILE-DO, REPEAT-UNTIL and FOR-DO which allow only a single entry. However, it can be realized using a GOTO statement which may allow multiple entries. In terms of execution control, the loop is characterized by two parameters: the number of entry points from an external point and the type of branches occurring inside the loop. The flow of control can be altered by IF, CASE, GOTO, CALL and RETURN statements let alone the loop constructs. The type of branch can thus be distinguished.

The properties of a microprogrammable loop are bound by the following constraints for effective implementation:

1. A single entry,

2. No call to the procedure or function which can not be expanded in line.

A microprogrammable loop must be entered through the first instruction. Although it is not impossible to synthesize a multiple entry loop as a single instruction as illustrated in Liu and Mowle [3], the overhead involved in the process of identification and synthesis, especially in case of nested loops, is considered prohibitive. A microprogrammable loop does allow multiple exits.

No procedure call must be made to the procedure which can not be expanded in line; nor must such a function be referred to. Several factors account for this constraint. A called procedure may be either too large to fit available control memory, external so that it is not available at compile time, or an ENTRY procedure as in FORTRAN. If a "Branch to Subroutine" instruction is microprogrammed together with other machine instructions, the RETURN linkage becomes difficult to handle, if not impossible, because control is returned to the calling procedure via the program counter or address of machine instruction. In the multiprogramming environment, a call to system I/O routine may be regarded as a possible breakpoint for job swapping. If this is

the case with a microprogrammed loop the outcome would be disastrous since the machine is not usually capable of saving the control store address during swapping. Thus, no procedure calls are allowed inside the microprogrammable loop unless they are to be expanded in line.

3. Identification of Microprogrammable Loops

As discussed, the microprogrammable loop is a single entry loop without any call to non-inline-expansible procedures. The single entry condition can be determined effectively using graph theoretic tools. To begin with, a canonical graph model of program control flow called a flow graph [9] is introduced briefly to aid in identification of microprogrammable loops.

A program can be partitioned into groups of statements such that once executed the first and the last statements are always executed without possibility of branch except at the last statement. Such a group of statements or instructions is called a basic block. The basic blocks and their successor relationships are represented by a directed graph (V,E). A flow graph with initial node s is designated by G=(V,E,s), where V is a vertex set and E is an edge set whose elements represent basic blocks and flow of control, respectively. In G, the initial node s≤V can reach every node. (The symbol "≤" denotes "is contained in.") An edge e is an ordered pair of vertices, (v1, v2), where e is incident out of v1 and incident into v2. Node v1 is said to be the predecessor of node v2, and v2 the successor of v1. A flow graph is strongly connected if there is a path between all pairs of nodes. An example of a flow graph is shown in Fig. 1.

In a flow graph, the microprogrammable loop is defined as a collection of nodes which is strongly connected and has a unique entry. To search for microprogrammable loops, a flow graph is partitioned into intervals as described by Allen [8]. Given a flow graph G and a node h≤V, an interval I(h) is a single entry subgraph for which h, called the header node, is the entry node. The interval can also be defined by the construction algorithm as shown in PROCEDURE Interval. Further, a flow graph is uniquely partitioned into disjoint intervals based on the algorithm illustrated in PROCEDURE Partition. The intervals thus obtained exhibit two important properties: I(h) is entered only at the interval header and every loop, if any, contains the interval header. These properties provide the necessary clues to the identification of microprogrammable loops.

Once the intervals are found, the loop inside the interval is identified by backtracking from the header node as shown in PROCEDURE DetectLoop. From the graph theoretic point of view, a loop in the interval is microprogrammable because its single entry condition is satisfied. To meet the second requirement concerning a CALL statement, information on the called procedure is needed so

3

that size, location and type of task may be available when a procedure call is encountered in the loop. Thus, PROGRAM written in the PASCAL-like language uPLoop provides the algorithm for constructing the microprogrammable loop. For example, as shown in Figs. 1a and 1b, a loop consisting of the nodes 4, 5, 6 and 7 in I(4) is microprogrammable since the subroutine SWAP can be expanded in line.

The detected loop is the inner loop unless the procedure to be expanded in line contains a loop. In case of nested loops, outer loops can be derived by utilizing the reducibility of a flow graph that has been partitioned into the intervals [8,9]. Such a flow graph can be reduced to another flow graph in which a node represents an interval of the former graph. The recursive application of the algorithms in PROGRAM uPLoop to the reduced graph will enable one to find outer loops as shown in Fig. 1c.

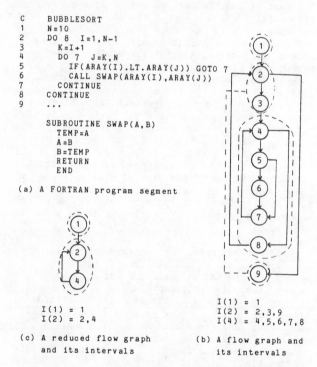

```
C      BUBBLESORT
1      N=10
2      DO 8  I=1,N-1
3         K=I+1
4         DO 7  J=K,N
5            IF(ARAY(I).LT.ARAY(J)) GOTO 7
6            CALL SWAP(ARAY(I),ARAY(J))
7         CONTINUE
8      CONTINUE
9      ...

       SUBROUTINE SWAP(A,B)
       TEMP=A
       A=B
       B=TEMP
       RETURN
       END
```

(a) A FORTRAN program segment

I(1) = 1
I(2) = 2,4

(c) A reduced flow graph and its intervals

I(1) = 1
I(2) = 2,3,9
I(4) = 4,5,6,7,8

(b) A flow graph and its intervals

Figure 1. Construction of a flow graph and its intervals: An example

With all the inner and outer loops identified, the two important parameters can be estimated: the frequency of execution and the size of microprogram to be synthesized. Since it is assumed that no execution profile is known a priori, the accurate frequency of execution may not be determinable, especially in the case of WHILE and REPEAT loops. However, frequency of execution can be projected based on the the depth of nesting, i. e., the more outer loops an inner loop has, the higher frequency of execution is projected. Upper and lower bounds of the microprogram size can be determined assuming optimization is not done on the microinstruction stream. A machine instruction is usually

```
PROGRAM uPLoop;

  PROCEDURE Interval(h,I(h));
    BEGIN
      I(h) := [h]
      REPEAT
        IF v ≰ I(h) AND v ≠ s AND all
           predecessors of v ≤ I(h)
        THEN I(h) := I(h) + [v̄];
      UNTIL all successors of the vertices in
           I(h) have been examined;
    END;

  PROCEDURE Partition(SI);
    BEGIN
      SH := [s];  {a set of header nodes}
      SI := [];   {a set of intervals}
      WHILE SH ≠ [] DO
        BEGIN
          Interval(v,I(v));
          SI := SI + [I(v)];
          SH := SH - [v];
          Add to SH any node which has a
            predecessor in I(v) but which is
            not already in SH or in one of
            the intervals in SI
        END;

  PROCEDURE DetectLoop(I(h),SL);
    BEGIN
      SP := [];   {a set of predecessors}
      SL := [h];  {a set of nodes in loop}
              {pred(x): a predecessor of x}
      IF l = pred(h) ≤ I(h) THEN
        BEGIN
          SL := SL + [l];
          SP := [l];
          WHILE SP ≠ [] DO
            BEGIN
              SP := SP - [n]; {n≤SP: any node
                               to be tested}
              FOR each p = pred(n) ≰ SL DO
                BEGIN
                  SL := SL + [p];
                  SP := SP + [p]
                END;
            END;
        END;
    END;

{Main program}

  BEGIN
    Partition(SI);
    WHILE SI ≠ [] DO
      BEGIN
        SI := SI - I(h);
        DetectLoop(I(h),SL);
        WHILE SL ≠ [] DO
          BEGIN
            SL := SL - [n]; {n≤SL: node
                             to be tested}
            IF node n contains a call to a
               non-inline-expansible procedure
            THEN loop is not microprogrammable;
          END;
      END;
  END.
```

interpreted by three microroutines: instruction fetch, instruction decode/operand fetch, and execution. Let F, D[i] and E[i] denote the number of microinstructions in the respective microroutines of the i-th instruction in the loop. When n instructions are combined into one instruction only one instruction fetch is needed instead of n fetches. Further, a microroutine for instruction decode and operand fetch may be either eliminated or reduced in size, depending on the synthesis environment where operands located in the main memory may be assigned to local working registers. Hence, the number of microinstructions for the newly synthesized instruction, L, is

$$F + \sum_{i=1}^{n} E[i] <= L <= F + \sum_{i=1}^{n} (D[i]+E[i])$$

4. Implementation Strategies

In general, implementation of problem oriented architecture synthesis involving the loop consists of three phases: microprogrammable loop identification phase, instruction synthesis phase, and microcode loading phase. In this section each phase is discussed, and three synthesis and loading techniques are described.

4.1. Loop Identification

Unquestionably, the loop can be identified during compilation of source programs. Most part of this process overlaps the code optimization of a compiler since loops must be identified before any optimization actions are taken [10]. In this case, loop identification does not impose any significant load on the compilation process if the compiler performs code optimization. On the other hand, identification may be implemented independently without compiler assistance. This type of implementation requires the execution time of $O(|E|)$ where $|E|$ is the number of edges in a flow graph [8].

4.2. Synthesis and Loading of a New Instruction

A new instruction is synthesized in microcode to replace the microprogrammable loop before execution occurs. Operands residing in the same location of the main memory throughout the loop execution may be assigned to local registers to obviate the main memory reference. Once the loop execution is completed, the operands whose values have been changed must be written back into the main memory. To perform these operations, extra microcodes must be appended before the loop entry and after the loop exit. In addition, instruction fetch and decode phases can be eliminated if the loop is implemented in microcode. During the synthesis process, microcode optimization strategies may be incorporated, such as elimination of redundant and negated microoperations, microcode motion, overlapping and other optimization techniques [1].

The synthesis activity may be performed either before or at run time, i.e., static

synthesis or dynamic synthesis. The static synthesis may be implemented during compilation or independently [2,4]. Likewise, a new instruction may be loaded into the control memory statically or dynamically. Based on these criteria, the implementation strategies may fall into three groups as follows:

		Synthesis	
		static	dynamic
Loading	static	Type I	--
	dynamic	Type II	Type III

The first implementation scheme Type I consists of static synthesis and static loading; Type II consists of static synthesis and dynamic loading; Type III consists of dynamic synthesis and dynamic loading.

4.3. Comparison of Implementation Schemes

The three implementation schemes for architecture synthesis perform functionally identical computations on the same computer. For this reason, overhead or time spent on loop identification, instruction synthesis and loading are approximately the same on a given architecture. However, there are many differences as discussed below.

For the Type I implementation (static/ static), the loops are microcoded and then loaded into the control memory until there is no more control memory space available. Time savings is a function of the size of writable control memory [3]. For a large application program which benefits the most through architecture synthesis, control memory size is likely to be a bottleneck, although current advances in memory technology alleviate this limitation to some extent. If such a constraint exists, priorities may be assigned to loops based on their execution frequency and size so that the loop with the highest priority is embedded first. If there is no provision to save the synthesized loop in another storage unit, it is volatile when job swapping occurs. Static/static implementation is inappropriate in multiprogramming environments and the repeated use over an extended period of time.

Type II implementation scheme (static/ dynamic) requires that the loops be microcoded and saved in the main memory, and then loaded into the control memory at run time when the need arises. A microprogrammed loop in the main memory must be properly tagged so that during execution it may be identified upon the detection of the instruction in the program. Higher overhead is incurred when the microcoded loop is written into and read from the memory. Each microcoded loop is loaded into the control memory, only when it is referred to, so this scheme requires relatively small amount of control memory. Non-volatility of synthesized microprograms makes this scheme suitable for the use in the multiprogramming environment and repeated use over an extended period of time. In case of repeated use, one-time overhead from the loop identification and synthesis process would be negligible thus maximizing the benefit of architecture synthesis.

Type III implementation scheme (dynamic/ dynamic) involves run-time synthesis of microcoded loop and its loading. For this scheme, loop bounds are marked by special arrangements such as an extended instruction or by trap in the loop identification phase. A routine which specializes in the synthesis is referenced when such an instruction is encountered during execution. This scheme needs no extra storage unit (like the main memory required for Type II) because synthesized microprograms are directly loaded into the control memory. Type III needs control memory space large enough to contain one loop so that program size does not affect the performance. It is as disadvantageous to the repeated use of a program as the Type I scheme because the microprogram for a loop must be synthesized each time the program is executed. Multiprogramming environment, however, is conducive to this scheme.

Type III is amenable to parallel processing where a separate processor synthesizes the microcode while the program is executed. An example would be where all the loops to be microcoded are listed at the entry of the program in the main memory. Upon the initiation of execution on the first processor the second processor starts to synthesize loops by fetching their bounds and identifying their location. The addresses of the microcoded loops are maintained in a table so that when the execution control reaches a loop the corresponding microprogram is loaded into the control memory. If the control reaches the loop before it is completely synthesized, it waits until the synthesis is completed. The first processor may be given a preemptive priority in access to the main memory.

5. Comparison with CPU Pipelining

The ultimate goal of the architecture synthesis is to speed up computations in the CPU and enhance the performance of a computer. A number of techniques have been directed to this goal; one of the common practices is pipelining or operation overlap in the CPU. It is useful as well as interesting to compare the time savings accrued from the CPU pipelining and the problem oriented architecture synthesis. For comparison purpose, Type I implementation scheme is selected, and the overhead incurred during loop identification and synthesis is neglected.

For the analysis of time savings accrued from the architecture synthesis, it is assumed that no optimization is performed except for the elimination of the instruction fetch and decode operations, and assignment of operands to local registers. Let

t = main memory cycle time,

n = number of machine instructions in the loop,
k = number of iterations the loop performs,
$m = an$ = number of operands assigned to working registers, $0 <= a <= 1$,
d = average time required to decode one instruction in main memory cycle time,
$P = b'mt = bnt$ = overhead in preloading and restoring operands where $b = b'a$.

The net time saving accrued, T, is the difference between the total time saving S and the overhead P, i.e.,

$$T = S - P = knt + kmt + kdnt - amt$$
$$= nt(k + ka + kd - b)$$

where knt = total instruction fetch time saved
kmt = total operand fetch time saved,
$kdnt$ = total decoding time saved.

For the calculation of the time saving accrued from the operation overlap, assume that there are no branches except at the end of the loop where the branch has been regarded as an unconditional branch by the CPU. Typically, a CPU consists of instruction unit (IU) and ALU, and CPU pipelining is accomplished by having instruction fetch, execution in IU and execution in ALU overlapped [9]. The IU performs decoding, effective address calculation and operand fetch besides the instruction fetch. For the pipelined operations, the unit time delay is the worst case time to execute the tasks in either instruction fetch, IU or ALU. Let

$t1$ = average execution time in IU,
$t2$ = average execution time in ALU,
$t' = max(t,t1,t2)$ = unit time delay,
t,k,n : as defined above.

Note that $t1 >= dt$. The maximum saving, T0, accrued from execution of n instructions is the difference between the execution time without overlap, A, and that with overlap, B, i.e., T0 = A-B. Without overlap, one instruction cycle is the sum of time spent on the three operations. Hence, $A = (t + t1 + t2)kn$.

First, consider the case of simple overlap where no overlap between IU operation and instruction fetch is allowed as shown in Fig. 2a. The execution time for kn instructions is $B1 = (1+2kn)t'$. Hence, the time saving T1 and the ratio R1 are

$$T1 = A - B1 = (t+t1+t2)kn - (1+2kn)t'$$

$$R1 = \frac{T}{T1} = \frac{(k+ka+kd-b)nt}{(t+t1+t2)kn - (1+2kn)t'}$$

Now consider the case of ideal overlap where overlap between IU operation and instruction fetch is allowed as shown in Fig. 2b. The execution time for kn instructions is $B2 = (2+kn)t'$. Hence, the saving T2 and the ratio R2 are

$$T2 = A - B2 = (t+t1+t2)kn - (2+kn)t'.$$

$$R2 = \frac{T}{T2} = \frac{(k+ka+kd-b)nt}{(t+t1+t2)kn - (2+kn)t'}$$

Compared with T1 and T2, T is more sensitive to the number of iterations k. Depending on the value of b, T may become negative at low k resulting in the reverse effect. Hence, for a small value of k, the CPU pipelining is superior in improving the performance. As k increases, the terms with k become dominant so the ratios given above are simplified:

$$R1 = \frac{(1+a+d)t}{t+t1+t2-2t'}, \quad R2 = \frac{(1+a+d)t}{t+t1+t2-t'}.$$

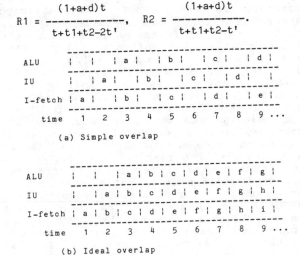

(a) Simple overlap

(b) Ideal overlap

Figure 2. The CPU pipelining

In the ideal case of pipelined operations, the delays in the stages are exactly the same. Hence, $t=t1=t2=t'$, $R1 = 1+a+d$ and $R2 = (1+a+d)/2$. Since $0\le a,d\le 1$, $1\le R1\le 3$ and $0.5\le R2\le 1$. These indicate that performance improvement through the architecture synthesis is always better than that through the simple overlap (up to 300 %), however, it can not be better than that through the ideal overlap. In the other extreme where $t' \equiv t+t1+t2$, the overlap schemes achieve no speedup whereas for $a=d=0$ the architecture synthesis scheme can still save instruction fetch cycles.

6. Conclusion

The problem oriented architecture synthesis based on microprogrammable loops involves three implementation issues: loop identification, new instruction synthesis, and loading of synthesized microcode into the control memory. A microprogrammable loop can be identified by partitioning the control flow graph into interval constructs. If performed during compilation, this process incurs only a moderate amount of overhead with respect to computation time. Implementation strategies are classified on the basis of the time when synthesis and loading are performed. In Type I implementation scheme, the loop is synthesized and loaded before program execution. The Type II scheme where the loop is synthesized before execution and loaded during execution is plausible as current technology produces cheaper and faster memories. The Type III scheme where both processes are performed during execution is amenable to parallel processing so program execution and architecture synthesis may be overlapped. Finally, to always outperform the CPU operation overlap, the problem oriented architecture synthesis has been found to require that the machine have the sufficient number of working registers to have more operands assigned locally, and that the microprogram be properly optimized.

Acknowledgements

The authors wish to thank Dr. A. J. Welch for his invaluable reviews and comments. They also gratefully acknowledge the insightful comments of two anonymous referees.

References

1. A. M. Abd-Alla and D. C. Karlgaard, "Heuristic synthesis of microprogrammed computer architecture," IEEE Trans. Comput. , C-23, pp. 802-807, 1974.

2. K. A. El-Ayat and J. A. Howard, "Algorithms for a self-tuning microprogrammed computer," Proc. 10th Annu. Workshop Microprogramming, IEEE-ACM, pp. 85-91, 1977.

3. P. S. Liu and F. J. Mowle, "Techniques of program execution with a writable control memory," IEEE Trans. Comput., C-27, pp. 816-827, 1978.

4. T. G. Rauscher and A. K. Agrawala, "Dynamic problem oriented redefinition of computer architecture via microprogramming," IEEE Trans. Comput., C-27, pp. 1006-1014, 1978.

5. E. Luque, A. Ripoll and J. J. Ruz, "Dynamic microprogramming in computer architecture redefinition," Euromicro J. 6, pp. 98-103, 1980.

6. W. G. Alexander and D. B. Wortman, "Static and dynamic characteristics of XPL programs," Computer 8(11), pp. 41-46, Nov. 1975.

7. D. E. Knuth, "An empirical study of FORTRAN programs," Software - Practice and Experience 1, pp. 105-133, 1971.

8. F. E. Allen, "Control flow analysis," ACM SIGPLAN Notices 5, pp. 1-19, July 1970.

9. M. S. Hecht, Flow Analysis of Computer Program, North-Holland, New York, NY, 1977.

10. A. V. Aho and J. D. Ullman, Principles of Computer Design, Addison-Wesley, Reading, MA, 1977.

11. J-L Baer, Computer System Architecture, Computer Science Press, Potomac, MD, 1980.

TOWARD TYPE-ORIENTED DYNAMIC VERTICAL MIGRATION

ROBERT I. WINNER and EDWARD M. CARTER

Vanderbilt University, Nashville, Tennessee

Abstract

The study of structured programming has shown that through data abstraction, program reliability and maintainability can be improved. At the same time, vertical migration has been shown to be an effective way to improve the performance of programs. Contemporary techniques, however, tend to address the needs of only certain classes of programs and therefore may overlook or even preclude certain optimization opportunities. Dynamic microprogramming can overcome the problem of applicability of a particular vertical migration by allowing the migration to be tailored for each particular application. This paper describes a project which is exploring the interactions of these three concepts of dynamic microprogramming, vertical migration, and data abstraction and how they can be integrated to form a coherent facility which provides automated redefinition of computer architecture for each application model.

Introduction

The programming architecture of a computer can be defined as the set of functions and interfaces which are available for use by programmers in typical programming languages such as assembler and procedure oriented languages. For our purpose, we can equate this to the set of operations provided by the instruction set and the data types on which these instructions operate. Since the advent of the von Neumann architecture in the late 1940's, little has changed in the basic schema of computer architectures except that more complex data types and instructions are being provided. This set of types and operations is still established by the computer architect and restricts the applications which can be implemented efficiently to those that can be mapped efficiently onto this set.

In the last ten years increasing scrutiny has been given to this restricted set of data types and operations as well as to the effect it has on reliability and maintainability of software. Some measures have been attempted which have to date resulted in working, yet not efficient, architectures for solving this problem. For the most part, only modifications to the basic von Neumann architecture have proven to be successful. This paper outlines a course of research which is being pursued to apply the recent advances in programming methodology to computer architecture through problem-oriented redefinition. This redefinition of a computer's architecture results in a model oriented architecture with a rich and applicable set of data types and operations which are tailored for the particular problem being addressed. In this research we are looking at dynamically redefining the architecture of computers to match the model being described by the programmer. The major premise of the research is that through the use of data abstraction facilities of programming languages, new data types can be discovered and migrated into the computer's architecture through dynamic microprogramming.

This paper will introduce the abstraction oriented redefinition technique under study at Vanderbilt University. The first section of the paper will review the major concepts which are being adapted to architectural redefinition including dynamic microprogramming, vertical migration, and data abstraction. With these concepts in mind the next section will describe how these techniques can be used for automated redefinition of computer architecture. This section will include a discussion of what has been done and the preliminary results. The final section will address the continuing research plan and the expected results of our analysis.

Background

This section of the paper is intended to review the three concepts of data abstraction/encapsulation, vertical migration, and dynamic microprogramming. These areas will not be studied in depth but will be highlighted with emphasis on application to architecture redefinition. The research is seeking to show that the interaction of these techniques will yield a total improvement in reliability and maintainability as well as performance which is greater than the sum of the individual contributions of each technique. Within each discussion some of the contributing research will be discussed which has particular application for this study.

Data Abstraction and Encapsulation

One of the largest strides in programming methodology in recent years has been the drive towards the utilization of structured programming techniques. Perhaps the best known of these techniques is that of information-hiding. In information hiding, presented in [1], the major goal is to "hide" the representation of data within a capsule or module which provides controlled access to the data through a set of entry points. In this way, the programmer who is using the encapsulation need know only the available entry points and the parameters used in calling the entry points as well as the returned values to use a data facility.

The facility may be as simple as an integer type or as complex as a stack of records each of which is of dynamic length. The former of the facilities is normally provided directly in the computer architecture and we will refer to these as primitive types. The latter of these is specific to the application and we will call these abstract types. An abstract data type is simply a representation of a class of objects and the operations which can be performed on them. These operations define a set of invariant properties and must maintain these properties for the type. An example of one of these properties is that all of the data values must come from a well defined set of allowable values. The presence of these invariant properties as part of the type description provides a useful tool for axiomatic verification of program behavior. This verification can be extremely useful where types may be migrated into firmware and which effectively become part of the computer architecture for the particular problem under study.

Some of the earliest work on abstract data types is described in [2] and [3]. In these reports Dijkstra and Wirth demonstrate that a program is simply a model of some physical or abstract system which is iteratively refined until it is implementable on a computer. In each of the iterative steps, some information about the model is simplified or deleted to yield a new abstract description of the model. This description is called an abstraction of the model. For the duration of the paper, model and abstraction are used interchangeably.

Horning in [4] lists some useful properties of data abstraction facilities. Each of these facilities can be seen to provide a useful tool for dynamic microprogramming. These properties are:

1) Avoidance of repetition

2) Modular program structure

3) A basis for structured programming

4) Conceptual units for understanding and reasoning about programs

5) Clearly defined interfaces that may be precisely specified

6) Units of maintenance and improvement

7) A language extension mechanism

8) Units of separate compilation

The first property provides for a simple method of compacting programs by avoiding repetitive sequences of instructions. The entire sequence is replaced by a mapping instruction which causes the appropriate action to be performed on an object of the abstract type. The concepts of modularity and conceptual units form the basis for a type mechanism by tightly specifying the representation of the type and the operation which can be performed on the objects of the type. The remaining concepts give us a syntactic basis for encapsulating a type such that controlled access to the objects of the type and hence possible migrated code can be enforced.

Data abstraction, therefore forms a new set of types, let us call this set the types of interest for this particular model. The components of the objects of the types of interest are formed by combining the primitive data types and implementing procedures to manipulate these items to simulate the abstract type. It is the responsibility of the programmer to describe the operations on this type object as well as its representations. It is the job of the compiler to translate this representation and operations into a coherent set of directives or machine instructions which can be understood by the architecture of the host computer.

Data encapsulation is the process of grouping the elements of the abstract data type together. In modern programming languages this is done by describing a user defined data type or structure and the procedures which access the elements of this type. Another requirement of encapsulation is that the objects of the abstract type must be protected from unauthorized access. The only method of creating, updating, or deleting these objects must be through the provided routines. It is these procedures which define the set of operations which maintain the invariant properties of the objects of the abstract type.

Vertical Migration

A computer system can easily be seen as a hierarchy of interpreters. From the end-user's perspective, the computer may seem to be a transaction processing facility which operates on user requests. From a high-level language programmer's perspective, the system may appear to be a programming language interpreter which is based on the particular programming language which he is using. This hierarchy can be followed down through the levels of language until one eventually can view the computer as a microprogrammed engine which interprets macrocoded instructions. This type of system has been studied extensively by Stankovic in [5,6,7] and Stockenberg and van Dam in [8]. The collection of levels has come to be known as a multi-level software/firmware hierarchical system and research has shown that moving functions between these levels can enhance the performance of the system as a whole. Furthermore, the previously mentioned research has also shown that the interaction between migrations can often result in less marginal improvement from one particular migrated object than the improvement gained from that migration taken alone.

This technique known as vertical migration provides a generalized n-level hierarchy which can be used for tuning a computing environment. Note that the concept of vertical migration allows both for a downward migration of functions to a lower level as well as a horizontal migration of functions to the same layer of the interpretive structure. Several results including [9,10,11] and [12] have shown that significant performance enhancement can be achieved through vertical migration by user microprogramming. In this technique the user microcode becomes a part of the architecture in that it is available as a service to the user in the same way as any macrocode instruction.

Included in the research which has been accomplished in this area are a review of methodologies used in determining what functions to migrate. Rauscher [13] brought to light the gains that could be made through dynamic microprogramming coupled with vertical migration. He showed that contemporary function-based and instruction-based schemes could be adapted for dynamic vertical migration decisions by a compiler. Most of the other methods however, are static decisions and once made apply globally to all applications. Furthermore, sequences of instructions are often grouped solely by their physical proximity in the examined code and may tend to be unrelated. For this reason parameterization of migrated code may be impossible and further inhibit microcode compaction. An enhanced migration decision technique such as abstraction-oriented migration seems to offer a great opportunity for increased system performance without a large increase in complexity when the correct functions are chosen for migration. In this way, sequences of related instructions are migrated where parameterization will be possible and further compaction enhanced.

In a panel discussion reported by Stankovic in [14] an informal discussion of how much of an application to migrate yielded a discussion as to why migrate anything at all. The ensuing discussion produced the following reasons:

1) To improve performance

2) For security support

3) For proprietary reasons for the manufacturer

4) For protection and privacy of data

5) To experiment with alternate machine architectures

6) To complete a feedback loop that allows the proper set of primitives to be chosen for the proper level.

It is the latter two of these reasons which are of interest to our research. We propose to make the feedback loop extremely tight with the compiler and programmer being the only participants. Furthermore, we propose that the experimentation with alternate architectures be carried out by the compiler and that the experiment produce a model-dependent architecture.

The majority of the literature on vertical migration concentrates on two important classes of migrations. Holtkamp in [15] reports on these two classes. The first class consists of those migrations which are function-oriented. In this class the migrated objects are functions (much like those in programming languages).

The second class consists of those migrations which are instruction-oriented. In this class sequences of instructions that occur more than once in a machine or intermediate language program and/or that are frequently executed are candidates for migration. Holtkamp further states that regardless of which of these these two classes is used for a migration strategy, the following four steps must be performed.

1) Identify suitable migration candidates

2) Predict the performance improvement

3) Migrate the objects

4) Verify the system's behavior

Research has been carried out in each of these areas. Rauscher in particular has investigated the correct choice of migration objects. Stockenberg and Stankovic have investigated performance prediction in depth. Several efforts have been applied toward automated migration of objects once the correct object has been chosen. Finally, much has been written about verification of program behavior outside of microcode, but these techniques seem readily adaptable to microprogramming as well.

Dynamic Microprogramming

For this paper, we will define dynamic microprogramming as the ability of a system user to place microcode dynamically into a writable control store thus effectively extending the programming architecture of the machine. The emphasis we place in this area is specifically architecture synthesis. According to Stockenberg and van Dam in [8] there are two types of architecture synthesis, manual and heuristic. The most well known synthesis technique is manual synthesis and has been seen in numerous applications such as language accelerators, operating system assists , and migrations of specific user functions to firmware. This type of migration is very often quite complex and is usually restricted to only a small class of programs. The second type of architecture synthesis is of most interest to our research. In heuristic synthesis an attempt is made to discover what portions of the program should be microcoded to yield the best performance improvement. This search is made in an automated or semi-automated procedure so that the complexity is reduced and the applicability of the procedure can be

greatly expanded. Earlier work by Abd-Alla [16] and El-Ayat [17] have also found that techniques can be described for dynamically redefining computer architecture in an automated manner.

Abstraction Oriented Migration

The term abstraction oriented migration refers to the ability to redefine dynamically the computer architecture to match the model that the programmer is attempting to simulate on the computer. Other researchers have been able to enhance the performance of systems through vertical migration, however these systems have used function-oriented or instruction-oriented techniques as the basis for migration decisions. In other words, the decision for vertical migration was made as a result of statically and/or dynamically examining a sequence of operations and determining which parts of the code should be migrated into microstore to provide the greatest degree of performance improvement. This type of analysis can often be very complex and may preclude analysis of a large number of application programs. In addition, most migration techniques seek to find new global primitives which can be applied across a system as a whole rather than for a particular program or application system.

It is the intent of this research effort to capitalize on the gains which have been made in both software and firmware engineering in order to produce a working facility for abstraction oriented migration. Our research goal then, can be summarized as follows.

The goal of this research is to investigate the feasibility and applicability of dynamically migrating abstract data types into the architecture of the machine through microprogramming. This migration will be model or program specific as opposed to the practice of migrating commonly used functions or instructions. Migration will be automatic and will be oriented towards the implementation of abstract data types in the user architecture.

This research proposes to decide dynamically which code should be migrated into firmware to provide the best opportunity for increased performance. The unit of migration will be the abstract data type. The programmer will directly influence the migration decision by describing abstract data types and performing the operations provided in the abstract type facility. The migration decision may be affected by such issues as at what lexical level the type is described, how many objects are created of this type, how many times are the operations of the type used, etc. The result will be a system where the types of interest will be the same as the types supported by the computer architecture. The programming architecture now, however, is changed to match the programmer's abstraction rather than the programmer being required to refine further his abstraction or model to gain an efficient implementation.

For a system to provide this type of capability three major questions must be answered.

1) What is the most appropriate method for describing the abstract data type ?

2) How is binding of abstract type to runtime reference to be accomplished in a dynamic manner ?

3) What are the requirements of the micro-machine to support the implementation of this system ?

Each of these areas will be addressed separately below.

Abstract Type Definition

In this area, we must consider what type of notation is most appropriate for describing the encapsulation facility for the abstract data type. Many different languages have provided abstract data type facilities including Modula, Modula-II, Ada, Clu, Alphard, Simula, C, and Mesa. Each of these languages provides a facility for hiding the representation of data from the user and providing controlled access to that data. Each language however, adds its own rules of scope and visibility to provide a slightly unique facility. The first stage of the research then is to determine what requirements must be provided by the data abstraction language. If no existing language exists which can be enhanced to provide these capabilities, then a new language facility must be described.

Kurki-Suonio in [18] proposed a method for using microcode to include abstract data types in the architecture of a computer. In his research, he concentrated mainly on defining a machine independent language which could be used to "bootstrap" a higher-level language, that language again being used to add the next higher-level language and so on. This technique results in new primitive data types rather than abstract model oriented data types. An excellent use could be made of this language, known as Lukko, for the output from the abstract data type

specification language compiler to support machine independence.

Gligor in [19] investigated architectural implications of what the implementation of abstract data types would require. This work has brought to light the problem of protection in automatic migration of encapsulated code.

The study of data abstraction itself also greatly influences this research and a study of current notations for representations of abstract types in programming languages was required. The following languages support abstract typing facilities and are summarized in the accompanying works: Clu [20], Alphard [21], Simula [22], Ada [23], C [24], Modula [25], Modula-II [26], and Mesa [27].

In addition to the language specific research being accomplished, other researchers have been investigating techniques for specifying, implementing, and testing abstract type facilities. The major works in this area are: Gannon [28], Thatcher [29], Jones [30], and Herlihy [31].

Binding

Binding is the process of linking a reference to the object named. In this context we are required to bind an abstract operation to the code to perform that operation as well as binding an object name to the object that is named. In the proposed system, binding of names to objects must be homogeneous without regard for the level, macrostore or microstore, at which the encapsulated code is implemented. Further the binding of operation names to actual code must be dynamic to allow for both microcoded and macrocoded implementations of an abstract type to exist. Furthermore, a method must be described for handling the effects that changes in scope may have on a particular program as well as managing a changing microstore.

Machine Requirements

The machine which supports this system will be required to provide a certain degree of flexibility which is not common in microprogrammable architectures today. This system can be implemented on current microcode architectures, but efficiency may suffer. These machine requirements will outline both optional and mandatory requirements for supporting this environment. Examples of what must be studied include microstore management techniques, sharing of control store, and protection of programs and users both in the microstore and macrostore. Research is currently being done in this area with regard to migration of operating system primitives and is reported in [32] and [33]. Results in these studies can be applied to the migration of abstract types as well.

An Example: Stack Migration Using Abstract Data Types

In this example a simple stack structure is being migrated into the firmware. The language used is C (without the class structure [24]). The representation of the stack is as a structure containing a top-of-stack pointer and an array of integers. The two stack operators, push and pop, are provided which accept the address of the stack to be used and in the case of push, the item to be placed on the stack. Pop returns the popped item through the normal C return mechanism. The code for the stack manipulation program is shown in figure 1. Figure 2 illustrates the simulation of the stack abstract data type.

The next step was to produce a microcoded version of the stack package. This version was produced by manually simulating the migration algorithm using the assembly language produced by the compiler as a base. Subsequent to this preliminary study, we have completed an automated migration package and are experimenting with other abstract types. In our migration package we are using the machine language version of the program as a basis for our migration algorithm.

Due to previous research at Vanderbilt, we had available a set of microprogramming tools which aided in the migration. A micro-assembler and micro-loader as documented in [34] were used for the language translator and micro-image builder. In order to provide for program dependent architectural redefinition, we exploited the capabilities of the virtualized writable control store on the Perkin-Elmer 3220 under UNIX* as described in [35].

The results of our initial studies for the stack example are shown in table 1. In the table the column "number of trials" refers to the actual number of pop and push operations. The columns labeled "stack" and "stackw" represent the time in execution for the non-microcoded and microcoded versions, respectively. Note that these times are for the entire iteration which includes macrocode for the for statement as well as the microcode entry instruction and the actual microcoded operation. The final column represents

*UNIX is a Trademark of Bell Laboratories.

the resulting percentage improvement. All times are reported in seconds. The clock granularity is 20 milliseconds and the resulting run times are reported using this clock. The results for runs less than 250 trials were sporadic due to this large clock granularity and therefore are not shown. Table 2 shows the size in bytes of the resulting programs. It is interesting to note that the execution size of the microcoded version is 146 bytes less than the macrocoded version. Thus, 146 bytes of macrocode became 648 bytes of microcode. This result is close to the expected four to one expansion ratio as described in [36] when migrating functions into microcode from macrocode.

Research Outline

The research being carried out is addressing the following questions.

1) What is the best notation to use for describing abstract data types with a target of microprogrammed implementation ?

2) What are the characteristics of a microprogrammed architecture which are necessary for an implementation of the above system ?

3) What performance improvement should be expected ?

4) How much more reliable is the software ?

5) What is the best algorithm for determining which types should be migrated and which types should not, assuming that microstore contention arises ?

6) How will compiler complexity change ?

7) When and how should the actual binding occur ?

8) To what degree is protection compromised in such a system ?

These questions form a general outline for a research effort which will eventually lead to a complete system for abstraction oriented migration. In the initial efforts we will be concentrating on the performance evaluation aspects of the research. Our stack migration study shows that there is potential for performance improvement and we feel that through exploitation of the inherent facilities of block-structured programming languages and work being done on global and local microcode compaction we can achieve significant performance improvement ratios as compared to the effort expended for manual migration.

Within these studies, we expect our greatest performance improvement to come on systems where no cache memory is available. In these systems, migrated code will in effect serve as cache for those operations which are included in the abstract type which has been migrated. In addition to the cache-like aspects, we feel that through global and local compaction such as in [37] and [38] we can achieve an even greater performance improvement. This improvement will come in the later stages of the research when we generate microcode from the intermediate code rather than the machine language program. The current programs generate code from the linked machine language and consequently the intent of the program has been obscured by the machine language architecture by this time. This restricts the opportunities for compaction as well as for initial optimization efforts using typical compiler optimization techniques. For machines with cache, we feel that the compaction opportunities will also enhance their performance as well as the improvement through decreasing instruction fetch overhead, even though this is not as great an opportunity as in systems without cache.

Since most microstores are relatively small in comparison to main memory we anticipate that not all abstract data types can be simultaneously in microstore. As part of our early research, we will investigate ways to manage the microstore with respect to what types to migrate. Several approaches are currently being considered. One of these approaches is to migrate as many types as possible with the most global types being of higher priority. Another and more interesting approach is to recognize that the execution environment of a program changes with time. In other words as a program changes from one scope to another the types of interest will possibly change as defined by the semantics of the programming language. For this reason the microstore may also change as each scope changes. Possibly a technique employing both of these methods will prove to be best.

Research Tools

Our current work is oriented to building a model which can be used to simulate different migration techniques. The model is being built on the Perkin-Elmer 3220 under UNIX. As part of the model we have implemented a facility which is used to instrument programs and which determines the characteristics of basic blocks such as number of instruction fetches, number and types of instructions, and general program flow. This facility

produces a flow-graph for a program which is later used in test runs to determine the control flow as well as the number of block uses for a particular data set. The block description is then merged with known parameters such as number of microinstructions needed in the current machine emulator to implement the instruction to form a complete description of the program. This then serves as the basis for performance improvement estimation through parameters including cache size, microcode compaction/expansion factor, and microstore/main memory speed ratios.

We have completed the first phase of the language translation portion of our research. This effort has produced a program which drives a series of data collection steps which prepares a C program for automated migration into microstore. The first step is to compile the target C code and to capture the generated assembly code. This code is then analyzed and labels inserted which indicate control points as well as address constants used for switch statements. The next step is to compile and link all of the code required for the program to run including C libraries. The final step is to examine this machine language program and to generate both the microcode and the microcode entry instructions for the operations to be migrated.

Two factors in this method are of note. First, the linked machine language code is used as the basis for our migration for simplicity. We found that it is much easier to migrate code one level, machine language to microcode, than it is to migrate across several levels, C to microcode or assembler to microcode. This technique resulted in a fast implementation of this facility. Second, we decided to provide both for macrocode to microcode and microcode to macrocode branching. In this way a facility to be migrated can fully utilize the system facilities provided at higher levels such as operating system calls and still return to microstore for the remainder of the migrated routine.

As just mentioned, we have completed the first phase of our migration facility but anticipate improving our generated code performance by the following three steps. The first effort will be to base our migrated code on the intermediate code as suggested by Rauscher [13]. The second step will be to utilize typical compiler optimization techniques on the intermediate code before creating our generated code. Finally, we will attempt to migrate as many data structures into the microstore as possible; for example, temporary variables can be allocated to microregisters. These steps will provide better migrated code. In combination with the choice of the correct types to migrate, we feel that a favorable performance improvement can be achieved with a small overhead in performing the migration.

An Aside

In our investigation of computer architectures, we have rediscovered, as many have, the fact that it is very difficult to describe the correct architecture for a machine. In other words, it is difficult, if not impossible, to find the correct set of primitive data types and operations which will support the set of all applications which can be run on a particular computer system. Some designers feel that it is necessary to find only a small set of primitives and let the compiler designer implement the set of more complex types and operations as required by the applications. Others feel that without the support of complex instructions such as are implemented on many modern architectures, many programs will not perform as well as possible and may in fact not even be efficiently implementable on today's computers. This debate has been described as the RISC/CISC, reduced-instruction set computer/complex-instruction set computer, controversy and can be seen in two of the initial articles [39] and [40]. We feel that the proposed abstraction-oriented migration techniques provides the facilities of both of these classes of machines. This could be viewed as an alternative approach to an adaptive machine as described in [41].

Need for This Research

The result of this study can be a significant step in closing the gap between programmers, languages, and architectures. The works mentioned above have not, nor were they intended to, close this gap; but to address symptoms of it. The combination of these techniques into a single coherent facility can significantly narrow this gap. This gap also is evident in other levels of a layered hierarchical system and can be narrowed in these areas through proper encapsulation of system types such as processes, messages, etc.

This approach is not a revolutionary change but an evolutionary one. It seeks to combine successful programming methodologies with a proven architectural feature to provide a model-specific runtime environment. The system is flexible in that it allows the programmer himself to make architectural decisions which affect the runtime environment of his program. An intuitive notion leads us to believe that if a programmer took the time and trouble to describe an abstract or

user defined type then the objects of that type must be of some importance. This approach simply seeks to take that intuitive feel one step further and to realize in the machine architecture the model which the programmer wants to simulate. The result will be a model oriented architecture which is tuned for a specific application rather than a model which has been made to fit an already established inflexible architecture.

References

1. D. L. Parnas, "On the Criteria to be Used in Decomposing Systems into Modules," Communications of the ACM Vol. 15(12), pp.1053-1058 (December 1972).

2. E. W. Dijkstra, A Discipline of Programming, Prentice-Hall, Englewood Cliffs, New Jersey (1976).

3. N. Wirth, Algorithms + Data Structures = Programs, Prentice-Hall, Englewood Cliffs, New Jersey (1976).

4. J. J. Horning, "Some Desirable Properties of Data Abstraction Facilities," ACM SIGPLAN Notices Vol. 8(2), pp.60-63, Proceedings of Conference on Data: Abstraction, Definition, and Structure (March 1976).

5. J. A. Stankovic, "The Types and Interactions of Vertical Migrations of Functions In A Multilevel Interpretive System," IEEE Transactions on Computers Vol. C-30(7), pp.505-513 (July 1981).

6. J. A. Stankovic, Structured Systems and Their Performance Improvement through Vertical Migration, UMI Research Press (1982).

7. J. A. Stankovic, "Good System Structure Features: Their Complexity and Execution Time Cost," IEEE Transactions on Software Engineering Vol. SE-8(4), pp.306-318 (July 1982).

8. J. Stockenberg and A. van Dam, "Vertical Migration for Performance Enhancement in Layered Hardware/Firmware/Software Systems," IEEE Computer Vol. 11(5), pp.35-50 (May 1978).

9. A. B. Tucker and M. J. Flynn, "Dynamic Microprogramming: Processor Organization and Programming," Communications of the ACM Vol. 14(4), pp.240-250 (April 1971).

10. P. F. Wilk and G. M. Bull, "A Strategy, Method, and Set of Tools For A User, Dynamic Microprogramming Environment," pp. 54-61 in Systems Architecture: Proceedings of the Sixth ACM European Regional Conference, Westbury House, Surrey, England (1981).

11. W. A. Wulf, "Reliable Hardware-Software Architecture," ACM SIGPLAN Notices Vol. 10(6), pp.122-130, Proceedings International Conference on Reliable Software (June 1975).

12. H. G. Baker and C. Parker, "High Level Language Programs Run Ten Times Faster in Microstore," ACM SIGMICRO Newsletter Vol. 11(3&4), pp.171-173, MICRO-13 Proceedings Thirteenth Annual Workshop on Microprogramming (September-December 1980).

13. T. G. Rauscher and A. K. Agrawala, "Dynamic Problem-Oriented Redefinition of Computer Architecture via Microprogramming," IEEE Transactions on Computers Vol. C-27(11), pp.1006-1014 (November 1978).

14. G. Chroust and J. R. Muhlbacher, Firmware, Microprogramming, and Restructurable Hardware, Elsevier North-Holland, New York, New York (May 1980).

15. B. Holtkamp and H. Kaestner, "A Firmware Monitor To Support Vertical Migration Decisions In the Unix Operating System," ACM SIGMICRO Newsletter Vol. 13(4), pp.153-162, MICRO-15 Proceedings Fifteenth Annual Workshop on Microprogramming (December 1982).

16. A. M. Abd-Alla and D. C. Karlgaard, "Heuristic Synthesis of Microprogrammed Computer Architecture," IEEE Transactions on Computers Vol. C-23, pp.802-807 (1974).

17. K. A. El-Ayat and J. A. Howard, "Algoritms for a Self-tuning Microprogrammed Computer," ACM SIGMICRO Newsletter Vol. 8(3), pp.85-91, MICRO-10 Proceedings Tenth Annual Workshop On Microprogramming.

18. R. Kurki-Suonio and J. Heinanen, "A Data Abstraction Language Based on Microprogramming," ACM SIGMICRO Newsletter Vol. 11(3&4), pp.154-161, MICRO-13 Proceedings Thirteenth Annual Workshop on Microprogramming (September-December 1980).

19. V. D. Gligor, "Architectural Implications of Abstract Data Type Implementation," ACM SIGARCH Computer Architecture News Vol. 7(6), pp.20-30, Proceedings Sixth Annual Symposium on Computer Architecture (1979).

20. B. Liskov, et. al., CLU Reference Manual, Springer-Verlag, Berlin (1981). Computer Science Lecture Series No. 114

21. M. Shaw, ALPHARD: Form and Content, Springer-Verlag, New York, New York (1981).

22. M. Ohlin, The CLASS and Pointer Concepts in SIMULA, Swedish Research Institute of National Defense, Stockholm Sweden (31 July 1975). C10045-M3(E5)

23. J. Ichbiah, "Rationale for the Design of the Ada Programming Language," ACM SIGPLAN Notices Vol. 14(6) (June 1979).

24. B. Stroustrup, "Classes: An Abstract Data Type Facility for the C Language," ACM SIGPLAN Notices Vol. 17(1), pp.42-51 (January 1982).

25. N. Wirth, "Modula: A Language for Modular Multiprogramming," Software - Practice and Experience Vol. 7(1), pp.3-35 (January 1977).

26. N. Wirth, Modula-2, Institut fur Informatik ETH, Zurich, Switzerland (December 1980). Nr. 36

27. C. M. Geschke, et. al., "Early Experience with Mesa," Communications of the ACM Vol. 20(8), pp.540-552 (August 1977).

28. J. Gannon, et. al., "Data-Abstraction Implementation, Specification, and Testing," ACM Transactions on Programming Languages and Systems Vol. 3(3), pp.211-223 (July 1981).

29. J. W. Thatcher, et. al., "Data Type Specification: Parameterization and the Power of Specification Techniques.," ACM Transactions on Programming Languages and Systems Vol. 4(4), pp.711-732 (October 1982).

30. A. K. Jones and B. H. Liskov, "A Language Extension for Controlling Access to Shared Data," IEEE Transactions on Software Engineering Vol. SE-2(4), pp.277-285 (December 1976).

31. M. Herlihy and B. Liskov, "A Value Transmission Method for Abstract Data Types," ACM Transactions on Programming Languages and Systems Vol. 4(4), pp.527-551 (October 1982).

32. M. Maekawa, et. al., "Firmware Structure and Architectural Support for Monitors, Vertical Migration and User Microprogramming," ACM SIGARCH Computer Architecture News Vol. 10(2), Proceedings Symposium on Architectural Support for Programming Languages and Operating Systems.

33. N. Kambiyashi, et. al., "Heart: An Operating System Nucleus Machine Implemented by Firmware," ACM SIGARCH Computer Architecture News Vol. 10(2), pp.194-204, Proceedings Symposium on Architectural Support for Programming Languages and Operating Systems (March 1982).

34. J. E. Roskos and R. I. Winner, "Toward User Sharing of the Microprogramming Level Under UNIX on the Perkin-Elmer 3220," ACM SIGMICRO Newsletter Vol. 12(4), pp.67-73, MICRO-14 Proceedings Fourteenth Annual Workshop on Microprogramming (December 1981).

35. R. I. Winner and L. B. Reed, An Overview of Sharing the Control Store Under UNIX, Submitted to SOFTWARE: Practice and Experience, August 1983.

36. A. G. Olbert, "Crossing the Machine Interface," ACM SIGMICRO Newsletter Vol. 13(4), pp.163-170, MICRO-15 Proceedings Fifteenth Annual Workshop on Microprogramming (December 1982).

37. A. Nicolau and J. Fisher, "Using an Oracle to Measure Potential Parallelism in Single Instruction Stream Programs," ACM SIGMICRO Newsletter Vol. 12(4), pp.171-182, MICRO-14 Proceedings Fourteenth Annual Workshop on Microprogramming (December 1981).

38. J. F. Martinez-Carballido and V. M. Powers, "General Microprogram Width Reduction Using Generator Sets," ACM SIGMICRO Newsletter Vol. 12(4), pp.144-153, MICRO-14 Proceedings Fourteenth Annual Workshop on Microprogramming (December 1981).

39. D. A. Patterson and D. R. Ditzel, "The Case for the Reduced Instruction Set Computer," ACM SIGARCH Computer Architecture News Vol. 8(6), pp.25-33 (October, 1980).

40. D. W. Clark and W. D. Strecker, "Comments on 'The Case for the Reduced Instruction Set Computer'," ACM SIGARCH Computer Architecture News Vol. 8(6), pp.34-38 (October, 1980).

41. R. I. Winner, "Adaptive Instruction Sets and Instruction Set Locality Phenomena," in Proceedings of IEEE International Workshop on Computer Systems Organization (March 1983).

```
#include <sys/types.h>
#include <sys/timeb.h>
struct stack {
                int top;
                int data[10];
                };
struct stack s1;
main(argc,argv)
int argc;
char **argv;
{
     int i;
     int secs;
     int millisecs;
     int num;
     struct timeb tbstart;
     struct timeb tbstop;
     int pop();
     int push();

   /* Set the number of trials */
     if (argc == 1)
             num = 100;
     else
             num = atoi(argv[1]);

   /* Get the starting time */
     ftime(&tbstart);

   /* Perform the number of calls required */
     for (i=0;i<num;i++)   {
             push(&s1,i);
             pop(&s1);
     }

   /* Get the completion time */
     ftime(&tbstop);

   /* Calculate the resulting times */
     secs = tbstop.time-tbstart.time;
     if (tbstop.millitm >= tbstart.millitm)
             millisecs = tbstop.millitm - tbstart.millitm;
     else {
             secs--;
             millisecs = (tbstop.millitm+1000) - tbstart.millitm;
     }
     printf("Time for %d trials is %d seconds + %d milliseconds\n",
             num,secs,millisecs);
```

figure 1. C Main Program

```
push(where,who)
struct stack *where;
int who;
{
        if ((where->top < 10) && (where->top > -1))
                where->data[where->top++] = who;
}

pop(where)
struct stack *where;
{
        if ((where->top > 0) && (where->top < 11))
                return(where->data[--where->top]);
}
```

figure 2. Abstract Data Type Stack

table 1. Execution Comparison

number of trials	stack (secs)	stackw (secs)	(stack-stackw)/stack
250	.032	.027	.156
1000	.114	.094	.175
2500	.285	.229	.196
5000	.580	.447	.229
10000	1.160	.900	.224
50000	5.760	4.500	.219
100000	11.520	8.987	.220
500000	57.593	44.900	.220
1000000	115.233	89.827	.220
2500000	288.007	224.540	.220
5000000	575.953	449.080	.220
10000000	1151.900	898.140	.220
100000000	11516.700	8980.980	.220

table 2. Size Comparison

program name	stored size	execution size
stack	6912	6500
stackw	6648	6344

IMPROVING THE PERFORMANCE OF UCSD PASCAL VIA MICROPROGRAMMING ON THE PDP-11/60

MARK T. SCHAEFER and YALE N. PATT

Computer Science Department
San Francisco State University

ABSTRACT

UCSD Pascal is implemented as a machine-independent virtual machine. This virtual machine is usually interpreted on a host computer by machine language instructions, which, in turn, are often interpreted by microcode. Performance of a virtual machine is generally a function of the number of levels of interpretation required to perform a computation. By bypassing one or more of these layers, it should be possible to enhance performance.

To test this hypothesis, a Pascal interpreter was written for the PDP-11/60. After analysis of the Pascal machine, changes were made that interpreted selected portions of the virtual machine directly in microcode.

This paper describes the microcode which was added, and discusses the improvements which resulted.

1.0 INTRODUCTION

One scheme for the translation and execution of Pascal language programs is shown in Figure 1. Initially Pascal language source code is translated by a compiler into **pseudo-instructions** or **pseudo-code (p-code)** for a pseudo-machine (**p-machine**). Next, the p-code is interpreted by the machine language of a **host** computer. The machine code is, in, turn interpreted by microcode. Finally, the microcode causes the hardware to perform the desired computation.

The generation of pseudo-code has the advantage that it is not hardware specific. Writing an interpreter for a given host machine is generally easier than rewriting or modifying the compiler to generate machine code for that machine. Thus, a p-code compiler is machine independent and relatively portable. Both are highly desirable qualities. However, interpretation of p-code on the host computer is usually inefficient, unless the host computer is designed specifically to implement the pseudo-machine architecture.

Three schemes for the execution of Pascal pseudo-code are shown in Figure 2. A circle (o)

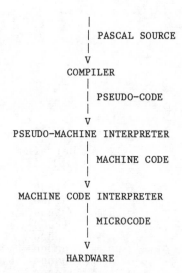

FIGURE 1 - A Layered Scheme for the Execution of Pascal

at a particular junction signifies a translation step. A star (*) indicates a translator input or output. The first scheme is equivalent to that of Figure 1. The second scheme shows a real machine that is built to execute pseudo-code directly in hardware. The cost of this increased efficiency is a more complex host architecture [5]. In the third scheme (see Figure 3 also), pseudo-code is interpreted directly in microcode, bypassing the machine language of the host. This approach, which has been used previously for other hosts [13], is the technique we used in this study.

This paper is divided into six sections. Section 2 describes the implementation. Section 3 delineates the workload which we used to determine where to provide microprogramming enhancements. Section 4 analyzes these workloads. Section 5 enumerates the microprogramming enhancements. Section 6 discusses the results of these enhancements.

© 1983 ACM 0-89791-114-8/83/0010/0140$00.75

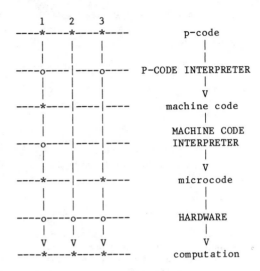

```
    1    2    3
----*----*----*----           p-code
    |    |    |                 |
----o----|----o----    P-CODE INTERPRETER
    |    |    |                 |
    |    |    |                 V
----*----|----|----        machine code
    |    |    |                 |
    |    |    |            MACHINE CODE
    |    |    |             INTERPRETER
----o----|----|----             |
    |    |    |                 |
    |    |    |                 V
----*----|----*----          microcode
    |    |    |                 |
    |    |    |              HARDWARE
    |    |    |                 |
----o----o----o----             |
    |    |    |                 |
    V    V    V                 V
----*----*----*----         computation
```

FIGURE 2 - Three Translation Schemes
for the Execution of P-code

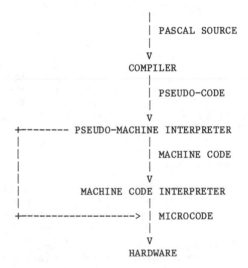

```
                    |
                    | PASCAL SOURCE
                    |
                    V
                COMPILER
                    |
                    | PSEUDO-CODE
                    |
                    V
+-------- PSEUDO-MACHINE INTERPRETER
|                   |
|                   | MACHINE CODE
|                   |
|                   V
|       MACHINE CODE INTERPRETER
|                   |
+------------------->| MICROCODE
                    |
                    V
                HARDWARE
```

FIGURE 3 - A Modified Scheme for the
Execution of Pascal

2.0   IMPLEMENTATION DETAILS

The Resource Sharing Time Sharing Extended operating system (RSTS/E or simply RSTS) is a multi-user timesharing system available on many of the Digital Equipment Corporation (DEC) PDP-11 line of minicomputers [12]. The PDP-11/60 is the only model which supports both RSTS and user microprogramming (with the addition of a special writable control store or WCS). UCSD Pascal is a complete Pascal language based run time and development system based on a pseudo-machine architecture. This system was originally developed under the direction of Professor Kenneth Bowles at the University of California at San Diego (UCSD) and is now maintained and distributed by SofTech Microsystems of San Diego [3,4,9]. The Computer Science Department of San Francisco State University (SFSU) has a WCS equipped PDP-11/60 running under RSTS.

2.1   Steps In Implementation

The 11/60 microprogramming tools [10] were transported from RSX-11 to RSTS. Meanwhile, a completely new Pascal interpreter was written for the RSTS environment. While based on the original UCSD Pascal interpreter for the PDP-11, it was completely rewritten. Five Pascal programs were established to serve as benchmarks to evaluate the pseudo-machine and establish a performance baseline. The interpreter was modified and a set of software tools developed to measure and report dynamic (run time) instruction frequencies. The results of this analysis were applied by writing microcode for the 11/60 to "assist" the Pascal interpreter. The interpreter was then modified to interface with the microcode. The benchmark programs were run again to measure any changes in performance.

2.2   The UCSD Pascal Pseudo-machine

The UCSD pseudo-machine is based on the Zurich P-2 pseudo-machine [8]. It is a stack-oriented machine consisting of a set of registers, a memory (which is partitioned into a stack and a heap), and a set of executable instructions. A word of memory is 16 bits in length. The total possible memory available with this scheme is 32768 words (32KW) though somewhat less is usually available to the user.

A detailed description of the pseudo-machine is available in [16]. The remainder of this document assumes that the reader is familiar with this description. All future references to the "p-machine" refer to the UCSD Pascal version II.0 pseudo-machine.

2.3   The Interpreter

The interpreter simulates the pseudo-machine. It is implemented as a RSTS **run-time system** (RTS). The RTS is read-only and is sharable. It is mapped into the last 4KW of each user's virtual address space and is swapped separately from the user job image.

All future references to "the interpreter" refer to the RSTS-based interpreter written for this project.

2.4   The PDP-11/60 Microarchitecture

The PDP-11/60 is a user microprogrammable computer. The base machine (PDP-11) architecture is implemented by microcode in 2560 words of read-only control store. In addition, there are 1024 words of writable control store. All words are 48 bits in length.

The data path is composed of three sets of "scratchpad" registers (ASP,BSP, and CSP), an ALU, an ALU result register , a shift register , a shift tree, and a bus address register. There is a rewrite path from the ALU result register back to the A and B scratchpads. These two scratchpads contain the base machine general registers, floating point accumulators, and other working registers. The C scratchpad contains constants required by the base machine.

One microcycle requires approximately 170 nanoseconds. Data can be read from the scratchpads, operated on by the ALU, and rewritten to the scratchpads in one microcycle. Memory data is read into a special register in the C scratchpad. It is written to memory from the ALU result register. A memory read takes two microcycles if the data is found in the cache. Otherwise, a delay of 1.1 microseconds (typical) is required while the data is fetched from main memory.

Locations in the writable control store are entered as the result of a special group of PDP-11 instructions reserved for this purpose. These are known as extended function code (XFC) instructions. Further information on the PDP-11/60 microarchitecture may be found in [11].

Given the limited size of WCS, only a portion of the p-machine can be in microcode. Note that the PDP-11 "base machine" microcode remains in read-only control store. Portions of the p-machine not directly in microcode continue to be simulated by sequences of base machine instructions. Thus, direct emulation of the p-machine in microcode is interspersed with simulation by PDP-11 machine language sequences.

3.0 THE WORKLOAD

In this study we are especially interested in the "university computer science" environment. We place primary importance upon the process of compilation, since student programs are repeatedly compiled during development. Second, we are interested in evaluating non-numeric computational performance.

Five sample programs were used in order to evaluate the p-machine. These sample workloads range from an artificial benchmark to test simple control and arithmetic functions to a somewhat exotic program to build a parse table for a grammar. All but one of these programs was based on its relevance to the "university computer science" environment. The five programs are described below.

3.1 Artificial Benchmark I

This program (see Figure 4) consists of nested FOR loops, a single conditional statement, and a single integer arithmetic operation. The FOR loops have been adjusted through trial and error to yield a run time of about 100 seconds on the 11/60 without any microcode assist. After

FIGURE 4 - Artificial Benchmark I

```
program AB_I;

var     I,J,K,INDEX    : integer;

begin
   for I := 1 to 20 do
      begin
         for J := 1 to 6 do
            for K := 1 to 6250 do
               if K <> I then
                  INDEX := INDEX + 1;
         write('.');
      end;
end.
```

every iteration through the two inner loops, a brief message is printed out. However, the program remains highly compute bound. This program consists primarily of one-word loads and stores, integer compares, jumps, and integer addition. These operations are extremely common in most applications. It is useful for evaluating performance enhancements to basic control operations.

3.2 Quicksort (recursive)

This program generates and sorts 5000 integers using a recursive quicksort algorithm. The algorithm is that of Wirth [17]. This benchmark tests general integer manipulation, array access, and control functions.

3.3 Modified Whetstone

The authors of this artificial benchmark claim that it is an accurate model of scientific computation [7]. The original benchmark was modified to eliminate several features not

available in UCSD Pascal or in the interpreter. (For example, trigonometric functions are not currently implemented in our interpreter). Because of this it is difficult to compare our results with benchmark results from other systems. However, it is still useful for evaluating the effects of certain performance enhancements on general scientific computing.

3.4 Compilation (2411 Lines)

This benchmark consists of compiling a large system program (SYSTEM.FILER). It represents a comprehensive test of non-numeric computation in general, and compilation in particular.

3.5 Parse Table Generator

This program generates an SLR parse table. The method used is that described by Aho and Ullman [2]. Input was a grammar for a simple, Pascal-like language used in a graduate compiler course at SFSU [15]. Again, this benchmark is a test of non-numeric computation.

4.0 MEASUREMENT AND ANALYSIS OF THE WORKLOAD

In order to decide which features to enhance with microcode, it was necessary to first measure and analyze the workload described in section 3. Cook [6] and Tannenbaum [14] have performed static analysis of university environment software. In addition to studying their data, we also wished to study the dynamic frequency and accumulated execution times of the byte codes executed by our five benchmarks. In the case of dynamic frequencies, our measuring system allowed us to obtain accurate counts. In the case of byte code execution times, our measuring system was inadequate. In this case, we performed a crude paper analysis.

4.1 Dynamic Frequency Of Byte Codes

Static analysis of source programs is insufficient to predict the run time nature of Pascal programs. This information must be obtained from measurement of **dynamic** byte code frequencies for a set of benchmarks. The interpreter was modified to do this.

The results of this analysis are now discussed in the context of individual benchmarks. Table 1 combines the results for all benchmarks in order to facilitate comparison.

4.1.1 Artificial Benchmark I

Table 1 shows the results for Artificial Benchmark I. Over 41% of the byte codes perform global one-word loads and stores. Nearly 12% of byte codes are constant loads (almost exclusively the number 1). Jumps and integer addition each comprise 11.8% of byte codes. The remaining byte codes are divided evenly between one word local loads and a conditional test (<=). Putting local and global loads and stores, jumps, and conditional testing directly into microcode should increase the execution speed of this program.

4.1.2 Quicksort (recursive)

Analysis of the Quicksort benchmark shows a similar distribution pattern with a few additions. The random numbers are stored in an array. Each array access consists of a load of the array base address (LAO), a load of the array bound limits, a check of the array bounds (CHK), and computation of the index (IXA). The actual array access requires the addition of the base address to the index. This is accomplished by the indirect load and store byte codes (SINDxx,IND,STO). Array related byte codes comprise some 30% of total byte codes. Placing these array related operations into microcode should increase the speed of this sort.

4.1.3 Modified Whetstone

Analysis of the Whetstone benchmark shows a slightly different pattern. Thirty-four percent of byte codes are still loading either constants or global or local variables. However, a more varied and even distribution of the remaining byte codes reflects the more realistic nature of this program. Over 15% of the byte codes load and store multiple words (LDM,STM,LDC). These byte codes are used to manipulate real values (which are two words in length). Eleven percent of the byte codes load address pointers (LLA,LAO). These are required both for the manipulation of real numbers and arrays. The importance of the constant 1 can be seen from the frequency of SLDC1 (13.2%). The importance of addition, subtraction, and multiplication (integer and real) are clear (SBI,ADR,ADI,MPR,MPI - 14%). The high frequency of integer subtraction (SBI) is something of an anomaly at 6%. Note that procedure calls and returns become significant for the first time at a frequency of 2.4%.

4.1.4 Compilation (2411 Lines)

Clearly the compilation of 2411 source lines is the most realistic benchmark yet discussed. The variety and distribution of byte codes is greatly increased over previous benchmarks. Nearly fifty percent of byte codes are constant loads (SLDCxx - 15.2%), global loads and stores (SLDOxx,LDO,SRO - 22.6%), or local loads and stores (SLDLxx,LDL,STL - 11.2%). The constants 0, 1, 13, and 47 are very important. Conditional testing and branching byte codes (EQUI,NEQI,FJP,UJP) comprise some 20% of byte codes. Note that testing for equality exceeds testing for inequality; the two combined far exceed the frequency of the next most common test byte code (LEQI - 0.5%). Integer addition (ADI - 3.2%) is by far the most common operator, followed by set inclusion (INN - 1.1%). Procedure calls and returns (CALLxx,RNP - 4.7%) are even more prominent than in the previous benchmark. Load global and local address byte codes (LAO,LLA - 2.5%) are not insignificant. The importance of set operations is underscored by the frequency of the load multiple word byte code (LDM - 1.1%); there is no real arithmetic performed by the compiler. Finally, note the presence of two byte codes of no significance in any of the previous benchmarks. These are the load byte (LDB - 3.4%) and case jump (XJP - 1.1%) byte codes. The load byte byte code is important in the scanner as it examines successive input characters. The frequency distribution of the compilation benchmark agrees very closely with the static analysis of Pascal source programs cited earlier.

4.1.5 Parse Table Generator

Almost half the byte codes (46.1%) for this benchmark are local or global loads and stores or constant loads. However, in a departure from

TABLE 1 - Byte Code Frequencies of the 5 Benchmarks (percent)
(Cumulative SLDL,SLDO,SIND only. Frequencies < 1.0%
not included.)

| | | | BENCHMARK | | | |
NAME	DESCRIPTION	COMPILE	SLR	WHET	SORT	AB1
SLDCxx	SHORT LOAD CONSTANT WORD (TOTAL)	15.2	15.1	19.9	14.9	11.8
SLDOxx	SHORT LOAD GLOBAL WORD (TOTAL)	14.8	1.9	–	–	29.4
FJP	JUMP ON FALSE	9.6	7.1	2.7	5.3	11.8
SLDLxx	SHORT LOAD LOCAL WORD (TOTAL)	8.8	17.9	3.4	18.6	5.9
EQUI	INTEGER TEST EQUALITY	5.7	1.5	–	–	–
SRO	STORE GLOBAL WORD	5.4	–	3.0	–	11.8
SLDC1	SHORT LOAD CONSTANT 1	4.8	3.1	13.2	3.1	11.8
UJP	UNCONDITIONAL JUMP	3.8	3.1	2.6	1.3	5.9
LDB	LOAD BYTE	3.4	–	–	–	–
ADI	ADD INTEGER	3.2	2.7	2.3	2.3	11.8
SLDC0	SHORT LOAD CONSTANT 0	2.4	9.0	–	10.7	–
STL	STORE LOCAL WORD	2.4	4.3	–	4.3	–
LDO	LOAD GLOBAL WORD	2.4	1.3	10.8	1.5	–
CALLxx	CALL PROCEDURE (TOTAL)	2.4	–	1.2	–	–
RNP	RETURN FROM NON-BASE PROCEDURE	2.3	–	1.2	–	–
SINDxx	SHORT LOAD INDEXED WORD (TOTAL)	1.9	4.9	–	4.9	–
SLDC4	SHORT LOAD CONSTANT 4	1.5	–	5.2	–	–
LAO	LOAD GLOBAL ADDRESS	1.3	6.5	5.6	6.9	–
LDCN	LOAD CONSTANT NIL	1.3	–	–	–	–
NEQI	INTEGER TEST INEQUALITY	1.3	–	–	–	5.9
LLA	LOAD LOCAL ADDRESS	1.2	–	–	–	–
SLDC47	SHORT LOAD CONSTANT 47	1.2	–	–	–	–
CXP	CALL EXTERNAL PROCEDURE	1.1	–	–	–	–
LDM	LOAD MULTIPLE WORDS	1.1	–	8.4	–	–
XJP	CASE JUMP	1.1	–	–	–	–
INN	SET INCLUSION	1.1	–	–	–	–
SLDC13	SHORT LOAD CONSTANT 13	1.1	–	–	–	–
CHK	CHECK ARRAY BOUNDS	–	7.6	4.8	10.7	–
IXA	INDEX ARRAY	–	7.4	4.8	7.0	–
LDCI	LOAD INTEGER CONSTANT	–	5.6	–	10.9	–
LEQI	INTEGER TEST LESS THAN OR EQUAL	–	2.6	1.7	1.2	5.9
LAND	LOGICAL AND	–	2.3	–	–	–
LNOT	LOGICAL COMPLEMENT	–	1.9	–	–	–
EQU	COMPLEX COMPARE EQUALITY	–	1.1	–	–	–
SBI	SUBTRACT INTEGER	–	–	6.0	1.4	–
STM	STORE MULTIPLE WORDS	–	–	4.3	–	–
ADR	ADD REAL	–	–	2.8	–	–
LDC	LOAD MULTIPLE WORD CONSTANT	–	–	2.5	–	–
MPR	MULTIPLY REAL	–	–	1.7	–	–
MPI	MULTIPLY INTEGER	–	–	1.2	–	–
LESI	INTEGER TEST LESS THAN	–	–	–	3.2	–
STO	STORE INDIRECT WORD	–	–	–	2.1	–

previous benchmarks, local loads and stores (SLDLxx,STL - 22.2%) are much more common than equivalent global operations (SLDOxx,LDO - 3.2%). The program is atypical in several other respects as well. Array accessing is very important as can be seen from the frequency of array related byte codes (CHK,IXA,LAO,SINDxx - 26.4%). The most common test operation is not for equality or inequality (EQUI,NEQI - 1.9%) but rather the less than or equal test (LEQI - 2.6%). It is not clear whether this reflects the importance of FOR loops or explicit comparisons. Procedure calls account for only 0.3% of all byte codes. Set operators are virtually non-existent (<0.1%). Integer addition and logical operations are of slightly greater importance than in the compilation benchmark (ADI,LAND,LNOT - 6.9%). This benchmark does not fit the static picture of non-numerical Pascal programs cited earlier. It is not known whether this is the result of an atypical programming style or reflects the underlying algorithms.

4.2 Time Distribution Of Byte Codes

While dynamic byte code distribution statistics are useful and informative, they do not reveal where the processor actually spends most of its time during interpretation. For example, consider the frequency statistics for the compilation of 2411 lines. The most common byte code is the short load constant group (SLDCxx) comprising about 15% of the total. This operation runs very fast, consisting only of a push of the byte code value. The procedure call group (CALLxx) comprises only 2.4% of total byte codes. Building a procedure activation record is much more complex than the short load constant operation, involving many pushes to the stack. Depending on the disparity in execution time between the two byte code groups, the interpreter may actually spend more time performing procedure calls than loading short constants.

A full analysis of the time distribution of byte codes requires specialized hardware support. Such support is not currently available on our machine.

5.0 MICROPROGRAMMING ENHANCEMENTS

As mentioned earlier, there are 1024 words of writable control store on the PDP-11/60. WCS is a limited resource. The interpreter functionality to be placed in microcode must be carefully selected in order to maximize performance improvement. Several approaches were taken.

One enhancement strategy involves placing into microcode a complete byte code operation. Very frequent and/or time consuming operations (such as global loads and stores and procedure calls) are the most obvious candidates.

A second strategy is to microcode only the most time consuming portions of such operations.

For example, instead of microcoding each procedure call byte code, it is probably nearly as effective to code only the building of the activation record common to all call byte codes. Another example would be to microcode the test for set inclusion. This operation is a loop which operates on successive members of each set. Other aspects of the set operation would remain in machine language.

A variation on this strategy is to place into microcode operations which are common to multiple pseudo-machine instructions. The best example is the interpreter fetch cycle. It is the single most common sequence in the interpreter. It requires several machine language instructions and is very time consuming. Operand fetching is another important example of this type. Operands are fetched throughout the interpreter. A block move instruction would also fall into this category. Several multiple-word loads and stores perform this operation.

Certain operations may be designed to "assist" the interpreter or the run-time system. For example, a multiple register save/restore internal to the CPU can simplify numerous interpreter sequences. A block clear of the RSTS I/O parameter blocks would probably improve the performance of certain I/O bound programs.

More than 256 words of microcode were written and debugged. Table 2 shows the function and size of the microcode. Table 3 shows the results of running the five benchmarks with and without the microcode. Note that the best performance improvement occurs with Artificial Benchmark I. This benchmark is running almost totally in microcode. Finally, Table 4 shows the relative sizes of the two interpreters. The microcode displaces over 600 words of the machine language interpreter.

The single most important sequence of microcode is the fetch sequence. The fetch sequence is entered initially via an XFC instruction. The next byte code is fetched. If it is in the range 0 to 127 it is a short load constant (SLDC); the byte code is simply pushed (the value of the operand is implied and is equal to the byte code). Short load constants are easily recognized since the sign bit of the byte code is always 0. Otherwise, the byte code is used as an index into a memory resident dispatch table. The dispatch address can be either a memory address or an address in WCS. Control is then transfered to the proper location. Macro addresses always have a high order bit of 1 since the interpreter resides in the virtual address space 160000(8) to 177777(8). Micro addresses range from 6000(8) to 7777(8). They always have a high order bit of 0 even after being shifted left 3 bits before being placed into the dispatch table (this saves a microinstruction at dispatch time). Byte codes interpreted in machine code terminate with a fetch XFC instruction. Byte codes interpreted in microcode reenter the fetch sequence directly without returning to the base machine. Here the fetch sequence checks whether

TABLE 2 - A Description of the Microcode

NAME	DESCRIPTION	uWORDS DEDICATED/SHARED
	INTERPRETER FETCH SEQUENCE	18/4
	GET UNSIGNED BYTE OPERAND	2/8
	GET WORD OPERAND	2/14
	GET BIG OPERAND	2/21
	GET SIGNED BYTE OPERAND	0/10
	LOAD PCP FROM SCRATCHPAD	1/1
	STORE PCP TO SCRATCHPAD	1/1
	LOAD SGP FROM SCRATCHPAD	1/1
	STORE SGP TO SCRATCHPAD	1/1
	STORE HPP TO SCRATCHPAD	1/1
	LOAD CPU CONSTANTS	8/0
SLDC	SHORT LOAD CONSTANT (ALL)	2/4
LDCN	LOAD CONSTANT NIL	1/6
LDCI	LOAD ONE WORD CONSTANT	1/21
LDL	LOAD LOCAL WORD	2/30
LDO	LOAD GLOBAL WORD	2/30
LLA	LOAD LOCAL ADDRESS	2/29
LAO	LOAD GLOBAL ADDRESS	2/29
STL	STORE LOCAL WORD	2/29
SRO	STORE GLOBAL WORD	2/29
SLDL	SHORT LOAD LOCAL WORD (ALL)	3/8
SLDO	SHORT LOAD GLOBAL WORD (ALL)	2/8
UJP	UNCONDITIONAL JUMP	1/21
FJP	FALSE JUMP	6/21
EFJ	EQUAL FALSE JUMP	7/25
NFJ	NOT EQUAL FALSE JUMP	7/25
EQUI	TEST EQUALITY	7/9
NEQI	TEST INEQUALITY	7/9
LEQI	TEST LESS THAN OR EQUAL	3/15
LESI	TEST LESS THAN	3/15
GEQI	TEST GREATER THAN OR EQUAL	3/15
GRTI	TEST GREATER THAN	3/15
ABI	ABSOLUTE VALUE	7/7
ADI	ADD INTEGER	2/11
NGI	NEGATE INTEGER	3/7
SBI	SUBTRACT INTEGER	3/10
LAND	LOGICAL AND	2/11
LOR	LOGICAL OR	2/11
LNOT	LOGICAL COMPLEMENT	3/7
NOP	NO OPERATION	1/4

TABLE 3 - CPU Time for Five Benchmarks (seconds)

BENCHMARK	NO uCODE	uCODE	GAIN (%)
ARTIFICIAL BENCHMARK I	100.0	55.4	44.6
QUICKSORT (RECURSIVE)	23.5	15.1	35.7
MODIFIED WHETSTONE	17.7	13.7	22.6
COMPILATION (2411 LINES)	45.7	33.5	26.7
PARSE TABLE GENERATOR	76.2	52.2	31.5

TABLE 4 - Interpreter Size (words)

RTS	SIZE
UCSD01.RTS (NO U-CODE)	3188
UUCSD3.RTS (U-CODE)	2500

a service condition exists. If so, it returns to the base machine after reloading the PC with the address of a known fetch XFC. If not, the next byte code is fetched.

The fetch sequence is a good example of a routine that could be more efficient if the 11/60 microarchitecture was less restrictive. The instruction register (IR) is loaded with an XFC when the fetch sequence is entered. Only word aligned requests may be issued to memory if the IR contains this instruction. In order to fetch the next byte code (which is byte aligned), two to three extra microinstructions are required to test for a possible odd address and compute a word aligned address. For the compilation benchmark, 2 extra microinstructions per byte code cost over 1 second of CPU time This is over 2% of the total CPU time.

The operand fetch microcode is also very important. Again, the restriction on memory requests results in needless delays in microcode. Operand fetch subroutines are called directly by byte code routines in microcode. These same subroutines are called by microcode invoked by XFC instructions for use in byte code routines interpreted by machine language.

Since there are more pseudo-registers in the pseudo-machine than available general registers in the PDP-11 base machine, three pseudo-registers are kept in memory by the interpreter. The microcode assisted machine keeps copies of these pseudo-registers in scratchpad registers for fast access by microcode. In order to maintain the consistency of both copies of the pseudo-registers, we implemented in microcode a set of load and store assist instructions. The load PCP instruction moves the current procedure code section pointer from its scratchpad location to one of the general registers (specified by the destination field of the XFC). The store PCP instruction performs the reverse operation. The load and store SGP instructions operate in an analogous fashion with the current segment pointer. It is not known whether the slowdown caused by the use of these instructions is recovered by performance gains in access of these registers by microcode. We expect to eliminate the memory resident copies eventually by placing all byte code routines that access them in microcode.

A potentially important interpreter assist function is performed by register save/restore microcode. These routines move the contents of PDP-11 general registers R2 through R5 to/from a group of scratchpad registers used by the base machine as floating point accumulators. These four general registers normally contain important pseudo-machine context (e.g., R4 is used as the interpreter program counter). By executing the save/restore XFC's any machine language routine (except one that executes a floating point instruction) can use any or all of these registers without the need for additional memory accesses. Note that this microcode has been debugged but was not used in any of the reported benchmark tests.

One other interpreter assist routine is implemented. It is invoked by an XFC. Its function is to load three scratchpad registers reserved for WCS microcode with specific constants. These constants are used in several important routines to save a microword. For example, the fetch sequence assumes the address of the memory resident dispatch table is in one of these registers. The address of a dispatch table entry can be computed in a single word by adding the value of the current byte code (as a sign-extended word offset) to the (constant) table address.

The next group of microcode routines implements all local and global one word loads and stores, including the load address byte codes. This group is extremely important to enhanced performance in almost all environments. Implementation is straightforward.

Two jump byte codes are implemented in microcode. The unconditional jump and false jump (UJP,FJP) byte codes have an average frequency of about 10% of byte codes for all benchmarks.

All of the integer compare byte codes are implemented in microcode. Test equality and test inequality (EQUI,NEQI) are important in almost all programs. Three of the four remaining byte codes are relatively insignificant for most workloads (the exception is LEQI). They could easily be eliminated if space in WCS were not available.

Implementation of the signed comparison byte codes is relatively difficult under the PDP-11 architecture. The condition codes are clocked differently depending on the instruction in the instruction register. Following the initial entry into the interpreter fetch sequence, the IR contains an XFC instruction. However, for the condition codes to be clocked correctly in the case of a signed branch, a PDP-11 compare (CMP) instruction must be loaded into the IR. This is done in a common subroutine. The microbranch is performed based on the state of the condition codes in the processor status word and the contents of the instruction register. The correct PDP-11 branch instruction must therefore be clocked into the instruction register before the microbranch is finally taken. This is all very awkward.

Four integer arithmetic byte codes were placed in microcode. Addition and subtraction were implemented due to their workload frequency. The absolute value and negate byte codes were implemented due to their relative simplicity.

Four logical byte codes (LAND,LOR,LNOT) were implemented, primarily due to their frequency as a group in the compile and parse table benchmarks.

The microcode is written to be sharable just like the interpreter. This implies careful observance of base machine conventions regarding scratchpad usage and the recognition of service conditions.

6.0 DISCUSSION OF RESULTS

6.1 Artificial Benchmark I

This benchmark shows the best performance gain (44.6%). This is not surprising since it is running almost totally in microcode. As such it seems to represent an upper limit for enhancement of "simple" operations in microcode on the 11/60 architecture.

Microprogramming folklore [1] says that a performance enhancement factor of at least 5 is expected from a pseudo-machine microengine. This benchmark shows a disappointing performance improvement of about 2. There are at least four reasons for this. First is the relatively low semantic content of the pseudo-instructions implemented so far. Microcoding of more CPU intensive pseudo-operations should yield a better performance gain. Second, the PDP-11/60 microarchitecture fails to provide several features which are important to efficient implementation of a byte oriented pseudo-architecture. We have already mentioned the problems associated with fetching bytes from memory and performing signed compares. Third, the existence of a hardware cache may affect instruction fetching overhead. In other words, because the interpreter runs part of the time in WCS microcode, fewer macro level instructions are fetched. The cache hit ratio for those portions of the interpreter that remain in machine code is improved over the machine code interpreter. Finally, there is no guarantee that microprogramming folklore is correct. Further work is required to properly test these ideas.

6.2 Quicksort (recursive)

Here again performance improvement is significant (35.7%). It is probable that the CPU spends more time executing the array index byte code (IXA) than any other. Implementing two array specific byte codes in microcode (CHK,IXA) will undoubtedly boost performance to a level close to the artificial benchmark.

6.3 Modified Whetstone

As expected, performance enhancement of this benchmark is the lowest of any benchmark (22.6%). This is due primarily to the frequency of real arithmetic operations (LDM,STM,ADR,MPR,DVR) as well as procedure calling. None of these operations are currently implemented in microcode. Floating point arithmetic is performed by microcode in the base machine.

6.4 Compilation (2411 Lines)

This benchmark shows a 26.7% improvement. The primary source of overhead is procedure calling. Set and character related byte codes (LDM,INN,LDB) also contribute to this overhead.

6.5 Parse Table Generator

This benchmark shows a 31.5% improvement. The increase in performance over the compilation benchmark reflects the reduced importance of procedure calling and set operations, in concert with the increase in arithmetic and logical operations.

6.6 Conclusions

The run time behavior of all benchmarks but one conformed to our expectations based on the work of Cook and Tanne um. Interpretation of pseudo-code directly i. microcode resulted in a significant performance improvement in all benchmarks. However, the degree of improvement was not as high as expected. For this reason, we expect to concentrate our future microcoding effort on operations with a higher semantic content.

REFERENCES

[1] Ahlstrom, J., Personal communication.

[2] Aho, A. and Ullman, J. **Principles of Compiler Design**, Addison-Wesley, Reading, MA, 1978.

[3] Bowles, K. A (nearly) machine independent software system for micro and mini computers. **Byte** 3 5, (Mar. 1978) 46.

[4] Bowles, K. **Microcomputer Problem Solving Using Pascal**, Springer-Verlag, New York, NY, 1977.

[5] Colon Osorio, F., and Patt, Y. RISC and CISC - Two different perspectives to an identical problem. Presented at IEEE CompCon Conference, San Francisco, CA, Spring, 1983.

[6] Cook, R. and Lee, I. A contextual analysis of Pascal programs. **Software Practice and Experience** 12 2, (Feb. 1982) 195-203.

[7] Curnow, H. and Wichmann, B. A synthetic benchmark. **The Computer Journal** 19 1, (Feb. 1976) 43-49.

[8] Nori, K., and Ammann, U., et al. The Pascal (P) compiler: implementation notes. **ETH Zurich** Technical Report 10, 1974.

[9] Overgaard, M. UCSD Pascal: a portable software environment for small computers. **Proc. 1980 National Computer Conference** 747-754.

[10] **PDP-11/60 Microprogramming Tools Reference Manual**, Digital Equipment Corporation, Maynard, MA, 1976.

[11] **PDP-11/60 Processor Handbook**, Digital Equipment Corporation, Maynard, MA, 1977.

[12] **RSTS/E Documentation Directory**, Digital Equipment Corporation, Maynard, MA, 1981.

[13] Smith, G., and Anderson, R. LSI-11 writable control store enhancements to U.C.S.D. Pascal. **Proceedings of the Digital Equipment Computer Users Society** 5 2, (Fall 1978) 813-817.

[14] Tannenbaum, A. Implications of structured programming for machine architecture. **Comm. ACM** 21 3, (Mar. 1978) 237-246.

[15] Terry, D. A SLR Parser Generator (Pascal Program), University of California at San Diego, Winter, 1979.

[16] **UCSD (Mini-micro Computer) Pascal Version II.0**, Institute for Information Systems, University of California at San Diego, La Jolla, CA, 1979.

[17] Wirth, N. **Algorithms + Data Structures = Programs**, Prentice-Hall, Englewood Cliffs, NJ, 1976.

Session VI
Microcode Verification and Synthesis

AXIOMATIC PROOF RULES FOR A MACHINE-SPECIFIC MICROPROGRAMMING LANGUAGE

ALAN WAGNER

Department of Computing Science, University of Alberta, Edmonton, Alberta, Canada

SUBRATA DASGUPTA

Department of Computer Science, University of Southwestern Louisiana, Lafayette, Louisiana

ABSTRACT

In recent years, much effort has been devoted to the design and implementation of high level microprogramming languages. One of the goals for such languages is to facilitate the formal verification of microprograms using Hoare's inductive assertion method. Essential to the use of this method is an axiomatic definition of the microprogramming language.

In this paper, we describe the axiomatization of the machine dependent microprogramming language S*(QM-1) [12]. This language is an instantiation of the machine independent language schema S* [3,4], for the Nanodata QM-1 "nanolevel" architecture. We show that, in spite of the complexity of the QM-1, with its variety of side-effects and special conditions, a small and uniform set of proof rules can be constructed.

1. INTRODUCTION

One of the explicit goals in developing high level microprogramming languages [4,5,19] is to provide a basis for the *formal verification* of microprograms. The practical importance of this issue is clearly obvious; since firmware constitutes one of the lower levels in the hierarchic, multilevel structure of computer systems, any errors in the microcode could have serious and costly repercussions on the reliability of all the higher levels of software executed on the machine.

As in the case of software, microprogram correctness can be approached using either *formal* verification or *empirical* testing. The advantages of each of these approaches are well documented [1,2] and will not be further discussed here. Clearly, both approaches are necessary and play complementary roles in the design of reliable firmware.

Many of the approaches to microcode verification directly draw upon the work on software verification, in particular, on the Floyd-Hoare inductive assertion method [8,10]. Essential to the use of this method is an axiomatic definition of the microprogramming language. Earlier efforts in this direction include Patterson's STRUM system [18], the combination of assertions with *symbolic simulation* as developed by Carter et al [2,15], and Mueller's work on automatic microcode synthesis [16]. It has also been argued convincingly by several authors that the axiomatic method can be used in the *design* of correct programs [6,9]. In this situation the (micro) program and its proof of correctness can be developed hand in hand. A *sine qua non* for this to be practical is an elegant, easy to use formal deductive system which the (micro) programmer can use in the *derivation* of proofs.

In this paper we describe the axiomatization of the *machine dependent* microprogramming language S*(QM-1) [12]. This language is an *instantiation* of the machine - independent microprogramming language *schema* S*[3,4], for the Nanodata QM-1 "nanolevel" architecture [17]. We shall show that, in spite of the complexity of the QM-1, with its horizontal nanoword, a wide variety of side effects, and numerous idiosyncrasies, a relatively small and uniform set of proof rules can be obtained.

2. FOUNDATIONS

The construction of correctness proofs relies on a deductive system which captures the semantics of the (micro) programming language. A Hoare-type deductive system consists of formulas in the predicate calculus along with formulas $\{P\}S\{Q\}$ where P, Q are predicates and S is some legal program statement. The formula $\{P\}S\{Q\}$ is to be read as : if the state of the machine is such that the assertion P is true before execution of S then the execution of S leads to a state such that Q is true when (and if) S terminates. This is a statement of *partial* correctness. A proof of *total* correctness requires, in addition, evidence that S terminates. P and Q are often called the *pre-condition* and *post-condition*, respectively, of the statement S.

In addition, Hoare logic consists of inference rules for the predicate calculus along with rules of inference which describe the effects of the execution of composite statements in the language. We shall express these inference (or proof) rules in the usual notation

$$\frac{H_1, H_2, \ldots, H_n}{H}$$

which states that if the premises $H_1, H_2, \ldots, H_n$ are valid then the conclusion H is also valid.

151

The primary problem in constructing a deductive system for micro-program verification lies in that microprograms - even those expressed in a high level language - are *inherently machine specific* [4]. Consequently, the proof rules and axioms for such programming languages as Pascal [11] are simply not sufficient nor, in some cases, necessary in the microprogramming domain since the various conditions that actually arise in the host micro-architecture *must* be taken into account when one considers microcode verification. For example, the structure of a typical host machine causes diverse side-effects to be generated in the execution of even the most innocuous micro-operations. Thus, axiomatization of a microprogramming language poses problems that do not readily occur in the case of a programming language.

The most important differences between our work on the axiomatization of S*(QM-1) and earlier efforts appear to be the following:

1. S* and, therefore, any language instantiated from it contains a rather rich set of data structuring capabilities. It also contains a number of constructs for expressing low-level parallelism appropriate for monophase, polyphase, and multicycle time schemes.

2. The feature known as *residual control* [7] present in the QM-1 poses rather unique problems in constructing proof rules. Since residual control is present in several other machines [13,14,20], our solution to this problem is expected to be useful in a wider context than for the QM-1 alone.

3. The highly horizontal nature of the QM-1, as well as the presence of nearly a dozen buses around which the QM-1 data flow is organized raises issues concerning *side-effects* which must be reflected in the axioms and proof rules. To our knowledge, no other verification system has addressed this critical issue.

3. AN OVERVIEW OF S*

Basically, the schema S* consists of the following features:

1. The primitive data types <u>bit</u> and <u>sequence</u> and a set of structured data types including, <u>array</u>, <u>tuple</u>, (which is identical to the Pascal <u>record</u>) and <u>stack</u>.

2. A set of *simple* statements which may be used to represent micro-operations i.e. the most primitive, indivisible units available to the microprogrammer. The principle simple statements include:

   a. a generic *assignment*, the syntax and semantics of which is not specified in S* - their valid forms and meanings are assumed to be machine-dependent and are determined during instantiation;

   b. the simple *selection* statement
   $$\underline{if}\ C_1 \Rightarrow S_1 \ || \ C_2 \Rightarrow S_2 \ || \ \dots \ || \ C_n \Rightarrow S_n \ \underline{fi}$$
   where the C_1's denote testable conditions and the S_1's are simple statements (other than selections). Here again, the construct merely provides a template for valid selections - the legal testable conditions C_i's and simple statements S_i are machine-independent and are deter-

mined during instantiation;

   c. the procedure <u>call</u> statement; and

   d. the <u>goto</u>.

3. A set of structured statements that allow for the composition of larger program entities. Most of these are adaptations of Pascal-like constructs and include the <u>case</u>, <u>while..do</u>, and <u>repeat..until</u> statements and, of course, sequential composition. In addition, constructs also exist for the parallel composition of statements.

4. The <u>synonym</u> declaration statement which allows the programmer to arbitrarily *rename* previously declared data objects or parts thereof.

As noted before, the syntax and semantics of the constructs in S* are only partially defined. An instantiation of S* to a particular host machine M specifically tailors the constructs in S* to M. The fully defined language S*(M) thus derived would contain the machine dependent information necessary for the efficient utilization of the micro-architecture. Such an instantiation was carried out by Klassen [12] for the Nanodata QM-1, resulting in the language we call S*(QM-1).

4. A SYNOPSIS OF THE QM-1 ARCHITECTURE

The Nanodata QM-1 [17] is a user-microprogrammable general emulation engine with two rather distinctive features: the *two level control store*, and the extensive use of *residual control*.

The higher of the control store levels is referred to, simply, as the *control store*. The *microinstructions* at this level may interpret conventional *machine instructions* residing in *main store*. The micro-instructions are 18-bit vertical words, and have no capacity for specifying concurrent operations. They are, in turn, interpreted by highly horizontal *nano-instructions* from the lower level control store known as *nanostore*. At this lower level, a high degree of parallelism is possible between *nano-operations*. S*(QM-1) is an instantiation of S* with respect to the QM-1 nanolevel architecture. A compiler would generate nanoprograms from a given S*(QM-1) source program.

The idea of *residual control*, [7] rests on the observation that in emulating a target architecture, a part of the control information, once "set up" will remain relatively invariant for significant periods of time. Thus, instead of holding this information in the microword (or, in the case of the QM-1, in the nanoword), it can be placed in special registers and held there for any desired period of time until it needs to be altered. By reducing the amount of control information that needs to be held in a micro(nano)word, the width of the latter can be significantly reduced. The states of these special *residual control* registers can, of course, be altered under micro(nano)program control. In the QM-1, the control function rests partly in the nanoword (providing what Kornerup and Shriver [13] termed "immediate" control) and partly in a set of residual control registers called *F registers*.

The nanostore consists of 360-bit wide nanowords each divided into 5 72-bit subwords (fig. 1). The first of these, called the *K vector*, contains

| K-vector | T-vector$_1$ | T-vector$_2$ | T-vector$_3$ | T-vector$_4$ |

Figure 1

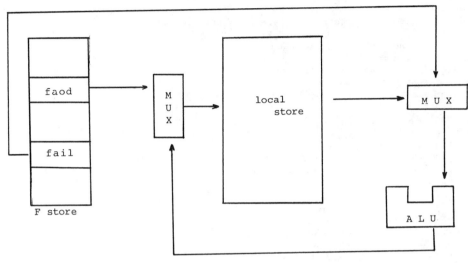

Figure 2

fields which serve to specify certain conditions and operations (e.g. ALU functions). The remaining subwords, the *T vectors* are identical in format and contain a number of fields that encode for the various nano-operations. When a T vector is activated, its fields are decoded and used to initiate specific hardware functions. At any given time, only *one* of the T vectors is active, while the K vector is active through the execution of all four T vectors in the associated nanoword. Thus, from a *logical* point of view, the combination of the K vector and the active T vector constitutes a single nano-instruction.

The bulk of residual control resides in the thirty-two 6-bit F registers. These can be set to values from certain fields in the K vector ("K fields") or from resources whose contents are only known at run time. For example, an F register may be loaded with values obtained from a micro-instruction residing in the control store.

The QM-1 also contains a *local store* consisting of 32 18-bit registers linked to other resources in the machine by a large number of buses. Precisely which local store register is connected to a particular bus is under the (residual) control of a specific F register. For example, one of the F registers called *faod* determines which local store register is connected to the ALU output bus (AOD), while the value in *fail* determines the local store source to the left ALU input bus (AIL) (Fig. 2).

Some of the F registers serve other control functions - e.g. specifying which of the local store registers 24 through 27 is to serve as the micro-

program counter for accessing control store. It should also be noted that since the K vector can remain unchanged over the scope of a nanoword, a certain amount of residual control also resides in the K vector.

Broadly speaking, the nanolevel architecture can be divided into an 18-bit domain (i.e. locations and data paths are 18 bits wide) and a 6-bit domain. The former consists of the thirty-two local store registers, thirty-two registers contained in an "external store," main memory, a control store, and a variety of arithmetic units. The micro-instruction register (local store register 31) can be accessed both as a single 18-bit location or as three 6-bit fields and thus provides the interface between the 18-bit and 6-bit domains. The 6-bit domain, dedicated to residual control, consists of the thirty-two F registers (collectively, the "F store"), certain K vector fields, and some special 6-bit locations.

5. S*(QM-1): ITS AXIOMATIZATION

The original instantiated language S*(QM-1) has been described elsewhere [12]. Basically, it defines within the framework of S* entities in the nano-architecture (i.e. data objects and actions) that are to be visible to the S*(QM-1) programmer. Since S*(QM-1) is machine specific, data objects and their names are predefined in the language (although synonyms can be used to rename them) and would appear in the data declaration block of a program. Each data object declaration, however, must be an instance of an S* data type.

As we have noted, using local store register 31 and other sources it is possible to load residual control registers with values which are not known prior to execution. In S*(QM-1) these F registers must also be declared as predefined variables in the data declaration part since, otherwise (i.e. if left undeclared) they would be invisible to the programmer. In the latter case, the programmer would be prevented from exploiting the parallelism available in the QM-1 by explicit control of these registers.

The need to declare residual control locations has had a major impact on the axiomatization and instantiation of S*(QM-1). S* was originally designed to be independent of control information [4]; yet, in S*(QM-1) this same control information is explicitly stated in the data declaration section. The part of the data declaration containing this information is prefixed by the keyword struct (structure) and it specifies the relationship between residual control registers and the source or sink locations that they select for data transfers; in effect, part of the QM-1 data path *structure* is specified in the language.

This is done by means of two constructs - the *array-with-pointer*, which was already present in S*, and a new construct, the *union-with-selector*. The general forms of these declarations are as follows:

(a) <id₁> : array[<dimension>] of <type> with
        <id> {,<id>}*[1]

where the with ... clause specifies identifiers of the only legal index variables for the array <id₁>. That is, the selection of the array element to be accessed is determined solely by values of one of the index variables.

Example 1

In the QM-1 a source of input data for the control store is one of 64 "logical" local store registers, and this would be determined by the setting of the 6-bit residual control register *fcid*. This relationship may be denoted by the declarations

    type ls_register = seq [17..0] bit
            . . . .
    control_store_source : array [0..63] of ls_
        register with fcid

Given this declaration the only legal reference to the above structure (say in an assignment statement) would be "control_store_source [fcid]".

(b) <id₁> : selector <id₂>
                union <id> : <type>
                    {<id> : <type>}*
                endun

---
[1] The notation {x}* denotes zero or more instances of the entity x.

Here <id₂> acts as a selector of one of the locations enclosed in the union clause. Thus, the union-with-selector type models a hardware multiplexer. However, it is illegal to reference the selector (<id₂>) explicitly. Rather, it is *side-effected* upon reference to a location inside the union. If the i-th (i≥0) of the locations is referenced, then <id₂> is set to i as a side-effect.

The locations within a union can only be of primitive types bit or seq. Structured types when present are considered to be decomposed into primitive elements.

Example 2

The control store input source of Example 1 can also be declared as:

control_store_source

        : selector fcid

            union

                local_store : array[0..31] of

                    ls_register

                all_ones   : array[0..31] of

                    ones

            endun

Given this declaration, a legal reference to the declared structure could be "control_store_source. fcid.local_store[12]".

Such a reference would, as a side-effect set *fcid* to the value 12. In fact, the object nanocode corresponding to this reference would first set *fcid* to 12, and then use this value in *fcid* to access local_ store. Note that the reference "control_store_ source.fcid.local_store[fcid]" would be illegal.

In summary, then, the union-with-selector data type allows the control function of F registers to be specified while the array-with-pointer allows references to storage locations using the preset values of the F register.

5.1 THE AXIOMS OF ASSIGNMENT

We shall use the following notation in defining the semantics of S*(QM-1).
1. Let P be an assertion. Then P[x/y] denotes P with all free occurrences of x being replaced by y.
2. Let P[x₁/y₁][x₂/y₂]...[xₙ/yₙ] denote the *simultaneous substitution* of the variables y₁, y₂, ... yₙ in P for all free occurrences of x₁, x₂, ... xₙ, respectively. Note that occurrences of some x₁ in expressions y₁, y₂, ... yₙ are not replaced. Furthermore, the substitution is invalid if the variables x₁, x₂ ... xₙ are not distinct.

The *simple assignment statement*

$$x := y$$

where x,y are locations satisfy the axiom:
        (A1)   {P[x/y][SEL/V]}

154

$$x := y$$
$$\{P\}$$

where SEL denotes all selector locations side-effected by reference (if any) to a union-with-selector type, and V denotes the set of values assigned to the selectors. That is, P[SEL/V] is equivalent to $P[sel_1/v_1][sel_2/v_2]....$

Example 3

Let "control_store_source" be declared as in Example 2, and let P be the assertion.

{control_store[addr] = control_store_source.fcid.

local_store[15] /\ fcid = 15}

Then by axiom (A1) we have the following formula:

{P[control_store[addr]/control_store_source.fcid.

local_store[15] [fcid/15]}

control_store[addr] := control_store_source.fcid.

local_store[15]

$$\{P\}$$

On substitution, this reduces to

$$\{TRUE\}$$

control_store[addr] := control_store_source.fcid.

local_store[15]

$$\{P\}$$

A necessary condition for any transfer to occur is the existence of a direct data path between the source and sink locations of the assignment: for each such statement in an S*(QM-1) program, there must, in addition, exist a mapping of the statement to nanoprimitive control fields. If this condition is not satisfied the statement is not compilable and a *mapping error* occurs upon compilation.

5.1.1 EXPRESSIONS IN ASSIGNMENTS STATEMENTS

The second class of assignments are of the form x:=E, where E is an expression.

As noted in section 4, a second group of residual control registers - the K vector fields - reside as part of every nanoword. During the execution of a nanoword each T vector is activated while the K vector remains active throughout. Fields in the K vector specify operations performed by the 18-bit functional units, mask values for test, and constants for injection into the 6-bit domain. An expression E in an S*(QM-1) program, containing an operator bound to some functional unit will, during execution, side-effect the relevant K vector fields by modifying or selecting the function to be performed.

Secondly, the output buses of several of the functional units in the QM-1 are declared as *pseudo-variables* in S*(QM-1). As a result, the evaluation of any expression involving the use of a device whose output lines are declared as a pseudovariable will set that pseudovariable to the value of the expression.

Thus an S(QM-1) expression can have a side effect.*

Example 4

Consider the expression

local_store[fail] 1<<s(5)

This will perform a single left logical shift of 5 positions on local_store[fail] and side effect the K vector fields $ksh\,c$ (which encodes the shift function) and $ksh\,a$ (which encodes the shift amount). Also the shifter output bus will be set to the value of the expression.

S*(QM-1) also permits *complex* expressions of the form

$$((expr_1)\ expr_2)$$

where the expressions are evaluated inside-out. Such expressions correspond to directly connected functional units. In the QM-1, the ALU and the shifter can operate independently or as a single unit performing double shifts on the output of the ALU and the shifter input (fig. 3).

Example 5

The expression

(local_store[fail]+local_store[fair]) local_store

[fsid] 1<<d(5)

specifies a double shift on the ALU output and the local store register pointed to by fsid.

The axiom for assignments involving expressions is:

(A2) $\{P[SEL/V_1][CNTR/V_2][MOD/V_3][MASK/V_4][OUT/E_1]$

$[x/E]\}$

$$x := E$$
$$\{P\}$$

where CNTR denotes K vector fields which are side-effected as a result of the operations and V_2, the values encoding these operations. MOD denotes any set of modifier fields side-effected by the operators specified in the expression and V_3 defines the corresponding modifier values appearing in E. MASK denotes the K-field side-effected in the evaluation of the expression if it is a boolean expression testing some condition in the QM-1 (cf section 5.2), and V_4 defines its corresponding mask value. Finally OUT denotes any pseudovariables (corresponding to output buses of devices used in E) which are side-effected in the evaluation of the expressions and E_1 denotes their corresponding expressions.

Example 6

Let P denote the assertion

{local_store[15] = local_store[13] 1<<s(5) ∧ kshc=

k_o ∧ ksha=5 ∧ faod=15 ∧ fail=13}

where k_o is a binary (or equivalent integer) valued constant; then, by axiom (A2) we have the formula

{P[faod/15][fail/13][kshc/k_o][shft_out_bus/local_

store[13]1<<s(5)] [local_store[15]/local_store

[13] 1<<s(5)]}

local_store[15] := local_store[13] 1<<s(5)

$$\{P\}$$

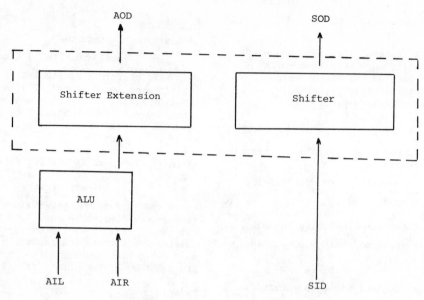

Figure 3

For convenience, the side-effects for expressions $[SEL/V_1][CNTR/V_2][MOD/V_3][MASK/V_4][OUT/E_1]$ will be denoted simply as $[EXPR]$.

5.1.2 MULTIPLE ASSIGNMENT STATEMENT

There are situations in the QM-1 where the action of functional units result in side-effects on other locations. For example, a write to control store also sets the control store output bus to zero. Such actions can be described using the multiple assignment statement which, in S*(QM-1), is of the form

$$x_1, x_2 := E_1, E_2$$

Example 7

control_store[addr],control_store_output_bus :=

   control_store[fcid],0

This same statement can be used to specify swapping of values of certain locations in a single time step.

    e.g. fcid,fcod := fcod,fcid

The validity of this statement rests on certain transfer-delay characteristics of the QM-1.

The axiom for the multiple assignment statement is:

(A3) $\{P[EXPR_1][EXPR_2][x_1/E_1][x_2/E_2]$
        $x_1, x_2 := E_1, E_2$
          $\{P\}$

Example 8

  $\{fsid=2 \wedge fail=3\}$ fsid,fail := fail,fsid
$\{fail=2 \wedge fsid=3\}$ where $(fail=2 \wedge fsid=3)$
$[fsid/fail][fail/fsid] \equiv (fail=3 \wedge fsid=2)$

5.2 PROOF RULES FOR CONTROL CONSTRUCTS

Unlike other variables, *testable locations* in the QM-1 are unstable. However, test conditions are not declared in the data declaration part of the program but are part of the language itself in the form of *test expressions*. Each legal test expression is bound to a particular machine condition.

Example 9

The machine condition OVERFLOW resulting from an ALU operation is defined by the S*(QM-1) test expression

   LOCAL OVERFLOW <u>of</u> (local_store[fail]+local_store

   [fair])

Test conditions in the QM-1 fall into three categories:
1. the so called "LOCAL" conditions generated from ALU and shift operations - CARRY, SIGN, OVERFLOW, RESULT, SHB, SLB (the latter denoting the high and low order bits of the shifter output bus);
2. These same conditions saved as GLOBAL conditions in a special F register (*fist*); and
3. SPECIAL conditions such as F_REG_ZERO, MS_BUSY and MS_DATA. The latter, for example, is set to 1 if a main store read or write is in progress.

In evaluating a test expression (of the form shown in Example 9, say) additional side effects may occur because of the 6-bit K vector fields ks, kt, and kx which are used as masks for testing, respectively, the local, global, and special conditions. The mask for local condition, for instance, is constructed by placing 1's in the bits corresponding to the conditions tested and zero elsewhere. The mask and the test condition are ANDed together with a 1 returned if the result is true, 0 otherwise.

Let "mask_sel" denote one of the keywords LOCAL, GLOBAL, SPECIAL and let "MASK" denote the pseudo-variable (i.e. ks, kx, kt) side-effected by the evaluation of the test expression B. Then the proof rule for the <u>repeat</u> statement is as follows:

(PR1) $\{P\}S\{Q \text{ MASK/V}][EXPR]\}$, $Q/\backslash \neg B \Rightarrow P$, COMPILABLE

    $\{P\}$ <u>repeat</u> S <u>until</u> mask_sel B <u>of</u> (E) $\{Q/\backslash B\}$

Proof rules of a similar nature have been defined for the _if_ and _while_ statements.

5.3 PARALLELISM IN S*(QM-1)

In the schema, S* [4] one of the ways for representing parallelism is by using the <u>cocycle</u> statement. Let

$$S_1 \; \theta \; S_2 ::= S_1 \; \square \; S_2 \mid S_1 \; ; \; S_2$$

where $S_1 \square S_2$ denotes the _parallel composition_ of statements S_1, S_2 while $S_1;S_2$ denotes the usual sequential composition. Then the <u>cocycle</u> statement is of the form

<u>cocycle</u> $S_1 \; \theta \; S_2$ <u>coend</u>

where S_1, S_2 can either be simple or composites of simple statements. The <u>cocycle</u> statement, in S*, indicates that the composite event $S_1 \; \theta \; S_2$ begins and ends in the same microcycle. Note that if θ is ";" then the microcycle is, by implication, polyphase.

Two additional properties of the general <u>cocycle</u> statement should be noted. Firstly, apart from the fact that the statement's execution begins and ends in a single microcycle (a property we call COCYCLIC), the composite statements $S_1 \; \theta \; S_2$ must also map onto a single microinstruction. We call this property COMPILABLE. Note that COCYCLIC does not necessarily imply COMPILABLE nor vice versa - S_1,S_2 may be COCYCLIC yet be encoded by the same field in the microinstruction hence they are not COMPILABLE; conversely, S_1,S_2 may be COMPILABLE but S_1 (for example) may require two or more cycles for its execution, - hence they are not COCYCLIC.

Secondly, in the case of the parallel version

<u>cocycle</u> $S_1 \; \square \; S_2$ <u>coend</u>

it is necessary for S_1,S_2 to be _dynamically disjoint_. Informally two statements S_1,S_2 are dynamically disjoint if during the time they are both in execution, there are no conflicts in their resource usage. We shall simply call this property DISJOINT. COMPILABLE, COCYCLIC and DISJOINT are all machine specific properties and are determined during instatiation.

In S*(QM-1) only the parallel version of the <u>cocycle</u> is instantiated. The COCYCLIC and COMPILABLE properties are interpreted in terms of the T step and the T vector respectively. The proof rule for the <u>cocycle</u> statement, then is:

(PR2) For all$(1\leq i \leq n)\{P_1\}S_1\{Q_1\}$, COCYCLIC, COMPILABLE, DISJOINT

$$\frac{}{\{P_1 \; /\backslash .. /\backslash \; P_n\} \; \underline{cocycle} \; S_1 \; \square \; S_2 \; \square \; ... \; \square \; S_n \; \underline{coend} \; \{Q_1 \; /\backslash .. \; /\backslash Q_n\}}$$

6. CONCLUSIONS

In a paper of this nature and size, we cannot hope to give the complete axiomatic semantics of S*(QM-1); thus, several other aspects of the axiomatization have been omitted in this discussion. These include, e.g., the treatment of data types and primitive control statements for invoking procedures, and the method of handling transient variables. For further details as well as examples of the use of the proof rules in deriving correct S*(QM-1) programs, the reader is referred to [21,22].

The work reported here demonstrates clearly the kind of issues that may arise in microcode verification. Given that these same issues are characteristic of micro-architectures in general we hope that our solution to these problems will have wide applications in other verification efforts. We have also shown that, in spite of the complexity of the QM-1 nanoarchitecture, it was still possible to construct a reasonably small and uniform set of axioms and proof rules.

As a final point, an indirect but pleasant consequence of this work is that the very act of formalizing the semantics of the language raised immeasurably, our understanding of the really important properties of the QM-1. The exercise of instantiating S* with respect to the QM-1 and deriving its axiomatic structure was worthwhile for this reason alone.

ACKNOWLEDGEMENTS

We thank Joseph Linn, Werner Damm and Bob Mueller for their critical comments on, and discussions of, this work. The first author (AW) was supported by a Natural Science and Engineering Research Council of Canada (NSERC) Postgraduate Scholarship.

REFERENCES

[1] Berg, H.K., "Correctness of Firmware - An Overview," _Firmware Engineering_, W. Giloi (Ed), Springer-Verlag, New York (1980).

[2] Carter, W.C., Joyner W.H., and Brand D., "Microprogram Verification Considered Necessary," _Proc. Natl. Comput. Conf._, pp. 657-664 AFIPS Press, (1978).

[3] Dasgupta, S., "Towards a Microprogramming Language Schema," _Proc 11th Annual Microprogramming Workshop_, MICRO 11, pp. 144-153 ACM/IEEE, (1978).

[4] Dasgupta, S., "Some Aspects of High-Level Microprogramming," _ACM Computing Surveys_ Vol. 12(3) pp. 295-324 ACM, (1980).

[5] Davidson, S., "High Level Microprogramming - Current Usage, Future Prospects," _Proc. 16th Annual Workshop on Microprogramming_, IEEE Comp. Soc. Press, N.Y.

[6] Dijkstra, E.W., _A Discipline of Programming_, Prentice-Hall, Englewood Cliffs, N.J. (1976).

[7] Flynn M.J. and Rosin R.F., "Microprogramming: An Introduction and Viewpoint," _IEEE Trans Comput._ Vol. C-20(7) pp. 727-731 (July 1971).

[8] Floyd R.W., "Assigning Meanings to Programs," _Mathematical Aspects of Computer Science_ Vol. xix, pp. 19-32 Amer. Math. Soc., (1967).

[9] Gries, D.G., _The Science of Programming_, Springer-Verlag, New York (1981).

[10] Hoare, C.A.R., "An Axiomatic Basis for Compu-

ter Programming," Comm. ACM, 12, 10, pp. 576-583 (1969).

[11] Hoare, C.A.R. and Wirth, N., "An Axiomatic Definition of the Programming Language Pascal," *Acta Informatica*, Vol. 2 pp. 335-355 (1973).

[12] Klassen, A. and Dasgupta, S., "S*(QM-1): An Instantiation of the High Level Microprogramming Language Schema S* for the Nanodata QM-1," *Proc: 14th Annual Microprogramming Workshop MICRO 14*, pp. 124-130 IEEE Comput. Soc. Press, (1981).

[13] Kornerup, P. and Shriver, B.D., "An Overview of the MATHILDA System," *SIGMICRO NEWSLETTER (ACM)* Vol. 5(4) pp. 25-53 (Jan. 1975).

[14] Kraley, M. et al, "Design of a User Microprogrammable Building Block," *Proc. 13th Annual Workshop on Microprogramming*, pp. 106-114 IEEE Comput. Soc. Press, (1980).

[15] Leeman, G.B., Carter, W.C., and Birman, A., "Some Techniques for Microprogram Validation," *Information Processing 74 (Proc. IFIP Congress)*, pp. 76-80 North-Holland, (1974).

[16] Mueller, R.A. and Varghese, J., "Formal Semantics for the Automated Derivation of Microcode," *Proc. 19th Design Automation Conf.*, Las Vegas, 1982.

[17] Nanodate Corporation, *QM-1 Hardware Users Manual, Third Edition, Revision 1*, Nanodata Corporation, Buffalo, N.Y. (1979).

[18] Patterson, D.A., "STRUM: Structured Microprogram Development System for Correct Firmware," *IEEE Trans. Comput.*, C-25, 10, Oct. 1976.

[19] Sint, M., "A Survey of High Level Microprogramming Languages," *Proc. 13th Annual Workshop on Microprogramming*, IEEE Computer Society Press, 1980, 141-153.

[20] Stritter, S. and Tredennick, N., "Microprogrammed Implementation of a Single Chip Microprocessor," *Proc. 11th Annual Workshop on Microprogramming MICRO 11*, pp. 8-16 ACM/IEEE, (1978).

[21] Wagner, A., "Verification of S*(QM-1) Microprograms," M.Sc. Thesis, Dept. of Computing Science, University of Alberta, Edmonton, Alberta, Canada (1983).

[22] Wagner, A. and Dasgupta, S., "The Use of Hoare Logic in the Verification of Horizontal Microprograms," Dept. of Computer Science, University of Southwestern Louisiana, Lafayette, LA, April 1983.

FLOW GRAPH MACHINE MODELS IN MICROCODE SYNTHESIS[*]

Robert A. Mueller   Joseph Varghese

Department of Computer Science
Colorado State University
Fort Collins, CO 80523

Abstract

Retargetability of microcode compilers is currently a major issue in microprogramming. We address the issue of local code generation from machine-independent specifications using weakest precondition semantics. The micromachine model used is a flow graph which is an abstract representation of the data paths of the machine. Examples of code generated by a prototype implementation are provided as an illustration of the method.

1. Introduction

One of the main problem areas in the development of microcode compilers is retargetability. Retargetability, in this context, denotes that property of a compiler which enables it to derive, for each construct in an intermediate language (which executes on a hypothetical machine known as the image machine), equivalent sequences of microcode for various microprogrammable machines (which are known as target machines). The problem is even more difficult than for ordinary compilers because of the large variation in microarchitectures as compared to macroarchitectures. Advances in hardware are more likely to be felt at the micro level and only gradually filter through to higher levels. The problem is made even more difficult because of the presence of concurrency and volatile machine resources. Also, stricter efficiency requirements for microcode virtually dictate the use of sophisticated tools for microcode generation.

Although many microcode compilers [Baba81,Sher81,MaLe81] have been designed and implemented, most of these are not truly machine-independent in that they require the manual

---

[*]This work was supported in part by NSF Grant #MCS-8107481

development of code generators for each target machine. Davidson [Davi80] proposes the use of a Pascal-like [Jens74] language in which resource binding constructs permit the programmer to specify the correspondence between program variables and target machine variables. Thus the problem is transferred from the compiler to the programmer who must adapt his programs to the target machine at hand.

Extensions of the application of Cattell's approach to automated code generation [Catt78] to microprogramming include the efforts of Marwedel and Zimmermann and those of Vegdahl. In the MIMOLA system [Marw79,Marw81,Zimm79] the target machine is described in terms of flow trees. Programs in a higher-level language are mapped into a similar representation and corresponding target machine instructions are derived through the use of pattern matching.

A related area in microprogramming is the problem of compacting microoperations (MOs) into microinstructions (MIs). An MI can be characterized as a set of nonconflicting MOs with certain timing relationships holding between them. Code generated for horizontal machines can be very inefficient unless it is compacted. Many local compaction [Land80,Ager76,Dasg76,Davi81] techniques and a few global compaction [Fish79,Poe80] techniques have been proposed in the literature. Vegdahl [Vegd82] also implemented a straightforward extension of Cattell's code generator generator and used it to demonstrate the need for coupling code generation with compaction in order to achieve a high degree of efficiency. In addition, he also showed that, contrary to the opinions held by some, the local compaction problem is far from solved.

Mueller [Muel80] has proposed the use of symbolic execution to simulate microprogram specifications by target machines. Local generation of microcode is effected by symbolically executing the microprogram specification, thus obtaining pre- and post-conditions for the specification, and then working backwards from the post-condition using only target machine instructions. As in [Vegd82] this method assumes that the high-level language has been syntactically analyzed and that the variables and operators of the microprogram specification have been bound to resources of the target machine, and is thus suitable for use as the code generation phase of a microcode compiler or as a code generator generator [Catt78]. In this paper we elaborate on this method and show how modelling the machine as a flow graph facilitates the local derivation of microcode.

2. Overview of the Method

In this section we present a basic overview of the method proposed by Mueller. Details of this method can be found in the references [Mue80,Mue82]. The proposed system has three components - a microprogram specification, a target machine description and a set of semantic rules to guide the derivation.

Microprogram specifications are assumed to be written by the microprogrammer in a high-level language, and translated using conventional parsing techniques into an intermediate representation [AhoU77]. The intermediate representation is processed by a data flow analyzer [Hech77] which partitions it into a flow graph of basic blocks, performs live/dead analysis on the blocks, and allocates target resources to the variable and operator resources.[1] Each basic block can be symbolically executed [Oakl79] to produce a symbolic representation of the block's function, which can be expressed in terms of values of the variables which are live upon entry to the block and the values of the variables that are defined in the block and live upon exiting the block.[2] For any block B, we refer to the former set as "USES(B)" and the latter set as "GEN(B)".

Thus, we can define the function of a basic block by associating with each variable in GEN(B), a symbolic expression in terms of the initial values of the variables in USES(B). This is the essence of the symbolic execution technique used in the symbolic verification of programs [King76] and microprograms [Birm74,Cart77,Joyn77, Croc77,Croc80]. The values associated with the variables in USES(B) are called "symbolic constants", which represent fixed but unknown values over a variable's data type domain. Likewise, a "symbolic expression" is an expression over symbolic and "hard" constants. We will use a_i's to denote symbolic constants and e_i's to denote symbolic expressions.

---

[1]Leverett discusses, in detail, machine-independent resource allocation algorithms that work with a target machine description [Leve81].

[2]A variable x is defined to be "live" at the top (bottom) of block B if and only if there is a definition-clear path for x from the top (bottom) of B to a use (reading) of x. A "definition-clear path" for variable x is a path containing no definitions (writes) of x. For a detailed discussion of the flow analysis of programs, see [Hech77].

A symbolic state vector (SSV) is an n-tuple, $ssv(m_1,...,m_n)$, where each m_i denotes a symbolic condition on a distinct machine variable ($1 \leq i \leq n$). Each such m_i is called a symbolic state mapping (SSM), and has the general form $ssm(X,e)$, where X is a machine variable and e is a symbolic expression. An example of an SSM is $ssm(A,plus(a,1))$ which represents the symbolic condition on A where A has the value a+1. An example of an SSV is $ssv(ssm(A,0),ssm(B,a))$ which represents symbolic conditions on the variables A and B where A has the value 0 and B the value "a". An SSV is a set of SSMs and represents symbolic conditions on a number of machine variables.

A symbolic assertion specification for basic block B is of the form

$$sa(ssv(ssm(X_1,a_1),...,ssm(X_m,a_m)),$$
$$ssv(ssm(Y_1,e_1),...,ssm(Y_n,e_n)))$$

where USES(B)=$\{X_1,...,X_m\}$ and GEN(B)=$\{Y_1,...,Y_n\}$.

We will refer to $ssv(ssm(X_1,a_1),...,ssm(X_m,a_m))$ as the "initial state vector" (ISV) of the symbolic assertion, and $ssv(ssm(Y_1,e_1),...,ssm(Y_n,e_n))$ as the "final state vector" (FSSV) of the symbolic assertion. The initial state vector represents the pre-condition and the final state vector the post-condition for the block represented by the symbolic assertion. An example of a symbolic assertion is

$$sa(ssv(ssm(A,a_1),ssm(B,a_2),ssm(C,a_3)),$$
$$ssv(ssm(A,plus(a_1,a_2)),ssm(B,a_3)))$$

The computation represented by the symbolic assertion above is the assignment to A of the sum of the initial values of A and B and the assignment to B of the initial value of C. Note that machine variables not assigned SSMs in the FSSV are assumed to retain whatever value they had in the initial state.

The target machine representation is discussed in more detail in the next section. At the highest level, we describe the target machine in terms of a series/parallel grammar which has the MOs of the machine as its terminal symbols. The timing relationships that hold between the MOs are modelled by terminal symbols denoting sequential or parallel execution. This description is sufficiently powerful to model most of the features of a microprogrammable machine. However, such a description may not be very efficient to manipulate for certain applications. Hence, for each phase, we may derive an alternate representation which has only the information required for that phase and is easier to manipulate. For the local code derivation phase we use a flow graph model of the machine which is an abstract representation of the data paths of the machine.

The semantic rules for the system are based on the weakest precondition operator defined by Dijkstra [Dijk75]. The weakest precondition operator wp takes as arguments a machine state S and a terminating machine operation M and finds a machine state T = wp(M,S) such that the machine is in state T before execution of M if and only if execution of the operation M leaves it in state S. In other words, the weakest precondition operator finds necessary and sufficient preconditions for the machine state such that the execution of an operation leaves it in a designated state. In our system, machine states can be represented as SSVs, and the machine operations over which the wp operator finds weakest preconditions are the MOs of the target machine. Axioms for handling sequences of operations that execute in series or parallel are also defined; thus we can find weakest preconditions with respect to MIs which are merely series/parallel sequences of MOs.

If the weakest precondition of the final state of a symbolic assertion with respect to a given sequence of MIs logically implies the initial state of that symbolic assertion then the MI sequence simulates the microprogram specification represented by the assertion. The goal of the synthesis system is to find such a sequence of MIs given the symbolic assertion and the target machine description. There are many additional rules which guide the synthesis. These can be classified as either validity rules which determine the applicability of target machine MOs in a particular situation or transformational rules that determine the transformational effect of these MOs when applicable. More details on the semantics of the system can be found in [Muel82].

3. Micromachine Models

In the past, micromachine models were developed primarily for use in microcode compaction and this is reflected in the emphasis placed on modelling MO conflicts and data dependencies while neglecting MO semantics. Two MOs can conflict if they attempt to use the same micromachine resource during the same minor cycle in a basic clock cycle [Agra76] or if they can cause the MI encoding to have two distinct values for the same field [Vegd82].

Data dependencies between MOs arise when one MO requires data produced by another. Models that handle data dependencies must account for the variable timing of MOs and the volatility of micromachine resources. Microoperation semantics can be modelled by assigning semantics to existing hardware description languages such as ISP [Barb77] as discussed in [Croc80]. However, these languages cannot accurately model all the timing features of micromachines [Sint81] and in addition, they are so general that they may lead to inefficient implementations of code generation or compaction algorithms.

Sint [Sint81] has proposed a language for MI description that can model very complicated timing and sequencing relationships between MOs, including asynchronous timing. This language is designed to be effective both in microcode generation and in microcode compaction but has, as yet, not been demonstrated in either application.

Vegdahl's [Vegd82] model is a direct extension of Cattell's mops (machine operations) [Catt78]. Some additional features have been added to adapt the machine description environment to microarchitectures. The micromachine model used has three main components - storage resources, MOs and conflict classes. The storage resources of the target machine are declared and their capacities described in terms of dimension (rank) and bit length. A MO description includes its transformational effect as well as some of the timing information. The timing information associated with a transformation gives the earliest and latest times for which the value assigned by the transformation is guaranteed to be stable. Conflict classes are used in compaction to determine the MOs of the machine that can reside in the same MI.

Mueller [Muel80] proposed the use of series/parallel grammars to model microprogrammable machines. This model has been shown to be sufficiently powerful to handle the features present in most microarchitectures [Muel81]. The terminal symbols of the grammar are the MOs of the target machine and these have two attributes - the transformational effect of the MO and its MI word encoding. Thus the MO semantics are represented directly in the terminal symbols of the grammar. The grammar generates only terminal strings that represent MIs consisting of valid combinations of MOs and the timing relationships that hold between these MOs are explicitly stated with the help of the sequencing terminals "next" and ";". However, our experiments have shown that microcode generation systems using the grammatical model directly can be very inefficient and may lead to exponential growth in the heuristic search tree. By extracting the important information and deriving the flow graph described in the next section, we can improve the efficiency of the code generation process.

4. Flow Graph Descriptions of Machines

The machine flow graph was defined with the code generation phase in mind. Hence it does not include conflict class or explicit data dependence information. Since only local code is being generated, sequencing information is not included and is assumed to be the responsibility of some other phase in the code generation process. The flow graph description of a target machine is an abstract representation of the data paths of the machine.

The flow graph is a set of nodes with directed edges between them. Each node represents a storage resource and has four attributes -

(1) a unique identifier

(2) the capacity information in terms of bit length and rank

(3) its visibility, which is either image or target, its retention characteristic and timing information. Image variables are those that are accessible to the machine language programmer. The values of these variables cannot be modified by the synthesis system unless the microprogram specification calls for such a modification. Target variables may be used by the synthesis system as temporaries. The retention characteristic is either permanent in which case the resource retains its value until explicitly modified or transient in which case the value assigned to it is only stable for a fixed period of time. The timing information associated with each resource includes the earliest and latest time that the value of the resource is stable after an assignment to the resource is made. Note that we assume that these times are a function of the resource and not of the MO which makes the assignment. This is a simplification, and the case where these times vary can be modelled by making conservative estimates of the earliest and latest times.

(4) a list of MOs which assign new values to this resource. There are two components in each MO - the functional transformation effected by the MO and the MI encoding that enables it. The value assigned to the resource could be an expression that includes constants and the values of other resources adjacent to this resource in the flow graph. The expressions are all assumed to be in prefix form. The encoding information can be used to determine conflict information, and data dependencies must be explicitly represented in the form of a partial order that will be discussed in the next section.

A sequence of data dependent MIs represents a path in the flow graph. A functional block is a node in the data flow graph and represents either a data resource or a functional unit resource. Transformations on data can take place only at functional blocks. For any two functional blocks there is a directed edge between them if the storage resource at the head of the edge has the other storage resource as an operand in one of its MOs. Thus, finding a sequence of MOs that transforms a given initial state to a given final state is equivalent to finding a path through the flow graph with the appropriate transformations at the nodes. This property of flow graphs will be exploited in the local code generation phase which will be described in the next section.

5. Microcode Generation Using Flow Graphs

In this section we describe the use of flow graphs in microcode generation. The emphasis is on clarity rather than completeness. As a result, we do not discuss all the details, and have opted to give only the basics required for comprehension of the method. A few examples are given to illustrate the method.

We assume that the microprogram specification is represented in the form of a symbolic assertion. Thus we have an initial and a final SSV and we are attempting to work backwards using weakest precondition semantics to transform the FSSV to the ISSV. The code produced is in the form of a partially ordered set of nodes such that data dependencies and anti-dependencies[3] are represented with the help of edges between nodes.

Given an FSSV we pick an SSM in it and look at its value component. This is an expression consisting of machine operators and constants which are either symbolic or "hard". Hard constants can only be generated in a finite number of ways and symbolic constants must be the value components of some state mapping in the ISSV. The task is now to find a path to each of these sources such that the MOs representing the paths perform the computation necessary to derive the state mapping (of the final vector) that is being considered.

If the expression consists only of a single constant, then the synthesis system has to find a path to the origin (source) of this constant such that no data transformations take place along this path. If the expression is more complicated, then we consider the leftmost prefix operator in the expression. The synthesis system then tries to find a path to a function block in which one of the MOs involves an assignment with an expression having the same operator. In general, the choice of function blocks selected in this manner may not be unique. The system picks the one which generates the shortest overall path, which is equivalent to picking the MO sequence having the smallest number of MOs. It should be noted that such a decision policy will not, in general, guarantee optimally compacted code, since we have concurrency and competition for resources.

If the MO we choose is of the form A <- B and the SSM being considered is $ssm(A,e_1)$ where e_1 is a symbolic expression, then the weakest precondition of this mapping with respect to the MO is the SSM $ssm(B,e_1)$[4].

---

[3] a MO is data anti-dependent on another if the former destroys information that is required by the latter [Vegd82,Bane79]

[4] In general, such an assignment can have other MOs as side-effects. Handling side-effects is a non-trivial task and a discussion of such a method would involve detailed descriptions of the implementation and is hence omitted.

If, on the other hand the SSM is of the form ssm(A,op(e_1,e_2)) and the MO we choose is A <- op(B_1,B_2) then the weakest precondition of this SSM with respect to the given MO is the SSV ssv(ssm(B_1,e_1),ssm(B_2,e_2)). If "op" is a commutative operator then we have two choices for the weakest precondition. Those SSMs that are derived in this way and which are also members of the ISSV can be deleted as we have found a path from the FSSV to one of its sources.

The SSMs of the FSSV are treated one by one in this way, until they reduce to a set of SSMs that are either in the ISSV or are SSMs involving hard constants such that the variable component of the mapping is the source of those hard constants. The resulting MO sequences cannot be compacted as they are generated because two MOs from different groups may use the same resource. Thus we have to perform live-dead analysis to determine the data anti-dependencies between MOs in different sequences. This aspect of code generation is independent of the flow graph and is hence treated in more detail in the next section.

The remainder of this section contains examples of synthesis. The machine model for these examples is shown in Figure 1. The image variables here are the registers in the register bank and the locations in the memory. Other locations are all target variables. The registers, the memory data register (MDR), the memory address register (MAR), and the instruction register (IR), can all pass data onto the source bus (s-bus). The inputs to the alu are the s-bus and the accumulator and the alu output is fed into a shifter which can perform various types of arithmetic shifts and rotates. The output of the shifter can be fed to the accumulator (acc) or to one of the inputs of the s-bus through the destination bus (d-bus). However, since the only input to the d-bus is the output of the shifter we model both elements with one resource and call it the shifter.

The alu, the shifter, and the s-bus are all transient elements and in this model, we assume that their values are stable for exactly one minor clock cycle after a value has been assigned to them. Examples of the flow graph representation of some of the functional blocks of the machine model are given in the Appendix. The examples given below illustrate the ideas presented, and the code shown as being generated was actually derived by a prototype implementation. The examples have also been kept simple for the sake of clarity.

Example 1 Consider the symbolic assertion

sa(ssv(ssm(r2,e_1),ssm(r3,e_2)),
   ssv(ssm(r1,e_1),ssm(r2,e_2)))

which conceptually represents the parallel execution of the statements r1 <- r2 and r2 <- r3. Let

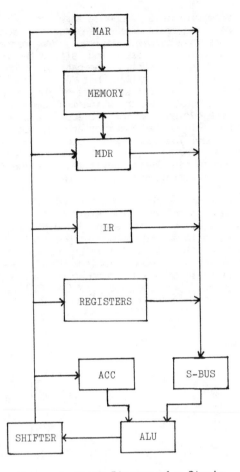

Figure 1. Block Diagram of a Simple Microprogrammable Machine

us first pick the SSM ssm(r1,e_1) from the FSSV. The symbolic constant e_1 is the value component of ssm(r2,e_1) in the ISSV. Thus r2 becomes the source for the SSM ssm(r1,e_1). The shortest path from r2 to r1 that passes data along without modification is r2 -> s-bus -> alu -> shifter -> r1. Thus we pass ssm(r1,e_1) back through the shifter using weakest precondition semantics to get ssm(shifter,e_1).

Now the source for ssm(shifter,e_1) is r2 and the shortest path from r2 to the shifter is r2 -> s-bus -> alu -> shifter. Thus we pass ssm(shifter,e_1) back through the alu to get ssm(alu,e_1). Continuing in this way we finally reduce this mapping to ssm(r2,e_1) which is part of the ISSV. Thus the code for this portion is

s-bus <- r2
alu   <- s-bus
shifter <- alu
r1   <- shifter

and it can be represented using a partial order as shown in Figure 2(a). Since some of the assignments made in this sequence are to volatile resources, the data from these resources must be used before they become undefined. We represent this constraint by assigning attributes to the directed edges representing the partial order. A directed edge (a,b) implies that MO a must execute before MO b. The first attribute of the directed edge is a number which is the minimum number of minor clock cycles that must elapse between the executions of the two MOs that are related by the partial order. The second attribute is the maximum such number, and if it is "inf", it indicates that the second MO can execute any time after the first subject to the minimum time constraint.

The code for the reduction of the second state mapping of the final state vector is shown in Figure 2(b). Note that some of the MOs from Fig 2(b) are data anti-dependent on MOs in Fig 2(a). For instance, the MO r2 <- shifter destroys data in r2 which is needed in the MO sequence for r1 <- r2. These data anti-dependencies are determined using live-dead analysis [AhoU77] and are discussed in the section on compaction related issues.

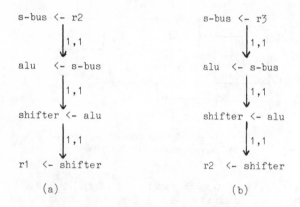

(a)   (b)

Figure 2. Microcode produced in Example 1.

Example 2 To demonstrate more complex derivations, let us take the example of an addition operation. Consider the symbolic assertion

$$sa(ssv(ssm(r1,a_1),ssm(r2,a_2)),ssv(r1,plus(a_1,a_2)))$$

which conceptually represents the operation r1 <- r1 + r2. The only SSM in the FSSV is $ssm(r1,plus(a_1,a_2))$ and its sources are r1 and r2 since they initially contain the values a_1 and a_2 respectively. Since the expression contains an operator we must find a path to a functional block which performs such an operation. The alu has an operation

alu <- plus(acc,s-bus)

and so we find a path from the alu to r1 which is alu -> shifter -> r1. Thus we move $ssm(r1,plus(a_1,a_2))$ back over the MOs r1 <- shifter and shifter <- alu to get a SSV containing the SSM $ssm(alu,plus(a_1,a_2))$. By moving this SSM back over the addition operation we get the SSV $ssv(ssm(acc,a_1),ssm(s-bus,a_2))$. We can now pick the SSM in this SSV one by one and work back to get the code derived in Figure 3.

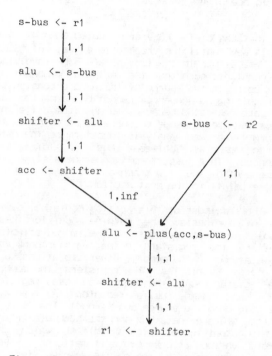

Figure 3. Microcode produced in Example 2.

Example 3 Consider the symbolic assertion

$$sa(ssv(ssm(r1,a_1)),$$
$$ssv(ssm(r1,con(bits(a_1,9,0),bits(a_1,15,10)))))$$

which conceptually represents the operation r1 <- rotate_left(r1,6). Here con is the concatenation operator and bits(x,y,z) represents bits y through z inclusive of x. The expression rotate_left(x,n) denotes the value obtained by rotating x left by n bits. Note that we do not explicitly assume a 16 bit architecture. The size declaration for r1 is assumed to have specified that r1 has bit length 16.

The only source for $ssm(r1,con(bits(a_1,9,0),bits(a_1,15,10)))$ is r1. Since the shifter is the only functional block in which a MO involves the con operator, we find the shortest path from the shifter to r1 which is shifter -> r1. We can thus derive the SSM

$$ssm(shifter,con(bits(a_1,9,0),bits(a_1,15,10)))$$

by passing the original state mapping back through r1. We now have a choice of the rotate operations that we can use. The machine model being used has rotates (both left and right) of one, two, four and eight bits. A left rotation by six bits is best achieved by either rotating left once by four bits and left once by two bits in any order or by rotating once by eight bits and right once by two bits. The choice is arbitrary since both take the same amount of time. We thus have four alternate sequences, two of which are given below.

```
r1 <- con(bits(r1,7,0),bits(r1,15,8))
r1 <- con(bits(r1,1,0),bits(r1,15,2))
```

or

```
r1 <- con(bits(r1,11,0),bits(r1,15,12))
r1 <- con(bits(r1,13,0),bits(r1,15,14))
```

6. Compaction and Related Issues

Microcode compaction is another area that is being intensively investigated [Davi78,Land80, Fish79,Poe80,Vegd82]. Code produced by compilers for horizontal machines must be compacted for efficiency and the code produced by the methods presented in the previous section are no exception. The code sequences that are derived are not yet ready for compaction because there are data anti-dependencies between MOs in different sequences. Sequences must be merged together to form one partially ordered set which has all the data dependency and anti-dependency information.

When two partially ordered sequences are to be merged together we have to use live-dead analysis to determine the new data anti-dependencies that have to be introduced. For instance, if a resource is assigned a value in each of two sequences then we might accidently destroy information if we ignored this anti-dependency in merging these sequences. We have to find the last use of this resource in one of these sequences and make any definition of this resource in the other sequence data anti-dependent on this one. Note that the order in which we select the sequences is not unique and hence the anti-dependencies introduced are not unique. For instance consider the two sequences

```
x <- y      x <- a
z <- x      b <- x
```

If we tried merging these two sequences we could end up with either of the two sequences given below.

```
x <- y      x <- a
z <- x      b <- x
x <- a      x <- y
b <- x      z <- x
```

This is one of many such analyses which introduce new data anti-dependency edges into the sequences generated by the code generator. The examples from the last section are merged and are shown in Figure 4.

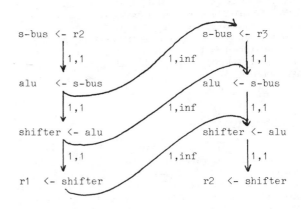

Figure 4(a). Microcode produced in Example 1 after merging.

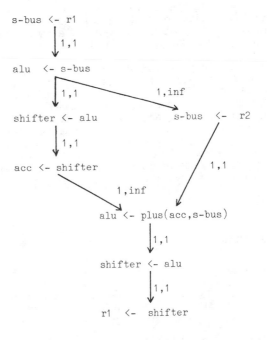

Figure 4(b) Microcode produced in Example 2 after merging.

The partially ordered set is still not ready for compaction. Most compaction algorithms assume that there is a linear ordering on the MOs. Vegdahl [Vegd82] has shown that this problem has not been adequately studied and we therefore use an algorithm given in his thesis. This algorithm does not always work but it will have to suffice for the present. Another fact demonstrated by Vegdahl is the necessity of coupling code generation with compaction. As of the time of writing we have not yet implemented this, but it is definitely one of the improvements that should be researched more thoroughly.

7. Conclusions

We have presented a method for modelling micromachines and shown how it can be used in local code generation. Examples of microprograms generated by a prototype implementation have also been included for illustration. While the flow graph model is general enough to handle most features of microarchitectures, it cannot model certain others. For instance, modelling interrupt handling is beyond the scope of most micromachine models. In some cases (e.g. writable control stores) the ability to model certain features of a microprogrammable machine cannot be effectively exploited by the code generation algorithm.

The code generated is not optimal. To achieve a significant measure of efficiency the code generator must be coupled to a microcode compactor. We are currently investigating the efficacy of coupling both existing and novel compaction strategies into the flow graph based synthesis system. Of particular interest are the recently reported reduction operator heuristic method of Henry [Henr83] and the use of symbolic covers pioneered by Reif and Tarjan [Reif81].

8. References

[Ager76]   Agerwala,T., "Microprogram Optimization: A Survey", IEEE Transactions on Computers, Vol. C-25, Number 10, 1976.

[Agra76]   Agrawala,A.K., and Rauscher,T.G., Foundations of Microprogramming: Architecture, Software and Applications, Academic Press, New York, 1976.

[AhoU77]   Aho,A.V., and Ullman,J.D., Principles of Compiler Design, Addison-Wesley, Reading, Massachusetts, 1977.

[Baba81]   Baba,T. and Hagiwara,H., "The MPG System: A Machine-Independent Efficient Microprogram Generator", IEEE Transactions on Computers, Vol. C-30, Number 6, 1981.

[Bane79]   Banerjee,U., Shen,S., Kuck,D.J., and Towle,R.A., "Time and Parallel Processor Bounds for Fortran-like Loops", IEEE Transactions on Computers, Vol. C-28, Number 9, September 1979.

[Barb77]   Barbacci,M., Barnes,G., Cattell,R., and Siewiorek,D., "The ISPS Computer Description Language", Technical Report, Carnergie-Mellon University, 1977.

[Birm74]   Birman,A., "On Proving Correctness of Microprograms", IBM Journal of Research and Development, Vol. 18, Number 5, 1974.

[Cart77]   Carter,W.C., Joyner,W.H., and Brand,D., "Microprogram Verification Considered Necessary", IBM Research Report RC7053(#29535), December 1977.

[Catt78]   Cattell,R.G.G., "Formalization and Automatic Derivation of Code Generators", PhD thesis, Carnergie-Mellon University, April 1978.

[Croc77]   Crocker,S.D., "State Deltas: A Formalism for Representing Segments of Computation", PhD thesis, University of California, Los Angeles, 1977.

[Croc80]   Crocker,S.D., Marcus,L., and van-Mierop,D., "The ISI Microcode Verification System", in Firmware, Microprogramming and Restructurable Hardware", edited by G. Chroust and J.R. Muhlbacher, North-Holland, Amsterdam, 1980.

[Davi78]   Davidson,S., and Shriver,B.D., "An Overview of Firmware Engineering", Computer, Vol. 11, Number 5, May 1978.

[Davi80]   Davidson,S., "Design and Construction of a Virtual Machine Resource Binding Language", PhD thesis, University of Southwestern Louisiana, 1980.

[Davi81]   Davidson,S., Landskov,D., Shriver,B.D., and Mallett,P.W., "Some Experiments in Local Microcode Compaction for Horizontal Machines", IEEE Transactions on Computers, Vol. C-30, Number 7, 1981.

[Dijk75]   Dijkstra,E.W., "Guarded Commands, Non-Determinacy, and the Formal Derivation of Programs", CACM, Vol. 18, 1975.

[Fish79]   Fisher,J.A., "The Optimization of Horizontal Microcode Within and Beyond Basic Blocks: An Application of Processor Scheduling", PhD thesis, New York University, October 1979.

[Hech77]   Hecht,M.S., Flow Analysis of Computer Programs, North-Holland, New York, 1977.

[Henr83]   Henry,S., "Reduction Operators in Microcode Compaction", M.S. thesis, Colorado State University, 1983.

[Jens74] Jensen,K., and Wirth,N., PASCAL User Manual and Report, Springer-Verlag, 1974.

[Joyn77] Joyner,W.H., Carter,W.C., and Brand,D., "Using Machine Descriptions in Program Verification", IBM Research Report RC6922(#29649), 1977.

[King76] King,J.C., "Symbolic Execution and Program Testing", CACM, Vol. 19, Number 7, 1976.

[Land80] Landskov,D., Davidson,S., Shriver,B.D., and Mallett,P.W., "Local Microcode Compaction Techniques", ACM Computing Surveys, Vol. 12, Number 3, 1980.

[Leve81] Leverett,B.W., "Register Allocation in Optimizing Compilers", PhD thesis, Carnergie-Mellon University, 1981.

[MaLe81] Ma,P-Y.R., and Lewis,T., "On the Design of a Microcode Compiler for a Machine-Independent High-Level Language", IEEE Transactions on Software Engineering, Vol. SE-7, Number 3, 1981.

[Marw79] Marwedel,P., and Zimmermann,G., "MIMOLA Report Revision 1 and MIMOLA Software System User Manual", Techn. Report 2/79, Institut fur Informatik and Prakt. Math., University of Kiel, 1979.

[Marw81] Marwedel,P., "A Retargetable Microcode Generation System For a High-Level Microprogramming Language", Proceedings of the Fourteenth Annual Workshop on Microprogramming, December, 1981.

[Muel80] Mueller,R.A., "Automated Microprogram Synthesis", PhD thesis, University of Colorado, 1980.

[Muel81] Mueller,R.A., and Varghese,J., "Grammatical Models of Micro-Instruction Set Processors", Technical Report CS-81-10, Department of Computer Science, Colorado State University, 1981.

[Muel82] Mueller,R.A., and Varghese,J., "Formal Semantics for the Automated Synthesis of Microprograms", Proceedings of the 19th Design Automation Conference, 1982.

[Oakl79] Oakley,J., "Symbolic Execution of Formal Machine Description", PhD thesis, Carnergie-Mellon University, 1979.

[Poe80] Poe,M.D., "Heuristics for the Global Optimization of Microprograms", Proceedings of the 13th Annual Workshop on Microprogramming, December 1980.

[Reif81] Reif,J.H., and Tarjan,R.E., "Symbolic Program Analysis in Almost Linear Time", SIAM Journal of Computing, Vol. 11, Number 1, 1981.

[Sher81] Sheraga,R.J., and Gieser,J.L., "Automatic Microcode Generation for Horizontally Microprogrammed Processors", Proceedings of the 14th Annual Workshop on Microprogramming, October 1981.

[Sint81] Sint,M., "MIDL - A Microinstruction Description Language", Proceedings of the 14th Annual Workshop on Microprogramming, October 1981.

[Vegd82] Vegdahl,S.R., "Local Code Generation and Compaction in Optimizing Microcode Compilers", PhD thesis, Carnergie-Mellon University, 1982.

[Zimm79] Zimmermann,G., "The MIMOLA Design System: A Computer Aided Digital Processor Design Method", Proceedings of the 16th Design Automation Conference, June 1979.

9. Appendix: Excerpts from the Flow Graph Representation of the Simple Microprogrammable Machine

```
function_block(r1,size(bits(15,0)),[image],
  [micro_op(assign(r1,shift),[enc(dest,1)])]).

function_block(r2,size(bits(15,0)),[image],
  [micro_op(assign(r2,shift),[enc(dest,2)])]).

function_block(ir,size(bits(15,0)),[target],
  [micro_op(assign(ir,shift),[enc(dest,13)])]).

function_block(mar,size(bits(15,0)),[target],
  [micro_op(assign(mar,shift),[enc(dest,14)])]).

function_block(acc,size(bits(15,0)),[target],
  [micro_op(assign(acc,shift),[enc(misc,3)])]).

function_block(alu,size(bits(15,0)),
  [target,transient],
  [micro_op(assign(alu,acc),[enc(alu,0)]),
   micro_op(assign(alu,s),[enc(alu,1)]),
   micro_op(assign(alu,plus(acc,s)),[enc(alu,2)]),
   micro_op(assign(alu,minus(acc,s)),
            [enc(alu,3)])]).
```

MIXER: AN EXPERT SYSTEM FOR MICROPROGRAMMING

Toru Shimizu and Ken Sakamura

Department of Information Science
Faculty of Science, University of Tokyo
7-3-1 Hongo, Bunkyo-ku Tokyo, 113 Japan

ABSTRACT

Microprogramming is an important technique to implement various functions on VLSI chips, and to adapt computers to application problems; but it is very difficult to generate an optimal and correct microcode, because each microarchitecture has its own peculiarities. This paper describes the effectiveness of an expert system based on a knowledge base for microprogramming. The purpose of the system is to give microprogrammers with a tool to develop microprograms without requiring that they have a deep knowledge of the microarchitecture, and to reduce microarchitecture learning time. The system is called MIXER. MIXER is a microprogram development system having as its knowledge base Texas Instruments' TI990 microarchitecture, and generates a TI990 microcode. This paper also describes the creation of a PASCAL-P machine emulator by applying MIXER.

1. INTRODUCTION

1.1. Why is microprogram development difficult?

Microprogramming has been established to design the control logic of a computer systematically. The technique is now used to implement highly complicated instruction sets on a single VLSI[1]. It is also used to adapt a computer to some special applications such as high-level languages[2] or program debugging[3]. Therefore, it is important to establish effective design techniques to develop optimal and correct microprograms.

The development of optimal and correct microprograms requires detailed knowledge of the hardware structure of the target machine, i.e. ALU operations, register functions, bus topologies, etc. A microprogrammer has to have a thorough knowledge of the functions of each microoperation. However, different machines have different structures and different functions, so a microprogrammer has to learn the microprogramming technique for the microarchitecture before writing his programs.

The conventional approach to the creation of microprograms is to develop a high-level language for microprogramming and compiling[4]; an optimizer then optimizes the microoperations. A high-level language enables microprogrammers to write microprograms in the form of syntactically high-level descriptions. For example, STRUM[5] and MPG[6] have syntaxes to represent resource names, arithmetic and logic expressions, and control transfers. An optimizing algorithm packs the microoperations generated by a microcompiler into a minimal number of microinstructions.

At present, there are some effective optimizing algorithms[7], but the high-level languages do not have sufficient descriptive power. Their compilers usually do not translate the description of what a microprogrammer wants to program into the best code for the microarchitecture.

For example, if the result of an operation is referred to as a memory address in the following step, the resulting value can be stored in the memory address register in parallel with the execution of the operation. But if a microprogrammer wants to generate such a code, he must specify this explicitly by performing a special operation. To take another example, if there are two operations that refer to the same source register, they can be merged into one by sharing that part in which a bus is set by a source data. After setting the bus, the two operations can fetch the data from the bus in parallel. Also in this case, if a microprogrammer wants to generate such a code, he must write, for example, a multi-destination operation instead of two operations.

The characteristics of the microarchitecture make it difficult to develop optimal and correct microprograms. Without a comprehensive understanding of the microarchitecture, a microprogrammer cannot determine which register to use or how to implement his problem, even if he uses a high-level language. There is no general purpose algorithm to map a microprogram specification onto a microarchitecture optimally. Thus, the conventional high-level language for microprogramming is

168

a sort of machine oriented high-level language. It is high-level only in terms of the syntax and not in the semantics.

1.2. Knowledge of microarchitecture and microprogramming techniques

When a microprogrammer programs his application problem, it is necessary for him to determine which registers and what microoperations to use. In order to select the appropriate registers or optimal microoperations, a microprogrammer must know the characteristics of the microarchitecture. We call this microprogramming knowledge.

Such knowledge may include the types of data transfer between registers that can be directly implemented as microoperations, the implementation options available for a given data transfer, or the operations which can be replaced by some other effective operation of equivalent meaning.

Each piece of knowledge has a special application condition and must be applied case by case. However, it is difficult to systematically manage this breadth of know-how, conventionally private province of highly skilled microprogrammers; therefore, an optimal and correct microprogram must be deviced by an expert microprogrammer.

We think that the use of such a knowledge base is the key to the effective development of microprograms. It is important to accumulate microprogramming know-how, to manage and share the knowledge base and to apply it selectively in the development of microprograms. In order to support the approach of microprogram development using a computer, we have developed the MIXER expert system for microprogramming.

MIXER generates the horizontal microcodes of Texas Instruments' TI990[8]. TI990 microprogramming know-how is obtained from an analysis of the TI990 microarchitecture and TI990 microcode in the control ROM. MIXER is applied utilizing a DEC system-10 PROLOG[9,10].

Users of MIXER can determine which register or what microoperation to use with only a cursory grasp of the characteristics of TI990 microarchitecture and its microprogramming techniques. Users address their queries to the knowledge base and receive the know-how of expert microprogrammers. The PASCAL-P machine emulator developed for TI990 demonstrates the effectiveness of MIXER in microprogram development.

The remainder of this paper is organized as follows. In section 2, our approach to the microprogram development process is defined. In section 3, knowledge categories and their applications in the preparation of a knowledge base to aid program compilation are presented. Section 4 describes our MIXER microprogramming system, which manages knowledge used for compiling and compiles automatically via a computer. Section 5 presents the results of experimental microprogram development employing MIXER, which shows it is both feasible and effective to develop an expert system

for microprogramming. Section 6 offers our conclusion.

2. DEVELOPMENT PROCESS OF A MICROPROGRAM

In order to manage microprogramming know-how and to employ it in microprogram development, we must first have an understanding of the know-how available. However there have been no research undertaken as to the knowledge required for the development of microprograms. This section describes the microprogram development process adopting our approach.

Microprogram development is, in general, the transformation of a source microprogram into an object microcode. In our approach, a microprogrammer does not have to be very familiar with microarchitecture when writing the source microprogram. The object microcode, however, consists of microoperations, and each microoperation controls the corresponding component in the microarchitecture. To solve the semantic gap between the description levels of a source microprogram and an object microcode, we break our development process down into two subprocess: compilation and optimization.

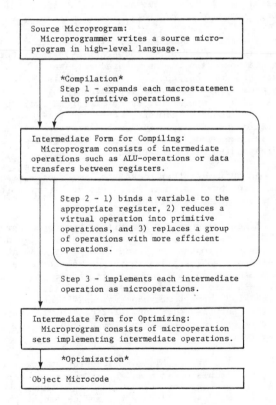

Fig. 1. MIXER Microprogram Compiling Process

First, a microprogrammer writes a source program using a high-level language. A high-level language is really a high-level of semantics. A microprogrammer can describe the specification of his microprogram in whatever format as he prefers. He can use variables and virtual operations which do not correspond to the real resources or real operations of the microarchitecture.

In the next stage, a compiler translates a user written source microprogram into a series of microoperations. We divide the compilation process into three steps. The first expands a user written macro statement into intermediate operations. The intermediate operation has a primitive function such as an ALU operation or a register transfer operation. For example, a multiplication is expanded into additions and shifts, and a memory reference is expanded into setting the memory address register and reading.

In the second step, a variable of the intermediate operation is bound to an appropriate register, and a virtual operation is executed as a set of primitive operations which can be directly implemented as microoperations. The second step also substitutes more efficient operations for those developed in step 1. For example, if a register transfer cannot be implemented directly, a temporary register is allocated to it. If there are two operations referring the same register, they are merged into one effective operation if possible. In other words, step 2 semantically optimizes the microprogram.

The third step expands an intermediate operation into a set of microoperations. The intermediate operation is implemented as a set of ALU, register, or bus controls in some timing. There are usually two or more implementations for an intermediate operation, which differ in their bus usage or control timings, but an intermediate operation cannot represent such differences; thus, it is expanded into one of the groups of corresponding microoperations in this step.

An optimizer then packs the microoperations generated by the compiler into as few microinstruction steps as possible.

Effective computer algorithms have been proposed to perform optimization, but there have not been many approachs to compilation by computer offered as peculiarities in the microarchitecture, which are not in the macroarchitecture, make it difficult to map a program specification as optimal and correct microoperations. There is no general purpose algorithm for determining which register or what operation should be used in microprogramming.

To solve the problem of microprogram compilation, we should develop an expert system by accumulating programming techniques and know-how. Moreover we can limit the machine dependent part in the knowledge base and create a general purpose system in accordance with this approach.

3. KNOWLEDGE OF MICROPROGRAMMING

In our approach of microprogram development, program compilation is executed by applying microprogramming knowledge. We define the follow-

ing three categories of knowledge to correspond to the three compilation steps.

3.1. Macro-knowledge

We define macro-knowledge as the knowledge used in the first compilation step. Macro-knowledge specifies how to normalize a user written statement as an intermediate operation, or how to expand a macro statement into corresponding intermediate operations. Fig. 2 shows an example of the macro-knowledge which expands a memory transfer statement into setting a memory address register and a memory read/write operation.

```
Source Statement:

    move memory(X) to memory(Y)
            Move data from memory addressed
            by X to memory addressed by Y

        ↓  is expanded to

Intermediate Operations:

    mar:=X      Set memory address register (mar)
                by X
    T:=mem      Read memory to variable T
    mar:=Y      Set mar by Y
    mem:=T      Write memory from T

        (A)  Macro-knowledge

macro_knowledge(
    [move,memory,X,to,Y],        Source pattern
    [[move,X,to,[r,mar]],        Object pattern
    [move,mem,to,T],             *Prefix r(egister)
    [move,Y,to,[r,mar]],         specifies resource
    [move,T,to,mem]]).           type.

        (B)  PROLOG Clause
```

Fig. 2. Example of Macro-Knowledge

The macro-knowledge describes typical macro translations. But if the macro-knowledge is managed systematically as a knowledge base, it is possible to append a new application oriented macro statement and share its definition among programmers.

Each piece of macro-knowledge is a combination of the source pattern of the macro statement it defines and the object pattern of corresponding intermediate operations. Macro-knowledge is implemented in the form of PROLOG clauses as follows:

```
macro_knowledge(
    Source pattern,
    Object pattern).
```

Fig. 2 also represents a PROLOG clause implementing a piece of macro-knowledge within the clause. There are about 100 pieces of macro-knowledge entered in the knowledge base.

3.2. Semantic knowledge

We define semantic knowledge as that

knowledge used in the second compilation step. Macro-knowledge and micro-knowledge transform the descriptive form of the microprogram syntactically, but semantic knowledge transforms the semantics of the microprogram.

Semantic knowledge allocates an appropriate register to a variable, maps a virtual operation as implementable operations in the form of microoperations, and replaces a group of inefficient operations by more efficient intermediate operations. Such transformations must be carried out case by case, based on how the variable is defined or referred, or what registers the operations are defining or referring.

Assert r is a variable or a register. We term the relationship of an operation defining resource r and those referring r as a DR-relationship. A microprogram includes many DR-Relationships. The semantic knowledge is applied on the matching of some DR-relationship.

Fig. 3 shows an example of semantic knowledge. This knowledge specifies that the two operations which increment a working register (W) and set the memory address register (mar) can be replaced by two other operations using a memory counter (mc). "mar:=W" in the source pattern and "mar:=mc" in the object pattern use different buses, so even if the "mar:=W" cannot be carried out in parallel with some other operations "mar:=mc" might be performed in parallel. Applying this knowledge, an existing microprogram can be transformed into a more effective one.

Semantic knowledge optimizes the microprogram semantically, but it is not always effective. Sometimes, the application of the semantic knowledge increases the number of steps. Moreover, there may be two or more pieces of semantic knowledge applicable to the same part of the microprogram; therefore, it must be applied by trial and error.

Each piece of semantic knowledge is a combination of the source pattern of a DR-relationship specifying its application condition, and the object pattern of operations which replaces operations by matching with the source pattern. Semantic knowledge is applied in the form of PROLOG clauses as follows:

        semantic_knowledge(
        Source pattern,
        Object pattern).

Fig. 3 also shows a PROLOG clause implementing a piece of semantic knowledge within the clause. There are about 200 pieces of semantic knowledge in the knowledge base.

3.3. Micro-knowledge

We define micro-knowledge as that knowledge used in the third compilation step. Micro-knowledge expands a primitive intermediate operation into a set of corresponding microoperations. Fig. 4 shows an example of the micro-knowledge which implements data transfer from the memory to register mdo, as a set of memory operations and two types of A-bus control operations.

Intermediate Operation:

    mdo:=mem   Read memory to register mdo

            ↓   is expanded to

Microoperations:

    read,   Read memory to TL bus
    abus2<tl,   Select TL bus as A bus
                    source in phase 2
    mdo<abus   Select mdo as A bus destination
                    in phase 2

        (A) Micro-knowledge

    micro_knowledge(
        [move,mem,to,[r,mdo]],   } Source pattern
                                   *Prefix r(egister)
                                    specifies resource
                                    type.

    [read,
     [abus2,tl],   } Object pattern
     [mdo,abus]]).

        (B) PROLOG Clause

        Fig. 4. Example of Micro-Knowledge

Each piece of micro-knowledge is a combination of the source pattern of an intermediate operation and the object pattern of corresponding microoperations. There are usually two or more sets of microoperations implementing the same

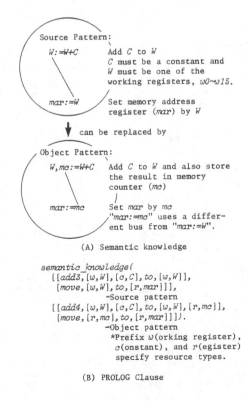

        (A) Semantic knowledge

    semantic_knowledge(
        [[add3,[w,W],[c,C],to,[w,W]],
         [move,[w,W],to,[r,mar]]],
                 -Source pattern
        [[add4,[w,W],[c,C],to,[w,W],[r,mc]],
         [move,[r,mc],to,[r,mar]]]).
                 -Object pattern
                  *Prefix w(orking register),
                   c(onstant), and r(egister)
                   specify resource types.

        (B) PROLOG Clause

    Fig. 3. Example of Semantic Knowledge

intermediate operation; a piece of micro-knowledge specifies one of these. Micro-knowledge is implemented as PROLOG clauses:

```
micro_knowledge(
    Source pattern,
    Object pattern).
```

Fig.4 also shows a PROLOG clause implementing micro-knowledge within the clause. There are about 800 pieces of micro-knowledge in the knowledge base.

3.4. Optimization of knowledge

The above three categories of knowledge are applied based on pattern matching of the source pattern of a statement, a DR-relationship, or an operation, with the description of a microprogram. The matching of an operation requires many condition checks, such as checking resource types matching with the template of a register; therefore, as even matching an operation requires a considerable period of time it is better to structure the application conditions of the knowledge and decrease the number of condition checks.

On the other hand, if the application conditions of the knowledge are structured, it is difficult to insert new knowledge into the knowledge base.

Therefore, it is better not to structure the knowledge representation. We refer to structuring the application conditions of the knowledge as the optimization of the knowledge. As there is an inclusion relationship among the source patterns of the knowledge, our system automatically optimizes the knowledge for relationship in the following way:

Assume A-->B and A'-->B' are knowledge items, where A and A' are source patterns, and B and B' are object patterns.

IF A=A' THEN
  replace A-->B and A'-->B'
  by A-->B;B'
("A--> B;B'" means "if A matches try B or B'."),

IF A is included in A' THEN
  replace A-->B and A'-->B'
  by A-->B;(A'-A-->B')
("A--> B;(A'-A-->B')" means "if A matches, try B, and moreover if A' matches, try B'."),

etc.

4. MIXER: AN EXPERT SYSTEM FOR MICROPROGRAMMING

4.1. System configuration of MIXER

We have developed an expert system for microprogramming called MIXER, which supports the development process of microprograms as described in the section 2. MIXER refers to a microprogram description and obtains the applicable knowledge about it from the knowledge base. It uses this knowledge during compilation in order to transform the description format of the microprogram or to determine which register is appropriate or what microoperations are best for the implementation of the microprogram. MIXER then generates a series of microoperations. MIXER also optimizes the microoperations and generates object microcode. That is, MIXER is a sort of microcompiler which compiles by applying microprogramming knowledge.

MIXER generates horizontal microcodes for Texas Instruments' TI990. Knowledge for TI990 microprogramming is gathered from the TI990 microarchitecture manual[8], and from an analysis of the microcode in the TI990 control ROM. The control ROM contains the microcode for the TI990 machine code emulator, which was developed by professional microprogrammers at Texas Instruments. Therefore, the microcode includes a substantial amount of knowledge about TI990 microarchitecture and the many techniques used program the TI990.

MIXER is implemented in the programming language PROLOG[9,10], which is a non-procedural language with mechanisms for pattern matching (called unification), and dynamic backtracking.

MIXER consists of a microcompiler, a microoptimizer, and a knowledge base (Fig.5). The microcompiler executes step 1-3 of the compilation. It obtains macro-knowledge, semantic knowledge, and micro-knowledge from the knowledge base, executes the compilation three steps, and generates a series of microoperations from a source description.

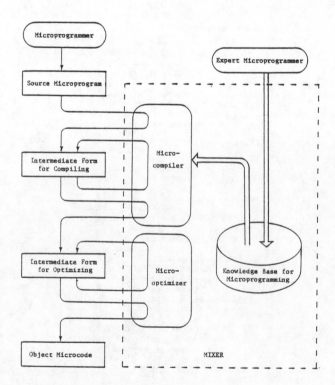

Fig. 5. MIXER System Configuration

Macro-knowledge is applied to the matching of the source pattern with a macro statement in the source microprogram. Semantic knowledge is applied to the matching of the source pattern of DR-relationships with operations of the intermediate form; finally micro-knowledge is applied to the matching of the source pattern with an intermediate operation.

The application of semantic knowledge needs context sensitive matching between a DR-relationship and operations. In the case of semantic knowledge and micro-knowledge, two or more pieces of knowledge may be applied to the same part of the microprogram in a nondeterministic manner. We have implemented such context sensitive and nondeterministic application mechanisms of the knowledge using the pattern matching and backtracking functions of PROLOG.

Generally, in the heuristic process of knowledge application, each piece of the knowledge must be evaluated to determine the best one to apply in a given situation. But in microprogramming, it is difficult to perform such an evaluation. Even if the number of microinstruction steps are minimized locally, this does not mean that the total number of steps in the microprogram has been minimized. Therefore, MIXER applies all possible knowledge, and after generating object microcode it selects the best object code. MIXER allows a microprogrammer to control the process of applying knowledge interactively.

The microoptimizer optimizes the microoperations generated by the microcompiler, and generates a series of microinstructions. The microoptimizer performs only local optimization, using the algorithm proposed by S.Dasgupta[11]. Some global optimization algorithms are also included as part of the semantic knowledge base.

4.2. Example of microcode generation by MIXER

We have developed a microcoded PASCAL-P emulator for the TI990 using MIXER. Fig.6 gives an example of microcode generated for a PASCAL-P load instruction (LDO). Although the part of the generation represented is deterministic, the real generation process includes application failures and non-optimal application of the knowledge base.

(1) LDO increments the value of stack pointer by 2, and pushes the memory data addressed by offset to the top of stack. A working register w0 acts as the stack pointer and the offset address is stored in the register mdi.

(2) Macro-knowledge is applied to the add-statement and the move-statement in the source microprogram transforming them into intermediate operations. In particular, the move-statement is a macro-statement and is expanded using the macro-knowledge shown in Fig.2 into (i) an operation that sets the memory address register (mar) to the source address; (ii) a memory read operation; (iii) an operation that sets the mar to the destination address; (iv) and a memory write

(1) Source Microprogram
  *This microprogram implements load operations in PASCAL-P, called LDO. Working register w0 is used as a *stack pointer*, and register mdi has *offset*.

  add 2 to w0   Increment *stack pointer*

  move memory(mdi) to memory(w0)
                       Push data from *memory* addressed by *offset*

        Step 1 : consulting macro-knowledge.

(2) Intermediate Form for Compiling

  w0:=w0+2   Add 2 to w0

  mar:=mdi   Set memory address register (mar) by mdi

  T:=mem   Read *memory* to variable T

  mar:=w0   Set mar by w0

  mem:=T   Write *memory* from T

        Step 2 : consulting semantic knowledge. Step 2 binds variable T to register mdo, and replaces 2 underlined operations.

(3) Intermediate Form for Compiling

  w0,mc:=w0+2   Add 2 to w0 and also stores the result in memory counter (mc)

  mar:=mdi   Set mar by mdi

  mdo:=mem   Read *memory* to mdo

  mar:=mc   Set mar by mc

  mem:=mdo   Write *memory* from mdo

        Step 3 : consulting micro-knowledge and optimization.

(4) Object Microcode
  *Consisting of 3 microinstructions.

  aluI.mc<a+b,a<abus,b<bbus,abus1<w0,
  bbus<2,w0<abus,abus2<sum,mar<cbus, } 1st
  cbus<mdi

  read,mdo<abus,abus2<t1,mar<mc   } 2nd

  write   } 3rd

Fig. 6. Example of Microcode Generation

operation. In the expansion, a new variable T is generated as a temporary register to save memory data.

(3) The semantic knowledge showed in Fig.3 is applied to the underlined part of (2) (Fig.6), and replaces it with the two underlined operations in (3) (Fig.6). The operation "mar:=mc" does not require control of the bus used in "mar:=w0", hence "mar:=mc" can be performed in parallel with other operations. There is another piece of semantic knowledge, which specifies the register to be allocated to the variable used for saving memory data. It is applied to the operations in (2) (Fig.6) defining or referring to variable T, and register mdo is selected from among the possible candidates.

(4) The intermediate operations in (3) (Fig.6) are sufficiently primitive to permit direct implementation as microoperations. Micro-knowledge, including the example shown in Fig.4, is applied to intermediate operations expanding each into microoperations. After optimizing the microoperations, an object microcode consisting of three microinstructions is generated.

If the semantic knowledge in Fig.3 is not applied in step 2 of program compilation, the generated microcode would require four microinstructions. The semantic knowledge shown in Fig.3 is effective in generating this microcode.

5. EVALUATION OF OUR APPROACH

We have generated a microcode to emulate 40 instructions for a PASCAL-P machine, including load, store, arithmetic and logic, and jump instructions.

We wrote a source microprogram for each instruction which were similar to the original PASCAL source. The allocation of all the registers to local variables was executed automatically by MIXER, but registers for global variables, such as the stack pointer and frame pointer, were specified by the user.

The source microprograms were compiled based on about 100 items of macro-knowledge, 200 items of semantic knowledge, and 800 items of micro-

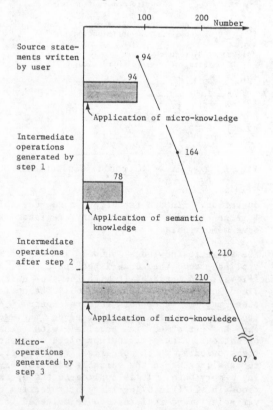

Fig. 7. Evaluation of Microcode Generation by MIXER

knowledge in the knowledge base. The microoperations generated were then optimized. The result of the microcode generation is shown in Fig.7.

The ratio of the numbers of source statements and microoperations generated indicates the "elevation" of the microprogram description level. The MIXER generated microcode was generally as efficient as hand-written microcode in terms of speed.

The above results indicate that it is both feasible and worth while to develop an expert system for microprogramming.

6. CONCLUSION

This paper has proposed a new approach to microprogram development, based on knowledge engineering. Our system uses a knowledge base in which various items of knowledge about micropro-gramming have been collected, and applies this knowledge during actual microprogram development. Using this approach a microprogrammer can select an appropriate register or an optimal microopera-tion without having to understand the microarchi-tecture in very great detail. This paper described an expert system for microprogramming called MIXER, which we developed based on our approach. We have also shown in this paper an example of the experimental development of microprograms for the PASCAL-P emulator running on the TI990, to illustrate the effectiveness of our approach.

Among current research in the field of knowledge engineering, there are some examples of expert systems used in such application areas as medical engineering[12]. There are also some languages which lend themselves to the development of expert systems, e.g. LISP and PROLOG[9]. Therefore, it is important to get more experience of developing effective and practical expert sys-tems for other application areas. From this point of view, we think our research contributes to future development of knowledge information pro-cessing systems as a practical application of knowledge engineering in this new area.

REFERENCES

[1] C.Ishikawa, K.Sakamura, and M.Maekawa, "Adap-tation and Personalization of VLSI-based Com-puter Architecture," Proc. of 14th Annual Microprogramming Workshop, 51-61(1981).

[2] K.Sakamura, T.Morokuma, and H.Aiso, "Automatic Tuning of Computer Architecture," Proc. of NCC, 499-512(1979).

[3] K.Sakamura, H.Kitafusa, Y.Takeyari, and H.Aiso, "A Debugging Machine - An Approach to an Adaptive Computer," Proc. of IFIP Congress 77, 23-28(1977).

[4] S.Dasgupta, "Some Aspects of High-Level Microprogramming," ACM Computing Surveys, 12, 3, 295-324(1980).

[5] D.A.Patterson, "STRUM: Structured Programming Systems for Correct Firmware," <u>IEEE</u> <u>Trans</u>. <u>on</u> <u>Computers</u>, C-25, 10, 974-985(1976).

[6] K.Baba, "A Microprogram Generating System - MPG," <u>Proc</u>. <u>of</u> <u>IFIP</u> <u>Congress</u> <u>77</u>, 739-744(1977).

[7] D.Landskov, S.Davidson, B.D.Schriver, and P.W.Mallett, "Local Microcode Compaction Techniques," <u>ACM</u> <u>Computing</u> <u>Surveys</u>, 12, 3, 261-294(1980).

[8] <u>Model</u> <u>990</u> <u>Computer</u> <u>MDS-990</u> <u>Microcode</u> <u>Development</u> <u>System</u> <u>Programmer's</u> <u>Guide</u>, Texas Instruments (1979).

[9] R.Kowalski, "Predicate Logic as Programming Language," <u>Proc</u>. <u>of</u> <u>IFIP</u> <u>Congress</u> <u>74</u>, 569-574(1974).

[10] L.M.Pereira, F.C.N.Pereira, and D.H.D.Warren, "User's Guide to DECsystem-10 PROLOG," University of Edinburgh (1978).

[11] S.Dasgupta and T.Tartar, "The Identification of Maximal Parallelism in Straight-Line Microprograms," <u>IEEE</u> <u>Trans</u>. <u>on</u> <u>Computers</u>, C-25, 10, 986-992(1976).

[12] E.H.Shortliffe, <u>Computer-Based</u> <u>Medical</u> <u>Consultations</u>: <u>MYCIN</u>, Elsevier (1976).

[13] R.M.Mueller and J.Varghese, "Formal Semantics for the Automated Derivation of Micro-Code," <u>Proc</u>. <u>of</u> <u>19th</u> <u>Design</u> <u>Automation</u> <u>Conferrence</u>, 815-824(1982).

Session VII
High Level Microprogramming:
Languages and Compilation

EXPERIENCE DEVELOPING MICROCODE USING A HIGH LEVEL LANGUAGE

R. Preston Gurd

Computer Graphics Laboratory
University of Waterloo
Waterloo, Ontario, N2L 3G1

Introduction

This paper describes a project in which every line of microcode developed was written in a high level language.

The project involved designing and implementing proprietary graphics and text primitives for a high performance, medium resolution (640 by 512 pixels) display processor developed by Electrohome, Ltd., of Kitchener, Ontario, for handling the North American Presentation Level Protocol Syntax (NAPLPS).

The language used was Microcode C, a subset of the C Language. The main difference between C and Microcode C is that, of the basic types, Microcode C supports only the type integer. The intent of this and other restrictions was to keep the compiler small, to minimize the complexity of the code generator, and to limit the set of operations allowed to those typically found at the microprogramming level.

There were two reasons for using a subset of an existing language, rather than designing a new language: to be able to cross-compile microcode programs for emulation on host systems, and to enable people who already know the existing language to be able to write microcode programs without any special training.

The target machine for this project is built from AMD bit-slice components. It uses four AMD2901 processor slices (making a 16-bit wide processor) and an AMD2910 sequencer. The system has a writable program memory of 2K 64-bit words. The processor has access to an eight bit per pixel image memory and a 16 bit per word scratchpad memory via a local bus. It can receive commands from a host MC68000 processor by reading a set of command registers and can initiate DMA transfers into or out of memories connected to the MC68000's bus.

Compiler Development

A compiler for Microcode C had already been implemented at the Computer Graphics Laboratory of the University of Waterloo for an AMD2903/2911-based processor for the Ikonas (now Adage) RDS-3000 graphics system [1]. The essential details of the language are summarized in Appendix A.

The compiler uses recursive descent to read in the source program. It builds expression trees, performs standard local optimizations on them, then traverses each tree recursively in order to allocate registers and translate the tree into a sequence of register transfer level operations (RTOs).

Before generating an RTO for a node, it is first necessary to evaluate its subnodes. In the call to evaluate a subnode, the node includes a specification as to where the subnode should put its result. It can ask for the result to be placed in any general register, in a specific general register, or in an external register (a "sink") to which the ALU output can be directed. For instance, if the operation is an assignment to a variable in memory, then the right hand side will be evaluated into the memory address register (MAR).

The set of RTOs can be thought of as a kind of higher level assembler. For instance, an RTO for a binary operation includes the operation (such as shift, add, or bit-wise and), the left operand register, the right operand register, and the destination register. For branching, there are RTOs to jump to a label, to call a subroutine, and make a conditional jump to a label.

As the stream of RTOs is being generated, each RTO is converted by a process very like macro expansion into a sequence of microoperations (MOs) which can be compacted into microinstructions. The conversion of one RTO may result in the generation of several MOs. For instance, an RTO which adds two registers and places the result in the MAR can be done in one instruction. However if the destination is a third register, (rather than the MAR), then the operation cannot be done in one instruction. Instead, the conversion will introduce an MO to move one of the registers to the destination register, then perform the operation using the other register and destination register as operands.

There are MOs defined for ALU operations, for sequencer operations, and for control of buses. A sequencer MO includes the sequencer operation (such as conditional jump), the condition code (if the operation is conditional), an address (if required), and a code indicating the form of the address (label, symbol name, constant, or offset relative to the current program counter). The basic ALU MO includes those fields which control the AMD 2901 ALU: the function code, the source operands, the "A" register, the "B" register, the shift/destination code, a code indicating the type of shift, and the selection of the carry input. If one of the source operands is the external "D" input, then it is also possible to specify which of the external source registers is to be selected as the D input.

As each MO is emitted it is passed into a compaction phase. In most cases, the compactor simply tries to place the new MO into the current MI; if this is not possible, it starts a new MI. However, for certain types of MO (such as one which shifts a register by one), it is possible to modify an existing MI, rather than start a new one. To make it possible to search backwards looking for an MI which can be modified, the compactor accumulates MIs for the current straight line code segment in a buffer.

All variables are allocated in the scratchpad memory. The compiler automatically generates the code sequences to set the Memory Address Register (MAR), to set the Memory Data Register, and to cycle the local bus as required. In order to access other devices, such as the image memory or the DMA control registers, special built-in functions are provided. For instance, in order to set a pixel at a given "x" and "y" address to the value "color", one can use the built-in function

    vmwr(x, y, color);

which will first set the video memory's X address register, Y address register and data register, then start a write cycle. However, there are instances in which this may be inefficient. For instance, when filling along a scan line, one might want to set the Y address and data only once, then do a series of writes, changing only the X address each time.

The compiler provides extra built-in functions to write to external registers (sinks), read from external registers (sources), and to explicitly cycle the local bus. These are

    input(source)
    output(sink)
    memcycle(type)

By using these functions in conjunction with register variables in important inner loops, it is possi-

ble to obtain efficient code without having to resort to using assembler.

Appendix B contains a sample program which includes the use of "vmrd", "output", and "memcycle".

Development work consisted of rewriting the code generator of the Ikonas version and creating the new set of built-in functions. Since the two machines were similar in many respects, it took about two weeks to do the rewrite and two more to visually inspect the generated assembly code and make needed corrections.

When the hardware was working well enough to try running programs on it, we were able to run compiler diagnostic programs, which checked out the code generated by the compiler for most operations. It took about a week to get these programs working. In the process, we found a couple of compiler problems, a couple of hardware problems, and a couple of places where there were differing concepts about what the hardware was supposed to be doing.

Initially, the plan was for the compiler to generate assembly code which would be uploaded to a floppy disk on the AMD SYS/10 Microcode Development System. Then it would be assembled by the AMD-supplied AMDASM assembler.

However, AMDASM turned out to be so slow assembling small test programs that we estimated assembly times for the full microcode NAPLPS program would be on the order of 45 minutes.

Therefore, we added an assembly pass to the compiler. Its input included: a file describing what each mnemonic means, in terms of what bits are to be turned on in the microcode word; a symbol table, giving the value for each constant and label; and a file of assembly code. The output was a file in the AMD object format which could be uploaded to the development system.

The result of this change was that we were able to compile 1800 lines of microcode, assemble it, and transfer it to the development system in less than fifteen minutes, greatly improving turnaround time on changes.

Application Software Development

Because the various features of the NAPLPS were subject to clarification and modification by the CSA, ANSI, and ISO standards committees, our understanding of the requirements of the NAPLPS changed and improved over time.

The microcode for NAPLPS is concerned with drawing lines, drawing filled or unfilled polygons, scrolling, setting attributes, scaling text, displaying text, and setting up user definable patterns. Attributes include such things as character size, foreground and background drawing colors, line texture, and polygon fill patterns. User definable patterns can be used for filling polygons or for creating custom characters, which are added to the Dynamically Redefinable Character Set (DRCS). Definables are created by turning on a definable mode such that, while in effect, subsequent text and graphics commands affect an invisible buffer, instead of the visible screen.

The largest single portion of the microcode is concerned with a proprietary algorithm for continuous scaling of text to any size specified by the user.

The graphics operations are made more complex by the need to be concerned with the size of the resolution independent "logical pel", which is set by the "information provider" as a binary fraction between zero and one. Depending on the resolution desired by the information provider and on the resolution available in the terminal, a logical pel may map into one pixel or it may map into a rectangular block of pixels.

In order to reach the market in a timely manner, we wanted to have the software ready go as soon as possible after the hardware was ready.

Having a subset compiler gave us the ability to debug most of the software on the host before the hardware was actually ready.

Since the built-in functions supported by Microcode C appeared just as procedure calls in the source code and since we at first used no inline assembly code whatsoever, it was a fairly simple process to provide procedures written in C to emulate each built-in function.

By compiling the microcode program with the host C compiler and linking it with an emulation library, we could run the microcode on the host, using all of the host's debugging facilities.

As a result, when the hardware was finally working, we could begin debugging knowing that most of the algorithms were correctly implemented.

The initial development of the application took about four months. At the end, we had about 1500 lines of Microcode C (including #defines and comments) which generated about 2000 words of microcode.

Hardware Development

Initial debugging of the bit-slice processor was done by the design engineer using programs written using AMDASM. Any of these programs could have been written in Microcode C, had the engineer known C and had the compiler been ready to use.

Once the board was more-or-less debugged, all subsequent programs were written in Microcode C. These included small, "one shot" programs written to pin down and reveal system problems, as well as more elaborate diagnostic programs written to check out the various system components and their interfaces with bit-slice board.

On several occasions, the design engineer made changes which affected the definition of bits in the microcode word. These were accommodated by trivial alterations to the code generator or to the assembly pass mnemonic definitions file. In one case, a change in the conventions for accessing external memories would have required many code alterations, had the code all been written in assembler. As it was, we accomplished the conversion easily by making a very simple change to the compiler.

Program development proceeded much faster than it could have using a microcode assembler. The reduction in coding and debugging time gained from using a compiler increased with the complexity of the program being written. For the one shot programs, there was little or no advantage. Larger programs of a hundred lines or so were written and debugged in a morning. The production microcode was about 80 per cent debugged before it was ever run on the machine. The NAPLPS microcode interpreter began working shortly after the hardware became operational.

This production code is presently written entirely in Microcode C. However, a small amount of inline assembly code may shortly be introduced. For one thing, there is no construct in C which maps naturally to the loop counter provided in AMD's sequencer chips. We expect to rewrite certain key inner loops in assembler to take advantage of this feature. For another, commands from the host are decoded by a series of "if-then-else" statements, whereas they could be more efficiently decoded using a jump table. Since there is no "switch" statement in the current compiler, it is likely that the decoding will get implemented as an assembler jump table.

Conclusion

There are a number of good things we can say about this experience. The code was easier to write, because the compiler took care of so many housekeeping chores (such as what register to use, or what name to give a label). The code was easier to debug, because we could debug higher level code using the more powerful tools available on the host and because the compiler translated it more correctly than a programmer could. The code was easy to modify, because its structure was neither constrained nor obscured by a morass of detail. And finally, the code was more comprehensible to others, because it was written in a language which could be understood by people who knew nothing about microprogramming.

Naturally, using a high level language instead of a microcode assembler is not without its disadvantages.

You need special expertise to create a code generator and debug it. Compiler bugs can be difficult to find and again require special expertise to fix. However, given that the expertise was available, it turned out that compiler bugs were only a minor source of errors and not unduly difficult to

181

solve.

Small size and efficiency are usually treated with the utmost importance in microprogramming. Unfortunately, the compiler generated code is somewhat bulkier and therefore less efficient than the best hand coding. In applications such as machine emulation, where absolute speed is of primary importance, using a compiler might not be advisable. However, there are other applications (such as the one discussed here) where the penalty paid for using a compiler instead of hand-coding is far smaller than the improvement gained by moving to a micro-architecture.

The work reported here does not claim to be suitable for all types of microcoding or all types of micro-architectures. However, we do believe that in this case the advantages gained from using a high level language far outweighed the drawbacks. It proved to be ideal for prototype development, giving us maximum flexibility to make changes in minimum time during system design and implementation. The first version of the microcode was so much faster than the MC68000 microcomputer code it replaced that the differences between the current version and possible hand-coding seem mostly academic.

References

[1] R. P. Gurd, *A Microcode C Compiler for the Ikonas Graphics System*. Waterloo, Ont.: University of Waterloo (Master's Thesis), 1983.

[2] J. D. Foley and A. van Dam, *Fundamentals of Interactive Computer Graphics*. Reading, Ma.: Addison-Wesley Publishing Co., 1982.

[3] B. W. Kernighan and D. M. Ritchie, *The C Programming Language*. Englewood Cliffs, New Jersey: Prentice-Hall, Inc., 1978.

Appendix A - Language Summary

Introduction

The language supported is a strict subset of C. The principle is that any Microcode C program can be compiled by a full C compiler. However, the reverse will definitely not be true.

You can use Kernighan and Ritchie's C Reference Manual [3] for further information about the syntax and semantics of C.

The compiler gives you access to hardware features by providing a set of built-in functions, which are replaced by in-line code. Because the compiler outputs assembly code, you also have the option of including assembly code.

Storage Class

If something is declared as "register", then it is kept in a machine register. If you declare a register array, then it is a pointer to the array which gets loaded in to the register. Local register variables are of course saved across function calls. Global register variables are always kept in their assigned registers. There is no enforced limit on the number of register variables you can declare, but keep in mind that, of the 16 registers in the machine, one is dedicated and at least one or two more are needed for expression evaluation.

Everything else is given a storage class of static, which means it will be stored in the scratch pad memory.

THERE IS NO RUNTIME STACK AND RECURSIVE PROCEDURE CALLS WILL NOT WORK.

Types

The only data types allowed are "int" and "struct". The type "char" is recognized but draws an error message and is treated exactly the same as "int". You can declare ints, pointers to int, or arrays of int, but not functions returning int.

You can declare structures, but not pointers to structures or arrays of structures. This restriction is imposed in order to avoid having to introduce hidden multiplications and divisions in pointer arithmetic. You can assign the address of a structure to a pointer to int, and you can use that pointer as the left operand of the "->" operation. If you need an array of structures, then you can handle extra scaling by using the sizeof operator.

You can use a structure name as the operand of "&", as the left operand of a "." operator, or else in a simple assignment statement whose left and right operands are structure members. You can take the address of a struct, or you can reference a member using the "." operator, or you can use it in a simple copy the contents of one structure to another. If you need to do a structure assignment using pointers to structures, you must use the "blkmove" built-in function to carry out the transfer.

There is no support for "enum", "typedef", or "union" types.

Statements

Statement types are shown in figure A-1. S, S1, S2, Sn are statements. Other words in upper case are keywords and may as usual be entered in lower case. Punctuation shown is required.

```
expression;
IF( expression ) S
IF( expression ) S1 else S2
WHILE( expression ) S
FOR( e1; e2; e3 ) S
BREAK;
CONTINUE;
RETURN;
RETURN expression;
{ S1 S2 ... Sn }
```

Figure A-1

Note that you cannot define a label and that there is no GOTO! Also, there is no SWITCH.

Expressions

The hierarchy of operators is shown in figure A-2.

```
= += -= /= *= %= <<= >>=
    &= |= ^=
||
&&
|
^
&
== !=
< <= > >=
<< >>
+ -
/ * %
unary ++ -- - ~ ! & *
-> . function calls, subscripting
(expr) name constant
```

Figure A-2

The right shift is a logical one, not arithmetic. However, if you really need to do an arithmetic shift, you can use the built-in function "ars".

The comparison operators generate a zero, if false, or a one, if true.

When calling a function, you must use the function name; you may not use an arbitrary expression. Also, the compiler issues an error message whenever it finds that you could have a function call nesting depth of greater than five, which is the maximum permitted by the AMD2910 sequencer.

When subscripting, the object being subscripted must be the name of either an "int" array or a pointer to "int". Otherwise, you will get a "can't subscript" error. For this reason, you cannot directly subscript a subscript.

In general, errors such as arithmetic overflow or out-of-bounds addresses go undetected and have undefined results.

Special Coding Techniques

Writing microcode in C can lead the the generation of fairly inefficient code if you are not careful. Although the generated code will not be as good as hand coding, with care you can still get very close.

The best way to reduce code size and improve running time is to use lots of register variables. However you should try to avoid doing so in a function which makes lots of function calls, since all local register variables must be preserved across function calls by storing them in memory before the call, then picking them up again on return.

Here is one way to reduce this overhead in function calling while still using register variables. Recall that C lets you declare new variables (but not functions) every time you begin a compound statement. If you declare a register variable inside a compound statement, then the register is kept on the save list only during the scope of that compound statement. Therefore if you can as much as possible limit the scope of register variables, you may be able to reduce the number which must be saved on any function call.

This leads to the type of construct shown in figure A-3.

```
proc()
{
    register xx;
    {
        register i;

        /* use register i, xx */
    }
    /* xx saved before call */
    function_call();
    /* xx restored.. */
    {
        register j, k;

        /* use xx, j, k */
    }
}
```

Figure A-3

An even better way of saving space and time is to keep things in registers which are globally accessible to all functions. This is the one point on which Microcode C is incompatible with C.

Microcode packages are often written to handle a variety of separate functions. For instance, in an emulation of a machine, you might have one logical function for each opcode. In such circumstances, it can be very convenient to have one group of global registers which can be used in different ways for different functions. Therefore, Microcode C lets you declare global registers.

However, you may also want to compile your Microcode C program using the regular C compiler, load it with some kind of emulation library and run it under the host system, so you can use its debugging facilities.

To be able to switch between C and Microcode C easily, declare any global registers like

    globreg x, y;

where "globreg" is defined for C as

    #define globreg int

and for Microcode C as

    #define globreg register int

Appendix B - Sample Program

The following is the compiler output for a simple program to draw a line on a raster display using an algorithm taken from [2]. The original source program text is included as comments in the output. The source code and generated code do not synchronize exactly, because generated code is emitted in a burst at the end of each straight-line segment of code.

```
MCC 2.0 - bres.c at Sat Aug 13 15:09:45 1983
CONT NOCLR CCL5 CCZERO MEMIG OR DZ NOP A0 B15 .
;/*
; * program to do a DDA using Bresenham's algorithm
; * as shown on page 436 of Foley and Van Dam.
; */
;#define WBSVMX 19 /* pixel X address */
;#define WBSVMY 20 /* pixel Y address */
;#define MEMWRB 4 /* write byte data */
;/*
; * endpoints and color are passed
; * in locs 0-4 of scratchpad RAM.
; */
;int x1, y1, x2, y2, col;
; x1 in spad 0 (0x0)
; y1 in spad 1 (0x1)
; x2 in spad 2 (0x2)
; y2 in spad 3 (0x3)
; col in spad 4 (0x4)
;main()
UJP  CCL4 MAIN
;main: EQU $
;{
;   register int dx, dy, incr1, incr2, d, x, y, xend;
; dx in reg 0
; dy in reg 1
; incr1 in reg 2
; incr2 in reg 3
; d in reg 4
; x in reg 5
; y in reg 6
; xend in reg 7
;   register color;
; color in reg 8
;   color = col; /* load colour into register */
;   dx = abs( x2 - x1 );
;   dy = abs( y2 - y1 );
;   d = 2*dy - dx;
;   incr1 = 2*dy;
;   incr2 = 2*(dy - dx);
;   if( x1 > x2 ){
;       /* start at point with smaller x */
;       x = x2;
;       y = y2;
;       xend = x1;
;   } else {
OR DZ    RCONST WBSMAR CCL7 MEMWT 0x0004 MEMRD
OR DZ RAMF B8  RBSMDR CCL7 MEMWT
OR DZ    RCONST WBSMAR CCL7 MEMWT 0x0000 MEMRD
OR DZ RAMF B9  RBSMDR CCL7 MEMWT
OR DZ    RCONST WBSMAR CCL7 MEMWT 0x0002 MEMRD
SUBR DA RAMF A9 B0  CAR1 RBSMDR CCL7 MEMWT
```

```
CJP  NCCNEG CCL4 0x0009
SUBS ZA RAMF A0 B0  CAR1
OR DZ    RCONST WBSMAR CCL7 MEMWT 0x0001 MEMRD
OR DZ RAMF B10  RBSMDR CCL7 MEMWT
OR DZ    RCONST WBSMAR CCL7 MEMWT 0x0003 MEMRD
SUBR DA RAMF A10 B1  CAR1 RBSMDR CCL7 MEMWT
CJP  NCCNEG CCL4 0x000f
SUBS ZA RAMF A1 B1  CAR1

OR ZA RAMU A1 B4
SUBR AB RAMF A0 B4  CAR1
OR ZA RAMU A1 B2
OR ZA RAMF A1 B3
SUBR AB RAMU A0 B3  CAR1
OR DZ    RCONST WBSMAR CCL7 MEMWT 0x0002 MEMRD
OR DZ RAMF B11  RBSMDR CCL7 MEMWT
SUBR AB A11 B9  CAR1
CJP  NCCGTZ CCL4 CC1
OR ZA RAMF A11 B5
OR DZ    RCONST WBSMAR CCL7 MEMWT 0x0003 MEMRD
OR DZ RAMF B6  RBSMDR CCL7 MEMWT
OR ZA RAMF A9 B7   UJP  CCL4 CC2
;CC1: EQU $
;       x = x1;
;       y = y1;
;       xend = x2;
;   }
;   vmwr( x, y, color );   /* first point on line */
OR ZA RAMF A9 B5
OR ZA RAMF A10 B6
OR ZA RAMF A11 B7
;CC2: EQU $
;   while( x < xend ){
OR ZA A8    WBSVMD CCL7 MEMWT
OR ZA A5    WBSVMX CCL7 MEMWT
OR ZA A6    WBSVMY CCL7 MEMWT  MEMWRB
;CC3: EQU $
;       ++x;
;       if( d < 0 )
;           /* choose Si - no change in y */
;           d += incr1;
;       else {
SUBR AB A7 B5  CAR1
CJP  NCCNEG CCL4 CC4
ADD ZA RAMF A5 B5  CAR1
SUBR DA A4  CAR1 RCONST  0x0000
CJP  NCCNEG CCL4 CC5
ADD AB RAMF A2 B4   UJP  CCL4 CC6
;CC5: EQU $
;           /* Choose Ti - increment y */
;           output( WBSVMY, ++y );
;           d += incr2;
;       }
;       output( WBSVMX, x );
ADD ZA RAMF A6 B6  CAR1
OR ZA A6    WBSVMY CCL7 MEMWT
ADD AB RAMF A3 B4
;CC6: EQU $
;       memcycle( MEMWRB );
;   } /* end while */
;}
OR ZA A5    WBSVMX UJP  CCL7 MEMWT  CC3 MEMWRB
;CC4: EQU $
UJP  CCL4 0x002c
```

AUTOMATIC ADDRESS ASSIGNMENT OF HORIZONTAL MICROPROGRAMS

Etsuo Takahashi, Kazutoshi Takahashi, Tatsushige Bito,
Tohru Sasaki and Kazuyoshi Kitano

Computer Engineering Division
NEC Corporation
Fuchu City, Tokyo 183
Japan

ABSTRACT

This paper presents a machine-independent address assignment program and its algorithm[7] for horizontal microprograms. An address assignment operation is performed on a symbolic microprogram called a "standard sequence microprogram." Microprograms which need address assignment are translated to this standard sequence microprogram.

The introduction of the standard sequence microprogram has made the address assignment tool applicable to various kinds of horizontal microprograms.

1. INTRODUCTION

Address assignment[1,2,3,4] is one of the toughest tasks specific to horizontal microprograms. An address assignment task must be carried out, taking into consideration various restrictions imposed upon microprogram words.
In addition, those restrictions are determined by a microprogram sequence-architecture. Because microprogram sequence-architectures are in most cases different from each other, it is very hard to implement a general-purpose address assignment program.

Hence, a standard sequence microprogram (SSM), whose language syntax is designed to describe the execution sequences for a microprogram, has been introduced. The address assignment program presented in this paper receives the SSM and assigns addresses to the words in the SSM. Any kind of horizontal microprogram can use address assignment service if it can be described in the SSM format.

The address assignment program is one component in a microprogram development support system, called MDS[5,6,7]. Figure 1 shows the relationship between the assignment program and other components in MDS. A microprogram written in a high-level language is stored in the microprogram source code file (SRC). The process definition file (PDF) contains the information which shows the syntax of the high-level language and tells the preprocessor how and what to output into the assembler interface file (AIF) and into the standard sequence microprogram file (SSF).

The address assignment program inputs the SSF and assigns addresses to the microprogram words in the file. An address assignment result is output to the address definition file (ADF). The information stored in the ADF is a list of microprogram word labels and their corresponding addresses in a microprogram address space.

The features of the address assignment program are:
(1) The microprogram address space compaction rate can be set in accordance with the user's request.
(2) Address ranges to be reserved for some reason can be omitted from an assignment operation.
(3) It is often the case that some modifications are needed for a microprogram. In order to cope with such a situation, there is an option that an address assignment service is only pertinent to the modified part of the microprogram, while the addresses of the non-modified part remain unchanged.
(4) An address assignment execution trace list, which is useful when an assignment result is unsuccessful, is output.
(5) An address assignment result in the ADF can be modified by hand, using a TSS terminal.

© 1983 ACM 0-89791-114-8/83/0010/0185$00.75

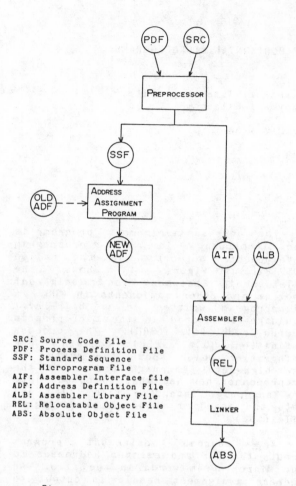

SRC: Source Code File
PDF: Process Definition File
SSF: Standard Sequence
     Microprogram File
AIF: Assembler Interface file
ADF: Address Definition File
ALB: Assembler Library File
REL: Relocatable Object File
ABS: Absolute Object File

Figure 1. Address Assignment Program
          and Language Processors in MDS

2.STANDARD SEQUENCE MICROPROGRAM

The sequence structure for a microprogram can be displayed in a graphical representation in which microprogram words are considered to be nodes and relations between words are considered to be branches. The standard sequence microprogram (SSM) is a microprogram graph model, whose nodes and branches have the information necessary for address assignment.

The information held by nodes are:
(1) A label attached to a microprogram word.
(2) A fixed address request when a microprogram word must be placed at a fixed address.
(3) An address alignment request when a microprogram word is to be at a specific address; e.g., an address multiple of 2^2 or 2^4.

The information held by branches are:
(1) A notation that specifies a jump span between microprogram words.
(2) Jump methods, such as one-way, multi-way, increment, or a subroutine call jump.
(3) Bit positions to be tested for a multi-way jump.

In MDS, automatic address assignment is applicable to any kind of horizontal microprograms which can be translated to the standard sequence microprogram (SSM).

The assembler library file (ALB) tells the assembler the specifications for the microprogram words, such as word length, field configuration for each word category, and so forth. The assembler translates a symbolic microprogram in the AIF to a relocatable object microprogram, referring to the ADF and ALB. An address for each microprogram word is given by the ADF. The relocatable object file (REL), in which an assembler result is stored, is an input to the linker. The linker makes the absolute object file (ABS), in which an executable microprogram is stored.

The standard sequence microprogram (SSM) will be presented in Section 2. In Section 3, the algorithm used in the address assignment program will be explained and, in Section 4, the address assignment program configuration will be presented.

3. ALGORITHM

The algorithm for the address assignment program is divided into two phases; i.e., an analysis phase and a placement phase. In the analysis phase, a standard sequence microprogram model, which has a network structure, is analyzed and translated to some separate trees. The placement phase gives addresses to the trees made in the analysis phase, one by one. Detailed explanations for the two phases are presented in 3.1 and 3.2.

3.1 ANALYSIS PHASE

As described before, an original standard sequence microprogram (SSM) has a network structure.
However, a network structure has the following characteristics which are unsuitabale for address assignment.

. All the restrictions to be imposed upon each node cannot be determined, unless all the routes in the network are traced.
. It is difficult to decide the address assignment order for the nodes; i.e., where to start and in which direction. Howerver, the assignment order for the nodes has a great affect on address assignment result.

It is not a good idea to resolve the above problems in an actual microprogram word placement stage because many trial and error operations are made during the microprogram word placement process. The analysis phase is to resolve the above problems beforehand in order to avoid a complicated placement algorithm and save execution time.

Figure 3 is an example of the analysis phase. An explanation of the analysis phase is given below.
(1) The network structure for a standard sequence microprogram model is recognized. (See Fig. 3(a).) A freely accessible branch is a branch with no restriction. If nodes are linked by a freely accessible branch, a jump span between the nodes has no limitation in regard to a microprogram address space.
(2) The restriction imposed upon each node is updated by a sort of logical AND operation of the node's original restriction and the restrictions on the branches which point the node.
(3) Nodes which have to be dealt with, as if they were one node, are redefined as a "group node." Those which have to be redefined as a group node are, for example, multi-way jump destinations or a pair of words connected by an increment jump. G1, G2, and G3 in Fig. 3(b) are such group nodes.
(4) Nodes which are not included in any group node, which was defined in (3), are also redefined individually as a group node. G4, G5, G6, G7, G8, G9, G10 and G11 in Fig. 3(b) are such group nodes.
(5) Multiple branches between two group nodes are unified so that the number of the branches between two group nodes becomes one, as shown in Fig. 3(b).
(6) Cut out freely accessible branches. Four freely accessible branches are cut out in the example. (See Fig. 3(c).)

(7) Branches that make loops are cut off. B65, which links G6 and G5 in Fig. 3(c), is such a branch.
(8) Modify branches until all the group nodes have one or no input branch. Assume that group node Gk has input branches; Bik from a group node Gi, and Bjk from Gj. (See Fig. 2 (a).) If the degree of the restriction imposed on Bik is less than that on Bjk, branch Bik is modified so as to go from Gi to Gj and is redefined as a branch Bij. (See Fig. 2 (b).) On the other hand, if the restriction degree for Bjk is less than that for Bik, Bjk is modified and redefined as a branch Bji which goes from Gj to Gi. This operation is repeated until all the group nodes have only one or no input branches.
The original logical relations between microprogram words are preserved because branches to be modified are those which connect group nodes. The original branches that connect individual nodes are kept unchanged.
In Fig. 3(c), B31 used to link G3 and G1 at first. As a result of comparison with B51, B31 has been modified and has been redefined as branch B35, connecting G3 and G5. This operation has made the group node G5 have two branches, B45 and B35. The B45 comparison with B35 is made, and finally B35 is redefined as a branch B34 connecting G3 and G4.
(9) By the steps from (1) through (8), an input microprogram with a network structure is converted, to some separate trees as shown in Fig. 3(d). In this example, the original microprogram has been converted to two trees; i.e., a tree with root G8, and another tree with root G10.

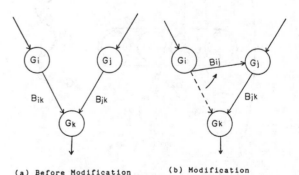

(a) Before Modification   (b) Modification

Figure 2. Branch Modification

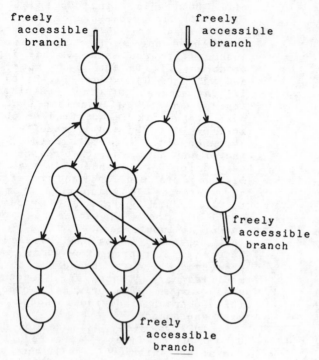

(a) Network structure

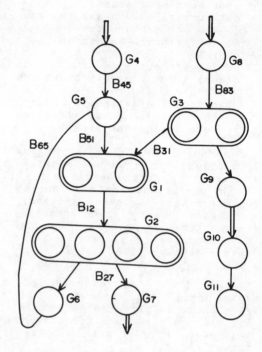

(b) Grouping and branch unification

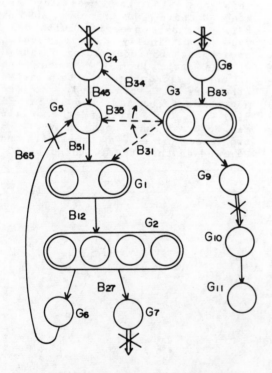

(c) Cut-off and modification

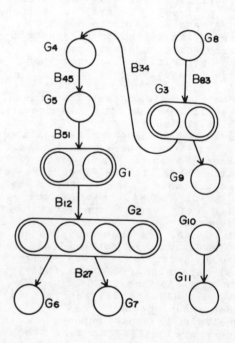

(d) Trees

Figure 3. An Analysis Phase Example

Trees made in the analysis phase
have the following characteristics.
. All the restrictions to be imposed
  upon each group node have already
  been calculated. This means no
  group node restriction calculation
  is needed in the placement phase.
. There is no loop contained in a
  tree, and each group node for the
  tree, has one or no input branch.
  This simplifies the
  group node trace of a tree, and
  consequently saves placement phase
  execution time.
. Trees do not have any direct
  relations with each other, from an
  address assignment standpoint.

3.2 PLACEMENT PHASE

In the placement phase, trees made
in the analysis phase are selected one
by one and are assigned addresses.
After the address assignment for one
tree is finished, the next tree is
selected and is assigned addresses. The
basic philosophy for the placement
phase, common to both trees and the
nodes in a tree, is "a severe
restriction is always considered
first." Figure 4 is a placement phase
process flow.

A tree assignment priority is
determined by the following measures:
(1) If there is a node with a fixed
    address request in a tree, the tree
    has a top priority in the placement
    phase.
(2) Among the trees without any fixed
    address node, the larger the tree
    size (number of microprogram words
    in a tree) is, the higher the tree's
    priority is.

An address assignment order for the
group nodes in a tree is determined by
the following measures:
(1) If a group node has a fixed address
    element in it, this group node is
    dealt with first of all in the tree.
(2) Among the group nodes with no fixed
    address element, the number of the
    nodes included in a group node
    decides the assignment order; i.e.,
    a larger group node is given a
    higher priority.

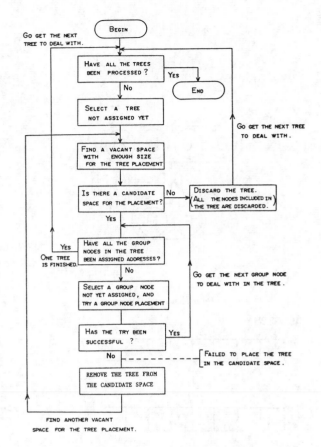

Figure 4. Placement Phase Process Flow

Figure 5 shows an example of a tree
placement. Fig. 5(a) shows a tree
structure, Fig. 5(b) indicates the
restrictions imposed upon the nodes and
branches of the tree, and Fig. 5(c)
shows a placement process.

. The group node to be treated first
  is G2, because the number of nodes
  included in G2 is the largest.
  Nodes B, C, D and E are placed at
  the addresses which satisfy all
  the restrictions imposed on the
  nodes in G2.
. The group node to be treated next
  is G3. Nodes in the group node G3
  must share the same address
  boundary block (size=2^4) with
  the nodes in G2. F and H in G3
  are placed at the addresses which
  meet the restrictions imposed upon
  F and H.
. The final one is G1. Node R in G1
  can be placed at any address as
  long as R shares with the nodes in
  G2 the same address boundary block
  (size=2^4). The address
  assignment for the tree comes to
  an end, when R is assigned an
  address, as shown in Fig. 5(c).

(a) Tree Structure

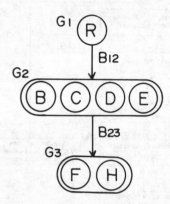

(b) Restrictions

G1:
    R must be located at XXXXXX. (Note 1)
G2:
    B must be located at ***0*0. (Note 2)
    C must be located at ***0*1.
    D must be located at ***1*0.
    E must be located at ***1*1.
G3:
    F must be located at *****0.
    H must be located at *****1.
B12: A link between G1 and G2 must be
     within the $$XXXX range (Note 3)
B23: A link between G2 and G3 must be
     within the $$XXXX range.

(Note 1)
  "X" takes a value of either 0 or 1.

(Note 2)
  "*"s at the same bit position
  must have the same bit value in
  a group node.

(Note 3)
  Two group nodes connected by a branch
  must be in the same address boundary block
  with the 2^n size; where n is the number of X's.
  "$$" is an address boundary
  block number, and takes either 00, 01, 10 or
  11 value in this case.

(c) Placement Process

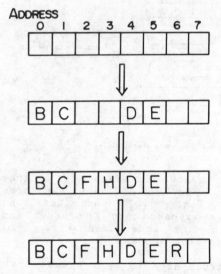

Figure 5. A Tree Placement Example

4. PROGRAM CONFIGURATION

Figure 6 shows an outline of the address assignment program.
As mentioned before, the standard sequence microprogram file (SSF) has a normalized or standardized microprogram model made by the preprocessor. The address definition file (ADF) has a label-address list which indicates the microprogram words and their corresponding physical addresses given by the address assignment program.

An assignment result is output to the new address definition file (NEW ADF), which becomes an input to the assembler (see Figure 1). The old address definition file (OLD ADF) is read in, when some modification has been made to the microprogram source code and when the addresses for the non-modified part ought to remain unchanged.
If the OLD ADF is not input, in the above case, both modified and non-modified parts will be re-assigned new addresses.

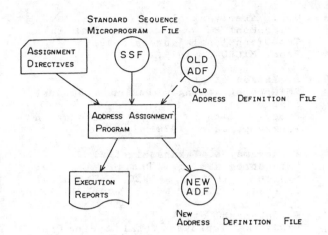

STANDARD SEQUENCE
MICROPROGRAM FILE

ASSIGNMENT
DIRECTIVES

SSF

OLD
ADF

OLD
ADDRESS DEFINITION FILE

ADDRESS ASSIGNMENT
PROGRAM

EXECUTION
REPORTS

NEW
ADF

NEW
ADDRESS DEFINITION FILE

Figure 6. Address Assignment Program Outline

The assignment directives, prepared by the user, give the address assignment program the following information:

(1) An address space in which the microprogram words are to be placed.
(2) A compacion rate for the given address space for address assignment.
(3) A request to input the OLD ADF, if necessary.
(4) Address ranges to be reserved; i.e., addresses at which no microprogram word is placed.

Two kinds of execution reports are output.

(1) A label-address corresponding list whose contents are the same as the output to the NEW ADF.
(2) An execution trace list, which is useful when any microprogram word could not be assigned an address. The reason for the assignment failure can be found in the trace list.

5. CONCLUSION

The microprogram address assignment automation has released microprogrammers from complicated time-consuming tasks. The address assignment program has already been used in the developments of various NEC computers, such as the ACOS system 1000 (large scale computer), the ACOS system 450 (medium scale computer), the MS190 (super minicomputer), and so forth. Program execution time, which often depends on input data, is about 5 to 10 minutes per 1,000 words on the ACOS system 900.

When there are more than 1,000 microprogram words, the address assignment program work is better than manual work, in terms of compaction; i.e., an address space needed for automatic address assignment can be smaller than that needed for manual address assignment. For example, manual assignment needed a 1,345 address space for 1,265 microprogram instruction words, while automatic assignment needed a 1,273 address space for the same microprogram.

Several plans for improving the program are being carried out. They are:

(1) A revision in the standard sequence microprogram syntax to expand its ability to represent microprogram instruction sequences.
(2) An algorithm improvement:
 . The present algorithm, as represented in Section 3, assigns addresses to trees one by one. This method sometimes cannot assign all the trees, when some trees' characteristics are peculiar for the assignment program.
 . A new algorithm would get some trees together, according to a certain evaluation function or measure, and deal with those gathered trees simultaneously in the placement phase.

REFERENCES:

1. T. Tanaka et al.
    "Proposal on Efficient Address
    Allocation Algorithm for Horizontal
    Microprograms"
    Proc. MICRO-11, November 1978.

2. T. Baba; H. Hagiwara.
    "The MPG System : A
    Machine-Independent Efficient
    Microprogram Generator"
    IEEE Transactions on computers, Vol.
    C-30, No.6, June, 1981.

3. T.G.Szymanski.
    "Assembling Code for Machines with
    Span-Dependent Instructions"
    Communication of the ACM, Vol. 21,
    No. 4, April, 1978.

4. J.F. Wakerly at al.
    "Placement of Microinstructions in a
    Two-Dimensional Address Space"
    Proc. MICRO-8, 1975.

5. A. Yamada et at.
    "Microprogramming Design Support
    System"
    Proc. 11th Design Automation
    Workshop, June, 1974.

6. T. Aoyama; K. Takahashi et al.
    "Microprogramming Design Support
    System (MDS)," NEC Technical
    Journal, Vol. 34, No. 5, June, 1981.

7. K. Takahashi et al.
    "MDS: An Improved Total System for
    Firmware development"
    Proc. MICRO-15, October, 1982.

High Level Microprogramming - Current Usage, Future Prospects

Scott Davidson

Western Electric Engineering Research Center

ABSTRACT

High level microprogramming languages have been studied extensively, but no widely accepted HLML exists to date. We examine the classes of HLMLs, giving examples. We then give some reasons as to the current lack of an accepted HLML, and give some suggestions how to solve this problem. The existence of a HLML would allow work on higher level microprogramming and firware engineering to proceed more rapidly. A possible microprogramming environment, based on a HLML, is presented.

1. INTRODUCTION

Higher Level Microprogramming Languages (HLMLs) are an extremely active field of research. So far, however, the results of this research has not led to a widely accepted HLML. There is far from general agreement on the need for a HLML. In the software area, not only are a (large) number of High Level Languages (HLLs) accepted, but the need to use these languages for software development is also universally accepted.

What is the definition of a HLML, and how are HLMLs different from HLLs? First, a *microprogramming language* is a language designed to be compiled into microcode. The possibility that the language is also interpreted or compiled into machine language level code is not excluded. A *higher level microprogramming language* has the properties that one statement in the language can be compiled into more than one microinstruction, and that the language contain constructs not directly supported by the target machine. These constructs are typically control constructs, such as *for* loops. These properties are necessary for a language to be a HLML, but not sufficient. We can say that a HLML must have some of the data and control structuring features of HLLs, but this is not a precise definition.

In theory, the only difference between HLMLs and HLLs is that HLMLs are compiled into microcode. A sufficiently clever compiler could generate microcode from any HLL. However, many common features of HLLs such as floating point arithmetic, pointers, and input/output are not usually useful for microcode. Therefore a HLML usually has the features found in a Systems Implementation Language (SIL), and has no features that cannot be efficiently translated into microcode.

In this paper we will explore the current and future status of HLMLs and their relation to the microcode development process. This is not a survey; a good survey of microprogramming languages was done by Sint [23]. We will first argue for the need for a HLML, and briefly explore why we do not yet have one. We will

then discuss a taxonomy of HLMLs, to attempt to define the structure of a language that could be widely accepted. We also present an example microprogram written in several languages to demonstrate the differences between language levels. Next we will introduce some cases of HLML use in industry. We will close by discussing the effects of a HLML on firmware engineering [8], attempting to define an ideal microprogramming environment.

Why do we need a HLML? The reasons are really the same as those justifying the use of HLLs, only more so. The first reason is to make large microprogramming projects more manageable. The second is to increase microprogrammer productivity. We must consider these two points together. Increased productivity means that fewer microprogrammers must be assigned to a project, decreasing the number of interactions required between microprogrammers, and thus further increasing productivity. Perhaps if adding more programmers to a late project makes it later [2], reducing the number of programmers will make it earlier, given a constant collective rate of code production. Having fewer microprogrammers also reduces the number of interactions required with others, such as hardware designers. HLMLs, by reducing the number of lines of code written, will ease the maintenance task, and will also simplify the training of new microprogrammers. Given a machine independent microprogramming language it might be possible to share microprograms, further increasing productivity. Arguments as to the effect of language level on the code development process also hold true for HLLs, and need not be considered further here.

Another reason for the adoption of HLMLs is their increased reliability. The same is true of HLLs, of course, but assembly level microprograms are even more difficult to understand than machine language programs. The microprogrammer must deal exclusively with resources at the hardware, not algorithm, level, while the assembly language programmer can at least give mnemonic names to variables residing in memory. The number of operations required to perform one operation at the algorithm level (such as an assignment) is greater at the microcode level than at the assembly language or HLL level. Thus the microprogram written at a low level is more difficult to understand. The need to grasp more levels of abstraction makes it more difficult to write and learn microcode.

Another advantage of a HLML is that it will allow us to use many of the tools developed in software engineering. We will cover this advantage in more detail in the final section of this paper.

Given all these advantages, why is there not a widely accepted HLML? We can identify several reasons. First, a compiler requires a significant lead time before it becomes available. Microcode development is at an early part of the critical path for a processor development project, therefore waiting until a compiler is developed would lengthen the critical path, delaying the project. The use of simulation means that the microprogramming can be done in parallel with hardware development. The current state of the art is such that a compiler development project would require significant staffing, which would further delay the microprogramming. Only a large organization can afford to develop a compiler in the expectation that it will be required later.

This scenario assumes that microprogramming will be done to emulate the machine instruction set during processor development. We might call another type of microprogramming "applications microprogramming". Applications microprograms perform functions that have been traditionally done in software, operating system functions, for instance. This type of microprogramming results in microprograms larger than emulators. Changes in this microcode would have less of an impact on the system, and therefore maintenance in the form of extensions to the functionality of the system would be more likely. Such a project might find a compiler more cost effective, first because more microcode may have to be written, and second because the project scheduling may not be so tight. We will see that this appears to have been the case.

The difficulty of writing a compiler for a HLML is not the main cause of lack of progress, however. The perceived need for efficient microcode has meant that most HLMLs have been machine dependent. A compiler for such a language cannot be used for a different target architecture without significant, and probably manual, reworking. Many of these languages have been produced in an academic environment, where, though they are made public, they are not supported. If they are developed in an industrial environment, they are often classified as proprietary and not announced. Even if they are released, industrial resistance to user microprogramming means that they are not likely to be supported. The user who does microprogram, of course, rarely has a big enough project to justify writing a compiler, even given a description of a language.

The small size of many microprograms has another effect. This is that assembly-level microprogramming techniques do produce working microprograms. For these projects, the economics still favor lower level tools.

Finally, there is a perceived need for efficient microcode. This has two effects. First, many believe that HLML compilers cannot do as good a job as a microprogrammer writing in assembly language. Second, the need for efficiency makes the job of writing the compiler more difficult, since optimization is not an option, but a necessity. HLL compilers have produced better code than assembly language programmers can write for some time now, but this is not the case for the microcode compilers reported in the literature. There are indications that a HLML might produce better code than assembly language (by taking advantage of high level improvements to the algorithm [18]), but this has still been a stumbling block.

These negative arguments will fall when microprograms become large enough for the productivity increase expected from a compiler to cover the cost of building the compiler. We are just beginning to see this happening, as will be seen in the third section of this paper. HLML compilers will be developed when there is no other alternative.

2. A TAXONOMY OF HLMLS

In this section, we will attempt to classify microprogramming languages according to two criteria. The first is the level of the language, high or low. The second is whether the language is machine dependent, machine independent, or a mixture of the two. These categories are not new, but we will attempt to clarify the distinction between high and low level. Again, we will mention several languages as examples; the reader is directed to Sint's paper [23] for a description of some of these languages. We will also present an example microprogram written in four different languages to help illustrate the differences among the languages.

2.1 Low Level and High Level Languages

What is a low level language, what is a high level language, and what are the differences?

A low level language typically includes those operations that can be performed in one microinstruction of the target machine. These include simple arithmetic and logical operations, as well as data transfers between registers and between registers and memory. All memory references have to be explicitly specified in some fashion. Typically low level languages are machine dependent, but some, like YALLL [19], are machine independent except for the need to specify target machine registers explicitly. Because of this explicit reference to target data resources, low level languages have few data structuring facilities.

Low level languages contain some structured control mechanisms, typically some kind of *while* loop. Gotos are usually also allowed, as is some type of multiway branch mechanism, of the sort commonly implemented by a microsequencer. In the past the presence of a looping mechanism has caused the authors of low level languages to have claimed them to be high level (see for instance many papers in [29]), but this is no longer the case.

High level microprogramming languages typically have several types of high level control structures, *for* loops as well as *while* loops. At least some register and storage allocation is done by the compiler instead of the user, though the user may be able to direct the placement of certain variables into registers. Some data structuring mechanisms are available, typically arrays but often others.

Some features can be found in all microprogramming languages. Bit operations (such as mask, or, etc.) are required to perform the low level data manipulation typically done at the microprogramming level. As mentioned above, some higher level control constructs can typically be found. Many low and high level languages allow explicit specification of parallelism, but there is some question whether local and global compaction algorithms [9,11,14] should be given the job of parallelism detection and exploitation.

The machine dependence or independence of the language of course has an effect on the level of the language. A totally machine dependent language requires that the allocation of variables to registers be done by the user, and therefore is not as high level a language as a similar machine independent one.

2.2 Machine Dependent and Independent Languages

A machine dependent microprogramming language can be defined as a language in which all operations and data elements defined in the language have a direct mapping to a resource of the target machine. Assembly languages are one class of machine dependent languages; however machine dependent languages can also support expressions of unlimited complexity. Data and functional resources of the target machine are bound at the language definition level, so the language is only useful for one target machine.

In a machine independent microprogramming language this binding is done by the compiler at a later stage of the translation process. The compiler must allocate storage for all variables in a pure machine independent language, and the control and data operations are not tied directly to the target microinstruction set. Thus, it is possible to translate a microprogram written in a machine independent language into microcode for several target machines, given a code generator for each.

Compilers for machine dependent languages are easier to write because the binding process, which is at the heart of compilation, is straightforward. The code that is produced by these compilers is likely to be efficient, since the programmer has the responsibility of making best use of target machine resources. However these compilers cannot be ported to other targets, which makes the compiler development effort have to pay off for only one application, which forces people using other targets to have to build new compilers from scratch. A compiler for a machine independent language can be ported to other machines by rewriting the code generator. However, these compilers must be much more sophisticated to generate good code. Thus they are cost effective only when a large number of different target machines are to be used, an uncommon situation.

Several techniques have been developed to get the advantages of both machine dependence and independence. The first is to design a language that is only somewhat machine dependent, perhaps using a standard set of operators and the data resources of a particular target. YALLL [19] is an example of this type of language. This strategy makes the compiler much easier to build, makes the compiler mostly portable, and keeps the language easy to use.

A second strategy is to design a machine independent language framework, that can be altered in a well specified way to produce a machine dependent language. The language schema S*, proposed by Dasgupta [6] is an example of this technique. The result is a set of machine dependent languages that can be understood by anyone understanding the schema. A next step in this approach would be an automatic compiler generator, using the schema and target machine description as input. As yet, this has not been done.

A third approach is to model the target machine resources that must be used by the source microprogram in terms of machine independent language features. The program remains machine independent, and thus portable, but the modeled target resources can be bound directly to those resources by the compiler. MARBLE, described by Davidson [7,10] is one example of this approach.

The common characteristic of all these approaches is to reduce the amount of work required to port the language and compiler by attempting to maximize the common features of what can be viewed as a set of different machine dependent languages. This is what we mean by "slightly machine dependent."

We see that there is no strict dividing line between machine dependent and independent languages. Most languages have machine dependent and independent features, and the proper mixture to obtain a proper degree of portability and efficiency is not yet known.

2.3 A Taxonomy of Microprogramming Languages

Given the discussion above, we can roughly divide HLMLs into 5 categories. Figure 1 illustrates the relationship of these language classes.

HIGH LEVEL MACHINE DEPENDENT	HIGH LEVEL MIXED	HIGH LEVEL MACHINE INDEPENDENT
LOW LEVEL MACHINE DEPENDENT	LOW LEVEL MACHINE INDEPENDENT	

Figure 1. A Microprogramming Language Taxonomy

2.3.1 An Example We will show the differences between language levels by means of an example, taken from [26]. This microprogram, for the Flynn machine, computes the product of two sixty-four bit numbers, represented in sign-magnitude format. Overflow is not checked for. Figure 2 gives the program.

A few words of explanation are in order. Capital letter variables represent main memory addresses, small letter variables represent microstorage addresses. In the Flynn machine these are in the same address space, with addresses 0-4095 representing the microstore and higher addresses representing the main store. The only difference between the stores is speed; they are addressed in the same way. M1 and M2 are registers containing masks, C means clear the destination before gating. U/F stands for underflow.

2.3.2 Low Level Machine Dependent Languages. In these languages the binding to target resources is done at language definition time. The control, data and functional primitives in the language closely match those available on the target, with perhaps an iteration construct added. They can allow renaming of registers to more closely match the usage of the registers by the algorithm, but storage allocation is done exclusively by the microprogrammer. An example is GMPL for a Hewlett-Packard microprocessor [12]. Figure 3 shows the multiply microprogram as it would be written in GMPL. GMPL was of course not designed for the Flynn machine, but we have substituted Flynn machine resource names for GMPL names to give a feeling for this class of language.

We can make several comments about this example. First, it is slightly easier to read than the assembly language version, because of the better format of the shift operation. The OUTPUT and WRITE operations are not really appropriate for the Flynn machine, but are a necessary part of GMPL. This shows the difficulty of using a language for one machine for a different machine. Finally, the structures of the examples are not too different. Well designed assemblers, for machines with good sequencing constructs, can look like a low level machine independent language. The boundary between language classes is not a clear one.

2.3.3 Low Level Machine Independent Languages. These languages implement a set of control and functional resources found on a wide range of targets. The data resources are simple, often a generic register type and arrays. Most binding is done by the compiler, but probably each implementation of a low level machine independent language includes some binding to specific target registers in the language definition, which makes programs in the language not really portable. An example of this type of language is YALLL [19]. Figure 4 shows the example written in YALL.

The three address format of YALLL is, I think, difficult to read, however YALLL was designed to serve as an intermediate language, so this is not an issue. We can see one of the problems of machine independent microprogramming languages in this example. The underflow flag, U/F, that was used in the previous two examples does not exist in YALL, so we had to rewrite the example to test the low bit of the variable *mier*. This was easy to do in this case, it might not be so easy for different machine resources. The sequencing for YALL is the same as assembly language, consisting of **if** statements and jumps. There is some machine dependence in this example, but it is limited to the registers. They are assumed to be 64 bits in width.

2.3.4 High Level Machine Dependent Languages. Control resources in high level machine dependent languages are usually bound to target control resources by the compiler, and are high level. The details of moving data between memory and registers is handled by the compiler, as is some of the detailed bookkeeping required by the target (such as checking for interrupts every so many cycles). Data and functional resources are bound at language definition time, though more complex expressions may be accepted than by low level languages. An example of a high level machine dependent language is microTAL [1].

This microprogram looks more high level than the previous microprograms. The machine dependent parts of this program are the use of the ACC as a predefined register, and the use of the U/F flag. Most of the program, however, consists of constructs familiar from high level programming.

2.3.5 High Level Machine Independent Languages. In these languages, all storage allocation is done by the compiler (though hints about which variables should be placed in registers may be given by the microprogrammer). Binding is done late, by the compiler. The operator repertoire will probably consist of those functions implemented or implementable by a wide range of targets. These languages often look like Systems Implementation

```
MPY:  y := B;                              y temporary storage for multiplier
      ACC := M1C / y;                      Sign of B in ACC (ACC := B & 100..0)
      ACC := ACC + A,                      Result sign in ACC
      x := M2C / A;                        Absolute value of multiplicand in x
;                                          Mask = 0111..1
      z := M1C / ACC;                      Set result sign and clear value.
      y := M2C / y;                        Multiplier absolute value in y.
MPY1: y := +1 / y;                         Shift multiplier right one bit.
      y := y+'00...0',                     Test if low bit was a 1.
      if U/F goto MPY3;
      if ZERO goto MPY4;                   Done?
MPY2: x := -1 / x,                         Shift multiplicand left one bit
      go to MPY1;
MPY3: z := x + z,                          Accumulate result
      goto MPY2;
MPY4: C := z;                              Store result
```

Figure 2. Microprogram Example - Assembly Language

```
INSTRUCTION Mult;
  Begin
                 READ (B);                 Read From Memory
                 INPUT WORD MREG ==> x;
  *                                        See Note 1 Below
                 y AND M1 ==> ACC;         Mask
                 READ (A);                 Multiplicand from memory
                 INPUT WORD MREG ==> x;
                 ACC + x ==> ACC;          Determine result sign
                 x AND M2 ==> x;           Magnitude of mcand in x
                 ACC AND M1 ==> z;         Sign to result register
                 y AND M2 ==> y;           Magnitude of multiplier in y
  * Beginning of loop. It is not a repeat because there is no variable
  * to increment or decrement
  MPY1:          SHIFT y RIGHT 1 ==> y;
                 IF U/F THEN MPY3;         A bit dropped?
                 IF ZERO THEN MPY4;        All done?
  MPY2:          SHIFT x LEFT 1 ==> x;
                 GOTO MPY1;
  MPY3:          x + z ==> z;              Accumulate result
                 GOTO MPY2;
  MPY4:          OUTPUT WORD z;
                 WRITE (C);
                 EXIT;
```

Figure 3. Multiply Microprogram in GMPL

Languages (SILs). An example is SUILVEN [24]. We present the example microprogram in MARBLE [7], using only the machine independent parts of the language.

This microprogram looks like a standard high level language program, which is the desired objective of microprogramming language design at this level. Language designers can take advantage of the experience of HLL designers. The problem with this class of microprogramming languages is not visible from this example; it is the efficiency of the produced code. Innocuous language features can cause grave efficiency problems. Consider the use of the variables *mcand* and *A* in the example above. A is resident in memory in the machine dependent versions of this program. The participation of A in the expression in the second statement of the procedure will force the compiler to allocate a register for A. If an assignment to mcand were made before this line no extra assignment need be made, an extra read from memory would not be done. A sophisticated optimizer could combine the reads and the registers, but this example shows how small perturbations of code can cause large problems that would not be problems in a HLL environment.

2.3.6 High Level Languages with Machine Independent and Dependent Components. These languages allow the inclusion of some machine dependence for efficiency reasons. This class is included in recognition that a little machine dependence can buy a lot of efficiency. Slightly machine dependent higher level languages may be included in this class, but we mean mostly machine independent languages or schemas that may be adapted for a given target. Examples are S* [6], MARBLE [7], and microAPL [13]. The example is given using the machine dependent capabilities of MARBLE.

Here we explicitly bind *mcand, mier* and *result* to the registers x, y and z. If binding were turned off they would again be simple variables. Explicitly stating the difference between these variables and A, B, and C would, we hope, encourage the programmer to pay more attention to register usage where necessary. The bound function UF allows this resource to be used by the MARBLE program.

We have briefly described five categories of microprogramming languages. In the next section we will examine several languages that are being used, and relate them to this taxonomy.

```
                 reg mcand = x
                 reg mier = y                          ; illustrates renaming feature
                 reg product = z                       ; x, y, and z are machine dependent

                 MPY:
                          load mier, B                  ; YALL cannot handle memory to memory
           ;                                              operations, so consider x,y,z as registers
                          and ACC,#100...00,mier
           ;                                            Clear ACC, set sign of B.  First operand is the
           ;                                              destination
                          load mcand, A
                          add ACC, ACC, mcand
                          and mcand,#011..1, mcand      ; Get mcand value
                          and product,#100...0,ACC      ; Set result sign, clear value
                          and mier,#011...1,mier        ; Get mier value
                 MPY1:    jump MPY3 if mier<0>=1        ; Test low bit
                          jump MPY4 if mier=0           ; Done
                 MPY2:    srl mier,mier,1
                          sll mcand,mcand,1
                          jump MPY1
                 MPY3:    add product,product,mcand     ; Accumulate product
                          jump MPY2
                 MPY4:    store product,C               ; Result to memory
                          rtn
```

Figure 4. Example Microprogram Written in YALL

```
proc MULT (A, B, C)

int  A, B, C, mier, mcand, result

begin
            ACC := (B and 100..0) + A
            mcand := A and 011...1
            mier := B and 011...1
            result := ACC and 100...0
            while mier <> 0 do
            begin
                mier := mier rshift 1
                if U/F  ! Machine dependent condition flag
                then result := result + mcand
                mcand := mcand lshift 1
            end
            C := result
end
```

Figure 5. Example Microprogram Written in microTAL

```
procedure multiply (in A, B: bit 64; out C: bit 64);

var         mier, mcand, result: bit 64;

begin
            mier := B;
            result := ((mier and <b>100...0) + A)
                and <b>100...0;
            mier := mier and<b>011...1;
            mcand := A and <b>011...1;
            while mier <> 0
            begin
                if odd(mier)
                then result := result + mcand;
                mier := mier rshift 1;
                mcand := mcand lshift 1;
            end;
            C := result;
end; /* of procedure multiply */
```

Figure 6. Example Microprogram Written in Machine Independent
    MARBLE

```
/* Global declarations of bound resources */
type                bound x,y,z = bit 64;
        /* Assumption: registers named x,y,z */

function bound UF returns boolean;
        bound;
            /* Representing the flag.  Could also be
                declared as a bound
                data resource if more appropriate */

procedure multiply (in A, B: bit 64; out C: bit 64);

var         mier: bound y;
            mcand: bound x;
            result: bound z;
begin
            mier := B;
            mcand := A;
            result := ((mier and <b>100...0) + mcand)
                and <b>100...0;
            mier := mier and<b>011...1;
            mcand := mcand and <b>011...1;
            while mier <> 0
            begin
                mier := mier rshift 1;
                if UF
                then result := result + mcand;
                mcand := mcand lshift 1;
            end;
            C := result;
end; /* of procedure multiply */
```

Figure 7. Example Microprogram in MARBLE Using Binding

3. HLMLS IN INDUSTRY

At the 1981 Microprogramming Workshop in Chatham, Massachusetts [16] a number of speakers described microprogram development in their projects. Most of these speakers described microassemblers, often coupled to sophisticated firmware engineering tools. Some of the speakers, however, discussed how HLMLs were being used in microcode development, and we will briefly describe these languages.

Bartlett [1] described MicroTAL, a high level machine dependent microprogramming language based on the SIL TAL. The purpose of the development of MicroTAL is to allow the migration of system and application functions written in TAL to microcode without extensive reprogramming. This would allow some debugging to be done before having to be involved with the low level target machine, effectively decoupling the debugging of the algorithm from the debugging of the hardware/firmware interactions. Another advantage of using a HLML in this application is that some of the bookkeeping required of the microcode could be handled automatically, inserted by the compiler. Parallelism exploitation, both through the overlaying of memory fetches and instruction execution and through compaction, is also done by the compiler.

The compiler has compiled a small procedure from a LISP interpreter into microcode that is almost as good as that produced by hand. Replacing six procedures from the interpreter with their microcoded equivalents has resulted in a 35% speedup.

Sheraga and Gieser [21] describe a machine independent higher level microprogramming language called HLL. They implemented HLL to allow the translation of computation intensive application programs, written in high level languages, into microcode. A number of different target machines are to be used, so machine independence is important, and they expect 100,000 lines of microcode to be generated, so a compiler was essential.

The microcode produced by HLL was compared with hand coded microprograms, and the compiler version was found to be from 5-10% longer than the hand coded version. Programmer productivity, also measured, was greatly increased by the use of HLL. In any case, they felt that it was infeasible to produce large amounts of microcode by hand.

A third example involves not a HLML compiler, but a microcode development strategy making use of a HLL. The microcode for the iAPX 432 [15] was developed using a top down approach. First, the high level algorithm was written in ADA. No binding to hardware was done at this point. The specification was very detailed; in fact ADA had to be extended somewhat for this task. Next, the specification was hand translated into a lower level version, using a subset of ADA, and making some hardware bindings. Finally, this version of the program was again hand translated into microcode, at the microassembler level. This method, though obviously taking longer than would be the case for automatic translation, had most of the advantages of using a high level language without the need for developing a compiler, and without loss of efficiency in the final code. Doing the translation to microcode took only 30% of the development effort, so this approach appears to be cost effective. A further advantage of this approach was that tests for the chip set were derived from the high level algorithm, which greatly simplified the job of test development.

3.1 Summary

The three examples cited above are certainly not the only cases of high level microprogramming language use in industry. IBM certainly has a microprogramming language; no information on it has been released to the best of our knowledge. Weidner [28] describes CHAMIL, developed at Sperry Univac. Poe, Goodell and Steely [20], are developing a lower level language at DEC.

We can, however, see some trends. The first is that people are realizing that very large microprograms make a language not a luxury, but a necessity. The second is that having one language framework for both system software and microcode development gives great advantages in the specification, migration and validation of microcode. Third, a microprogrammer developing an algorithm at a high level can make improvements to the algorithm at that level, and probably can obtain a faster microprogram than is available by tuning only at the low level. This lower level tuning is still necessary, and can be done by a compiler, if one is available, or by hand.

A HLML provides another advantage; a decoupling of the program from the lower level hardware. When changes to the hardware are made (which is inevitable during processor development) the microcode, but not the algorithm, must be changed. A high level version of the algorithm that does not have to be altered allows regression testing of the changed microcode. Sometimes the algorithm is affected by the changes to the hardware. When this happens the changes will be easier to make to the high level version than to the microcode.

A HLML is essential for large amounts of microcode, and useful for any microprogramming project. A HLML does not necessarily imply the existence of a HLML to microcode compiler. Hand translation, using a well defined set of rules, could provide better code for a smaller initial investment. It appears that we have not reached the break-even point for the development of a compiler for most microprogramming applications. The use of HLMLs before this point is reached allows experiments with these languages to be performed, and may help to clear up our rather murky understanding of HLMLs. Hand translation will also give us better insight as to what a successful HLML compiler should be. Finally, if enough microprogrammers grow used to the use of HLMLs, a demand should be created for a compiler.

4. THE FUTURE OF HIGH LEVEL MICROPROGRAMMING - TWO SCENARIOS

In this section we will discuss two methods of HLML language design, and then describe some microprogram development methods that we might see in the future. The goals that must be met are efficient target code, ease of portability of the language, ability to use software engineering tools and methods in microprogramming, and increased microprogrammer productivity.

One possible language is a completely machine independent HLML. This type of language can meet the goals of increased productivity and interface with software engineering tools just as standard HLLs have met these goals. The other goals are more difficult to meet. The goal of production of efficient code requires an extremely sophisticated compiler to detect sequences of source code that can be mapped to target microinstructions, to do register allocation considering the memory reference penalty found in most microprogrammable machines, and to do both local and global microcode compaction and optimization. To meet the goal of portability, the many machine dependent parts of such a compiler must be designed so that retargeting the compiler for another architecture does not require rewriting most of the compiler. The language must be designed so that the microprogrammer is confident that the compiler correctly deals with all the particularities of the target machine, including interrupt handling, exceptions, and nonstandard data and functional resources. No machine independent language and compiler now meets these specifications, and it is certainly not obvious if this problem is solvable. If it is not, perhaps machine dependent code sequences can be included in the microprogram. This is the strategy currently used by most software SILs.

Another possibility would be to design a retargetable compiler for a range of machine dependent high level languages. The machine dependence, we hope, will allow the compiler to produce efficient code without being as complex as the compiler for a totally machine dependent language. The retargetability of the compiler would make it portable. The language would have to be designed to be truly high level, especially the machine dependent parts of the language. It is not clear how low level functionality can be expressed in a high level way and remain reasonably understandable to someone reading the program who is not an expert on the target. S*, given a retargetable compiler (which does not yet exist) is a first step on this path.

Another difficulty with this approach is in the design of tools for microprogram development. Any tools that require semantic knowledge would have to be table driven, to be easily adapted to new target machines. Perhaps these tools would be driven by the microinstruction description that would certainly be a part of each compiler for this type of language. Much work has been done on these descriptions, [22] for example, so this approach is plausible.

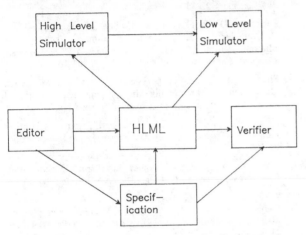

Figure 8. A Proposed Microprogramming Environment

We have briefly described two approaches to HLML design in the future. Given such a compiler, how can we further increase microprogrammer productivity? The experience of software design has showed us that a language is not enough; that a language must serve as the basis for a set of tools that further aid the development process. These tools have become known as programming environments [27]. What could be the structure of a microprogramming environment? One possible microprogramming environment is shown in Figure 6. The first part of the environment would be an intelligent microcode editor. This would serve the same function as intelligent editors for software [25], except that it would also include tutorials on the use of any machine dependent features that could be accessed from the HLML. The structure of the language itself should prevent the user from writing illegal microcode; if this is impossible in the machine dependent parts of the language the editor should flag any errors in usage.

Two other parts of the system are simulators. A review of some microcode simulators can be found in [8]. A high level simulator will interpret HLML statements and allow the user to trace a microprogram in terms of the HLML. A low level simulator would be able to simulate each microinstruction produced by the compiler and report on the effects of the execution of the microcode in both high and low level terms. This low level simulator is necessary first to debug a compiler for a new processor, and second to provide an aid to the microprogrammer at the hardware interface. It will be necessary in debugging the hardware of a new processor to have complete information about the effects of the microprogram at a low level; this simulator will provide this information. The low level simulator must be table driven to allow the simulator and thus

the programming environment to be easily reconfigured for other targets.

These simulators will provide, in addition to the ability to check the simulated data resources of the target, execution profiles and timing information. These are a great help in determining where the microprogram is spending its time, and are far easier to implement in the simulator rather than in a compiler. Another feature of the language and simulator should be assertions. Instead of being executable, the usual case, these assertions should compile into breakpoint specifications for the simulator. If this is done the real microprogram can be simulated, rather than one altered by the presence of code for the assertions.

Another part of the environment, which might be migrated into the language itself, should be a way of specifying the response of the microprogram to asynchronous events. In addition to this the specification must be able to specify the timing of the microprogram, in the sense that a certain microcode segment must execute within a certain amount of time. How to specify this information in an understandable way is a difficult problem; going from such a specification to code that satisfies the requirements is a still more difficult problem. Certainly research in real-time languages and systems will be valuable for microprogramming in the future.

Finally, a verification system might be included for some applications, but in general the cost of such a system, at least in the near future, would be excessive. This system would prove the correctness of the microprogram with respect to the given specifications. We can expect that it will be interactive, and will communicate with the microprogrammer through an interface similar to those used by the simulators. A great deal of work has been done on verification of microcode already, for instance [3,4,5]. This works suggests that a verification system, though expensive now, will become feasible for critical microprograms.

In summary, a microprogramming environment will include a language, an editor, a compiler, and several simulators. The language is the foundation of these tools, and to justify the cost of the environment over many systems, the language must be portable. With such a system, the practice of firmware engineering will at last approach the practice of software engineering.

5. CONCLUSION

In this paper we have argued that a HLML is the key to future progress in firmware engineering. Microprogram simulators are widely used, and are becoming well human engineered. Work in intelligent editors is progressing well in the software area and can be easily adapted for microprogramming. Languages are still our major stumbling block.

Currently, building a high level microprogram compiler is only economically justified if large amounts of microcode are to be produced. Academic research can show the way to reducing the cost of compiler construction, and provide a firm experimental and theoretical foundation for this work. Industrial use of HLMLs, even without compilers, can provide practical experience with the advantages and disadvantages of these languages. This work, we hope, can lead to a widely accepted paradigm for HLMLs, in the manner of the procedural language paradigm for HLLs. This is not to say that a microprogramming language should necessarily be procedural! We of course can never expect to see a universally accepted language. Given this paradigm, and several examples of successful languages, we can proceed with the job of developing the proper tools for productive and correct microprogramming.

6. ACKNOWLEDGEMENTS

I would like to thank the referees for their valuable comments on an earlier version of this paper.

7. REFERENCES

[1] Bartlett, J. F., "MicroTAL - A Machine-Dependent High-Level Microprogramming Language," *Proc. 14th Annu. Microprogramming Workshop*, pp. 109-114.

[2] Brooks, F. P. Jr, *The Mythical Man Month* (3rd ed.). Reading, Massachusetts: Addison-Wesley, 1975.

[3] Budkowski, S., and P. Dembinski, "Firmware versus Software Verification," *Proc. 11th Annu. Microprogramming Workshop*, pp. 119-127.

[4] Carter, W. C., W. H. Joyner, Jr., and D. B. Brand, "Symbolic Simulation for Correct Machine Design," *16th Annu. Design Automation Conf.*, June 1979.

[5] Crocker, S. D., Marcus, L., and D. van-Mierop, "The ISI Microcode Development System," *IFIP TC-10 Conference on Microprogramming, Firmware and Restructurable Hardware*, North-Holland, Amsterdam, 1980, pp. 243-249.

[6] Dasgupta, S., "Some Aspects of High Level Microprogramming," *Comput. Surv.*, 12 (1980), 3, pp. 295-324. Microprogramming Language Design,"

[7] Davidson, S., "Design and Construction of a Virtual Machine Resource Binding Language," Ph.D. Dissertation, Computer Science Department, University of Southwestern Louisiana, December 1980.

[8] Davidson, S., and B. D. Shriver, "Firmware Engineering: An Extensive Update," *IFIP TC-10 Conference on Microprogramming, Firmware and Restructurable Hardware*, North-Holland, Amsterdam, 1980, pp. 1-36.

[9] Davidson, S., D. Landskov, B. D. Shriver, and P. W. Mallett, "Some Experiments in Local Microcode Compaction for Horizontal Machines," *IEEE Trans. Comput.*, C-30 (1981), 7, pp. 460-477.

[10] Davidson, S., and B. D. Shriver, "Specifying Target Resources in a Machine Independent High Level Language," *AFIPS Proceedings of the National Computer Conference* (Vol. 50), 1981, pp. 81-85.

[11] Fisher, J. A., "Trace Scheduling: A Technique for Global Microcode Compaction," *IEEE Trans. Comput.*, C-30 (1981), 7, pp. 478-490.

[12] Guffin, R.M., "A Microprogramming Language Directed Microarchitecture," *Proc. 15th Annu. Microprogramming Workshop*, pp. 42-49.

[13] Hobson, R. F., P. Hannon, and J. Thornburg, "High-Level Microprogramming with APL Syntax," *Proc. 14th Annu. Microprogramming Workshop*, pp. 131-139.

[14] Landskov, D., S. Davidson, B. D. Shriver, and P. W. Mallett, "Local Microcode Compaction Techniques," *Comput. Surv.*, 12 (1980), 3, pp. 261-294.

[15] Lattin, W. W., J. A. Bayliss, D. L. Budde, J. R. Rattner, and W. S. Richardson, "A Methodology for VLSI Chip Design," *Lambda*, II (1981), 2, pp. 34-45.

[16] MICRO-14, *Proceedings of 14th Annual Microprogramming Workshop*, October 12-15 1981, Chatham, MA.

[17] Oestreicher, D. R., "A Microprogramming Language for the MLP-900," *Proc. ACM SIGPLAN-SIGMICRO Interface Meeting*, 1973, pp. 113-116.

[18] Patterson, D. A., "An Experiment in High Level Language Microprogramming and Verification," *Comm. ACM*, 24 (1981), 10, pp. 699-709.

[19] Patterson, D. A., K. Lew, and R. Tuck, "Towards an Efficient, Machine-Independent Language for Microprogramming," *Proc. 12th Annu. Microprogramming Workshop*, pp. 22-35.

[20] Patterson, D., R. Goodell, M. D. Poe, and S. C. Steely Jr., "V-Compiler: A Next-Generation Tool for Microprogramming," *AFIPS Proceedings of the National Computer Conference*, (Vol. 50), 1981, pp. 103-109.

[21] Sheraga, R. J., and J. L. Gieser, "Automatic Microcode Generation for Horizontally Microprogrammed Processors," *Proc. 14th Annu. Microprogramming Workshop*, pp. 154-168.

[22] Sint, M., "MIDL - A Microinstruction Description Language," *Proc. 14th Annu. Microprogramming Workshop*, pp. 95-106.

[23] Sint, M. "A Survey of Higher Level Microprogramming Languages," *Proc. 13th Annu. Microprogramming Workshop*, pp. 141-153.

[24] Sommerville, J. F., "Towards Machine Independent Microprogramming," *Euromicro Journal*, 5 (1979), 4, pp. 219-224.

[25] Teitelbaum, T., and T. Reps, "The Cornell Program Synthesizer: A Syntax-Directed Programming Environment," *Comm. ACM*, 24 (1981), 9, pp. 563-573.

[26] Tucker, A. B., and Flynn, M. J., "Dynamic Microprogramming: Processor Organization and Programming," *Comm. ACM*, 14 (1971), 4, pp. 240-250.

[27] Wasserman, A. I. (ed.), Special Issue on Programming Environments, *Computer*, 14 (1981), 4.

[28] Weidner, T. G., "CHAMIL, A Case Study in Microprogramming Language Design," *ACM SIGPLAN Notices*, 15 (1980), 1, pp. 156-166.

[29] Wexelblat, R. L. (ed.), *Proceedings of ACM SIGPLAN-SIGMICRO Interface Meeting*, 1973.

Panel Session VIII
Firmware Methodology and Practice

Chairman

S. Davidson
Western Electric

Panelists

To Be Determined

Session IX
Microcode Compaction and
Optimization II

ON AUTOMATED DESIGN OF COMPACTED MICROPROGRAMS

P. DEMBINSKI

Institute of Computer Science,
Polish Academy of Sciences
00901 Warsaw, Poland

ABSTRACT

A method of automated design of horizontal microprograms from their vertical specifications is proposed. It may be considered complementary to the known microprogram compaction algorithms in that it mainly deals with branching and looping structure of the source microprogram and not with its straight line segments. The method is based on systematic performance of a local microprogram transformation dynamically adjusted to the hardware derived constraints formulated separately.

INTRODUCTION

Reducing the size of control memory and/or minimizing the execution time are the general microprogram optimization objectives. When the execution time becomes the prevailing factor than parallelization of computations and horizontal organization of the store are of main interest. In this context the term "microprogram compaction" has been established to mean the activity of transforming vertically designed microprograms into equivalent horizontal solutions taking into account constraints resulting from specific hardware organization. In other wordsthe task is to 'pack' independent microoperations into horizontal microinstructions to minimize their number without changing the underlying algorithm.

Much of the work has been done in this direction. Compaction algorithms are primarily based on microprogram partition into its straight-line segments compacted separately, (so called local compaction techniques, e.g. [1],[10]. Various approaches to local compaction are surveyed and compared in [3,6,7]). More global approach of intersegment optimization was taken in [2] for not looping fragments , or by the project described in [8,9]. The trace scheduling technique proposed in [5] is based on truly global data flow analysis. However, even these global compaction methods do not take into account all of the compaction possibilities while manipulating the branching structure of a microprogram and/or introducing conditional microoperations. If the compaction procedure is thought off as a part of the design process (and not only as an optimization technique in a fixed hardware environment) it may be worthwhile to make a slight change in the disigned hardware (inserting a decoder of conditional microoperations into the control part may be an example) to achieve considerable gain in execution time of the whole microprogram. Even without such changes there are often unexploited compaction possibilities when branching and looping structure is altered. In this paper we concentrate on the above aspect of compaction.

To illustrate the problem let us consider the microprogram of floating-point addition presented in Fig.1 (floating-point addition of normalized numbers where both the exponents and fractions are represented by 8 bits in 2's complement system). This may be viewed a vertical version to be optimized. One can imagine that, in this case, the ultimate compaction goal is to minimize the number of microstatements whatever the price is to be paid in necessary hardware to implement such a maximally parallel solution. For such a task one can produce the horizontal microprogram of only 6 microinstructions given in Fig.2. But the compaction goal may be formulated differently. Given a specific structure the microprogram is to be implemented, produce an equivalent microprogram with reduced number of microstatements taking into account the constraints resulting from this specific hardware. These constraints may not, for instance, permit certain operations to be executed in parallel or may limit the use of conditional microoperations in situations when theoretically (i.e., according to the microprogram semantics) it was admissible. The structure the diagram of which is given in Fig.3 provides an example of such a constraint. It is not possible to add registers' values and to check their equality in the same step of a computation because both operations require a single adder of the structure.Another example is given by the AM 2901 microprocessor in which one control field controls three blocks in the microprocessor operational unit (this reduces the control word size) excluding thereby the simultaneous execution of some microoperations. The microprogram in Fig.4 satisfies the compaction goal formulated for the microprogram of Fig.1 and the possibilities of the implementing structure in Fig.3 (assumig an appropriate control unit).

The question arises whether the micro-program in Fig.2 and that in Fig.4 might be achieved from the initial one by a mechanical procedure. If so, then whether one can look for a single general algorithmic scheme from which, specifying some input parameters (restrictions in the above sense), one can obtain a compaction algorithm for a given hardware environment.

Such an algorithmic scheme is presented in this paper. It is based on a system of microprogram transformations defined in [4] and thought off as a step towards an automation of the microprogram design and verification. What we propose in this paper is a way of systematic use of the above transformations in order to get a compacted (with respect to the given hardware configuration)

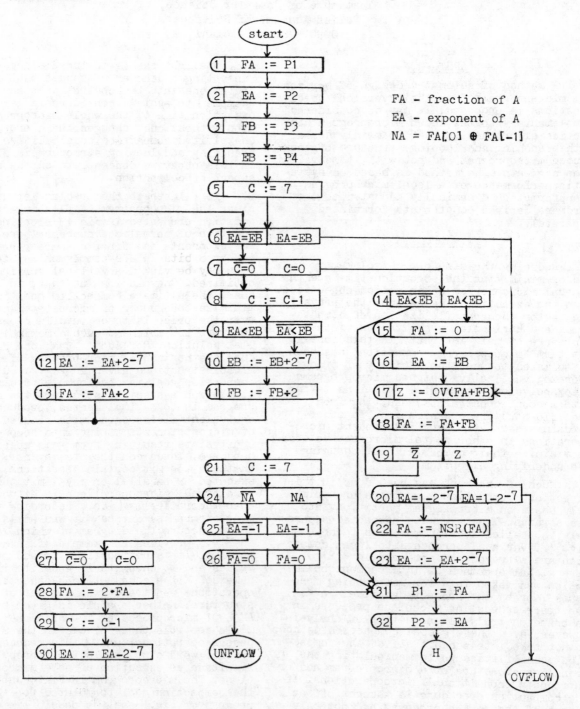

FA - fraction of A
EA - exponent of A
$NA = FA[0] \oplus FA[-1]$

Fig.1

and horizontal version of a vertical micro-program. If no restriction is stated the compaction algorithm reduces the number of the microprogram instructions to the extend allowed by the semantic description of the language in use and the possibilities of detecting parallelism in the microprogram by examining its syntax. It is important to stress that the transformations we are dealing with are strictly "syntax directed" which makes them effective and easy to im-plement but, at the same time, restricted in their nature.

Finally, one should mention that concentrating on the branching and looping structure of microprograms the presented algorithm may fail to produce the results as good as other methods if applied to the straight-line segments (only in presence of other than data dipendency constraints). The algorithm could be (labouriously) extended

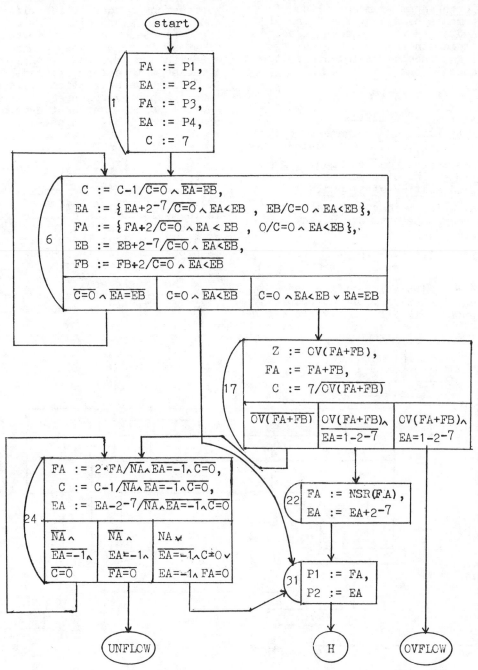

Fig. 2

to improve its performance also in these cases but for the sake of presentation simplicity of the main idea we have decided to omit this extention.

NOTATION AND SEMANTICS

We are going to use some convenient notation but niether syntax nor semantics of the language is fully or formally presented. Details can be found in [4].

By a <u>microprogram</u> we mean a list of labeled statements headed by the "<u>start L</u>" form which indicates the statement labeled by L with which the program begins its computation. Any labeled statement has the following general form:

$$L: co \underline{exit} Q_1.L_1,\ldots,Q_n.L_n \qquad (1)$$

where $L,L_1,\ldots,L_n$ are <u>labels</u>, co is a (possibly empty) list of assignments called <u>costatement</u>, and $Q_1,\ldots,Q_n$ are boolean expressions (predicates) called <u>branching</u> (or <u>exit</u>) <u>conditions</u>. The statement of the form "L:" is called <u>halting</u> <u>statement</u>.

Examples of flow-chart representation of programs and statements are given in Fig.1, 2 and 4.

<u>Assignments</u> are written

$$X := E \qquad (2)$$

where X is a variable identifier and E an expression. The only important property of costatements is that for every two assig-

nments $X := E$ and $Y := F$ occurring in the same costatement, $X \neq Y$.

<u>Expressions</u> are build up from simple <u>terms</u> and <u>predicates</u> by the conditional form. A <u>conditional expression</u> is written

$$\{E_1/Q_1,\ldots,E_n/Q_n\} \qquad (3)$$

where E_i is any expression and Q_i a predicate, i=1,..,n . If n=1 we often write E/Q instead of $\{E/Q\}$, and unconditional expression E can be identified with the conditional expression E/1 . Conditional expressions do not occur in terms or predicates. As it will be defined later on, the substitution of a conditional expression for a variable in a term or predicate, necessary to define transformations, yields a conditional expression or predicate respectively. We also assume that nesting conditional expressions may be eliminated by

$$\{E_1/Q_1,\ldots,E_n/Q_n\}/Q \equiv \qquad (4)$$
$$\{E_1/Q \wedge Q_1,\ldots,E_n/Q \wedge Q_n\}$$

The value of the conditional expression (3) for a given valuation of its variables is the value of its constituent expression E_i for which the predicate Q_i is satisfied. We say that the conditional expression is <u>proper</u> if all its predicates are pairwise disjoint.

The single assignment (2) changes the actual value of X into that of the expression E . If E is conditional of the form

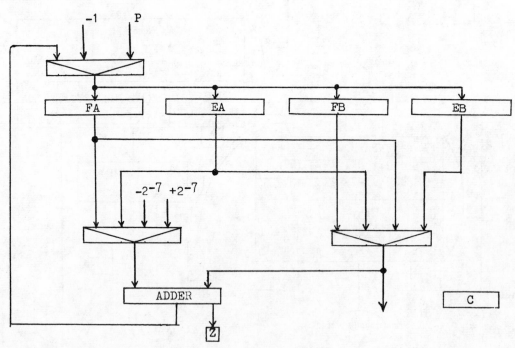

Fig.3

208

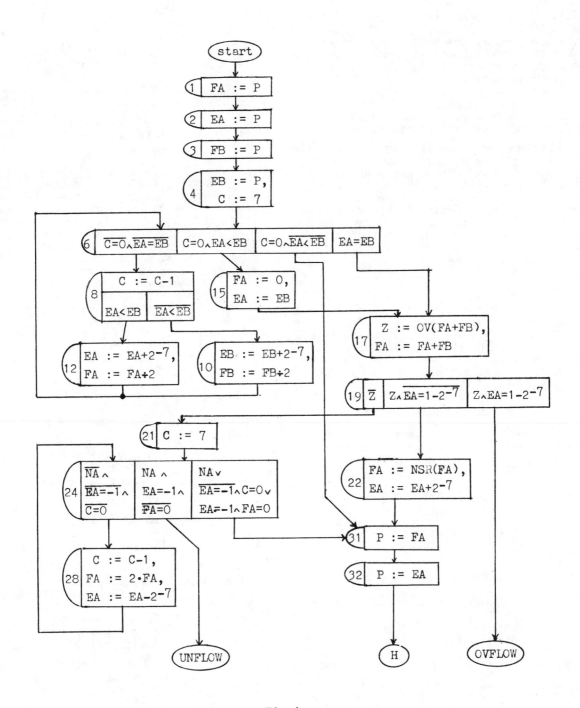

Fig.4

(3) and, for a given valuation, none of the predicates is satisfied then the value of X remains unchanged.

A costatement is interpreted to perform all its assignments simultaneously, and a statement in the form (1) simultaneously computes not only assignments of its costatement but also all its branching conditions. This means that although a variable may have its value changed by an assignment within the costatement, any of the statement branching conditions which refers to that variable is computed with respect to the initial value of the variable. This interpretation reflects the microprogram ideology which is based on the assumption that one microinstruction describes computation performed in parallel during one phase of a synchronizing clock.

A statement is called proper if all conditional expressions of its costatement are proper and its branching conditions are pairwise disjoint (branching is proper). A microprogram is proper if all its state-

209

ments are proper. The properness property is the only one semantical property assumed. The property is preserved, however, by the transformations which are to be used and it is satisfied by vertical microprograms we start with the compaction procedure. This means that properness does not influence further consideration of this paper.

Programs are semantically characterized by their input-output functions. The (partial) function is defined for a valuation v of the program variables and yields valuation v' iff there is a computation begining with the start statement of the program and the initial valuation v and ending in a halting statement with the final valuation v'.

Programs are said to be <u>semantically equivalent</u> iff their input-output functions are identical.

A program is called <u>vertical</u> iff all its non halting statements are those in the form "L: X:=E <u>exit</u> L'" or "L: <u>exit</u> $Q.L_1,\overline{Q}.L_2$" where E is an unconditional expression (each statement describes a single microoperation). Any other program is called <u>horizontal</u>.

BASIC TRANSFORMATION

Let co be a costatement and Q a predicate. By co/Q we denote the costatement co in which every assignment becomes conditional with respect to Q. For example,

co: $X:=\{E_1/Q_1,E_2/Q_2\}$, $Y:=E$

and, with (4),

co/Q: $X:=\{E_1/Q\wedge Q_1,E_2/Q\wedge Q_2\}$, $Y:=E/Q$

Denote:

var(co) – the set of all variables occurring in co

var(Q) – the set of all variables occurring in Q

lvar(co) – the set of all left-hand side variables of the assignments occurring in co

fvar(co) = var(co)- lvar(co) (free variables)

Let $co_1,..,co_n$ and $Q_1,..,Q_n$ be arbitrary costatements and predicates respectively. We define the new costatement $co = \bigoplus\limits_{i=1}^{n} co_i/Q_i$ as follows:

1. if $X:=E_{i_j} \in co_{i_j}$ for $1\leqslant i_j \leqslant n$, and $X\notin$ lvar(co_p) for $p\neq i_j$, $j=1,..,k\leqslant n$,

   then $X:=\{E_{i_1}/Q_{i_1},..,E_{i_k}/Q_{i_k}\} \in$ co

2. no other assignment belongs to co.

The following example illustrates the use of the operation:

co_1: $A:=F(A,X)$, co_2: $A:=G(A,X)$, co_3: $A:=H(A)$
$C:=C+1$ $C:=C+1$

If Q_1,Q_2 and Q_3 are arbitrary disjoint predicates then

$\bigoplus\limits_{i=1}^{3} co_i/Q_i$: $A:=\{F(A,X)/Q_1,G(A,X)/Q_2,H(A)/Q_3\}$,
$C:=C+1/Q_1\vee Q_2$

Consider two costatements co and co' and a predicate Q. Denote by $\hat{co}$ ($\hat{Q}$) a new costatement (predicate) which results from co (Q) by replacing each occurrence of a free variable X in co (a variable X in Q), such that $X:=E \in co'$, by the expression E. Notice that $\hat{co}=co$ ($\hat{Q}=Q$) if there is no such a variable. Writing $\hat{co}$ or $\hat{Q}$ we shall always add with respect to what other costatement they are constructed. In order to be precise we need to understand properly the above substitution rule when E is conditional. The following example seems to be sufficient to understand the rule and can be easily generalized. If

co : $Z:=X+Y/X<Y$

co': $X:=E/Q$

then, with (4) and some obvious logical rules,

co : $Z:=\{E+Y/Q\wedge E<Y, X+Y/\overline{Q}\wedge X<Y\}$

Consider the following set of statements:

L : co <u>exit</u> $Q_1.L_1,..,Q_i.L_i,..,Q_j.L_j,..,Q_n.L_n$

L_i: co_i <u>exit</u> $P_1^i.L_1^i,..,P_{n_i}^i.L_{n_i}^i$

$\vdots$ (5)

L_j: co_j <u>exit</u> $P_1^j.L_1^j,..,P_{n_j}^j.L_{n_j}^j$

<u>Theorem.</u> If, in a proper program $\mathbb{P}$, there is a set of statements of the form (5) such that, for each $k=i,i+1,..,j$,

lvar(co_k) $\cap$ lvar(co) = $\emptyset$

then the program $\mathbb{P}'$ which results from $\mathbb{P}$ by replacement of the statement labeled by L with

L: $co \cup \bigoplus\limits_{k=i}^{j} \hat{co}_k/Q_k$ <u>exit</u> $Q_1.L_1,..,Q_i\wedge\hat{P}_1^i.L_1^i,..,$
$Q_i\wedge\hat{P}_{n_i}^i.L_{n_i}^i,..,Q_j\wedge\hat{P}_1^j.L_1^j,..,$ (6)
$Q_j\wedge\hat{P}_{n_j}^j.L_{n_j}^j,..,Q_n.L_n$

is proper and semantically equivalent to $\mathbb{P}$ ($\hat{co}_k$ and $\hat{P}_m^k$, $k=i,i+1,..,j$, $m=1,..,n_k$, are formed with respect to the costatement co).

The proof of this theorem and various

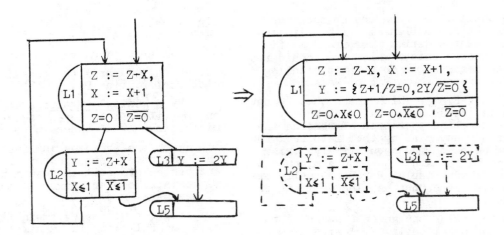

FOLD(L1;L2,L3)

Fig.5

program transformations resulting from it are given in [4]. We concentrate our attention on the main of these transformations, namely this defined by the replacement of (5) with (6). That one will be denoted

$$FOLD(L;L_1,..,L_j)$$

and an example of its application is given in Fig.5, where $n=2$, $i=1$, $j=2$ and $n_i=2$, $n_j=1$.

Observe, that after the transformation the statements L2 and L3 in the example of Fig.5 become isolated (i.e., without any entrance to them from another statement) and therefore can be removed without altering the semantics of the program. Furthermore, since properness of the new statement L1 is preserved, two branching conditions of L1 can be merged and the resulting condition $Z=0 \wedge \overline{X \leqslant 0} \vee \overline{Z=0}$ can be simplified, by logical rules, to $\overline{X \leqslant 0} \wedge \overline{Z=0}$ (we have already simplified the arithmetical expression $Z-X+X+1$ to $Z+1$, and the predicate $X+1 \leqslant 1$ to $X \leqslant 0$).

For that reason we introduce a convention which says that each FOLD transformation is immediately followed by the local simplification procedure which does the following:

- it removes those statements from among $L_i,..,L_j$ which become isolated
- it merges all branching conditions of the new L statement which can be merged
- it simplifies conditional expressions of the new L statement using (4)
- it simplifies new predicates and expressions occurring in the new L statement by known logical and arithmetical rules, and it deletes "false" components of conditional expressions and/or exit part of this statement.

While the first three actions are based on easy to implement syntactical rules, the last one requires an additional mechanism (checking the equivalence of predicates and terms) which is not subject of our interest but it is assumed to exist as a convenient supporting tool. In view of that convention the FOLD transformation presented in Fig.5 would result in the right-hand side diagram with all dotted components removed.

Now, it seems obvious that we are basing our compaction algorithm on repeated use of the FOLD transformation. It is not irrelevant to the result, however, what sequence of transformations is chosen. In the example of Fig.5 all three transformations FOLD(L;L1), FOLD(L;L2) and FOLD(L;L1,L2) are admissible but only the choice of the last one removes both L1 and L2 statements. The order of application is similarly important. Another difficulty arises when two instructions are in a loop which means that there is no clear order of execution. In the next section we present a solution to all these problems.

COMPACTION ALGORITHM

We start the algorithm with the following input:

- a vertical microprogram $\mathbb{P}$ to be compacted
- a finite set of constraints $\mathbb{C}$ the target (as well as the source) microprogram must satisfy. The only constraints we are talking about are those which can be formulated as a decidable property about the microprogram statements.

The output of the compaction procedure

$$COMPACT(\mathbb{P},\mathbb{C})$$

is a semantically equivalent to $\mathbb{P}$ horizontal microprogram which satisfies $\mathbb{C}$.

We shall illustrate the consecutive steps of the compaction algorithm with the floating-point addition microprogram of Fig.1. The constraints which are considered are those resulting from the implementing structure presented in Fig.3. Namely:

1. $P_1=P_2=P_3=P_4=P$, which means that we have single access to the external memory. Therefore, the operation of reading the operands and placing them into registers must be performed sequentially. This means in turn that any two assignments using the variable P are mutually exclusive and cannot be placed in one costatement.

2. The following assignments and/or conditions are mutually exclusive because of the "path resource conflict". We do not list all of them. The reader can easily complete the list.

    $EA:=EA \pm 2^{-7}$, $EA=EB$, $FA:=FA+FB$, etc.

3. No conditional microoperation (i.e., assignment) is allowed.

The compaction procedure is performed in two major steps

$$COMPACT(\mathbf{P},\mathbf{C}) = TSEQUENCE(\mathbf{P}); ADJUST(\mathbf{C})$$

This means that in the first step a sequence of FOLD transformations is produced as if there were no constraints, and then this sequence is performed and dynamically modified accordingly to the given set of constraints $\mathbf{C}$.

We are going to present the whole algorithm in five steps. The first four of them concern the TSEQUENCE part, the fifth describes the content of the ADJUST procedure.

STEP 1. <u>Find a minimal partition of P</u>

Obviously we can consider any program $\mathbf{P}$ as representing a graph $G(\mathbf{P})$ in which the program statements are nodes. We shall identify the graph nodes (statements) with their labels.

Let $M \in G(\mathbf{P})$. A subset $\mathbf{Z}$ of $\mathbf{P}$ is called <u>M-closed</u> iff

1. $M \in G(\mathbf{Z})$

2. if $L \neq M$ belongs to $G(\mathbf{Z})$ then, for all $L' \in G(\mathbf{P})$ such that (L',L) is an arc in $G(\mathbf{P})$, $L' \in G(\mathbf{Z})$

3. if $L \in G(\mathbf{Z})$ then L is not a halting statement in $\mathbf{P}$.

The condition 2 says that the only entrance to $\mathbf{Z}$ is through the node M .

As usual, we can talk about paths in the graph. A path $L_1,..,L_k$ is called <u>direct</u> iff it is repetition-free.

A M-closed subset $\mathbf{Z}$ of $\mathbf{P}$ is called <u>conflict-free</u> (ccf-subset) iff for each

direct path $L_1,..,L_k$ in $G(\mathbf{Z})$, such that $M=L_1$ and every $1 \leq i \neq j \leq k$,

$$lvar(co_i) \cap lvar(co_j) = \emptyset$$

where co_i denotes the costatement of the statement L_i in $\mathbf{P}$.

By a <u>minimal partition</u> of $\mathbf{P}$ we mean any partition into ccf-subsets with the minimal number of these subsets.

From the above definitions one can see that a minimal partition of $\mathbf{P}$ always exists and can be effectively determined. There may exist, however, many minimal partitions of the same $\mathbf{P}$.

For the microprogram in Fig.1 one can give the following two minimal partitions:

1. $\mathbf{Z}1=\{1-5\}$, $\mathbf{Z}2=\{6-16\}$, $\mathbf{Z}3=\{17-21\}$
   $\mathbf{Z}4=\{24-30\}$, $\mathbf{Z}5=\{22,23\}$, $\mathbf{Z}6=\{31,32\}$

2. $\mathbf{Z}1$, $\mathbf{Z}4$, $\mathbf{Z}5$ and $\mathbf{Z}6$ as above,
   $\mathbf{Z}2=\{6-17\}$, $\mathbf{Z}3=\{18-21\}$

STEP2. <u>For each ccf-subset $\mathbf{Z}$ in the minimal partition of $\mathbf{P}$ obtained in the STEP 1, find a loop-free reduct of $G(\mathbf{Z})$.</u>

Consider a ccf-subset $\mathbf{Z}$. Remove from the graph $G(\mathbf{Z})$ a number of arcs in such a way as to get a loop-free graph without isolated nodes. Any such graph which results from $G(\mathbf{Z})$ by the <u>minimal</u> number of removals will be called the <u>loop-free-reduct</u> of $G(\mathbf{Z})$ lfr $\mathbf{Z}$.

In the examplary microprogram of Fig.1 $\mathbf{Z}2=\{6-16\}$ is a ccf-subset. $G(\mathbf{Z}2)$ is presented in Fig.6 and its loop-free-reduct results by removing the dotted arcs (11,6) and (13,6). It happened, in this case, that lfr is a tree. In general, however, it may be a loop-free graph.

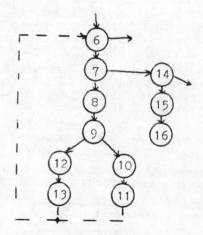

Fig.6

Again, there may exist more than one lfr. It is irrelevant for the algorithm which one is chosen.

STEP 3. <u>For each lfr obtained in the STEP 2 form the sequence of FOLD transformations</u>

For each inner node L in lfr(**Z**)(i.e. having at least one direct successor in lfr **Z**) define the transformation

$$\text{FOLD}(L;L_1,..,L_k) \qquad (7)$$

where $L_1,..,L_k$ are all direct successors of L in the graph lfr(**Z**). Every such transformation is well defined since **Z** is conflict-free. Assume the number of the above transformation to be n > 1 . Let us order all these transformations into a sequence which satisfies the following property:

- the transformation (7) may stand i-th in the sequence $1 \leqslant i \leqslant n$ if, for all $1 \leqslant j \leqslant k$, L_j is either a final node in lfr(**Z**)(i.e. without any direct successors in this graph) or the transformation FOLD(L_j;..) stands earlier in the sequence.

This property roughly says that the compaction transformations are performed "bottom-up" within each ccf-subset of **P**. This guarantees that none of the transformations may introduce a conflict.

Accordingly to the above rule the following two sequences of transformations might be created for the lfr(**Z**) in Fig.6. Again, arbitrary choice from among them is possible.

1. FOLD(15;16)	1. FOLD(12;13)
2. FOLD(14;15)	2. FOLD(15;16)
3. FOLD(10;11)	3. FOLD(10;11)
4. FOLD(12;13)	4. FOLD(9;10,12)
5. FOLD(9;12,10)	5. FOLD(8;9)
6. FOLD(8;9)	6. FOLD(14;15)
7. FOLD(7;8,14)	7. FOLD(7;8,14)
8. FOLD(6;7)	8. FOLD(6;7)

STEP 4. <u>Concatenate the sequences of FOLD transformations obtained in STEP 3</u>

STEP 5. <u>Perform ADJUST(**C**)</u>

Let FOLD($L;L_1,..,L_k$) be a transformation defined for the program **P** and **C** a set of constraints.

We say that the transformation is <u>reductive</u> if for each $1 \leqslant i \leqslant k$, L_i has no entrance to itself i.e., L_i does not occur in the exit part of the statement labeled by L_i .

The transformation is **C**-applicable if the resulting statement labeled by L satisfies all the constraints in **C** .

Now, it is obvious that if a microgram **P** satisfied the constraints from a given set **C** then a **C**-applicable transformation preserves this property.

ADJUST(**C**) : Let $T_1,..,T_n$ be the sequence of FOLD transformations

For i=1 <u>to</u> n <u>do</u>

 <u>if</u> T_i=FOLD($L;L_1,..,L_m$) is reductive and   **C**-applicable

 <u>then</u> perform T_i

 <u>else</u> <u>if</u> there is no subsequence $L_{i_1},..,L_{i_k}$ of $L_1,..,L_m$ such

    that FOLD($L;L_{i_1},..,L_{i_k}$) is

    reductive and **C**-applicable

 <u>then</u> <u>skip</u>

 <u>else</u> perform FOLD($L;L_{i_1},..,L_{i_k}$)

    where the subsequence is chosen to have the greatest k (if there are two or more of the same length an arbitrary choice is made)

If we assume the constraints defined earlier then application of the ADJUST procedure to the first of the examplary sequences obtained in the STEP 3 results in performance of the following sequence of transformations:

1. FOLD(15;16)
2. FOLD(10;11)
3. FOLD(12;13)
4. FOLD(8;9)
5. FOLD(7;14)
6. FOLD(6;7)

One can easily check that the sequence of FOLD transformations obtained in the STEP 4 and performed (with **C**=∅) on the vertical microprogram in Fig.1 gives the horizontal microprogram in Fig.2 with only 6 microstatements, i.e., ~84% reduction which must be paid, however, by probably unrealistic for the purpose hardware extention. With the examplary constraints the same sequence applied to the source microprogram reduces the number of its 32 statements to 17 (Fig.4) and can be realized in a very simple hardware configuration.

We end this section showing that some preparatory transformations on the source microprogram can improve the compaction result. The two changes in the microprogram are good illustration of the problem.

The two changes are both irrelevant for the floating-point addition algorithm. The first one does not alter the formal semantics of the microprogram and can be achieved by simple syntactical manipulations described in [4]. The second one, however, is changing this formal semantics and can be only done on the designer responsability. In the first case the compaction algorithm would eliminate the 9th microinstruction in the microprogram in Fig.4 (with approp-

213

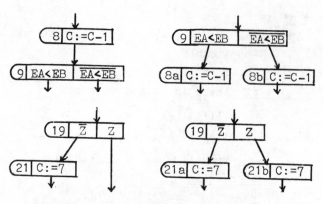

Fig.7

riate changes in 6th, 10th and 12th), and, in the second case, the 23th microinstruction would disappear (with a change in 17th). Of course, the two changes (or any of that sort) can only influence the result if there are any constraints assumed. For that reason they have no impact on the microprogram in Fig.2. These two simple examples seem to show, to some extend, flexibility, power and limits of the transformational approach to the compaction.

FINAL REMARKS

We have presented an algorithm of microprogram compaction which takes into account the overall flow structure of the compacted microprogram. It can be considered at many levels of abstraction and different sets of constraints can model appropriate hardware requirements. For the sake of clarity we have restricted our attention to the RTL microprograms and the monophase systems. The same ideology can be easily extended to deal with lower level descriptions and to include multiphase schemes. The lower level microprogram the more constraints are directly embedded into its description. To some extend, however, it seems advantageous to separate the microprogramming solution of a problem from some detailed hardware requirements (modelled by the constraints) to enable possible changes in the design.

We realize that one of the crucial point in this approach is the way the hardware knowledge is represented through the set of constraints. It is a separate and sometimes not easy problem. Another difficulty arises in cases when the algorithm is allowed to modify microinstructions simplifying the obtained terms. The kind of simplification illustrated in Fig.5 is only possible if real arithmetic is considered. This is not

the case in prctice and therefore a special attention must be paid to the problem. It becomes even more difficult if the assumption of the basic theorem is relaxed which is possible in some particular cases. At last, we recall that the method does not give optimal solutions and some preparatory transformations may help to improve the result. For all these reasons we would like to see the presented parallelization algorithm as component of a larger computer-aided system of microprogram design and not a separate entity. This would allow the designer to apply the algorithm at different stages of the design process (which is iterative in the nature) to look for some possibilities difficult to predict without this tool.

REFERENCES

1. S.Dasgupta, J.Tartar, The Identification of Maximal Parallelism in Straight-Line Microprograms, IEEE Trans. on Comp., C-25, October 1976

2. S.Dasgupta, Parallelism in Loop Free Microprograms, Proc. IFIP 77, B.Gilchriot ed. , N.Holland, 1977

3. S.Davidson, D.Landskov, B.D.Shriver, P.W.Mallet, Some Experiments in Local Microcode Compaction for Horizontal Machines, IEEE Tran. on Comp., C-30, July 1981

4. P.Dembiński, Microprogram Transformations, ICS PAS Reports,488, Warsaw 1982

5. J.A.Fisher, Trace Scheduling: A Technique for Global Microcode Compaction, IEEE Tran. on Comp., c-30, July 1981

6. D.Landskov, S.Davidson,B.D.Shriver, P.W. Mallet, Local Microcode Compaction Techniques, ACM Comp. Surveys, vol.12, September 1980

7. P.W.Mallet, Methods of Compacting Microprograms, PhD Thesis, University of S. Louisiana, 1978

8. M.Tokoro, T.Takizuka, E.Tamura, F. Yamaura, A Technique of Global Optimization of Microprograms, Proc. Micro 11, 1978

9. M.Tokoro,E.Tamura, T.Takizuka, Optimization of Microprograms, IEEE Trans. on Comp., c-30, July 1981

10. M.Tsuchiya, M.Gonzalez, Toward Optimization of Horizontal Microprograms, IEEE Trans. on Comp., C-25, October 1976

11. G.Wood, Computer Aided Design of Microprograms, PhD Thesis, University of Edinburgh,1979

A RESOURCE REQUEST MODEL FOR MICROCODE COMPACTION

TORE LARSEN
University of Tromsø
Tromsø, Norway

DAVID LANDSKOV and BRUCE D. SHRIVER
The University of Southwestern Louisiana
Lafayette, Louisiana

ABSTRACT

A new approach to resource conflict analysis in microcode compaction has been developed. This paper begins with a description of the resource binding problem in microcode compaction and an analysis of earlier solutions. Then a new specification technique is presented and related to a standard problem in combinatorial theory. This new technique allows microoperations to be specified with resource choices, the actual binding to specific resources being delayed until compaction time. A polynomial-time algorithm for analyzing resource conflicts under this model is explained. Further extensions to the algorithm to support more complex machine models are suggested.

1.0 INTRODUCTION

The resource request model presented here extends microcode compaction to support a more general concept of machine resources. An associated algorithm to efficiently analyze resource requests has also been developed.

Microcode compaction is the conversion of microcode specified in terms of microoperations (MOs) into microcode specified as a list of microinstructions (MIs), each of which contains one or more MOs. MOs are compacted by placing several MOs in each MI, subject to the dual constraints of data dependency in the code and legal resource usage in the host machine. The compaction process attempts to produce code that will execute as fast as possible on the host machine.

The case of compacting a block of jump-free code is called the local compaction problem [LAND80]. In the absence of jumps, the fastest execution time can be obtained by compacting to the fewest number of MIs. This is similar to the unit-time execution problem of scheduling theory [COFF76]. Current efforts at solving the more difficult global compaction problem involve sophisticated algorithms that use local compaction subalgorithms [e.g. FISH81a]. These global compaction algorithms are not part of standard scheduling theory. Additional discussion on the general microcode compaction problem can be found in [FISH81b].

Another way in which microcode compaction is distinguished from other problems in scheduling theory is the relative complexity of possible resource usage. As the compaction process tries to place MOs into the same MI, it checks the MOs' resource needs. Examples of machine resources are registers, ALUs, buses, and clock cycles. Two MOs that need the same unshareable resource at the same time are said to conflict. Conflicting MOs cannot be placed into an MI together. If an MO can potentially be satisfied by different combinations or resources, then resource conflict analysis becomes a more difficult problem.

This paper examines the entire resource usage question and provides a framework for discussing the issues involved. By providing a concept of "equivalent resources", the resource request model presented here allows MOs to be specified with a choice of resources. The model supports this generalized use of resources in a microcode compaction system in a more efficient way than has previously appeared in the literature. An algorithm is presented that binds requests to resources in polynomial time.

This research was supported in part by the Norwegian Research Council's NAVF Grant D.07.01.22 and NTNF Grant 0405.05503.

Resource requests can also be used as a technique for analyzing resource needs of benchmark programs and thus are a potential design aid for microprogrammable architectures. Using requests can provide feedback on the effectiveness of various resource replications and interconnections.

This paper concludes with a discussion of possible extensions to the model.

2.0 RESOURCE CONFLICT ANALYSIS

A set of MOs whose resource needs cannot be satisfied when the MOs are placed in the same MI is said to have a resource conflict. A set of MOs that do not have a resource conflict is said to be conflict-free.

In order to detect resource conflicts, two things must be known about each MO:

a) The resources required by the MO. For a given machine, the set of machine resources, R, can be determined by examining all MOs. Any machine resource whose use by an MO can prevent another MO from being executed at the same time must be included in R. Each MO in a compacted program will use some subset of R during its execution.

b) The time period for which each resource is used. This period is measured relative to the instruction cycle in which the

MO is scheduled. For the purpose of discussion in the next few sections, temporarily assume that each resource is used for exactly the instruction cycle in which the MO is scheduled. A subsequent section will discuss timing.

In the MO Tuple model of machine behavior [MALL78], for example, the basic representation of an MO's resource requirements is a list of resources associated with the MO. For timing, a machine cycle is divided into an integral number of phases. MO timing is represented by a list of the clock phases that the MO is active.

2.1 Forming Complete Instructions

An algorithm that examines a set of microoperations and constructs

conflict-free microinstructions from them is called a Form Complete Instructions algorithm (FormCI). The compaction algorithm that invokes FormCI ensures that no MO in the set is data preceded [LAND80,FISH81b] by an unplaced MO. This means that any register reads or writes that must precede the MOs in the set will already have been placed in the compacted program. The set is called the Data-Ready Set (DSet).

Resource conflicts are usually detected by a conflict analysis subalgorithm within the FormCI algorithm. An MI is complete with respect to a set of MOs if adding any additional member of the set to the MI causes a resource conflict; otherwise the MI is incomplete. It is well known that, as long as MOs are not bundled across MI boundaries [VEGD82], only complete instructions need be considered when compacting [YAU74]. An algorithm that forms complete instructions is used in some form by all of the standard local compaction algorithms except the First-Come, First-Served algorithm [LAND80]. Thus most global compaction algorithms, which are based on

local compaction, will use a FormCI algorithm [e.g. FISH81a].

A study of FormCI behavior reveals the use that compaction makes of conflict analysis. A particular FormCI algorithm, Binary FormCI [LAND80], is briefly reviewed in this section. Other algorithms are possible, but their differences are not important for the purpose of this discussion.

Binary FormCI selects MOs from the DSet one at a time and alternately considers them as included in or excluded from the MI (see Figure 1). The MOs that have not yet been selected are called the remaining DSet. The combination of MOs that is under consideration is called the partial instruction.

A partial instruction can be rejected as a potential complete instruction because of (1) resource conflict, or (2) incompleteness. Each time an MO is added to the partial instruction, the conflict analysis algorithm is called. Each time an MO is excluded from the partial instruction, the completeness analysis algorithm is called. For a discussion on the detection of incompleteness, see [LAND80].

The recursive invocations of the Binary FormCI algorithm can be represented as a tree (see Figure 2). Each node on the tree corresponds to a MO considered for inclusion or exclusion. An include node is represented by having the name of

```
              Binary FormCI

(Let I represent the current partial
instruction.  Before any calls to
Binary FormCI have been made, I is
empty and the remaining DSet is
equal to the DSet.)

If the remaining DSet is not empty:

  Select an MO from the remaining DSet.
  Consider including this MO in I.  If
  there is no conflict in I, reapply
  this procedure with this MO in I.

  Consider excluding the MO from I.
  If this does not make I incomplete,
  then reapply this procedure with
  this MO excluded from I.

If the remaining DSet is empty:

  Place I in the list of complete
  instructions.
```

Figure 1. High-Level Description of
Binary FormCI Algorithm

the MO in parentheses. An exclude node is
represented by having a minus sign and the
name of the MO, all in square brackets.
An arrow from a node to the box labeled
"Complete Is" represents the addition of a
partial instruction to the list of
complete instructions. Inside the box, an
instruction is represented as a set of
MOs. The "backup" in the example is an
incompleteness failure that is detected
without having to invoke the completeness
analysis algorithm. Notice that the
partial instruction at a node is
identified by the path from the root to
that node.

2.2 A Choice of Resources

Often, an MO can use any one of
several resources. For example, an MO
might be able to use either of two ALUs.
If the ALUs are not identical in speed,
functionality, and interconnection to
other resources, then the choice of which
one to use should be delayed until
compaction time. Otherwise, the premature
selection of a particular ALU might later
cause a conflict that could be avoided
simply by using the other ALU.
Unnecessary conflicts are highly
undesirable because they can force extra
MIs to be created.

Example 1. Suppose MO1 can use
either MI field F3 or F4, and in addition
it uses field F2. If no other MO being
analyzed for conflict needs either F3 or
F4, then the choice of which one is used
by MO1 does not affect the compaction. On
the other hand, if MO2 uses F4, then an
advance choice of F4 for MO1 introduces an
unnecessary conflict and may force an
undesirable extra MI in the final
compaction.

Example 2. Suppose that fan-out
restricts a bus to being read by no more
than two registers at a time. This
situation can be modeled by considering
the bus to be two equivalent resources:
busRead1 and busRead2. A single MO
needing to read the bus can use either
busRead1 or busRead2, but three such MOs
together do not have enough bus-reads to
share. In this model it is a mistake to
prebind MOs to particular bus-reads. Such
a binding introduces artificial conflicts,
such as two MOs conflicting over busRead1
when busRead2 is available.

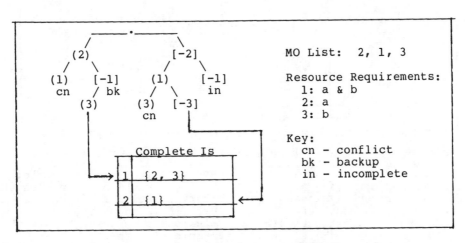

Figure 2. Example of Binary FormCI Execution

An MO specified with a choice of resources is said to be an <u>unbound</u> MO. An unbound MO that specifies all possible resource choices is said to be an <u>MO template</u>. An MO for which all choices have been made is said to be <u>bound</u>, and the choices are called a <u>binding</u> (1) of the MO. The compaction process starts with MO templates and ends with a list of MIs containing bound MOs. A set of bound MOs that originated from the same MO template are <u>versions</u> of the MO template.

In the past, conflict analysis over MOs with a choice of resources was done using the version concept at the FormCI level [LAND80, DAVI81a]. In case of conflict, each version of an MO was tried in combination with the versions of the other MOs in order to determine which versions gave the best compactions. An example of the combinatorial explosion involved may be seen in Figure 3, which is a simple extension of the problem in Figure 2. Here MO 1 can choose either resource c1 or resource c2, so it has two versions, 1A and 1B. These versions cause extra nodes on the tree to be created, even though resources c1 and c2 are not involved in a conflict. With the version concept, Binary FormCI does not live up to its name, since it certainly does not develop a binary tree.

The FCFS local compaction algorithm, which does not use a FormCI subalgorithm, has been extended to handle a choice of resources by a technique known as <u>version shuffling</u> [DAVI81a]. This technique is

extremely inefficient. In version shuffling, all possible versions of each MO are generated, and then all combinations of the MO versions are compared, regardless of detected conflicts. An upper bound on the computational complexity of this approach gives an idea of its inefficiency. The worst case for an individual MO occurs when the MO needs j resources but does not care which resource is chosen from k possibilities. In this case, version shuffling checks k resources j times, or k raised to the jth power bindings for one MO alone.

An efficient conflict analysis algorithm needs a method to describe and analyze resource choices that avoids blindly generating unnecessary combinations. The problem with version analysis is that the choice is kept at the MO level, while an MO may involve several independent choice situations.

3.0 RESOURCE REQUEST SETS

3.1 Delaying Resource Binding

Having FormCI check multiple versions of each MO can be avoided if the analysis of resource choices is performed by the conflict analysis subalgorithm. The subalgorithm does not have to actually bind resources to MOs; it has only to determine if there exists at least one binding that allows the set of MOs to be in the same instruction. For this

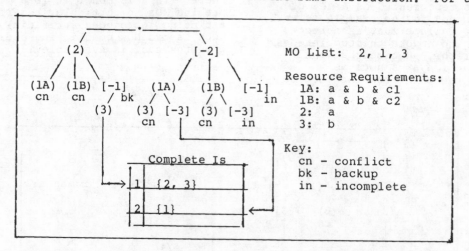

Figure 3. Example of Binary FormCI Execution with Versions

(1) Binding as discussed here is a different concept from resource binding discussed in [DAVI81b]. In that work, high-level source language constructs are bound to target virtual machine (i.e. host) resources.

determination to be possible, the resource conflict function can no longer be a binary relation as it has been in the past. This inadequacy of a binary relation is demonstrated by the simple example of three MOs, each wanting one copy of two equivalent resources. These

218

MOs are pairwise conflict-free but conflict when considered as a threesome.

Thus when FormCI invokes the conflict analysis subalgorithm, it passes as a parameter a set of unbound MOs. The subalgorithm analyzes whether or not the set conflicts. In addition, the subalgorithm can report which MOs are involved in the conflict. FormCI can use this knowledge to avoid considering the exclusion of an MO unnecessarily. Information about possible bindings can be kept between invocations of the conflict analysis subalgorithm and used to speed the analysis process. Only after FormCI has finished finding the complete instructions will a final binding of resources be made. The conflict analysis subalgorithm, however, should save information that makes this binding easier.

The elimination of the version concept in the FormCI algorithm is a valuable simplification. The Binary FormCI algorithm, for example, is reduced back to a true binary tree. However, there remains the fundamental problem of avoiding unnecessary combinations. The resource request model solves this problem.

3.2 The Request Set Concept

This section introduces a new technique for specifying an MO's resource needs. The technique is based on the idea that a set of resources can be functionally identical for a given MO. Functionally identical means that:
1) regardless of which resource is used, the MO has the same semantics, and
2) whenever the MO can gate data to one of the resources, it can also gate that data to the other, and the outputs of the resources can be gated to the same destinations. An MO can use any functionally identical resource when it requires a resource of that type. Resources that are functionally identical relative to one MO might not be functionally identical relative to another.

In this specification technique, resources that are functionally identical for a given MO are grouped into a set called the resource request set. During its execution, the MO must use resources from each of its request sets. To make resource analysis consistent, a resource that is not functionally identical to any other resource for an MO is placed in a request set by itself. Each MO is associated with a list of resource request sets rather than with the individual resources themselves.

To save the compaction process unnecessary analysis, binding different resources from the same request set is not considered except when another MO needs one of the same resources. This is possible because if resources are functionally identical for an MO and no other MO needs one of the resources in the same cycle, then the choice of which resource is used cannot affect the quality of the compaction. It is not significant for the MO if the resources are active during different time intervals, as long as none of them use more than one machine cycle.

Example 1, Revisited. Suppose MO1 can use either MI field F3 or F4 and in addition it uses field F2. Then MO1's request sets for these particular resources are {F3, F4} and {F2}. If MO2 has a request set {F4}, then how {F3, F4} is bound for MO1 can make a difference in the final compaction.

The request set concepts may be defined more formally. For a particular machine, the set of all possible resources, R, is determined. A request is defined to be a two-tuple of the form:

$$\langle A, d \rangle$$

where A is a subset of R, called the request set, and d is a nonnegative integer, called the demand. Each MO is associated with a list of requests. A request is interpreted to mean that the MO needs d resources from the request set A.

By examining the repertoire of MOs on the machine, all possible request sets can be enumerated (with no duplication of sets). Indexes into this request set vector can be used to specify request sets, thus simplifying the analysis of requests.

During compaction, the conflict analysis algorithm is presented with a set of MOs and must determine if a resource binding exists over this set. This motivates the following definitions: For a given set of MOs, there is a request family of k requests, $\langle A[1], d[1] \rangle$, $\langle A[2], d[2] \rangle$, ..., $\langle A[\underline{k}], d[\underline{k}] \rangle$, formed by listing one after another the request lists for the MOs in the set. A resource binding for the set of MOs is a family of resources:

$$a[1,1], a[1,2], ..., a[1,d[1]],$$
$$a[2,1], a[2,2], ..., a[2,d[2]],$$
$$...$$
$$a[\underline{k},1], a[\underline{k},2], ..., a[\underline{k},d[\underline{k}]]$$

such that:

1) a[i,j] is an element of A[i] for
   1<=j<=d[i] and 1<=i<=k, and

2) all of the a's are distinct.

In general, there is a need for an
algorithm that examines a request family
and finds whether or not a resource
binding exists for it. Such an algorithm
is said to solve the resource request
binding problem, in which resources are
bound to requests instead of directly to
MOs.

4.0 A CONFLICT ANALYSIS ALGORITHM

The formulation of the resource
binding problem in terms of requests is
related to a standard problem in
combinatorial theory. An algorithm for
this combinatorial problem provides the
basis for a more advanced algorithm that
solves the resource request question. The
resource request algorithm is presented
and explained with an example.

4.1 Systems of Distinct Representatives

A restricted subproblem of the
resource request binding problem involves
the combinatorial theory problem of
finding a "system of distinct
representatives" (SDR). But simply
applying an SDR algorithm directly to the
request binding problem has the following
deficiencies:

1) Each request can need only one
   resource,

2) The model of machine resource
   usage cannot be too
   sophisticated. In particular,
   all MOs must execute in one
   cycle, so that no time sharing
   of resources is possible. No
   other kind of resource sharing
   can be possible.

3) Only one conflict analysis of an
   MO set can be performed. This
   is inappropriate for resource
   binding, since the FormCI
   algorithm may invoke the
   conflict analysis algorithm many
   times. A call differs from the
   previous call only in the
   addition (or deletion) of a few
   requests. The data collected
   during one conflict check can be
   reused. It is possible to save
   not only the partial binding of
   the requests, but also
   information to guide future
   searches. How to accomplish
   this is one of the challenging
   questions in the design of a

good conflict analysis
algorithm. A considerable
savings of computation effort is
possible.

4) Each MO can be associated with
   just one request, so that the
   interaction between conflicting
   requests and the removal of MOs
   is avoided.

5) No identification of which
   requests are involved in a
   conflict can be reported.

Subject to the above restrictions,
there is a correspondence between some of
the terminology of resource binding and
that of combinatorial theory. A
successful resource binding of a request
family is analogous to a matching of a
bipartite graph, and the resources used in
the resource binding are known as a
transversal of the request sets, or a
system of distinct representatives for
them. [LAWL76, BRUA77, MIRS71]

In combinatorial theory, the marriage
theorem [BRUA77] is fundamental to the
study of systems of distinct
representatives. It characterizes when a
system of distinct representatives exists
and is the inspiration for many of the
more advanced results of transversal
theory. It is interesting to state this
theorem in the terminology of resource
binding. Essentially, the condition
stated in the theorem is that every
subfamily of the requests must contain in
its request sets at least as many
resources as the sum of its needs. This
condition is obviously necessary to have a
conflict-free MO set; perhaps surprising
is that it is also a sufficient condition.

Theorem. (The Marriage Theorem). A
family of requests, <A[1],d[1]>, ...,
<A[n],d[n]>, is conflict-free if and only
if the following condition is satisfied:
   For each k = 1,2,...,n and for each
   choice of i1,i2,...,ik with
   1<=i1<i2<...<ik<=n,

   |A[i1] U A[i2] U ... U A[ik]| >=
      d[i1] + d[i2] + ... + d[ik]

For a proof, see [BRUA77, MIRS71].
Perhaps the most elegant proofs are based
on matroid theory [LAWL76]. The
inequalities for each subfamily of
requests are collectively known as Hall's
Condition. They are minimal in the sense
that none of them are implied by the
others [MIRS71, p. 26].

4.2 The Concepts Behind the Binding Algorithm

The algorithm demonstrated will identify a conflict-free resource binding if one exists. Otherwise it will identify exactly which requests are conflicting with each other. The relationship between request sets and resources is characterized by the following two invariants:

1) Every request set contains one or more resources.

2) For a given request family, every resource can be used by at most one of the request sets of which it is a member.

A data structure represents all possible request sets and resources. A resource is either "free", meaning it is not used to meet any requests, or it is "allocated" to a request, meaning it is associated with one of the requests of which it is an element of the request set. The allocation is a temporary binding that might have to be changed as more requests are considered.

The algorithm treats the requests sequentially, trying to allocate enough resources to meet the demand. Once the demand is met, a resource will not be released from the request unless a substitute resource is found. The basic algorithm for allocating resources to a request $\langle A,d \rangle$ is described by the following two steps:

Allocate Resources(A,d)

1) Allocate free resources in A until either d resources are allocated or there are no free resources left in A. Terminate if d resources were allocated.

2) Consider reallocating resources that are elements of A but are currently allocated to other (intersecting) requests. Assume that the resources $a[1]$, $a[2]$, ..., $a[n]$ are the elements of A that are allocated to other requests. Suppose that $a[1]$ is allocated to B. $a[1]$ can be reallocated only if a substitute resource can be allocated to B. The search for such a substitute resource is done by invoking (recursively) Allocate Resources(B,1). This implies checking for free resources in B and, if necessary, issuing new invocations of Allocate Resources. If a substitute resource for B is found, $a[1]$ is reallocated. The

reallocation terminates when enough resources are reallocated or all n resources in A have been considered.

4.3 The Validity of the Basic Algorithm

The validity of this basic algorithm will be demonstrated before considering further extensions. The recursive search for resources and substitute resources for a request A involves a specific subfamily of the request family. This subfamily is called A's search family, SF(A). SF(A) consists of:

1) A itself.

2) Every request set B that is allocated a resource that is also an element of a request set in SF(A).

It should be noted that the content of the search family is dependent on the actual allocation of resources. Reallocating one resource might influence the membership of more than one request set's search family.

The algorithm terminates when enough resources are found or it is impossible to reallocate more resources to a request A. In the latter case a conflict-free resource binding is impossible since SF(A) violates Hall's Condition. That is, the total demand exceeds the number of distinct resources in the associated request sets. This is established by the following argument.

Suppose a request, $\langle A,d \rangle$, cannot be satisfied. This means that d exceeds the number of resources allocated to $\langle A,d \rangle$. No request in SF(A) is allocated more resources than its demand. It follows that, if Hall's Condition is not violated, there has to be a request B in SF(A) such that B contains at least one resource, $r[0]$, satisfying either one of the following conditions:

1) $r[0]$ is allocated to a request not in SF(A).

2) $r[0]$ is free.

The first condition is contradictory to the definition of the search family. In the second case $r[0]$ would either be in A or not. If $r[0]$ is in A, it could be allocated to A, which contradicts the termination criterion for the algorithm. If $r[0]$ is not in A, it follows by the definition of search family that there exists $\underline{k}$ resources $r[1],r[2], \ldots r[\underline{k}]$ for $1 <= \underline{k} <$ "number of request sets in SF(A)", such that:

1) r[1] in A,
2) r[$\underline{i}$] allocated to B[$\underline{i}$] for 1<=$\underline{i}$<=$\underline{k}$,
3) r[$\underline{i}$] in B[$\underline{i}$-1] for 2<=$\underline{i}$<=$\underline{k}$, and
4) r[0] in B[$\underline{k}$].

By reallocating r[0] to B[$\underline{k}$], r[$\underline{k}$] could be reallocated to B[$\underline{k}$-1]. This could be repeated until finally r[1] is reallocated to A. This again contradicts the termination criterion.

Hence it is demonstrated that the algorithm works if it terminates. Since the request family represents a finite graph, termination is assured by not searching through loops in the graph.

4.4 Extensions and Adaptations of the Basic Algorithm

The algorithm works for any initial allocation of resources done in Step 1 of Allocate Resources. The amount of necessary reallocation, however, depends on the initial allocations and other requests that are in the request family. One approach is to allocate resources arbitrarily with the exception that free resources are preferred over resources that are already allocated. That is, reallocation is postponed for as long as possible. However, the algorithm can easily be modified to implement other strategies for initial allocation and reallocation. These strategies could allocate resources according to heuristics preferring resources that are in lower demand. Such strategies might find a conflict-free binding faster if one exists. However, a complete search is always needed to detect that no binding exists.

Step 2 presents a choice of different strategies when searching for substitute resources. The search can be done "depth first" or "breadth first". "Depth first" indicates that no request set gives a negative answer until it has checked all request sets with which it has a nonnull intersection (its neighboring request sets). "Breadth first" indicates that all the neighboring request sets of the considered request set answer without in turn checking any of their neighboring request sets. If the demand is still unsatisfied after they all answer, then their previously unasked neighboring request sets are also asked, and so on, until the demand is met or all request sets have been asked.

For this description of the algorithm, "depth first" was chosen, since it closely reflects the recursive definition of the search family. Search strategies are discussed further in

Section 4.6.

As mentioned earlier, there are algorithms in the literature that search for a matching of a bipartite graph. However, the resource binding problem differs from the classical matching problem in several respects. These differences have inspired the following extensions to the known algorithms:

1) Mechanisms are provided to search for more than one resource when traversing the request sets.

2) Mechanisms are provided to modify the request family after an attempt to find a mapping has been made. The new request family is treated as a modification of the old. This implies that the search for a mapping over the new request family will use the maximal mapping over the old request family as a starting point.

3) The result of each search for substitute resources is recorded. These results are used to prune later searches within both the current and later request families.

4) The search family for each unsatisfied request is identified. A search family of an unsatisfied request is called a "conflict family". Only by reducing the demand on any request in the conflict family is it possible to allocate more resources to the unsatisfied request. Different conflict families may intersect; this indicates that more than one request might be satisfied by reducing the demand on a request in the intersection. The content of a conflict family is not known until after the search for substitute resources terminates unsuccessfully.

To support these extensions every request is associated with the following information:

A) The request set.

B) The number of resources required.

C) The set of resources actually allocated.

D) The search family.

E) The neighboring request sets. That
   is, the request sets that have a
   nonempty intersection with this
   request set.

F) The "unavailable" neighbors. These
   are neighbors that could potentially
   release resources but have been
   discovered to be unable to do so.

G) A number indicating the position in
   the current search path. A flag is
   sufficient to detect loops in the
   search path. However, the sequence
   number of the node already in the
   search path is used to determine if a
   neighbor can safely be regarded
   unavailable. Assume that the request
   A has invoked an unsuccessful search
   for substitute resources for B. If
   no search loop was detected from B, B
   can safely be regarded unavailable
   for A. If a search loop was detected
   however, B can only be regarded
   unavailable if the loop did not
   involve a request earlier than A on
   the search path.

4.5 An Example of Executing the Algorithm

Bipartite graphs will be used to
illustrate the algorithm. The allocation
of a resource to a request will be
indicated by a mark (O) on the edge
between the resource and the request. For
convenience, the number of resources
required (RR) and the unavailable
neighbors (UA) will be indicated for each
request.

The example uses the following
request family:

$$\langle A,1\rangle \ , \ \langle B,1\rangle \ , \ \langle C,1\rangle \ , \ \langle D,2\rangle$$

where the request sets A, B, C, and D are
defined:

$$A = \{a,b,c,d\}$$
$$B = \{a\}$$
$$C = \{a,b\}$$
$$D = \{b,e\}$$

The algorithm treats the requests in
sequence, A first. Initially the resource
a is allocated to the request A. The
resulting allocation is shown in Figure 4.

Next the request B is treated. The
only resource that can be used by B is a,
which is allocated to the request A. B
will ask A to release one resource from
the intersection between A and B. In this
example the only possible resource is a.
Since A still contains free resources, b
is allocated to A and the resource a is
reallocated to B. The resulting
allocation is shown in Figure 5.

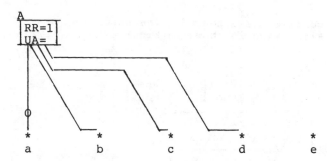

Figure 4. Bipartite Graph After Including
           Request A

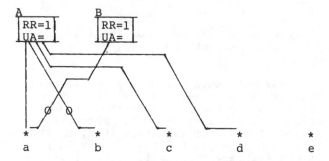

Figure 5. Bipartite Graph After Adding
           Request B

The request C is treated. All the
resources in C are already allocated to
other requests, so it is necessary to ask
neighboring requests. A neighboring
request is selected by picking a resource
in C and seeing to which request that
resource is currently allocated; this is
called asking the request "through" the
resource. Assume intersecting requests
are asked through resources from left to
right in the figure. B then is asked
through a. B contains no free resources
or resources allocated to intersecting
requests. Hence B cannot release any
resources. No loops were detected from B,
and B can safely be regarded unavailable
for C.

C then asks A through the resource b.
A still contains free resources, so c is
allocated to A and b is reallocated. The
resulting allocation is shown in Figure 6.

The request D is added. D requires 2
resources. The resource e is free and is
allocated to D. D will ask C to release
the resource b. C contains no free
resources and has to check for
reallocations. The only other resource in
C is a which is allocated to B. B
however, is unavailable from C. Hence C
cannot find any substitute resources and
has to be regarded unavailable from D. D
has exhausted its possibilities without
being allocated enough resources, hence a

conflict is detected. The resulting
allocation is shown in Figure 7.

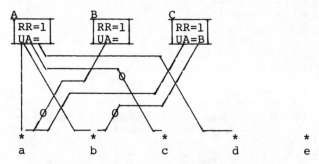

Figure 6. Bipartite Graph After Adding
Request C

The only unsatisfied request in this
example is D, it defines the conflict
family "B, C, and D". The total request
on B, C, and D is 1+1+2 = 4. The total
number of distinct resources in B, C, and
D is |B+C+D| = |{a,b,e}| = 3. According
to the Marriage Theorem it is not possible
to allocate enough resources to satisfy
the request family <B,1>, <C,1>, <D,2>.

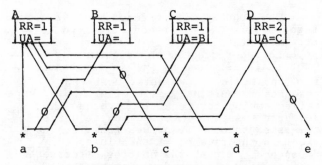

Figure 7. Bipartite Graph After Adding
Request D

4.6 Complexity of the Algorithm

Given a request binding problem, let
the number of requests in the request
family be represented by |requests|.
Similarly, let |resources| represent the
number of machine resources. Define the
term

$$\text{total\_demand} = \sum_{i=1}^{|\text{requests}|} \text{demand}[i]$$

where demand[i] is the demand of the ith
request. Let |request set[i]| represent
the cardinality of the request set from
the ith request and define the term

$$\text{linkage} = \sum_{i=1}^{|\text{requests}|} |\text{request set}[i]|$$

The algorithm presented in the preceding
sections solves the request binding
problem in
O(min(total_demand, |resources|) * linkage)
time.

This time bound is established by the
following argument. Any request binding
can have no more than min(total_demand,
|resources|) edges. Since each level 1
execution of Allocate_Resources increases
the number of bound requests by at least
1, there can be at most min (total_demand,
|resources|) executions of
Allocate_Resources. The time bound will
be established if the complexity of
Allocate_Resources can be shown to be
O(linkage). Searching for free resources
(and reallocating them) does not repeat
any edge, hence it requires O(linkage)
time.

An algorithm of less time complexity
exists for the request binding problem.
This algorithm is based on reducing the
bipartite matching problem to the max-flow
problem for simple networks and then
applying an efficient max-flow algorithm.
This approach allows the request binding
problem to be solved in
O(total_demand**(1/2) * linkage) time.

The salient difference of the
max-flow based algorithm is that its
search for new bindings proceeds in
stages. In any one stage, the length of a
path in the search family is limited.
This limit is simply the length of a
shortest path that successfully satisfies
a request. Thus, for example, the first
stage binds requests to resources without
any attempt to reassign resources at all,
since the shortest successful path is
length one. The limit is
straightforwardly calculated. During the
setup for each stage, a breadth-first
search, starting at all unsatisfied
requests, proceeds through the graph.
Each node (request or resource) is labeled
with the search depth. Already labeled
nodes are not relabeled. This search
identifies the shortest path length to
satisfy any request.

In addition the max-flow approach
builds an auxiliary graph of just the
vertices and edges that were used in the
breadth-first search. This auxiliary
graph is then the graph that is searched
during a stage. The stage search itself
can be depth-first, if desired.

Once as many requests as possible have been satisfied, the stage finishes. Each new stage increases the limit by one or more requests. The algorithm finishes when all requests are satisfied or all resources are assigned.

The lower complexity of the max-flow approach arises from each stage having a limit on the length of a path in the search family. The max-flow based algorithm is the asymptotically fastest algorithm known for the bipartite matching problem. The choice of which algorithm to use should be based on the expected number of requests and the average request set size. The simpler algorithm should be adequate for sufficiently restricted problem domains.

5. EXTENDING THE MODEL

There are several common machine characteristics that should be supported in a general microcode compaction model. Certainly multiphase cycles should be supported at least to the level that it is possible to write to a register and then read from that register in the same cycle. This time-sharing of resources adds considerably to the challenge of resource conflict analysis. Similar questions are raised by the general sharing of resources, such as the sharing of an MO field by two MOs that happen to use the same literal value.

Before discussing these extensions to the model, a general specification technique is needed to provide the framework for later discussion.

5.1 Resource Expressions

It is useful to develop a notation that allows the specification of an MO's resource needs as a logical expression.

Suppose that a, b, and c are machine resources and that a particular MO is being discussed. "a & b" is written to indicate "a and b are both used" by the given MO. Similarly, "a v b" indicates "either a or b is used". Let a propositional calculus expression [MEND70] using & and v and symbols representing machine resources be called a resource expression.

Each set that satisfies a resource expression is a legal combination of resources that allows the associated MO to execute. For example, the expression a & (b v c) is satisfied by the sets {a, b} and {a, c}.

Resource expressions can be related to requests by associating each request with an expression over the resources in its request set. For example, the set notation request ⟨{a,b,c}, 1⟩ would be written ⟨a v b v c, 1⟩. Another possible request is ⟨a v (b & c), 1⟩. In this case either binding a to the request, or binding both b and c, would satisfy the request.

Resource expressions for different requests cannot be combined. For example, the expression a v b for one request and b v c for a second request are not equivalent to the expression (a v b) & (b v c). The latter expression can be satisfied logically by binding b to both requests, but such a binding is illegal in the request model, since different requests cannot share the same resource.

Resource expressions for requests can be modified to be more compatible with the resource binding algorithm of the previous section. To accomplish this, the expressions are converted to disjunctive normal form. In this form, an expression is either a fundamental conjunction or a disjunction of fundamental conjunctions. A fundamental conjunction is either a resource or a conjunction of resources, no two of which are the same. Examples of resource expressions in disjunctive normal form are:

$$(a \& b) \lor (b \& c) \lor d$$
$$a \lor b$$

It is well known that a noncontradictory logical expression is equivalent to an expression in disjunctive normal form [MEND70].

5.2 Sharing Resources

The resource request model can be extended to support resource sharing by different MOs.

An important example of sharing occurs in machines with multiphase timing. Such machines can be modeled by associating with each resource and MO the phases of the machine cycle that the MO uses the resource (if any). For example, MO1 might use a resource during phases P1 and P2, while MO2 uses the same resource during phases P4 and P5. At least for this resource, MO1 and MO2 are compatible.

There is some bookkeeping associated with specifying phases, but the more difficult added complexity comes from the fact that MO1 and MO2 can both be allocated the same resource at the same time. If MO3 wants that resource, for example, both MO1 and MO2 must be asked if they can release it. Thus two searches have to be made instead of the usual one. This branching of searches can occur repeatedly.

The multiphase use of resources can be modeled using the request expressions of the previous section. Suppose the machine cycle has n phases. Each resource is divided into n copies of that resource, each associated with a particular phase. A request for a resource from phase i to phase j is interpreted to be a request for the conjunction of the ith through jth copies of the resource.

Request expressions can also be used to model resource sharing in general. In this case, however, a resource is broken up into as many copies as there are potential requests for the resource, since it is not known in advance how many shareable requests will be made. Any request for one of the copies is analyzed by a special routine that tests the conditions for shareability.

6. CONCLUSIONS

The suggested approach to resource allocation provides an effective support for compacting unbound microprograms. An algorithm for the request model of resource usage, while not as efficient as the elementary approach of resource-vector analysis, nevertheless can execute in polynomial time. Thus machines that exhibit the "resource choice" property can be modeled in an effective way. It is of interest to pursue the suggested expansions of the concept as these might provide a unified means of handling the more powerful general resource expressions.

It is also interesting to note the symmetry between resources and requests. When identifying the conflicting requests, the described algorithm also identifies precisely the resources that could be duplicated to resolve the conflict. This information could be used by an integrated firmware development system, aiding in the design of new architectures.

REFERENCES

BRUA77 Brualdi, R. A., _Introductory Combinatorics_, North-Holland, New York, 1977.

COFF76 Coffman, E. G., Jr., ed., _Computer and Job-Shop Scheduling Theory_, New York: Wiley, 1976.

DAVI81a Davidson, S., D. Landskov, B. D. Shriver, and P. W. Mallett, "Some experiments in local microcode compaction for horizontal machines," _IEEE_ _Trans._ _Comput._ C-30, 7 (July 81), 460-477.

DAVI81b Davidson, S., and B. D. Shriver, "Specifying target resources in a machine independent higher level language," in _AFIPS_ _Conf._ _Proc._, Vol 50: _1981_ _National_ _Computer_ _Conf._, AFIPS Press, Arlington, Va., 81-85.

FISH81a Fisher, J. A., "Trace scheduling: a technique for global microcode compaction," _IEEE_ _Trans._ _Comput._ C-30, 7 (July 81), 478-490.

FISH81b Fisher, J. A., D. Landskov, and B. D. Shriver, "Microcode compaction: looking backward and looking forward," in _AFIPS_ _Conf._ _Proc._, Vol 50: _1981_ _National_ _Computer_ _Conf._, AFIPS Press, Arlington, Va., 95-102.

LAND80 Landskov, D., S. Davidson, B. Shriver, and P. W. Mallett, "Local microcode compaction techniques," _Comput._ _Surv._, 12, 3 (Sept. 80), 261-294.

LAWL76 Lawler, E. L., _Combinatorial Optimization:_ _Networks_ _and_ _Matroids_. New York: Holt, Rinehart and Winston, 1976.

MALL78 Mallett, P. W., "Methods of Compacting Microprograms," Ph.D. dissertation, Univ. of Southwestern Louisiana, Lafayette, Dec. 1978.

MEND70 Mendelson, E., _Theory_ _and_ _Problems_ _of_ _Switching_ _Circuits_. Schaum's Outline Series. New York: McGraw-Hill, 1970.

MIRS71 Mirsky, L., _Transversal_ _Theory_, New York: Academic Press, 1971.

PAPA82 Papadimitriou, C. H., and K. Steiglitz, _Combinatorial Optimization:_ _Algorithms_ _and_ _Complexity_, Englewood Cliffs, NJ: Prentice Hall, 1982.

VEGD82 Vegdahl, S. R., "Local Code Generation and Compaction in Optimizing Microcode Compilers," Ph.D. dissertation, Carnegie-Mellon Univ., Dec. 1982.

YAU74   Yau, S. S., A. C. Schowe, and M. Tsuchiya, "On storage optimization for horizontal microprograms," in _Proc._ _7th_ _Annual_ _Workshop_ _on_ _Microprogramming_, ACM, IEEE, New York, 1974, 98-106.

Panel Session X
Working Session on Firmware Engineering

Chairman

B.D. Shriver
University of Southwestern Louisiana

Panelists

To Be Determined

Author Index